Under the editorship of H E R O L D C. H U N T

Charles William Eliot Professor of Education, Harvard University

Teaching the Young

METHODS OF PRESCHOOL

AND PRIMARY EDUCATION

Lillian M. Logan

Lecturer in Education, Evansville College
Kindergarten Director, Evansville Public Schools

HOUGHTON MIFFLIN COMPANY · BOSTON
The Riverside Press · Cambridge

Child

Cover drawing by Joan Baldwin

LB
1507
.L83

The Riverside Press

CAMBRIDGE, MASSACHUSETTS

PRINTED IN THE U. S. A.

She pictured to herself ... how she would gather about her other little children, and make their eyes bright with all their simple sorrows, and find a pleasure in all their simple joys.

LEWIS CARROLL

Editor's Introduction

ALTHOUGH THE RECENT widespread attention to education has been focused primarily on the secondary school, an inevitable consequence has been an ever-growing realization of the importance of early childhood education. So important are the early formal educational experiences of the child that unless these are built upon established psychological principles, with adequate provisions for programing, staffing, housing, financing, and evaluating, the accomplishments of both the elementary and secondary schools will fall far short of what is desirable and necessary.

It is to the full and optimum realization of the role of early childhood education that the author addresses herself in *Teaching the Young Child*. After considering the desirability of a nursery-school program, the author discusses the primary school in its individual and component parts. Not only is the history of early childhood education reviewed in tracing the design of today's basic structure but the influence of pioneer thinkers is documented and evaluated. Research findings are consistently utilized, and the text is replete with illustrative material covering every phase of these important childhood years.

Beginning and experienced teachers alike will find *Teaching the Young Child* practical and informative, for Dr. Logan is herself a master teacher. Currently a Lecturer in the Department of Education of Evansville College, she serves as critic-teacher for both Evansville College and Indiana University in conjunction with her duties as Kindergarten Director in the Evansville Public Schools. Dr. Logan has taught children in nursery school, kindergarten, and the primary grades for twenty years; in addition, during the past eight years she has taught the college course in early childhood education. She has served as supervisor of teachers-in-training and as chairman of preschool education on the college level and has worked with graduate seminars and workshops.

Mrs. Logan's doctoral dissertation at the University of Wisconsin won for her the Pi Lambda Theta Research Award for Women in Education in 1952. This book, too, is a contribution that will not only enrich the literature of the field but, more importantly, help to strengthen the early childhood education program.

Herold C. Hunt

Preface

TEACHING THE YOUNG CHILD was written out of the experiences of many years of teaching young children in nursery school, kindergarten, and the primary grades, in guiding preservice students in teacher education, and in working with inservice teachers in many sections of the country in workshops and conventions. It was written primarily for students preparing to teach in nursery school, kindergarten, and the primary grades. It was written, too, for experienced teachers who are looking for ways of revitalizing and improving practices through a creative approach to teaching, and for administrators who are on the lookout for a book that will help to stimulate thought and improve the quality of teaching through an inservice program in the school. The writer is concerned with the "why" and "how" as well as the "what" and "when" of curriculum for young children.

The book deals with teaching the young child from two to nine years of age. It considers the total pattern of child development, curriculum, learning, method, and guidance in an integrated course. Problems, projects, questions, and bibliography appear in each chapter to stimulate discussion and experimentation in the college classroom and in inservice teacher education. The book discusses and illustrates principles essential to success in teaching young children. The incidents are real and vital, and they reflect situations that challenge the teacher to creativity in her day-to-day tasks.

Part I is concerned with the significance and development of the child in the nursery school and kindergarten. The essential elements of early childhood education appear in a setting in which the teacher learns to understand the development, growth characteristics, and behavior of the children she teaches, gains insight into problems of guiding them successfully through the formative years, and learns to understand herself and her role.

Part II deals with the key task teachers face — that of selecting, organizing, planning, developing, and evaluating learning experiences. How to organize a program in terms of daily living and learning in the classroom, how to decide what centers to use in program planning, and how to evaluate a good day or a good year at each educational level, all are discussed. Ways of working effectively with parents in evaluation procedures are stressed.

Part III deals specifically with curriculum areas. How to organize and develop learning experiences in communication, how to increase social understandings, how to broaden concepts about the world in which the child lives, how to develop an understanding of numbers, and how to foster creative expression in the arts, all are considered. Curriculum areas are examined on the basis of learning experiences appropriate for the different age levels.

Part IV is concerned with problems we face in teaching. Discipline in the classroom, problems arising from large classes and crowded quarters are examined and suggestions for possible solutions are presented.

Each teacher must find the design for good teaching that best fits the needs of her situation. There is no rule of thumb the teacher can use to solve her problems; however, there are certain basic principles. The warp and woof are the same, but the design is developed differently by the different teachers and by the same teacher as she works with different groups of children. The pattern each child weaves is his own, but on each pattern is the imprint of the teacher.

For the questions about childhood education that a thoughtful critic can ask, for the challenge to my thinking, for aid in polishing the manuscript, and for sharing the responsibility of proofreading, I am deeply indebted to my husband. His constant encouragement and help were an inspiration throughout the writing and completion of the book.

Lillian M. Logan

Contents

Part IV

THE PROBLEMS WE FACE

Teaching the Young Child

EARLY CHILDHOOD

EDUCATION

I

Early childhood education has come into its own. Every educational movement is composed of all that has gone before plus the influences of the present. The significance of the formative years as they affect the child's future adjustment and personality is now generally admitted.

A knowledge of the past should inspire us in three directions: to respect the achievements of educational leaders who have made worthwhile contributions; to strive to reach beyond their accomplishments, resourcefulness, and courageous effort, however significant and far-reaching those contributions have been; and to avoid the mistakes that have been made in the past.

The essential elements of early childhood education appear in Part I. The historical setting merges with the present as today's teacher meets the boys and girls who will be in her classes. She will learn to understand their development, characteristics, and behavior; she will gain insight into problems of guiding them successfully through the crucial years; she will discover, too, that she must understand herself and evaluate her strengths and weaknesses in such a way that the strengths become predominant and overshadow the weaknesses. To that end the teacher should recognize the contributions of the past in order to build upon them and improve them.

1

The Nursery School Comes of Age

*The new institutions of human culture constitute moments
of equilibrium between the past and the future.*

— FRANCISCO LARROYO

In our fast-moving space age many children have exhausted the resources of
the modern home long before they are six. Their bursting curiosity, boundless
energy, creative imagination, growing abilities, and eternal "why" demand
outlets that the home cannot always supply. Inadequate play space, crowded
housing, and working mothers make it necessary to provide experience for
children outside the home. Parents who formerly assumed responsibility
for the child's early years are now looking to the nursery school or kindergarten to provide a suitable environment and worthwhile educational experiences for their children. The decision to send a child to nursery school
may be arrived at after long deliberation; it may, on the other hand, come
suddenly, at the point of desperation, when a mother decides, "I can't do anything with Johnny; I'll send him to a nursery school."

The wisdom of encouraging group experiences for some children at the age of three or thereabouts, although not universally accepted, is widely admitted. Research shows that young children may benefit from social experiences with others of their age. Psychologists have emphasized the significance of adjustment in early years and the long-reaching effects of unfortunate conditions during the formative years.

A nursery school is not a parking place; it supplements and enriches the basic experiences that a good home offers. In the nursery school children are encouraged to broaden their horizons, to develop new interests, to experience the stimulation and satisfaction of exploring, manipulating, and creating. They discover people — people of their own age to play with and adults who like and respect them. They discover that they can work and play and be happy away from home. They gain confidence in meeting new situations, adjusting to people, and finding that the first step toward maturity is an exciting adventure.

Development of Nursery Education in America

ANTECEDENTS

The beginning of the nursery school can be traced to schools established in Europe in the nineteenth century. The educational significance of early childhood was first noted by Comenius who, in 1654, published the first illustrated textbook, which was adapted for teaching children. Near the end of the eighteenth century, in 1790, Robert Owen established an "infant school" in connection with his cotton mills in New Lanark, Scotland. In the socialistic experiment in New Harmony, Indiana, the constitution proposed by Owen was adopted, and in 1826, a school was established

> . . . where over one hundred children from two to six could be amused, play games, and dance and sing. They were to be out-doors as much as possible, to learn when their curiosity induced them to ask questions, and not to be annoyed with books! [1]

When the children became five, they were promoted from the infant school into the higher, or Pestalozzian, school. The children boarded in and did not return to the home of their parents at night; in fact, they seldom saw their parents but slept in an upper room or loft over the workshop.[2]

These schools, envisioned as places where children could be rationally educated through delightful experiences in a happy environment, were not nursery schools as we think of nursery schools today. The teachers were not trained for working with young children, the groups were extremely large, and parents were excluded.

[1] George B. Lockwood, *The New Harmony Movement* (New York: D. Appleton and Company, 1905), p. 242.
[2] *Ibid.*, p. 243.

The New Harmony movement died within a year, and with it died the idea of public education for the youngest children in an environment where love, kindness, and activity dominate. Infant schools continued to exist in the United States until 1840, but they gradually merged into the primary schools and eventually ceased to exist. Not until almost a century later did the nursery school come into its own in America.

THE MODERN NURSERY SCHOOL

In 1909, the first real nursery schools were established in England by Rachel and Margaret McMillan. In 1915, the faculty wives of The University of Chicago established a cooperative nursery school. In 1919, the Bureau of Educational Experiments in New York started one and, in 1921, the Teachers College of Columbia University opened a nursery school. In 1922, Miss Abigail Eliot, upon her return from six months of study in England with the McMillan sisters and Miss Grace Owen, opened the Ruggles Street Nursery School in Boston.

The motivation behind the early nursery schools in America was primarily educational. In the 1920's, with help from various foundations, child development research centers were established. Then came university nursery schools, which served as pilot centers and leaders in demonstrating the kinds of learning experiences young children needed. Among the other early research-oriented and experimentally minded nursery schools established in the 1920's were the Merrill-Palmer School in Detroit and the Iowa State College Nursery School. In 1925, Cornell University and the Ohio State University opened schools. The Franklin Public School Nursery in Chicago was started the same year. In 1926, the Yale Psycho-Clinic Guidance Nursery opened; Vassar College, Smith College, and Antioch College also initiated nursery schools that year. In 1927, the Mills College Nursery School opened, and the Pacific Heights Nursery School was founded by Rhoda Kellogg in San Francisco.[3] By 1930, about 300 nursery schools had been established, a few of them integrated with the public schools.

The objective of the research center nursery schools was maximum development of children. Students of child development, home economics, and teacher education participated in nursery-school educational experiences. From 1925 to the beginning of the Second World War efforts were made to turn every day nursery into a nursery school. In an increasing number of cases the nursery-school pupil in the day nursery was studied, guided, and educated — not merely watched over.

FEDERALLY SUBSIDIZED NURSERY SCHOOLS

With the onset of the depression economic forces began to operate: 3,000 nursery-school units serving 65,000 needy children were organized under the

[3] Rhoda Kellogg, *Nursery School Guide* (Boston: Houghton Mifflin Company, 1949), p. 7.

The Ruggles Street School, established in 1922, used outdoor as well as indoor play.

Federal Emergency Education Program. Between 1934 and 1935 more than 1,900 nursery schools with an enrollment of 75,000 were reported.[4] Some 1,500 of these nursery schools were administered under the Works Projects Administration, which had 150,000 families enrolled in a Family Life Education Program.

The industrial employment of women in the Second World War created conditions similar to those existing at the beginning of the industrial revolution, when Robert Owen established his schools in Scotland. Once more the welfare of the preschool child was threatened. Child-care centers were hastily organized to meet another emergency. These emergency periods, with their inevitable strains and tensions, admittedly provided inadequate programs for young children. They did, however, focus attention on the responsibility of society for providing adequate educational experiences for its youngest citizens.

[4] National Advisory Committee on Emergency Nursery Schools, *Emergency Nursery Schools During the Second Year, 1934–35* (Washington, D.C.: The Association for Childhood Education, 1936).

Types of Nursery Schools in America

In its most characteristic and desirable form, the nursery school in the United States is a cultural agency for supplementing and strengthening the normal functions of a normal home.

A look at the development of the nursery school makes it clear that various factors, situations, and needs have created a variety of types of nursery schools. Among those that exist at the present time are nursery schools associated with research centers in universities and colleges, private nursery schools, cooperative nursery schools, child-care centers, day nurseries, nursery schools for handicapped children, and neighborhood play groups.

Nursery schools associated with research centers in universities and colleges. These continue to offer some of the best educational experiences both for young children and for adults. Research in child development, psychology, curricula, and guidance is an integral function of such centers. Children who enroll in the centers frequently come from relatively high socioeconomic levels of society. The educational program reflects the experimental approach to problems and practice. Opportunities for observing, planning, and developing activities with children provide valuable learning experience for children, parents, and prospective teachers.

Private nursery schools. These range from mere parking places bearing such descriptive names as "Tiny-Tot Motel" to well-organized, effectively supervised nursery schools meeting high educational standards. The wide variation in purposes, programs, organization, and qualifications of staff members is a persistent problem. The number of good private nursery schools fails to meet the demand. Because of the high cost of maintaining qualified staffs, limiting the number of children, and providing adequate facilities and equipment, the good private nursery school frequently serves only the children of the more privileged classes.

The cooperative nursery school. This is one answer to the problem of finding a good nursery school within the reach of the average family's purse.

In a speech at the Biennial Conference of the National Association for Nursery Education in Minneapolis, Minnesota, October 1953, Myra Woodruff pointed to the unity of purpose within a framework of diversity in the pattern of the cooperative nursery school, when she said:

> The good cooperative nursery school embodies all of the things we work for in good nursery education. . . .
>
> Some cooperative nursery schools are organized primarily for the worthwhile group experience which can be offered the children. Others are set up with their major purpose to provide a laboratory for parent education activities.
>
> Some cooperatives are sponsored by churches, others by welfare agencies, some by neighborhood centers, some by boards of education, by teachers, by housing

The Antioch College Nursery School has grown from 12 children in 1929 to 45 today.

developments, adult education departments, junior colleges. . . .

The pattern of financing such schools is widely different. Some are stock incorporations with stock being sold. Others are supported primarily by parent fees. Some are financed by parent fees and funds raised by the parent body. . . . Still others are supported by state adult education funds supplemented by parent fees. And there are many combinations of these financing patterns.

There is just as wide variation in the staffing of cooperative nursery schools. In some the organization plan calls for a well-qualified director who is assisted by parents. In others there is a trained director assisted by experienced teachers, so that parents do not participate in the actual teaching. In these schools parent assistance takes the form of carrying major responsibility for the administration of the program. There are still other schools where there are no trained teachers, and where parents make up the teaching staff, sometimes after one or two preparatory courses.[5]

Child-care centers, or day nurseries. Child-care centers, which were established during World War II, are still operating, in some cases under state

[5] Myra Woodruff, Chief, Bureau of Child Development and Parent Education, New York State Department of Education, "The Cooperative Nursery School — A Significant Trend." Resumé of speech, October 1953.

and local support. Some of the centers have the characteristics of a good nursery school. Too often, however, they provide custodial care but offer a limited educational program and are fraught with hazards to safety and health. Children suffer from the effects of overstimulation, overcrowding, and unqualified teachers. Although the day nursery provides daytime care for children from less privileged homes, it also considers itself responsible for the mental as well as physical care of its charges. Attempts are made to organize the program so that it is educationally as well as custodially oriented.

Nursery schools for the handicapped. These schools offer opportunity for rich first-hand experiences to children with special needs. In many places schools are being designed and equipped to meet requirements of children with orthopedic, neurological, speech, and vision handicaps. The average school is not equipped to meet the needs of such children.

Neighborhood play groups. These are informal in nature and are usually organized by parents who are striving to meet the needs of the neighborhood children. Such groups are characterized by a wide age range and limited equipment; they are supervised by mothers and others for the convenience of the neighborhood. A characteristic beginning comes when one mother, faced with a transportation problem, a slim budget, and too little time, observes that in her immediate neighborhood there are other children within a year of the age of her own four-year-old. At her suggestion the children come over to her house one day with their mothers and a few small babies. Over a cup of coffee the mothers plan a nursery program. The group meets perhaps three days a week, giving each mother only one turn in two weeks.

Certification of Teachers in Nursery School and Care Centers

An examination of the types of programs for young children reveals the variations in educational qualifications of teachers. It is possible in many parts of the United States for anyone, with or without essential qualifications, to work in or even operate a center for young children.

A recent survey to determine certification required in various states for nursery-school teachers shows that none of the fifty states requires certification for all types of places providing group care for normal children under five.[6] Two-thirds of the states have some regulations for professional preparation of nursery teachers, but less than one-third issue certificates for these teachers. Much remains to be done to ensure adequate educational requirements for those who teach the youngest children. Until more stringent standards are set, until nursery schools of all types are supervised and staffed with qualified teachers, parents must be qualified to evaluate a nursery school.

[6] Leora Bently Bliss, "Certification of Teachers in Nursery School and Day-Care Centers," *Childhood Education Journal*, February 1958, p. 275.

A small group allows the child to develop social characteristics without becoming overstimulated.

Characteristics of a Good Nursery School

When a parent asks, "Shall I send my child to nursery school?" what he or she often wants to know is, "How can I be sure of finding a good school?"

A good nursery school is a school in which worthwhile learning experiences are selected and organized for children from two to four years of age, based on knowledge of growth needs for these ages and developed under the guidance of qualified teachers working together with the parents.

There are certain evidences of concern that the good nursery school has maintained throughout its development. Among these are: (1) respect for the child's way of learning; (2) concern for the child's inner feelings, implying the need for an evaluation of learning experiences and climate in terms of their effect on the child's personality development and mental well-being; (3) regard for parent participation and contributions to the nursery school.

Factors for Consideration in Selecting a Nursery School

There are a number of specific factors for which a parent can look in selecting a nursery school or kindergarten. Among these are the number of children in the group, the teacher-pupil ratio, the age range within the group, the length of day, provisions for the child's health and safety, the educational and personal qualifications of the staff, and the physical set-up.

In a good nursery school the number of children is small. When groups are large, children become overstimulated, strained, and tense. As a result, behavior problems that negate the benefits of group experience arise. At least one teacher is needed for every eight children, and there should be two adults present in each group at all times. It is possible, but not desirable, to operate a school with only one fully qualified staff member, assisted by aides.

The experience and maturity of children within a group varies with the age range, and the program will be tailored to fit the children. Many children are not ready for nursery school before three years of age. The small number of children to which the two-year-olds can adjust, the short day from which they can profit, and the amount of individual attention they require make education for the two-year-olds almost prohibitive in cost.

The length of day varies. Three or four hours a day seem to be long enough for most young children. In the case of a full-day schedule, therefore, the program must include a long nap. Only if these needs are considered can the nursery school fulfill its function, as delineated by Nelly Wolffheim:

> The nursery school should help the child with the task of freeing itself from its early surroundings. It may save an only child from a life-long dependency. A nursery school can, however, only be a help if it is conceived in the right lines. If a child is placed in a large nursery school, the transference is made more difficult, as the conditions for close contact with his nursery school teacher or for friendships with other children are not favorable there. The same might be said of the old style nursery schools, in which free play and free movement were rarely customary and most of the time was spent in sitting still and being occupied with communal tasks. This disadvantage of the large or unfavorably organized nursery schools . . . must not be ignored if the liberation of the child from its close family ties is one of the tasks of the nursery school.[7]

Summary

This brief survey of the development of the nursery-school movement indicates that the nursery school in the United States is educationally oriented and developed in response to the mental and emotional needs of the child in a complex industrial society. The early nursery schools in Europe, in contrast, were concerned primarily with relieving social conditions and only secondarily with providing educational experiences.

[7] Nelly Wolffheim, *Psychology in the Nursery School*, translated by Charles Hannam (New York: Philosophical Library, Inc., 1953), pp. 32–33.

As social conditions changed in America, the problems of caring for children increased, and a pattern of nursery schools developed to meet needs for custodial care as well as for education for the children.

Today's nursery school is the result of the interaction of cultural and social forces that have necessitated the use of agencies outside the home to provide worthwhile learning experiences and care for the young child. The types of nursery schools existing today include research centers, private nursery schools, cooperative nursery schools, child-care centers or day nurseries, nursery schools for handicapped children, and neighborhood play groups.

The modern concept of education takes into consideration the principle of continuity in the growth process. It recognizes the fact that babyhood persists to a certain degree throughout the period of childhood and that growth is a gradual process. The nursery school, the kindergarten, and the primary school attempt to provide a natural environment in which a young child can grow and develop. The extension of the school downward to include the nursery and the kindergarten, and outward to encompass the broadened range of interests of the primary child, presents a challenge to the teacher to understand the child in the entire cycle of development of childhood education.

QUESTIONS AND ACTIVITIES

1. Trace the development of the nursery school in the United States.

2. List some present-day conditions that necessitate the use of nursery schools for the nurture and education of young children.

3. How would you go about changing a day nursery into a nursery school? What social values would be derived from such a change? What educational values would be derived?

4. What happens to the parent-child relationship when children are enrolled in nursery school before they are ready for the separation?

5. In what way does a good nursery school supplement the child's home experience? Observe in a nursery school and use your observation as a basis for answering this question.

6. What factors should parents consider in selecting a nursery school for their child?

7. Visit three of the types of nursery schools described in the chapter and evaluate them in terms of the definition of a good nursery school.

SELECTED READINGS

Brunot, James, Florence S. Derr, and Bess Goodykoontz. "Federal Programs for Children," *Childhood Education*, 19:170–176, December 1942.

Close, Kathryn. "Day Care up to Now," *Survey Midmonthly*, 79:194–197, July 1943.

Committee on the Infant and Preschool Child, White House Conference on Child Health and Protection. *Nursery Education: A Survey of Day Nurseries, Nursery Schools, and Private Kindergartens in the United States.* New York: The Century Co., 1931.

Davis, Mary Dabney. *Schools for Children under Six.* U.S. Office of Education, Bulletin No. 5. Washington, D.C.: Government Printing Office, 1947.

Davis, Mary Dabney, and Rowena Hansen. *Nursery Schools, Their Development and Current Practices in the United States.* U.S. Office of Education. Washington, D.C.: Government Printing Office, 1932.

Forest, Ilse. *Early Years at School.* New York: McGraw-Hill Book Company, Inc., 1949.

Forest, Ilse. *Preschool Education: An Historical and Critical Study.* New York: The Macmillan Company, 1927.

Henry, Nelson (ed.). *Early Childhood Education.* Forty-Sixth Yearbook of the National Society for the Study of Education, Part II. Chicago: The University of Chicago Press, 1947.

History of the Kindergarten Movement. Washington, D.C.: The Association for Childhood Education, 1935.

Kellogg, Rhoda. *Nursery School Guide.* Boston: Houghton Mifflin Company, 1949.

Langdon, Grace. "Developments in the Field of Emergency Nursery Schools," *School Life*, 23:242–243, March 1938.

Lockhead, Jewell. *The Education of Young Children in England.* New York: Bureau of Publications, Teachers College, Columbia University, 1932.

Lockwood, George B. *The New Harmony Movement.* New York: D. Appleton and Company, 1905.

McClure, Worth. "Education of Children," *Social Change and Education*, pp. 213–234. Thirteenth Yearbook of the Department of Superintendence. Washington, D.C.: National Education Association, 1935.

McMillan, Margaret. *The Nursery School.* New York: E. P. Dutton & Co., Inc., 1921.

Moustakas, Clark. *The Nursery School and Child Care Center.* New York: William Morrow & Company, Inc., 1955.

National Advisory Committee on Emergency Nursery Schools. *Emergency Nursery Schools during the First Year, 1933–34.* Washington, D.C.: The Association for Childhood Education, 1935.

Our Cooperative Nursery School, Revised Manual. Silver Spring, Md.: Silver Spring Nursery School, 1954.

Owen, Grace. *Nursery School Education.* New York: E. P. Dutton & Co., Inc., 1920.

Read, Katherine. *The Nursery School,* Second Edition. Philadelphia: W. B. Saunders Company, 1955.

Rudolph, Marguerita. *Living and Learning in Nursery School.* New York: Harper & Brothers, 1954.

_2_

The Kindergarten in the
Educative Process

*The intrinsic charm and curiosity of childhood make of
the preschool a source of never-ending delight.*

— Rosaura Zapata

In 1837, in a small Thuringian village in Blackenburg, Germany, Friedrich
Froebel founded a school for children between the ages of three and eight.
To it he gave the incredible name of *Kleinkinderbeschäftigunganstalt.*[1] In
time the term was shortened to *kindergarten.*

In the kindergarten at Blackenburg Froebel experimented with his concept
of children engaged in a happy social enterprise in an outdoor environment.
His basic principles included self-activity, social participation, creativity, and

---

[1] *Klein,* little; *Kinder,* children; *Beschäftigung,* occupation; *Anstalt,* institution; hence,
"an institution for the occupation of little children." Adolph Meyer, *Development of Education in the Twentieth Century* (Englewood Cliffs, N.J.: Prentice-Hall, Inc., 1950), p. 24.

motor expression. The kindergarten had individual development as its aim, motor expression as its method, and social cooperation as its means.

The kindergarten has played a significant role in the development of modern concepts of early childhood education. It has enriched the lives of children in many parts of the world. The same decades that saw the evolution of scientific theory and practice in the nursery-school movement witnessed the culmination of the struggle of the kindergarten to free itself from old-world domination. The kindergarten emerged from the struggle shorn of its old-world rootings — an American institution, ready to stand on concepts tested and proven on American soil.

The Kindergarten Comes to America

Nowhere was the kindergarten more heartily welcomed than in America. Tradition credits a German woman, Mrs. Carl Schurz, with opening the first kindergarten in the United States in Watertown, Wisconsin, in 1856. A student of Froebel, Mrs. Schurz established a private kindergarten in the German language and in the Froebelian spirit.

The first English-speaking kindergarten opened in Boston in 1860 under the direction of Miss Elizabeth Peabody. Miss Peabody, the dominant figure in the pioneer period of the American kindergarten, went to Germany in 1867 to study and observe Froebel's kindergarten. She returned to America a devoted disciple and spent her life maintaining the Froebelian theories.

In 1873, the concept of the kindergarten filtered into the public schools. Under the leadership of William T. Harris, the first public kindergarten was opened in St. Louis with Miss Susan Blow as director. By the end of the century kindergartens — public and private — were firmly rooted in American soil, but not in American tradition. Though kindergartens were here to stay, they still had the flavor of the old world.

Miss Blow devoted her life to studying, expanding, and defending Froebel's theories. She developed the "Blow Program," quite generally accepted in the kindergartens of the eastern United States for more than thirty years. The program was organized around the Froebelian materials, mother-play sequences, games, and gardening.

Theoretically, Froebel conceived of the kindergarten as a free and happy place where children could learn through play, unfolding as naturally as plants in a favorable environment. In practice, however, his theories as they were interpreted by his American exponents led to rigid and systematized formulas. His followers clung to his materials and methods and neglected his principles. Far from being free to follow natural impulses and develop initiative, the child was prohibited from freely expressing his ideas or using his own resources to solve problems. Froebel's ideas of freedom disappeared; the system became dogmatic. Teachers required the children to use the materials in a specific, prescribed, and rigid manner.

Froebelian Materials and Method

According to Froebel, education is the unfolding of the "child germ." He believed that by playing with the symbols of the mental content implicit in the germ, the child would attain the objective of education — a full knowledge of unity with God. This knowledge, which according to Froebel is present at birth in the "mind germ," merely needs to be permitted to unfold through the use of certain symbolic materials.

Materials, which were used in a stereotyped manner, consisted of three types: the gifts, the occupations, and the mother-play or nursery songs. The gifts and occupations were permanent play materials designed to stimulate the child's motor expression. Technically, the gifts were materials whose forms were fixed, such as blocks, cubes, spheres, sticks, and cylinders, designed to familiarize the child with geometric forms and their derivations. Play with the gifts was prescribed in rigid detail day by day in the Blow Program. Precise instructions to the kindergarten director made original thinking or experimentation not only unnecessary but nearly impossible.

The rigidity with which the materials were used defeated the purpose for which they were intended. The blocks were arranged in a unit inside a box; from this box the child removed them according to directions, and to it he returned them when the formal lesson was completed. As the gift was handed to a child, he was expected to wait for a given signal, turn the box on its top, pull out the cover, and raise the box with a steady hand, thus leaving the whole cube standing before him. This was done in order to be certain that through the play the child would comprehend the laws of unity and diversity.

Although Froebel's symbolism is no longer accepted, the circle is still often used as a teaching aid.

The symbolism that permeated the use of the materials in the Blow Program is illustrated in the following example. The first gift, a ball, the symbol of unity and wholeness, was presented to the child on a string. He was told to play with it in such a way that the directions, "up and down," "side to side," "back and forth," and "round and round" became clear to him and related to his knowledge of God.

The activities in connection with the occupations were also prescribed and teacher-directed. These included clay modeling, drawing, perforating, bead-stringing, embroidering, sewing, coloring, paper-folding, pasting, weaving, interlacing, making chains, and peas-work. Although some of these activi- ties are still found in kindergartens, their use is neither prescribed nor cir- cumscribed.

Not even the games escaped symbolic interpretation. Froebel had a com- plicated interpretation of the value of the circle in kindergarten procedure. He believed that the pleasure with which children played circle games had its basis in a "presentiment of what is symbolic and significant in the games." He asked the question, "May not their delight in these movements, for exam- ple, spring from longing, and the effort to get an all-round-all-sided grasp of an object?" [2] To Froebel, the circle was a specific means of making the child feel his identity with his social group and ultimately his unity in the absolute.

As the mentor of the conservative element in the kindergarten, Miss Blow clung tenaciously to the mysticism and symbolism of the Froebelian theories. In defense of her program, which was the personification of these theories, Miss Blow stated in 1908 that "in its conception of the child, its symbolism, and its heritage of free-activity with ideal values, the Froebelian kindergarten reveals a lineage from the philosophy of idealism." [3]

As was inevitable, however, the movements shaping education at the turn of the century had their impact on the kindergarten. The introduction of the kindergarten into public schools, beyond the sphere of influence of the Blow Program, brought a questioning attitude toward kindergarten practices and led to divergent philosophies of childhood education. A movement toward the modification of practice in harmony with scientific concepts was to spring up within the ranks of the kindergarten theorists.

Leaders of the Modern Kindergarten in America

The influence of such leaders as Miss Patty Hill, Miss Anna Bryan, and Miss Alice Temple provides a fascinating chapter in the development of the kindergarten.

Miss Patty Hill was fortunate enough to have come under the influence of

[2] H. C. Bowen, *Froebel and Self-Activity* (New York: Charles Scribner's Sons, 1913), p. 64.

[3] Susan Blow, *Educational Issues in the Kindergarten* (New York: D. Appleton and Com- pany, 1908), p. xiii.

Miss Anna Bryan, a director of a kindergarten in Louisville, Kentucky, who, because she took her training in Chicago, did not come under the ultra-Froebelian influence. Both Miss Hill and Miss Bryan believed that the Froebelian materials and method were limited and stereotyped and that adherence to the Froebelian system made progress impossible.

During her childhood Miss Hill had decided to devote herself to young children and, when an opportunity to enroll in Miss Bryan's training school for kindergarten teachers presented itself, she lost no time in registering. Watching children experiment with materials in the kindergarten, these leaders became firmly convinced that until such schools concerned themselves with the needs of children and, indeed, until they became integrated with the elementary school, they were doomed to failure. Miss Hill, Miss Bryan, and Miss Alice Temple were among those who dedicated themselves to developing a program based on a scientific knowledge of children.

Miss Bryan took a critical attitude toward the Froebelian theories. At a meeting of the National Education Association, in 1890, she read a paper entitled "The Letter Killeth." In it she explained the principles of the creative gift sequences with which Miss Hill had been experimenting in Louisville. This experiment was an attempt to make the gifts more meaningful to children. In connection with the fourth gift (eight rectangular blocks, $2\frac{1}{2}'' \times 1'' \times \frac{1}{2}''$) the children were given problems to encourage thinking; for example, they were asked to make a bed for a paper doll cut out by the teacher, or two beds for two dolls, or to follow some similar idea. Instead of dictating the building of the cube from the rectangular blocks of the fourth gift, Miss Hill began to suggest the possibility of constructing a doll bed, a table, or a barn.

CONSERVATIVES VERSUS LIBERALS

Gradually, however, the Louisville kindergarten became a threat to the dedicated Froebelians, and a bitter battle ensued. The records of the meetings of the International Union from 1892 to 1908 give a clear picture of the intensity of the struggle.

The conservatives felt impelled to defend the Froebelian theories. Criticizing the liberals, in 1904 Miss Blow asserted, "In its jubilant sense of conformity with nature, and in its swift surrender to fatal impulses, the free-play kindergarten repeats in its tiny circle the self-destructive sweep of naturalism. In its tendency to conceive the child as shaped and fashioned by the historic process, in its reaction from intellectualism to an exaggerated voluntarism, the industrial kindergarten betrays the influence of pragmatism." [4]

The liberals believed that progress was desirable and inevitable. They had at least one asset that could not be denied by even their most bitter enemies: from the beginning they had allied themselves with the projects of such leaders in the child study movement as G. Stanley Hall, William H. Burnham, and John Dewey. The Froebelian kindergarten in America had been little

[4] *Ibid.*, p. xiii.

Dissatisfaction with the Froebelian gifts led to the development of the Patty Hill building blocks.

concerned with the physical needs of the child. The liberals emphasized health and studied the effects of so rigid a program on mental health.

By the turn of the century Miss Hill had become the recognized leader of the liberals, while Miss Blow continued to give allegiance to the conservative theories. In what amounted to a personal contest for leadership at Teachers College, Columbia University, Miss Hill and Miss Blow taught simultaneously, giving their students entirely opposite views of childhood needs and education. In 1910, Dean Russell called Miss Hill to become chairman of the Kindergarten Department there, in order to introduce the new ideas of kindergarten education to the East, where the work had been extremely conservative. In this position she was able to carry out her ideas based on a socialized approach to the nurture and education of young children. She regarded both nursery school and kindergarten as the logical testing ground of scientific progress in the education of young children.

In the early 1890's her concern for the welfare of the youngest ones had prompted her to enroll babies in her kindergarten in Louisville. Almost from the beginning of her teaching career at Columbia University, Miss Hill opened demonstration groups of three-year-olds in connection with her graduate course in childhood education. She emphasized the significance of understanding and working with the threes as well as with the fours and fives. Her interest in nursery education led her to follow the work done in government nurseries for children of munitions workers in World War I and to study records of nursery-school education in England. In 1921, Miss Hill succeeded in bringing Miss Grace Owen, a prominent English nursery-school educator, to lecture at Teachers College, Columbia University.

Her interest in children from infancy through the entire cycle of childhood reflected a philosophy based on the developmental approach to child study. Her leadership, coming at a period when the kindergarten was under the influence of a small number of individuals blinded by faith in a system, resulted in an objective look at kindergarten theories and practice. Her belief in continuous evaluation led the way for experimentation. Her conviction that there are better ways of guiding children, and that when better ways are found they should be used, was the starting point of a scientifically grounded education for young children. Under such leadership it was inevitable that the liberals in the kindergarten movement should have gained ground and eventually triumphed.

The New Look in the Kindergarten

A general clarification of objectives, methods, and curriculum followed as the leaders examined the kindergarten program in terms of the growth of the child. Many significant modifications took place in the curriculum:

1. Organization of a curriculum based on the child's needs for physical and mental health, activities centered around problem-solving, and experiences based on real-life situations.

2. Revision of play materials, development of new materials designed to meet the need for use of large muscles, elimination of activities requiring use of small muscles and fine muscle coordination.

3. Substitution of creative activities for formal, teacher-directed handwork activities.

4. Flexibility in the scheduling of activities, longer periods based on the interests and needs of the children.

5. Provision for informal experiences in language in place of the morning talks outlined in the Blow Program.

6. Unification with the primary school instead of the former policy of isolation, achieved by intergrade visits of teachers, development of new techniques of evaluation, and an attitude of cooperation among teachers of young children, the concept of continuity of growth, a realization that children in nursery school, kindergarten, and primary grades are so nearly alike that it is not feasible to draw a sharp line of demarcation.

7. A new approach to parent education and home and school relationships based on a realistic study of the child.

8. A broadened base for teacher education founded on a knowledge of the humanities, social sciences, anthropology, child development, and educational psychology.

Contributors to the Kindergarten Movement

Our consideration of the development of the kindergarten in the educative process has already revealed the influence of Friedrich Froebel on the American kindergarten. Froebel's theories were unchallenged until John Dewey made his impact felt. The progressive kindergarten leaders, who came to share Dewey's ideas, gradually developed an American point of view in the kindergarten.

The modern kindergarten organizes learning experiences around problems that are significant to children.

Miss Hill recalled the beginning of Dewey's influence on her own philosophy and practice in the kindergarten. "I read in his writings," she said, "that 'a mode of expression apart from a vital idea to express is barren and stultifying' — this was my starting point for getting away from the formalism of the traditional procedures. As soon as I could, I went to study with Professor Dewey." [5]

Dewey's outstanding contribution was in freeing the kindergarten from domination of the theories grounded and rooted in foreign soil. Early childhood education became the first proving-ground in this country of a philosophy of education based upon the idea of experience. Through Miss Hill's ability to grasp this experimentalist point of view, the kindergarten became an institution dedicated to meeting the needs of children in a vigorous, dynamic society.

Among Dewey's ideas that influenced the education of children were:

(1) Experiences children are having now are important because the present is significant to the child.

(2) Education is not merely preparation for life; it is life.

(3) Interest is a motivating factor in learning.

(4) The curriculum must be oriented to real experiences of childhood in a social setting rather than to experiences selected because they are supposed, by adults, to be proper and valuable for children.

William Kilpatrick summarized Dewey's contributions to childhood education in the following statement:

When Dewey first began to influence education Froebel reigned supreme in the kindergarten. Only those who know at first-hand the curious and mystical

[5] Patty Hill, "Forty Years in the Kindergarten," *The Survey*, 58:508, September 1927.

cult of the Froebelian doctrines as interpreted by his disciples or the unsympathetic management of the former primary school can appreciate the advance made in childhood education.[6]

An examination of kindergarten development would be incomplete without a reference to Dr. Maria Montessori, a physician who worked with young children in Rome in the *Casa dei Bambino*. Her influence, though not widely recognized in America, was responsible for two important concepts of childhood education: the need for the child to have responsibility for practical housekeeping activities in the school and the role of the teacher as a passive guide rather than a domineering force in the kindergarten. The didactic materials she developed were based on the importance of sense training, but her emphasis on the use of the materials and her belief in the transfer of training lessened her influence on the American kindergarten.

[6] William Heard Kilpatrick, "What John Dewey Meant to Childhood Education," *The Association of Childhood Education Journal*, 27:380, April 1950.

Self-activity, social participation, creativity, and motor expression are evident in the modern kindergarten.

Promising Practices in Today's Kindergarten

Based upon beliefs about democracy, the way children develop, the nature of effective learning, and the function of the school in the education of effective citizens, the modern kindergarten emphasizes educational experiences that promote group living and develop individual potentials. In a democratic society, experiences must be provided that will result in more effective, more satisfying, and more responsible living. Growth potential is in every individual, but each child grows in his own unique way. He brings to his first educational experience his individual background, needs, capacities, and interests. The school must provide experiences that will contribute to his optimum physical, intellectual, social, and emotional development.

Among the promising practices that are in the kindergarten today are the following:

(1) Provision for individual differences in children, through varying the learning activities, the material, the equipment, and the methods to meet individual needs.

(2) Provision for the child's total experience through activities that are related to those of his out-of-school life; implied here is a close relationship with parents and the community.

(3) Organization of the learning environment on a democratic basis, so that children learn group processes through experience in sharing, cooperating, planning, communicating, and problem-solving.

(4) Organization of learning experiences around problems, tasks, or interests that are significant to children and relevant to their educational development in a complex, changing society.

(5) Use of firsthand experiences, visual aids, and personal resources to enrich the child's experiences and broaden his horizons.

(6) Broadening of the base of evaluation to include more than scores on readiness tests; growth and learning are thus measured in terms of behavior changes.

(7) Recognition of the desirability of housing the nursery, kindergarten, and primary children in a unit of their own in order to meet their needs for security and recognition and to provide space for activities.

(8) Limiting the number of children taught by one teacher to a reasonable number, in order to prevent such problems as arise from overstimulated children in overcrowded classrooms.

(9) Staggering the enrollment in kindergarten in such a way that the first days permit a gradual introduction to the group situation.

Summary

Looking back on the development of the kindergarten, the following four distinct stages can be identified:

(1) The naïve stage, in which the kindergarten in America was simply the concrete expression of the educational ideals of Friedrich Froebel.

(2) The arrested development stage, in which kindergarten directors as a whole formed an exclusive, self-satisfied, and rather intolerant group.

(3) The rivalry period, in which strife between the conservatives, under the leadership of Miss Susan Blow, and the liberals, led by Miss Patty Hill, was the rule.

(4) The coming-of-age period, in which many of the leaders were "ready to forswear both the name and the system when better ones are found." [7]

It was at the fourth stage that the "kindergarten was ready to adopt and nurture a sister institution, the nursery school, which as a newer form of child education was presently to take the place of the kindergarten in caring for the needs of the youngest children." [8]

As a result of the willingness of forward-looking leaders to accept scientific truths as they found them, today's kindergarten has emerged with a program of education based on a developmental philosophy and an understanding of the principles of growth, learning, and behavior.

QUESTIONS AND ACTIVITIES

1. Explain the theories of the educational value of play held by Friedrich Froebel, Susan Blow, and Patty Hill.

2. How did Froebel's lessons in gifts and occupations violate the principles of child psychology?

3. Form a panel and discuss the role of the kindergarten teacher as conceived of by Susan Blow, Patty Hill, and Maria Montessori.

4. What are the criticisms of the Froebelian kindergarten as it developed in America? Are they valid?

5. Trace the development of the influence of John Dewey on the American kindergarten.

6. Why were the theories of Montessori not widely accepted in the American kindergarten?

7. Observe in a kindergarten of your choice and determine evidences of the practices of Froebel, Montessori, or Dewey.

8. What is the attitude of the kindergarten teacher whom you observed toward her own practices? What evidences of self-evaluation did you observe?

SELECTED READINGS

Blow, Susan. *Kindergarten Education,* Monographs on Education in the United States. Edited by Nicholas Murray Butler. Albany: J. B. Lynn Company, 1900.

[7] Patty S. Hill, "Kindergartens of Yesterday and Tomorow," *Kindergarten–Primary Magazine,* 29:46, September 1916.
[8] Ilse Forest, *Early Years at School* (New York: McGraw-Hill Book Company, Inc., 1949), p. 37.

Davis, Mary Dabney. *General Practice in Kindergarten Education in the United States*. Washington, D.C.: National Education Association, 1925.

Davis, Mary Dabney. *Kindergarten-Primary Education*, U.S. Office of Education, Bulletin No. 30. Washington, D.C.: Government Printing Office, 1930.

Froebel, Friedrich. *Education by Development*. Translated by J. Jarvis. New York: D. Appleton and Company, 1900.

Froebel, Friedrich. *Education of Man*. Translated by Hartmann. New York: D. Appleton and Company, 1892.

Froebel, Friedrich. *Mottoes and Commentaries of Friedrich Froebel's Mother-Play*. Translated by H. R. Eliot. New York: D. Appleton and Company, 1908.

Froebel, Friedrich. *Pedagogics of the Kindergarten*. Translated by J. Jarvis. New York: D. Appleton and Company, 1895.

Garrison, Charlotte, Emma Sheehy, and Alice Dagleish. *The Horace Mann Kindergarten*. New York: Bureau of Publications, Teachers College, Columbia University, 1937.

Hill, Patty S. "Changes in Curriculum and Method in Kindergarten Education," *Childhood Education*, 2:99–106, November 1925.

Hill, Patty S. (ed.). *A Conduct Curriculum for the Kindergarten and First Grade*. New York: Charles Scribner's Sons, 1923.

Hill, Patty S. "Kindergartens of Yesterday and Tomorrow," *Kindergarten-Primary Magazine*, 39:4–6, September 1916.

International Kindergarten Union, Committee of Nineteen. *The Kindergarten*. Boston: Houghton Mifflin Company, 1913.

Kilpatrick, William H. *Froebel's Kindergarten Principles Critically Examined*. New York: The Macmillan Company, 1916.

Montessori, Maria. *The Montessori Method*. Translated by Anna George. New York: Frederick A. Stokes Co., 1912.

National Society for the Study of Education. *The Kindergarten and its Relation to Elementary Education*, Sixth Yearbook, Part II. Chicago: The University of Chicago Press, 1907.

National Society for the Study of Education. *The Coordination of Kindergarten and Elementary Schools*. Seventh Yearbook, Part II. Chicago: The University of Chicago Press, 1908.

Prüfer, Johannes. *Frederico Froebel*. Buenos Aires: Editorial Labor, S.A., 1930.

3

Understanding the Children You Teach

The ever-enduring process of perfecting, maturing, refining, is the aim of living.

— John Dewey

"Why do you teach?" the writer asked an elementary teacher who had spent twenty years in the classroom. "Because," she replied, "after twenty years, it still intrigues me; it still provides fresh challenges and offers unexpected rewards. Each September I feel like a captain setting sail with an untried crew, over uncharted seas."

Understanding children is challenging; it involves the social climate, one's philosophy, many organizational and learning activities; it influences child-teacher-parent relationships; and it determines the evaluation processes. Understanding children is significant; it can change a drab classroom in a shabby, antiquated building into a cheerful laboratory for learning.

In this chapter we shall attempt to review some principles of human development, to lay a foundation for a psychological approach to an understanding of child behavior, and to present the developmental tasks of children in infancy, early childhood, and middle childhood.

Understanding Growth and Development

From the day he toddles off to nursery school to the day he is ready to leave the primary school, a youngster has traveled a long way toward maturity. In order to guide her charges along this path, a teacher must have knowledge of the way a child grows. Anyone concerned with teaching is increasingly dedicated to understanding and applying basic principles of growth, development, and learning. Just as a parent who recognizes that growth follows in an orderly sequence will not try to force the child in his physical, mental, or emotional growth, so the teacher who recognizes individual differences in rate of growth among children will provide for such differences in the learning activities in the classroom.

PRINCIPLES OF CHILD GROWTH AND DEVELOPMENT

Longitudinal studies of growth during recent decades have furnished us with a great deal of information about its nature. Genetic studies of child development have provided additional information about the general principles of development during the early years of life. These studies form the basis of the principles presented here.

Development is continuous, gradual, and orderly. What occurs at one stage of growth carries over and influences the following stages. The process takes place not by leaps and bounds but at a slow, regular pace. Each stage in the development of an individual is an outgrowth of an earlier stage. Hence, a teacher of young children must have not only a specific knowledge of children from nursery school through the elementary school but also a general knowledge of development from infancy to adulthood.

Development is not a haphazard affair. Each child has his own design. Frank has expressed the individuality of development in this way:

> The life career is a broad highway along which every individual must travel. Each individual with his unique heredity and nature will travel at his or her own rate of progress and will attain the size, shape, capacity, and developmental status which are uniquely his or her own at each stage in the life career. Because the rate of development remains fairly constant, development can be predicted early.[1]

Such prediction makes possible long-range planning for educational and vocational careers.

[1] L. T. Frank, "The Concept of Maturity," *Child Development*, 21:21–24, 1950.

On the other hand, evidence obtained from genetic studies indicates, as Gessell points out, that development follows an orderly sequence of growth:

Although no two individuals are exactly alike, all normal children tend to follow a general sequence of growth characteristic of the species and of the cultural group.[2]

Development proceeds from general to specific responses. In all phases of development, the child's responses are general before they become specific. In muscular responses, for example, the newborn infant moves his whole body at one time, instead of moving any one part of it. Random kicking precedes coordination of leg muscles in crawling, creeping, or walking. A similar pattern is seen in the child's use of his eyes. He sees large objects before he sees small ones; as he reaches for an object, he responds with his whole body. In learning new tasks such as dressing or undressing the whole body wiggles and responds.

The same sequence is seen in development of language. The infant babbles before he can say words. When he does use words, he uses general ones before specific. He says "dog" before he says "cocker spaniel." Concept formation, too, follows a similar pattern. For example, the baby distinguishes living from inanimate objects, then human beings from animals.

[2] Arnold Gesell, "Growth Potentialities of the Human Infant," *Scientific Monthly*, 68:252–256, 1949.

Growth follows an orderly and coherent pattern, but the pattern varies for each child.

The significance of this principle for the teacher is easy to see. She must provide the child with an opportunity to react to situations with his whole body, giving him a chance to use his large muscles before expecting him to participate in activities demanding the use of the small muscles. In concept development she must go from the simple to the complex, until the child gains skill by building upon what he already knows.

Development is interrelated. Most traits are correlated with others. The child who is gifted intellectually is generally above average in size, appearance, and sociability. Mental defectives, on the other hand, tend to be smaller than normal children.[3] It is not true that the child who is above average in one trait will be below in others and vice versa. Although the rate of development of different parts of the body may differ, they are compensatory; below-average growth in height during one period may be accompanied by above-average increase in weight.

The teacher needs to keep in mind that every aspect of growth is affected by every other aspect. For example, in learning to read and spell, the child's emotional self, social self, physical self, and other selves are all involved, along with his intellectual self.

Growth varies among individuals. Although children follow an orderly pattern of growth and development, it should be emphasized that a child grows at his own rate, and his rate of growth is consistent. The rapid developers continue to develop rapidly and the retarded children continue their slow pace. As the years progress, the chasm between the rapid developers and the retarded children widens. In general, this principle holds true in behavior patterns as well as in physical and mental development.

Development proceeds at different rates for different parts of the body. Not all parts of the body grow at the same rate, nor do all aspects of mental growth proceed at the same pace. To expect a child to make equal progress in all phases of development is futile. At-age-level achievement and maturity for each child in each phase of development is an impossibility.

Every individual normally passes through each major stage of development. The rate and time required to complete the characteristics of each stage of development differ from one child to another, but by the time the individual reaches twenty-one years of age the development will, except in unusual cases, be completed. Inability to pass through all the developmental stages is often correlated with low intelligence. Although other factors, such as unfavorable environment, ill health, and lack of motivation, may retard the normal rate of development, their influence is not permanent.

[3] Elizabeth B. Hurlock, *Child Development* (New York: McGraw-Hill Book Company, Inc., 1956), p. 38.

Each developmental stage has characteristic traits. At each age, certain traits develop more rapidly and more obviously than others. A dominant pattern, a leading characteristic gives that stage its coherence and unity. Each age has a characteristic pattern of its own that is consistent from child to child. The behavior of any given child at any given age is colored partly by his own individuality and partly by the pattern of this age level. The pattern does not consist so much of what the child can accomplish as it does of the way in which he behaves.[4]

In such a growth pattern, there are phases characterized by equilibrium and others characterized by disequilibrium. In the former, the child is "in focus." He is making a good adjustment and is easy to live with. In the latter, his adjustments are difficult; he appears to be torn by inner tensions, insecurities, indecisions. Environmental factors as well as inner conditions precipitate behavior problems. In any given child, periods of equilibrium and disequilibrium alternate.

Genetic studies have revealed the predictable ages of disequilibrium and equilibrium. Most obvious are the periods of disequilibrium at two-and-a-half, three-and-a-half, and just before the onset of puberty. Ilg and Ames have formulated a schematic presentation of age changes from two to adolescence:

2 years	5 years	10 years	Smooth, consolidated
2½	5½–6	11	Breaking up
3	6½	12	Rounded, balanced
3½	7	13	Inwardized
4	8	14	Vigorous, expansive
4½	9	15	Inwardized, outwardized, troubled, neurotic
5	10	16	Smooth, consolidated [5]

Obviously, such broad descriptions of behavior at various age levels must be treated with discretion, inasmuch as individuals vary in the actual age at which these periods of equilibrium and disequilibrium appear. Yet a cursory examination of the growth characteristics of children from two to ten will be useful in orienting the student to young children.

Many problems are normal behavior for the age in which they occur. Each developmental age is accompanied by certain undesirable forms of behavior that are unique to that age and are outgrown as the child moves on to subsequent stages of development. Look, for example, at the three-and-a-half-year-olds; they reveal emotional instability, insecurity, extremes in behavior, stuttering, and nail-biting. At this age there is a developmental spurt, especially in boys who have been slow in starting. Behavior then becomes well organized, and a period of equilibrium follows.

[4] Frances Ilg and Louise Ames, "The Three and a Half Year Old," *Journal of Genetic Psychology*, 75:21–31, September 1949.

[5] Frances Ilg and Louise Ames, *Child Behavior* (New York: Harper & Brothers, 1955), p. 12.

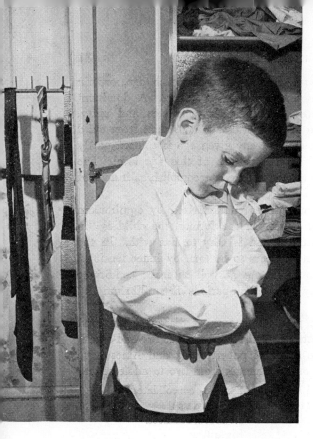

Achieving personal independence helps a child maintain a state of emotional equilibrium.

The five-year-old again is in focus, but this period of equilibrium is followed by disequilibrium — a difficult age in which the child is aggressive, explosive, fresh, rude, argumentative, and insulting.

During all this and later development, children exhibit many forms of behavior that will be modified or abandoned in the course of time. "This principle of development," says one observer, "implies the idea that behavior activities which are useful to the child at one level of maturity are modified or abandoned, as the case requires, at another stage of development in favor of responses more useful and harmonious with the child's developmental level." [6]

If teachers and other adults concerned with guiding boys and girls would inform themselves as to the developmental problems of children and be patient enough to follow the sequences of growth patterns, many of the problems of being a teacher or parent would be lessened.

Indeed, a lack of understanding of such normal behavior at various ages is at the root of much frustration of teachers and of much friction between child and parents. Adults need to understand and tolerate, but also guide, the normal behavior patterns of children. They must accept children in terms of the social and behavioral standards of their growth and guide them through difficult periods.

[6] Karl C. Garrison, *Growth and Development* (New York: Longmans, Green & Co., Inc., 1953), p. 71.

Growth creates needs. Needs, motives, and personal-social drives of children are the result of years of living in a particular environment. They are not wholly determined by growth. The kind of culture that emerges from a specific environmental pattern determines to a significant extent the pattern of behavior and the growth of personality.

Implied in such a concept is an interaction between the child and his environment. At birth the infant is concerned solely with satisfying the basic needs for maintaining life. When he has food, warmth, and protection to an adequate degree, administered by friendly hands, he responds by growing and developing. But as growth continues, new needs, new demands arise. Such continuing and ever-broadening growth of needs and their satisfaction motivates development. Needs are the products of intrinsic growth factors (the results of heredity), plus extrinsic factors in the culture.

Herein lies the challenge. The idea implies that the school contributes to growth and development, that its influence upon the child creates new needs, good or bad, and that, having created them, it satisfies them in part or in whole.

Growth is modifiable. Although the urge to grow is innate, under certain conditions it may be modified in rate or timing. Timing is one aspect of growth that is not susceptible to environmental change. When pressure is applied before a child is ready frustration may result. Even when applied during the developmental spurt or growth upswing, gain may be only temporary, tending to recede to the original rate when pressure is released.

In the ideal situation, it should be remembered, modification comes with the greatest permanent benefits as the result of a continuous effort to improve the total culture and environment within which the child lives and to provide a constant school environment that is conducive to optimum growth and learning.

IMPLICATIONS OF THE PRINCIPLES OF DEVELOPMENT

A knowledge of the principles of development is essential. It helps us to know what to expect and when to expect it. It gives the adult a clue as to when to stimulate and when not to stimulate development in the child. In short, it provides a basis for planning in such a way that the encouragement to achieve is present at the right psychological moment. Thus, when a child is beginning to walk, he must be given opportunities to practice walking and the necessary motivation. When he is beginning to talk, he should be encouraged to talk; if his wishes are always anticipated, his motivation for speech may be blocked.

Knowledge of developmental patterns also makes it possible for adults to prepare the child beforehand for changes that will take place in his body, his behavior, or his interests. The child who knows what is expected of him when he comes to kindergarten adjusts to school more readily than the child who has had no preparation.

Understanding Child Behavior

If the teacher applies her knowledge of growth and development and relates it to actual classroom situations, many frustrating situations may be avoided.

An understanding of the behavior of boys and girls can transform confused, harassed teachers into confident, competent, poised individuals able to organize profitable learning activities and develop them in a stimulating group situation. Many adults have trouble understanding children's behavior; they think of children as miniature adults. Assuming a child's reactions and patterns of behavior to be quite similar to their own, they interpret the child's activity in terms of adult standards and adult expectations of conduct. But children are not miniature adults. Their needs are somewhat different from those of adults; they are not mature physically, mentally, socially, or emotionally; they lack sufficient experience to make adjustments in a mature way; they live in the here-and-now, unable to foresee consequences of their actions; and they do not fully comprehend relationships of cause and effect. From all this, some general principles for the interpretation of child behavior have emerged:

1. Children's activity is directed toward satisfying needs.
2. Children's maturation patterns affect their behavior.
3. Problems of adjustment arise when the child cannot satisfy his needs.
4. Children attempt to meet their problems intelligently.
5. Children's behavior is caused.

Activity directed toward satisfying needs. Perhaps one of the most useful ideas for the teacher to remember about child behavior is that a child's activity is not haphazard. The child has, first of all, biological needs that must be satisfied. The infant's activity centers largely around satisfying such needs, which develop primarily out of the structure and dynamic mechanisms of the individual, chiefly those concerned with food, liquid, oxygen, warmth, rest, and activity. When a need is not met, tensions are built up, and the infant seeks to eliminate this tension. If he is successful, equilibrium is restored. The satisfaction of biological needs is learned at a relatively young age.

Social needs develop as the child grows older and feels the need for affection. He wants to trust adults and be accepted by them. He can satisfy his social needs only through association with others. As the infant or young child gains control over his biological needs, social needs become increasingly powerful in directing his activity. Satisfaction of social needs remains a major problem through childhood, adolescence, and adulthood. With increasing maturity the child seeks and often finds better ways of satisfying his needs. In order to help this process, the teacher should provide an environment in which the child can satisfy his need for acceptance, affection, recognition for achievement, and status in the group. The child must also have experiences in group responsibilities and privileges as he grows from dependence to independence, from irresponsibility to responsibility.

Children need to learn to face reality and to accept themselves as they are, with whatever strengths and weaknesses they possess. They need to accept, understand, and express their inner feelings. As they develop, they must also learn to control those feelings that are undesirable and to redirect their emotional outlets in ways that are socially acceptable.

Adults should provide children with experiences that will help them understand the forces operating in their world. Children need opportunities to achieve satisfaction and success. As they mature, they need, too, to experience failure in some ventures and to build inner strengths to meet disappointment. The teacher should provide a social climate that will encourage children to express themselves creatively, for only thus will they build their own inner reserves and strengths.

Maturation patterns and behavior. Maturation may be defined as growth of all types — physical, motor, sensory, mental — which occurs under normal, stimulating conditions.

From infancy throughout childhood, the maturation rate affects significantly

During the developmental years the need for security gives way to the need for social experience.

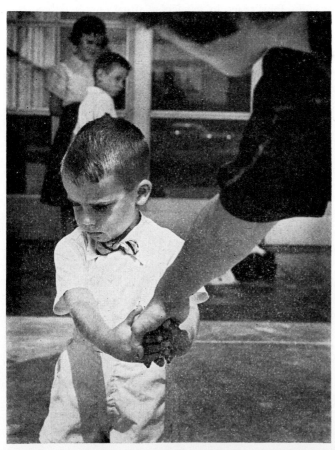

Whatever a child does, he does for a reason, although the reason may not be readily apparent to the adult.

what children can do, how they react in particular situations, and how they feel about themselves and others. What a child does, says, thinks, writes, expresses; how he feels about his physical size and appearance; how he reacts to his family and his age-mates; how he feels about his achievements; how he meets new situations; what defensive mechanisms he resorts to in frustrating situations; how he responds to satisfactions and frustrations, all are dependent upon his maturation rate. He carries with him his own timetable of growth, largely determined by hereditary factors; although he can be motivated, he cannot be pushed. A teacher must know the child in order to determine his maturational status and understand his behavior.

A striking example is found in the relationship between maturation pattern and the development of speech. For example, gifted girls begin talking at a mean age of 11.01 months; gifted boys at 11.74 months; normal children at 15.32 months; and feeble-minded children at 38.52 months.[7]

Adjustment problems and need satisfaction. Every need — biological, social, or personal — with its pattern of tension and demand for satisfaction, constitutes the motivation for the activity that follows. If that activity leads directly to satisfaction of the need, obviously no adjustment problem arises. But if satisfaction is not achieved, the need is still there; the tension remains, and the

[7] C. D. Mead, *The Relation of General Intelligence to Certain Mental and Physical Traits of Children* (New York: Teachers College Contributions to Education, 1916), p. 117; Lewis Terman, *Genetic Studies of Genius* (Stanford: Stanford University Press, 1926), Vol. I, p. 187.

child tries to reduce the tension. When he cannot do this, a problem of adjustment arises. When children cannot find socially approved ways of solving such problems of adjustment, they will resort to some other activity to satisfy the need, or they will withdraw, regardless of whether the teacher approves of their behavior. It is at this point that the teacher must help, for, we are told, "early childhood is the period of life predominantly concerned with the origin of neurosis." [8]

Activities that teachers consider serious behavior problems, such as lying, stealing, cheating, masturbating, fighting, and withdrawing, are symptomatic of unsatisfied needs and should be dealt with as such. Teachers should be aware of the conditions that block need satisfaction. Such conditions may exist in the child himself or stem from his relationship to age-mates and adults. Some result from the child's inability to achieve success in his academic work; others stem from conditions in his social environment. At times, conditions within the classroom itself make it impossible for him to satisfy his basic needs. For example, if the child's need for activity is not provided for in the daily schedule, he may burst out into undesirable behavior.

It is essential that the teacher provide an environment in which needs can be satisfied. Such an environment will not only permit but encourage bodily activity and motor experience by providing time for a variety of motor activities and will ensure a balance of activity and rest. It will provide a social climate that offers reasonable opportunities for communication, sharing, planning, and participation in experiences significant enough to bring some measure of satisfaction and success to the children.

Adjustment and intelligence. The normal child has potential for intelligent behavior, but how he uses this capacity depends largely on the adults around him. If he receives approval for solving problems intelligently, he tries to meet his problems intelligently.

Susan, the five-year-old who has been getting her way by temper tantrums since she was two, persists in this behavior as long as she considers it intelligent. When the kindergarten teacher fails to recognize it as intelligent behavior and Susan gains no satisfaction from her exhibitions, she may soon decide that they work at home but not in school.

Helping parents to understand that a child behaves as he does because he is honestly convinced it is an intelligent way of responding to a given situation is not always easy. Adults have difficulty in believing that a child who repeatedly bumps his head against the wall believes he is acting intelligently on the basis of past experience. As children are helped to find more satisfying and socially approved ways of meeting needs they will adopt them. The road to maturity is one in which the child adopts more intelligent behavior as he finds it a more suitable way of satisfying his needs.

[8] Catherine Landreth, *The Psychology of Early Childhood* (New York: Alfred A. Knopf, Inc., 1958), p. 6.

Behavior is caused. Everything a child does, he does for a reason. All of his activity has a cause. It stems from heredity, from his maturation pattern, from the situation to which he must respond, from his own inner satisfaction or frustration in meeting his needs, and from the learning he has achieved up to that time.

Much so-called misbehavior is symptomatic. The child is signaling that for some reason or other he cannot satisfy a need in a socially approved way. He may be trying to say that you are failing to give him the opportunity to satisfy his biological needs. He may punctuate his effort to tell you that you are failing him by all sorts of symptomatic behavior — whispering, throwing paper wads, sneaking out to the bathroom, running up to sharpen a pencil, tearing his books, throwing pictures away, and so on. In the face of such behavior a wise teacher will check up on herself to see whether or not she is providing adequately for the basic needs.

Developmental Tasks

Standards of what to expect at each age have been set up not as infallible guides but as aids in understanding sequences of development at various stages in the growth cycle. One of the most comprehensive standards has been formulated by Havighurst in his series of developmental tasks for different age levels. Havighurst defines a developmental task as one "which arises at or about a certain period in the life of an individual, successful achievement of which leads to his happiness and to success with later tasks, while failure leads to unhappiness in the individual, disapproval by the society and difficulty with later tasks." [9] Developmental tasks are set by both internal and external forces. There are three sources for such tasks: physical maturation, such as learning to walk; the cultural pressures of society, such as learning to read: and personal values and aspirations that are part of the personality of the individual, such as choosing and preparing for an occupation. Of course, these sources are not mutually exclusive.

The concept of developmental tasks is useful to educators for two reasons. Firstly, it helps in identifying and stating the objectives of education in the schools. For example, education may be conceived of as an effort of society through the school to help the individual achieve certain of his developmental tasks, or it may be conceived as society's way of helping parents control their children. Secondly, it aids in timing educational efforts. "When the body is ripe and society requires, and the self is ready to achieve a certain task, the teachable moment has come. Efforts at teaching which would have been largely wasted if they had come earlier, give gratifying results when they come at the teachable moment, when the task would be learned." [10]

[9] Robert James Havighurst, *Developmental Tasks and Education* (Chicago: The University of Chicago Press, 1948), p. 2.
[10] *Ibid.*, p. 5.

Developmental Tasks of Children

Approaching Four Years	The Four-Year-Old	The Five-Year-Old	Middle Childhood, Six to Twelve Years
Learning to walk	Learning initiative	Developing a wholesome attitude toward growing physical organism	Learning physical skills necessary for ordinary games
Learning to take solid foods	Developing conscience	Learning to get along with age-mates	Learning to get along with age-mates
Learning to talk	Learning tasks of locomotion	Developing concepts necessary for everyday living	Learning an appropriate sex role
Learning processes of caring for physical needs	Having initial experience in group participation	Learning to be a contributing member of a group	Developing fundamental skills in reading, writing, and calculating
Developing a basic sense of trust	Learning to find a place in family and peer group	Continuing to learn tasks of locomotion	Developing concepts necessary for everyday living
Developing a foundation for becoming an independent and self-directive person		Developing conscience as a moral guard	Developing conscience, morality, and a scale of values
Learning simple concepts of right and wrong			Achieving personal independence
			Developing attitudes toward social group and institutions

From Robert Havighurst, *Human Development and Education — Process of Elimination* (New York: Longmans Green & Co., Inc., 1953); *Developmental Tasks and Education* (Chicago: The University of Chicago Press, 1948).

Physical achievement is necessary to the social development of the young child.

Summary

In this chapter we have stressed the need for understanding child growth and development as a prerequisite to organizing the learning environment so that the design for development may be in the direction of patterns that are individually satisfying and socially approved. A knowledge of the principles of growth prepares the teacher to expect continuity, orderliness, and relatedness in development; it prepares her likewise for variation in the growth pattern, for the constant emergence of new needs, resulting in new tensions that must be resolved as the individual passes through each major stage of development.

Children are confronted with certain learning problems or developmental tasks because they are growing organisms, because they have basic needs that must be satisfied, and because the culture dictates how and when many of these must be met. An enumeration of the developmental tasks provides the teacher with a description of the major learning problems confronting a child at a given stage. Since not all children master these tasks at the same chronological age, the teacher must know the sequence of the developmental tasks.

Such a design emphasizes the developmental orientation toward growth and alerts the teacher to the need for looking back to previous experiences and forward to future goals of boys and girls as clues to present behavior. The orientation is one that points up the importance of interpreting behavioral changes in terms of an individual interacting with his environment.

QUESTIONS AND ACTIVITIES

1. Why is it important to know the principles of development?

2. How should the concept of individual differences influence the instructional program?

3. Analyze the five principles underlying a psychological basis for understanding children's behavior. What evidence of the application of these principles did you observe in your visit to a classroom?

4. In what way can the teacher make use of a knowledge of the developmental tasks in planning the curriculum for her children?

5. Visit a nursery, kindergarten, and a primary grade, and identify the developmental tasks common to the children at each of the three levels. In what way did the teacher aid the children in working on their developmental tasks? What did the teacher do to prevent maladjusted behavior in the classroom? What might she have done? Cite specific cases of maladjusted behavior you observed.

6. List the symptoms that teachers frequently classify as problem behavior.

SUGGESTED READINGS

Almy, Millie. *Child Development.* New York: Henry Holt & Company, Inc., 1955.

American Council on Education. *Helping Teachers Understand Children.* Washington, D.C.: American Council on Education, 1946.

Breckenridge, M. E., and E. L. Vincent. *Child Development.* Philadelphia: W. B. Saunders Company, 1950.

Cunningham, Ruth, *et al. Understanding Group Behavior of Boys and Girls.* New York: Bureau of Publications, Teachers College, Columbia University, 1951.

Forest, Ilse. *Child Development.* New York: McGraw-Hill Book Company, Inc., 1954.

Garrison, Karl C. *Growth and Development.* New York: Longmans, Green & Company, 1952.

Gesell, Arnold, and Frances L. Ilg. *The Child from Five to Ten.* New York: Harper & Brothers, 1946.

Gesell, Arnold, and Frances L. Ilg. *Infant and Child in the Culture of Today.* New York: Harper & Brothers, 1943.

Havighurst, Robert J. *Developmental Tasks and Education,* Second Edition. Chicago: The University of Chicago Press, 1948.

Havighurst, Robert J. *Human Development and Education.* New York: Longmans, Green & Company, 1952.

Hurlock, Elizabeth. *Child Development,* Third Edition. New York: McGraw-Hill Book Company, Inc., 1954.

Ilg, Frances L., and Louise B. Ames. *Child Behavior.* New York: Harper & Brothers, 1955.

Jersild, Arthur. *Child Psychology,* Fourth Edition. Englewood Cliffs, N.J.: Prentice-Hall, Inc., 1954.

Josselyn, Irene. *The Happy Child.* New York: Random House, Inc., 1955.

Martin, W. E., and C. B. Stendler. *Child Behavior and Development*. New York: Harcourt, Brace & Company, Inc., 1959.

Martin, W. E., and C. B. Stendler. *Child Development*. New York: Harcourt, Brace & Company, Inc., 1953.

Midcentury White House Conference on Children and Youth. *A Healthy Personality for Every Child*. Raleigh, N.C.: Health Publications Institute, Inc., 1951.

Millard, Cecil V. *Child Growth and Development*. Boston: D. C. Heath & Company, 1958.

Olson, W. C. *Child Development*. Boston: D. C. Heath & Company, 1949.

Sheehy, Emma D. *Fives and Sixes Go to School*. New York: Henry Holt & Company, Inc., 1954.

Terman, L. M. *Genetic Studies of a Thousand Gifted Children*. Stanford: Stanford University Press, 1952.

Thorpe, L. P. *Child Psychology and Development*, Second Edition. New York: The Ronald Press Company, 1955.

4

Guiding the Two- to Nine-Year-Old

The products of growth are envisioned as a fabric in which threads and designs are visible.

— ARNOLD GESELL

In the preface of a book published in 1923, Patty Hill wrote: "One might timidly venture to prophesy a better future for both school and society when the behavioristic concept of education shall be applied in the early, impressionable years of children."[1]

In 1946, Gesell and Ilg boldly stated that, "The task of child care is not to mold the child behavioristically to some predetermined image, but to assist

[1] Agnes Burke *et al.*, *A Conduct Curriculum for the Kindergarten and First Grade* (New York: Charles Scribner's Sons, 1923), pp. xxi–xxii.

him step by step, guiding his growth. This developmental philosophy does not mean indulgence. It is instead a constructive accommodation to the limitations of maturity." [2]

Today, so far have we progressed along this path, the question of how much guidance a child needs can be discussed on the basis of the characteristics of a two-year-old, a three-year-old, or a seven-year-old, with the understanding that the growth gradients are approximate norms of developmental sequence.

As we look at children from two to nine years old, we will focus on the three responsibilities the teacher must assume in guiding children's physical, social, emotional, and intellectual areas of behavior. Teachers must know the developmental characteristics and needs of children from two to nine years old in order to know what behavior to expect at the various levels of development; they must know how to apply their knowledge of developmental characteristics and needs in teaching children in nursery, kindergarten, and primary grades; and they must understand the nature of the learning process by which effective development proceeds, in order to provide the proper learning environment to facilitate optimum development of each child.

Developmental Characteristics

As the student observes the behavior of young children, she will come to know what a two-year-old is like, a three-, a four-, a six- or a nine-year-old. She will discover how the two's are alike, how they differ from each other, and how they differ from the other age levels. As she watches for cues, she will come to detect not only differences at a given age level but the relation of these differences to maturity. Gradually she will gain skill in classifying children and in guiding their growth and learning experiences.

As a prospective teacher, each student will want to know what children are really like, what to expect of them at various stages of development, what knowledge is essential, and what techniques are successful in guiding children's learning. Teaching young children is essentially guidance of physical and social development. The behavior guidance and general management of a young child should be based on the maturity level of his personal-social behavior — not on his chronological age. If the teacher observes that a four-year-old is operating consistently at the three-year-old behavior level, it will be an advantage to both teacher and child to treat him as a three-year-old and not hold him to four-year-old standards. Hence, one should be familiar with the characteristics of each age level.

In the final analysis the child is his own norm. He has his own self-regulatory mechanism of growth, which can only be aided by an understanding teacher. [3]

---

[2] Arnold Gesell and Frances Ilg, *The Child from Five to Ten* (New York: Harper & Brothers, 1946), p. 35.

[3] Arnold Gesell and Frances Ilg, *Infant and Child in the Culture of Today* (New York: Harper & Brothers, 1943), p. 72.

THE TWO-YEAR-OLD

The two-year-old brings something of a breathing spell to both the child and his mother. It is an age of rather marked equilibrium. At this age, the child is easier to control than he was or will be. His added maturity, his eagerness to conform, and his desire to do what he can do and to avoid what he cannot do, all make this a period of comparative ease in guiding the individual child.

Socially, he is interested in people, anxious to please and to be pleased by others. Sharing, however, is not for him, although he is willing to let children use toys other than the ones with which he is playing. His good nature, warm response, and interest in people are delightful. Increased ability to express himself in language contributes toward this improved behavior. He understands much of what others say to him, and he is beginning to use verbal communication to make his needs known and to gain his own ends. He is becoming a master of persuasion. Frustrations are less frequent, for language often takes the place of crying, shouting, and temper tantrums.

Motor-wise, the two-year-old is becoming more adept. He climbs more easily and loses his balance less frequently; he crawls, runs, and trots more often than he walks. But at two he is still an infant-child and in most cases is happier at home than in a nursery school.

THE TWO-AND-A-HALF-YEAR-OLD

The change that takes place between the two-year-old and the two-and-a-half-year-old is as bewildering and overwhelming for the child as for the parent. Perhaps the most exasperating aspect of the two-and-a-half-year-old is his predilection for "No!" This disturbs parents more than teachers.

The nursery-school teacher recognizes that "no" is a word that is fun for a child, because it evokes the strangest behavior in adults. A teacher knows that only a moment after a child has said, "No," most emphatically, he confidently takes her hand, smiles his most engaging smile, and proceeds to do what he just said he wouldn't do.

THE THREE-YEAR-OLD

Ilg and Ames picture the three-year-old as more conforming, more anxious to please than the two-and-a-half-year-old.[4] His motor control is improved and his interest in people has increased. Cooperative, imaginative, responsive to verbal guidance, beginning to share, the three-year-old is a joy to his teachers and parents. "We" has become an important word. It expresses his reaction to the new-found security and confidence he feels toward people. Socially, he gets along better with his age-mates, although he needs plenty of reassurance, encouragement, and guidance from adults. He feels he is a good boy, but he wants to be told about it.

[4] Frances Ilg and Louise Ames, *Child Behavior* (New York: Harper & Brothers, 1955), p. 27.

Interests have broadened: he enjoys a wide variety of play materials; he loves painting, clay modeling, and water play; he builds blocks with precision and forethought; he enjoys percussion instruments, especially the drum. He loves rhythms and vigorous outdoor play. Material of any sort serves as a whetstone for his dramatic abilities, and blocks become boats, trains, airplanes, or rockets.

Perhaps the most significant change in the three-year-old is his fluency in language. Now he can be controlled by language, not just entertained. He loves using words, any words, but especially new ones and big ones.

THE THREE-AND-A-HALF-YEAR-OLD

As he approaches three-and-a-half our happy, calm, assured three does a right-about-face. A great change seems to set in, ushering in a period of marked uneasiness, insecurity, poor motor coordination, and general disequilibrium. In part, this change is the result of his eagerness to conquer new worlds, to have new experiences, and to achieve. His vocabulary is inadequate for keeping up with this world of ideas. He tries so hard to express and to achieve that frequently he blocks and stutters. He often shows evidence of great emotional extremes. Shy one moment and boisterous the next, he has difficulty in taking social situations in his stride.

Obviously, in a period of strains and tensions the greatest need of the three-and-a-half-year-old is constant reassurance from the adults around him. He needs affection and patience as he approaches what some writers have called the "impossible fours."

THE FOUR-YEAR-OLD

"Out-of-bounds" is the most descriptive and most frequently quoted phrase concerning the four-year-old. Defiant, boastful, tough, swaggering braggadocio characterizes the four-year-old. In motor development he kicks, breaks things, runs away, and pushes.

Emotionally, too, he is out of bounds, exhibiting loud, silly laughter and aggressive behavior, alternating with temper tantrums and fits of rage. Verbally, he is almost impossible. Profanity and words relating to the bathroom and elimination are common. He rhymes, quotes, and dwells on an experience, particularly on an unpleasant experience that may embarrass his mother.

Socially, his behavior shows growth in group situations. He plays vigorously, talks incessantly, and enjoys imaginary companions. He likes to play with sand, clay, and fingerpaint. Blocks are becoming his prime interest. He can concentrate, and he now enjoys painting as a relief from vigorous play. Stories, music, puzzles, and picture books are beginning to fascinate him.

THE FOUR-AND-A-HALF-YEAR-OLD

Much to the relief of all concerned, the four-and-a-half-year-old is beginning to calm down. He is less boisterous, more interested in quiet activities such as painting and books. He is interested, too, in numbers and letters and in "reading" pictures. He engages in conversation, having developed elementary skills of discussion. "Know what I did last night?" or "What did you see on TV?" are common openings for lengthy conversations. According to Ilg and Ames, four-and-a-half is a catching-up time for some children, especially for boys who have been slow starters in language or motor development.[5] For them, indeed, it may be a period of rapid intellectual and motor development.

THE FIVE-YEAR-OLD

Many times a first-grade teacher, with a room full of six-year-olds, has said despairingly, "How do you get those five-year-olds to behave like that in kindergarten?" Mothers of the fives, too, breathe a sigh of relief as the unpredictable fours become the stable, sociable, cooperative fives.

The five-year-old loves kindergarten, his teacher, and life. Being good is easy for him, for he is not looking for new worlds to conquer. He is content to do what he can do. He is a good boy, satisfied with himself, with his world, and with the adults around him. He goes confidently to and from kindergarten. He has completed the first long lap on the pathway to maturity.

THE SIX-YEAR-OLD

After a year in kindergarten, the six-year-old emerges with certain characteristics and evidences of growth — physical, intellectual, emotional, and social — considerably advanced from those of his beginning days in kindergarten.

He has gained considerably in height. He can catch a ball, balance and hang from his heels on the jungle gym, handle scissors with ease, model in clay with gusto. He is improving in muscular coordination. His health is more robust; having built up a resistance to colds and common illnesses, he is absent less frequently than he was as a kindergartner. His random activity is being channeled into specific drives, and his need for increased outlets for physical, social, and creative urges is evident.

Intellectually he is more curious. "Why?" has given way to "How?" His speech is clearer and more complex; he has added many words to his vocabulary. As a rule, he listens well and carries out directions with more dispatch. Skill in auditory and visual discrimination is improved. His questions reveal a broadened curiosity and interest in his world. He is eager to explore, investigate, and experiment. He is more mature. He reads signs and pictures and asks, "What does this say?" Although he has had no formal training in reading in kindergarten, he may actually read books.

Ilg and Ames refer to the six-year-old as the "tumultuous six." "He is aggressive, vigorous, boisterous, and wants to be first!"[6]

---

[5] *Ibid.*, p. 33.
[6] *Ibid.*, p. 34.

Music is only one activity that stimulates the interest of the four-year-old.

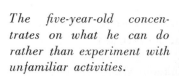

The five-year-old concentrates on what he can do rather than experiment with unfamiliar activities.

The need for increased outlets for physical energy becomes very important with the six-year-old.

Reading becomes significant to the child for the first time when he is seven.

Action is the key word for the eight-year-old, who is interested in exploring and manipulating his world.

The Seven-Year-Old

Each age brings with it changes in behavior. Seven is no exception. Whereas the six-year-old was aggressive, rough and ready, falsely sure of himself, meeting situations head-on, the seven-year-old is characterized by withdrawn behavior. He withdraws not only from conflict but from people. He enjoys solitude. He likes to read, watch television, and dream.

Emotionally, he is often upset. He demands too much of himself and of others. He is restless, fidgety, and dreamy. He can be caustic, contentious, and critical. Seven is also sensitive to his inner feelings and attitudes as well as to the feelings and attitudes of age-mates and adults.

The seven-year-old is talkative and he often exaggerates. He uses words as tools of persuasion instead of as blows in fighting. Full of energy, he nevertheless tires easily.

The Eight-Year-Old

The eight-year-old goes forth each day to joust with windmills. Nothing daunts him. Expansive, speedy, and active, looking for new worlds to conquer, he is not one to withdraw from the heat of battle.

Yet, for all his seeming brashness and bravado, he is more sensitive than the inexperienced teacher might expect. He needs help in setting realistic goals and in being tolerant of himself when he meets failure. He is exhilarant, arrogant, and ready, but he needs to identify himself with an understanding adult.

Action is the key word for the eight-year-old. In play, baseball and football give him an outlet for his energies. He is a gregarious, social creature. Boys play with boys, girls are "sissies," and so are boys who play with girls. The eight-year-old has many interests: television, books, science, stamp collections, building, sports, and so forth.

The Nine-Year-Old

When eight becomes nine, he has left the stage of early childhood behind him. Standing on the threshold of an uncertain period, his behavior is characterized by rebellion, withdrawal, complaint, and insecurity. His individuality is becoming more noticeable. He is quieter at work, but may annoy others by making sudden noises, such as banging on the desk top or making clicking sounds with his mouth.

Though competition in work and play excites him, he is afraid of failure. He wants to be independent of the teacher, but at the same time he wants to be able to refer to her for help. He may be self-conscious when reporting or reciting before the group. He knows when he is sure or not too sure of an answer. He is developing skills of evaluation and discusses how he can do things best. He concentrates for longer periods at a time. He enjoys grades and report cards and compares his grades with the others. He wants to be treated as an adult, but he is still, at times, a little boy.

Two Growth Periods

Two- to Five-Year-Olds

From the behavior profiles of the first five years of life we see that this period is characterized by the highest rate of growth. The child does practically as much growing in his first five years as he does in the next ten.

His main concern is with himself and with satisfying his basic needs. How he gets along socially depends on his place in the family, the family's place in the community, the opportunities for playing and working with other children, and his own behavior pattern. Language serves him as a useful social tool. By the time he is ready for first grade he has a speaking vocabulary of some 2,500 words and uses most of the forms of speech.

Most of his motor skills have been established, although he will need opportunity to practice them in order to develop increased confidence, coordination, and skill in the years ahead. He runs, skips, jumps, throws, and is able to handle his body fairly well. His eyes, ears, and voice are ready to respond and to do whatever he is able to learn at this point.

During this period he is learning to identify and accept himself, to be aware of the physical and social world around him, and to share his emotional world with others. He has made a beginning on the life-long task of learning to live with people. He has begun to meet and deal with some of the demands life places upon him. He has taken the first steps in responsible living.

Six- to Nine-Year-Olds

Perhaps the major task of the six-to-nine is to learn the social skills of living in groups of various size and complexity.

The period is characterized by the need of the child to learn the skills of communication, to read, write, speak, and listen. He is becoming skillful in the use of numbers. His interest in the world about him is growing. He wants to achieve, to succeed, and to please. Parents and teachers are important to him; he trusts them, depends upon them, and in general is in a stable stage of development. Relationships between mental age and chronological age are fairly constant, physical growth is at an even tempo, and the child feels able to take care of his needs in most activities requiring skills.

Teaching the Two- to Nine-Year-Olds

Teaching the Two-Year-Old

Because the responsibility that the teacher of the two- and two-and-a-half-year-old must assume is great, she must never be without an assistant. Many two-year-olds neither ask for help nor come to get it; therefore, the teacher must sense the needs of each child. Always she must be prepared to play her role as a mother-substitute, a friend, and a guide. She must give genuine affection and warm support.

The two-and-a-half-year-old needs much help in adjusting to his age group. He enjoys parallel play; the best way of organizing and guiding the play period is to provide the same equipment for several children. Each child can run his own game while the teacher engages in similar play nearby. Interest in the sandbox runs high, and manipulation is more varied. In doll play children show more imagination. Easel painting is popular.

A safe environment and careful supervision of all activity are imperative. Doors must be closed, stairs must be guarded, gates must be watched. The teacher of two-year-olds must be ready to account for her charges at any moment. Counting noses often is helpful. In addition, the teacher must notice what goes into ears, nose, and mouth.

The teacher is responsible for arranging the physical set-up in the playroom and for organizing the outdoor environment to afford maximum group enjoyment and participation and minimum group friction. Thus, she provides for individual differences in adjusting to the educational environment, establishes efficient and satisfying routines, and maintains warm teacher-child-parent relationships.

Guiding this youngest of students requires the teacher to be simultaneously tolerant and supporting, to be constantly alert to physical needs and safety, to arrange adequate play environment, to show confidence in each child's ability to grow in adequacy and social competence, and to be at once sensitive to the needs of the individual and of the group. Teachers of the youngest must possess physical stamina, intelligence, a genuine love for children, patience and poise sufficient to meet emergencies, and tact in working with parents.

TEACHING THE THREE-YEAR-OLD

Since this is a social, imitative age, it is wise for the teacher to stress the positive. She will say, for example, "We stand on the floor," not, "Don't stand on the tables." Letting a child who has a problem in his own group shift to another is a useful way of helping both him and the group. Isolation from his own group may be used, but only as a last resort. If it is used, it should be for only a brief period, and he should be accompanied by an adult and toys he likes.

Guidance of the three-year-olds requires arranging the best possible physical set-up both in the playroom and out-of-doors. It involves helping children to adjust to group living and to learn the developmental tasks of eating, sleeping, waking, dressing, undressing, and toileting.

The teacher of three-year-olds must be simultaneously permissive, supporting, confident in the child's ability to grow in adequacy and social competence, and vigilant in ensuring physical safety.

TEACHING THE FOUR-YEAR-OLD

Teaching the four-year-olds is a challenge. Some teachers are unable to cope with this age because of its personality characteristics. A combination of firmness and flexibility is what is needed — a recognition of the fact that out-of-bounds behavior is characteristic of the age. One needs to hold the reins loosely, but in such a way that they can be pulled up sharply at a moment's notice.

One teacher who has been particularly successful with this age recommends a mixture of holding the four-year-old firmly to the line and giving him the freedom he can use. She offers the following suggestions:

> Provide a variety of materials and activities.
> Be ready to reorganize groups if play deteriorates.
> Provide quiet periods balanced with vigorous play.
> Plan and evaluate the program in terms of the developmental characteristics and needs of the child.
> Use isolation as a means of relief from group stimulation, not as a punishment.
> Set limits on a child's behavior in terms he understands.

The teacher must provide a warm response to the child's overtures of friendliness, though she should be prepared for extreme emotions and a free display of feelings. The closer he comes to his fifth birthday, the more stable and predictable his behavior will be. If you can't accept him and enjoy him at four — wait! He'll soon be five!

TEACHING THE FIVE-YEAR-OLD

Teaching the five-year-old is a responsibility. It is only too easy for an unimaginative teacher to exploit a child's eagerness to please and to learn.

Arousing the child's curiosity through arranging a stimulating environment is the teacher's responsibility.

It takes far less effort to plan handwork lessons, formal reading readiness exercises, and teacher-directed games than it does to provide a rich environment with learning experiences broadened in scope to meet the five-year-old's need to explore, manipulate, experiment, solve problems, and create.

Creative teaching demands that the teacher provide stimulating experiences, new materials, time, space, and motivation for the five-year-olds, who are eager to expand their horizons. The good kindergarten teacher is concerned with the child's development intellectually as well as socially, emotionally, and physically. Parents have become aware of the value of the socializing and educational experience of a year in kindergarten and are its staunchest supporters. Kindergarten, according to Laura Zirbes, a well-known educator, "is important not because it prepares children for first grade, but because it prepares children who are going to be first graders." [7]

The kindergarten teacher who would successfully guide children during this significant year must be able to help the child develop basic understandings and concepts of the world in which he lives. She must know and understand basic fields of subject matter and methods of problem solving; she must inspire children in creative experiences. Her program should be based on the needs of the children, their experiential background, and the developmental stage during which an interest in academic matters makes itself felt.

Teaching the Six-Year-Old

Somewhere between five and six the child reaches out; he moves out from a world of comparative security, from a world of fancy, to a world of reality. The six-year-old is not merely a bigger and better five-year-old. He is a different child. On the positive side, his teacher finds him less timid, more ready to explore his world, vigorous, energetic, and eager for new experiences. He wants to win, to be first, and to be right. When he is not, he may pout. He changes quickly from an eager, aggressive, warm, enthusiastic lad to a negative, demanding child, subject to tears and tantrums.

The teacher who understands the six-year-old recognizes the new urges, drives, and temperament. She makes use of the child's eagerness to learn, to work, and to achieve difficult tasks. She assigns tasks that he can accomplish. She helps him accept himself, channel his energies, and utilize the upsetting emotional drive. Unobtrusively she guides him by making choices when he seems unable to choose between several possibilities.

The teacher who is successful with the six-year-old provides for his needs for status: on the playground she helps him find things he can do successfully; in the classroom she provides for his abilities so he can succeed at something. She accepts him as he is — shy or bold, noisy or withdrawn, good or bad.

Teaching the Seven-Year-Old

The teacher's opinion is important to the seven-year-old, for he is dependent on adult approval. He wants to be sure he has done the right thing.

[7] *Childhood Education*, 31:370, April 1955.

The teacher who is looking for a less strenuous job might try the second grade. By that time the child has made his adjustment to school; he has learned to work independently; he has learned to read fairly well; he wants to please the teacher.

Interests of the two sexes are becoming fixed. Girls play with girls, and boys with boys. Girls tend to show their interest in the boys by tattling. Boys want to know more about the world outside the school and the home. They all gain from excursions into the larger community. They are approaching what may be called the "maturity of childhood." The teacher who is not interested in stimulating and challenging the withdrawn seven-year-old might do well to remember that he will change. In the words of Ilg and Ames, "Though seven tends to be less happy and satisfied with life and shows it in special expression — with the inevitable pout, his fatigue will lessen, and he will be ready for almost any adventure by the time he is an eight-year-old." [8]

TEACHING THE EIGHT- TO TEN-YEAR-OLD

The teacher of the eight-year-olds needs to challenge, channel, and guide their many interests and to stimulate their curiosity. The eight-year-old is not so dependent on the teacher as was the seven-year-old.

Age-mates are more important now than the teacher. Because the eight-year-old is beginning to feel the influence and pressure of the group, the wise teacher uses her knowledge of group motivation to make her role that of a regulator and counselor. If she appeciates whole-hearted acceptance by the child, the eight-year-old will provide it. Never again, indeed, will the teacher find such acceptance of herself, her actions, or her motives. She can guide with humor, control with silence, and motivate by finding the true interests of this group and understanding their motivations. Before long, these eight-year-olds will be past the stage of early childhood.

Most of the children who have started school at six will have been promoted from the primary grades by the time they are nine. However, because a few enter late and others have been kept back, the teacher of the third grade may find a few nine-year-olds in her room. Teachers of the nine-year-olds often report that the fourth grade is difficult because the nine is such a rugged individualist and has such strong likes and dislikes.

If they are having trouble with school, nine-year-olds often need more individual attention than the younger ones do. On the other hand, many of them are able to analyze their abilities and weaknesses and, once started successfully on the road to intellectual achievement, they actually enjoy the intellectual effort demanded in perfecting skills and solving problems.

The guidance technique of isolation from the group is no longer effective. The teacher of the nine-year-old must help him find his problem and evaluate his progress, giving him help if he needs it. The relationship can be a very happy one if the teacher helps him find himself and is fair in her dealings. She must be aware of individual differences in children. Since "crushes" are

[8] Ilg and Ames, *op. cit.*, p. 37.

likely to begin at this time, children may be devoted to the teacher, but shy. They will have strong feelings about her: she is wonderful or she is terrible; she is fair or she is unfair.

Guiding Children's Learning

I learned to tie my shoes today,
I learned to ride my bike.
I learned to read a sign today,
I learned to dance last night.
    I learned to swim,
    I learned to add,
I learned to tie a knot.

And so it goes. Children are learning every day — in school and out of school, with or without instruction:

> The child learns many things quickly and permanently. Throughout his childhood years he is learning to communicate, to listen, to know and understand, and to speak more effectively. He is learning to be at home in his world, learning to read its signs and portents, learning to read people . . . learning to act less on impulse and more with purpose.[9]

In our effort to respect the importance of growth and development, we must not stop with encouraging physical and social growth. If we are to educate the child, he must do more than grow and remain healthy. He must learn, he must be oriented to the society in which he lives, and he must master the tasks society requires of him. Emphasis on encouraging and guiding growth does not preclude the need for learning or for mastering the skills needed in today's world.

One of the major tasks of the teacher is to guide learning. How can the teacher discharge this responsibility so that children will learn with increasingly less direction from her and more motivation from within?

A teacher's success in helping children learn will in large measure be determined by her skill in four areas:

1. The teacher must understand the nature of learning.
2. The teacher must be familiar with the principles of teaching and apply her knowledge in the classroom.
3. The teacher must help the child develop a respect for learning and for the satisfactions learning brings.
4. The teacher must evaluate her ability to provide a classroom environment that motivates optimum learning and growth.

THE NATURE OF LEARNING

The infant at birth has limited behavior response. He is limited in the types of adaptive responses he can make to stimuli in the environment. His be-

[9] Frank G. Jennings, "Most Dangerous Profession," *Saturday Review*, March 8, 1958, p. 22.

havior at two, three, four, and later years is, therefore, partly the result of learning. Learning in turn is affected by the maturity level at which a particular learned act or response is possible.

Learning theorists agree in describing learning as "a process in which a change in performance or behavior results from training, practice, or observation." [10]

How Children Learn

Learning does not occur in haphazard, unpredictable ways. With or without instruction, certain elements are present in every act of learning. Learning takes place when there is a drive, need, or motive, that is, an appropriate goal or incentive, the attainment of which will satisfy the motive or reduce the tension. In order for learning to occur, four essentials must be present. There must be *drive, cue, response,* and *reward.*

Douglas, a four-and-a-half-year-old, illustrates the way in which these elements combine in the learning act. When Douglas enrolled in kindergarten at four-and-a-half, he was one of fifty-nine children who attended the afternoon session. A cursory glance revealed that he was a slim, dark-haired, brown-eyed, shy youngster who seemed to enjoy being with other children. It was not long before the teacher realized that he was reading. He stopped to read all the signs on the bulletin board in the hall and on the street when the class took excursions. He read the books on the library table. When the teacher asked him, "When did you learn to read?" Douglas replied, "I can't remember when I didn't know how to read." Douglas had learned to read at

[10] Catherine Landreth, *The Psychology of Childhood* (New York: Alfred A. Knopf, Inc., 1958), p. 309.

The most important element in learning is the desire for knowledge.

three years of age, while his father was in the army. Each week the father wrote a letter, which Douglas wanted to read by himself.

The *drive* was there. Douglas wanted something. He wanted to interpret the symbols on the page himself.

The second element is *cue* or sign. The learner must notice something. The cues in this case were symbols that he had to learn in order to attain the goal. Once he knew what the symbols meant, he could read the letter his father wrote to him every week. He paid attention to the cues.

The third element is *response*. The learner must do something. Douglas needed to act upon the situation, to respond correctly to the symbols. He went about the process of interpreting the symbols and seeing relationships between written symbols and spoken words.

The fourth element is *reward* or reinforcement. As Douglas comprehended the meaning of the words that the symbols represented, he received a reward from the response. Because the correct response reinforced the learning, it ensured his making the correct response on the next occasion.

Learning is concerned with change of behavior and is affected by the total growth of the child. As far as the child is concerned, "Learning is a process of behavioral changes resulting from interaction between the child and his environment and moving in the direction of desired educational goals." [11]

Principles of Learning

There are many principles of learning that both teachers and parents should understand and apply in order to facilitate progress. Many students preparing to teach young children, and even teachers who have taught for some time, are familiar with these principles and yet do not put them into practice. Although they have been accepted for several decades, they are often ignored or violated in the classroom.

LEARNING IS CONTINUOUS

Children have lived several years before they enroll in nursery school, kindergarten, or first grade. The child's present stage of development is the result of past experiences. The child, therefore, must be understood in terms of his previous experience, his present development, and his future goals. Thus, unless the kindergarten teacher offers challenging experiences to the nursery-school graduate, the child is likely to become bored and dissatisfied. Kindergarten must be more than a year of socializing experience — it must be a year of stimulating new experiences in many areas of learning. In the course of a day, opportunities may arise for learnings related to science, numbers, the social sciences, geography, physics, geology, music, art, drama, or reading. The same, of course, applies to the first-grade child.

[11] V. E. Herrick, J. L. Goodlad, E. J. Estvan, and P. W. Eberman, *The Elementary School*, pp. 97–98. Copyright, 1956, by Prentice-Hall, Inc., Englewood Cliffs, N.J. Reprinted by permission of the publisher.

Each Child Learns at His Own Rate

Adults are becoming increasingly aware of the fact that children in the same classroom develop at different rates in different functions. Each child has his individual pattern of learning as well as his tempo of growth. By the time he comes to school, his rate of learning is fairly well defined. Thus, educational programs that are concerned with meeting individual needs substitute developmental tasks for minimum grade standards and provide for differences in ability among children by modifying teaching procedures to permit each child to function in the group or activity best suited to his individual interests and his abilities.

Learning is Optimum When Adjusted to the Level of Maturity

Efficient learning is most likely if it is based on readiness, in terms of a proper relationship between the demands of the activity and the characteristics of the child. Children learn best at certain points of maturity, and the teacher who tries to force learning before the child has reached the essential general maturity is unwise. She may set up an emotional block, with the result that the child will resist such learning when the teachable moment does arrive. Rebellion against reading in the first grade is frequently the result of a previous attempt to get the child to learn to read before he was ready. The successful teacher, in short, adjusts the tasks to the child's needs, interests, intelligence, and maturity.

Efficient Learning is Related to Pupil Purpose

"Learning takes place more readily if the child accepts as useful and important the activities in which he is expected to engage." [12] When a child sees some relation between what is expected of him and his own goals, he participates in the activity with interest and enthusiasm. The teacher is responsible for selecting purposes that have meaning for children.

This does not mean, however, that the teacher must stand by waiting for children to clarify their purposes. It does mean that children's purposes have a definite place in planning in the classroom and that the teacher must help them organize and clarify their thinking about purposes. Arranging a stimulating environment, creating situations that arouse children's curiosity and interest, and helping children to see a need for learning certain basic skills and using certain abilities — all this is a teacher's responsibility. Pupil purposes are the means, not the ends, of education. It is the responsibility of the teacher to help pupils develop worthwhile aims.

Children Learn Best Through Concrete Situations

Problem-solving activities under the guidance of the teacher offer the best learning experiences because they stimulate critical thinking. They place upon the children the responsibility for whatever conclusions are reached. First-hand participation in real-life experiences brings richer rewards than merely

[12] *Ibid.*, p. 107.

The good teacher plans her class work so that every child has an opportunity to succeed.

reading about them or seeing them on film. A school visited by the writer in Mexico provides a striking example of real-life activities leading to effective learning. Undernourished children from underprivileged families learned to plant, harvest, cook, and can nutritious vegetables; to wash and iron clothes; to polish shoes, and to clean and sew — for the express purpose of teaching those processes to their parents. Problems of absenteeism in both the schools and the factories decreased as a result of the school's effort to teach children to solve real and persistent problems.

In our own schools activities such as excursions, experiments, care of pets, school gardening, cooking, sewing, and woodworking give children opportunities to learn through participating in the activities of everyday life.

Efficient Learning Maximizes Understanding

Learning is achieved by maximizing the satisfactions a child gets from his learning activities, not by emphasizing drill or repetition. Practice does not make perfect; it makes permanent. Children need to get reward or satisfaction from a task well done, but rewards need not be extrinsic. Better by example than by precept, the teacher or parent can develop within the child a love of and a need for learning. Children discover gradually that learning creates a need for more learning, and that learning becomes its own reward. In the feeling of satisfaction the child gets from a task well done, a problem solved, or a skill learned — not in any concrete, visible product — lies his reward.

Evaluation of Progress

HELPING CHILDREN EVALUATE PROGRESS

"How am I doing?" "Did I read that story better today?" These are not rhetorical questions. The child wants to know how he is doing.

A teacher must help children gain skill in evaluating their progress in learning. One group of first graders, for instance, wanted to evaluate their progress over a six-week period, in learning to read, in learning to write, and in skill in numbers. At the end of each day they checked their work against the preceding day's work and marked a plus or minus on cards they had designed. At the end of the six weeks they took the reports home to their parents. Progress was obvious. Every child had shown growth in at least one area. He had learned to see his strengths and weaknesses and to evaluate both.

SELF-APPRAISAL FOR THE TEACHER

To be certain that she is providing conditions that contribute to maximum learning for all children, the teacher, too, needs to use evaluation techniques. As a check on whether she is providing conditions favorable to the development of her pupils, let her ask herself the following questions:

1. Do I provide an environment and learning activities suited to the abilities and needs of each student, so that he can succeed with reasonable effort in some area? Do I help children learn from failure?

2. Is my room free from an intensely competitive atmosphere? Do I help students get recognition for the use of their abilities?

3. Do my students feel free to express their feelings, thus avoiding tensions and clashes of wills that might divert their energy?

4. Do I really like the boys and girls in my room? Do I realize that much of the child's behavior that creates problems for the teacher represents the child's attempt to find a way out of a difficulty?

5. Do I treat my students with as much courteous consideration as I show my friends and my professional colleagues?

6. Do I respect each individual personality and show faith in the realization of his best potentialities?

7. Do I provide group experiences that give the children an opportunity to develop a sense of responsibility for group enterprise and get satisfaction from success of others?

8. Do I encourage children to discover and evaluate their own abilities, strengths, and weaknesses, and to meet difficulty or criticism in a constructive way?

9. Do I encourage children to discover the creative ability and talents which lie within their powers?

10. Do I postpone judgment instead of labeling a student on the basis of a single incident or limited observation?

11. Do I try to understand each boy and girl in my classroom? [13]

[13] Ruth Strang, *The Role of the Teacher in Personnel Work* (New York: Bureau of Publications, Teachers College, Columbia University, 1948), pp. 164–165.

Principles for Guiding Children

Among the useful principles that have recently emerged from examination of the research on the development of children and from experience in talking with boys and girls from two to nine years old, the following are worth pointing out:

Children must be understood and guided in terms of individual growth patterns and developmental levels. The wise teacher understands that children are complex; there is no simple formula for guiding them. She understands the behavior attitudes to which each age is subject and guides them accordingly.

Children have psychological needs that require consideration. Among these are the three "A's" — affection, acceptance, and achievement. A warm, friendly teacher can do much to help a child to find himself and accept himself, to express his inner feelings and satisfy his urge to know, to make decisions, to achieve, to create, to adventure, and participate with others in a variety of experiences.

All children need recognition. They need to succeed in at least one area of academic endeavor and to be recognized for the achievement. From about five years of age, achievement and mastery become important to children. The teacher must make every effort to discover the child's own area of accomplishment and interest.

Some children need special help. However conscientious the teacher may be, some children fail to respond. They exhibit withdrawn, negative, and unstable behavior. Such children need help from special teachers and agencies.

Summary

There are three major responsibilities of the teacher: (1) to know the developmental characteristics of the children she teaches; (2) to know how to apply that knowledge to guide children's growth; and (3) to understand the nature of learning and to apply that knowledge in directing the learning activities of children.

Since child guidance is essentially growth guidance, a developmental philosophy gives the teacher a perspective and a constructive frame of reference for making decisions about guiding children. It gives her, moreover, a tolerant understanding of what to expect of a child at a given level of maturity, regardless of chronological age.

Understanding the nature of learning is essential for effective guidance. Among the principles of learning the teacher must bear in mind are these: (1) learning is continuous; (2) each child learns at his own rate; (3) children do best when learning is adjusted to the learner's level of maturity; (4) children learn best when learning is related to pupil purposes; (5) children learn through real-life situations; (6) efficient learning comes from maximizing the satisfaction and understanding that learning affords the child.

Although the child, the group, the teacher, and the parent all play an important role in development and learning in early childhood, it is the child who must do his own learning. He must become increasingly skillful in evaluating his own progress and in seeing his goals and relating his behavior to them. The teacher's task is to assist, encourage, motivate, and support the child as he learns to control his environment and broaden his horizons.

QUESTIONS AND ACTIVITIES

1. From what you know about the developmental characteristics of children, at what age would you enroll a child in nursery school? In kindergarten?

2. Visit a nursery school and see how much time the teachers spend in observing children and recording their behavior.

3. Observe in a kindergarten in which children make something to take home every day. Observe in a kindergarten in which the work period centers around problem-solving activities and creative activities. In terms of what you know about the children's development, evaluate the two kinds of experiences for five-year-olds.

4. Visit several classes in the primary school and see whether you can find the purposes that underlie the kinds of learning experiences in which the children are participating.

5. Analyze the learning environment observed during a visit to a class, indicating weaknesses and strengths. Did you observe a child learning anything by himself? In a group situation?

6. What additional principles of learning would you add to the list given in the text? Why?

7. Why should a primary-grade teacher be concerned with the developmental characteristics and behavior of a nursery-school youngster?

8. Organize a discussion on the challenges and rewards presented in teaching at each level of childhood education.

9. List some of the important researchers in the field of child development, behavior, and learning, and indicate their contributions to childhood education.

SELECTED READINGS

Burton, William H. *The Guidance of Learning Activities*, Second Edition. New York: Appleton-Century-Crofts, Inc., 1952.

Cronbach, Lee J. *Educational Psychology*. New York: Harcourt, Brace & Company, Inc., 1954.

Frederick, Robert W., and William H. Burton. *How to Study Handbook*. New York: D. Appleton-Century Co., Inc., 1938.

Herrick, Virgil, John Goodlad, Frank Estvan, and Paul Eberman. *The Elementary School*. Englewood Cliffs, N.J.: Prentice-Hall, Inc., 1956.

Hilgard, E. R. *Theories of Learning*, Second Edition. New York: Appleton-Century-Crofts, Inc., 1956.

Ilg, Frances L., and Louise Ames. *Child Behavior*. New York: Harper & Brothers, 1955.

Jenkins, Gladys G., *et al. These Are Your Children.* Chicago: Scott, Foresman and Company, 1953.

Jersild, Arthur. *Child Psychology.* Englewood Cliffs, N.J.: Prentice-Hall, Inc., 1954.

Jersild, Arthur, *et al. Child Development in the Curriculum.* New York: Bureau of Publications, Teachers College, Columbia University, 1946.

Kingsley, H. L., and Ralph Garry. *The Nature and Conditions of Learning,* Revised Edition. Englewood Cliffs, N.J.: Prentice-Hall, Inc., 1957.

Landreth, Catherine. *The Psychology of Early Childhood.* New York: Alfred A. Knopf., Inc., 1958.

McGeoch, J. A. *The Psychology of Human Learning.* New York: Longmans, Green & Company, 1952.

Martin, William E., and Celia B. Stendler. *Child Development: The Process of Growing Up In Society.* New York: Harcourt, Brace & Company, Inc., 1953.

Millard, Cecil V. *Child Growth and Development in the Elementary School Years.* Boston: D. C. Heath & Company, 1958.

National Society for the Study of Education. *Learning and Instruction.* Forty-Ninth Yearbook, Part I. Chicago: The University of Chicago Press, 1949.

Reynolds, Martha. *Children from Seed to Saplings,* Second Edition. New York: McGraw-Hill Book Company, Inc., 1951.

Stendler, Celia B. *Teaching in the Elementary School.* New York: Harcourt, Brace & Company, Inc., 1958.

Strang, Ruth. *An Introduction to Child Study.* New York: The Macmillan Company, 1951.

5

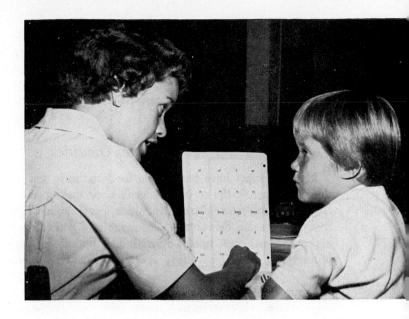

The Teacher Children Remember

*Those who educate children are more to be honored than
those who produce them; for these only give life, those
the art of living well.*

— ARISTOTLE

All teachers have the opportunity, and many have the power, to inspire
children to expand their horizons, to stretch their abilities, to reach goals, and
to achieve success. They have the power to guide children so that they "develop
into brave and wonderful adults instead of into dull, over-aged adolescents.
The results of teaching color, mold, and determine the shape of our nation and
the character of our people." [1]

In many schools pupils are met by a teacher who inspires them, a teacher
for whom respect and love can develop simultaneously. Such magic is possible whether the teacher faces a nursery school, a kindergarten, a group of
elementary children, or a seminar in a graduate school. It can happen if the

[1] Frank Jennings, "Most Dangerous Profession," *Saturday Review*, March 8, 1958, p. 22.

teacher has the ability to establish effective personal relationships with her pupils, if she retains the unquenchable thirst for knowledge, the insatiable appetite for wonder, and the ability to transmit these qualities. What kind of person is this teacher? What personal qualities, competencies, and knowledge does she possess?

Personal Qualities

Many attempts have been made to describe in terms of personal qualities the good teacher, the successful teacher, or the superior teacher. One list includes such items as "alert, altruistic, approachable, charitable, clean, cooperative, courageous, democratic, dependable, dignified, fair, faithful, generous, happy, honest, neat, noble, openminded, optimistic, patient, poised, positive, progressive, pure (morally), reverent, sensitive, tolerant, true, and truthful." [2]

Landreth suggests that "good health, a pleasing speaking voice with no marked accent, an attractive appearance (nursery school teachers should be at least attractive as the average mother), a broad human understanding, and a sense of humor are the characteristics generally agreed upon as desirable

[2] Josephine Foster and Neith Headley, *Education in the Kindergarten* (Yonkers-on-Hudson, N.Y.: American Book Company, 1948), p. 25.

Patience is an important personality trait for the teacher of young children.

in the nursery school teacher." [3] Hymes, too, points out that young children want teachers who are warm, tender, and motherly.[4] As one child expressed it, "My teacher is just like my Mom. I love her, and I think she loves me."

An examination of the literature on this subject reveals that love is the thread that runs through the woof and warp of design for development of children. Educators such as Owen, Pestalozzi, and Froebel emphasized the need of love in the environment for children. Many modern educators, too, subscribe to the belief that all children, and particularly those who are denied love at home, need a teacher who can and will give them affection.

In a speech to the delegates of the World Congress of Organización Mundial Educación Pre-escolar, Dr. Daniel Prescott stressed the important role of love in the education of young children. He pointed to the need for selecting as nursery-school teachers only persons who themselves have "achieved the security of knowing that they are loved, because persons who lack this security will be unable to build the kind of relationships needed by certain children." He went on to say:

> Children from homes where love is absent or ill-expressed need to find a personal relationship based on love in the nursery school and in the kindergarten. In fact, finding such a relationship is their main hope of avoiding later maladjustment and failure to achieve satisfactory love relationships as adults.[5]

Qualities Children Like

As children grow older they want a teacher they can talk to and who can help them with their work. One of the ways in which personality traits have been studied has been in questioning pupils regarding the qualities of teachers who seem to have effective relationships with children. Necessarily such a procedure involves children older than those we have been discussing, but is relevant to them.

Frank Hart made a study in 1934 in which he questioned all seniors in sixty-six high schools of various sizes and types, regarding the teachers they liked most or least, or found of most value. He found that boys and girls attach much importance to the personal qualities of a teacher. Eighty per cent indicated that the best-liked teacher was also the most effective teacher. Only about one per cent considered their most effective teacher to be the one they liked least. Their selection of the best-liked teacher was made on the basis of helpfulness in teaching. Next came such personality traits as cheerfulness, good nature, sense of humor, friendliness, fairness, and sympathetic understanding. Negative personality traits, such as crossness, grouchiness,

[3] Catherine Landreth, *Education of the Young Child* (New York: John Wiley & Sons, Inc., 1942), p. 18.

[4] James L. Hymes, Jr., *A Child Development Point of View* (Englewood Cliffs, N.J.: Prentice-Hall, Inc., 1955), p. 25.

[5] Daniel Prescott, "The Role of Love in the Education of Pre-School Children." Speech to the World Congress of Organización Mundial Educación Pre-escolar, September 10, 1956.

sarcasm, failure to smile, or losing one's temper, were ranked first among the least-liked teachers. Ineffectiveness as a teacher took second place in causing the rejection of a teacher by the pupils.[6]

Witty analyzed letters from 12,000 pupils of grades 2 through 12 all over the nation, on the subject, "The Teacher Who Has Helped Me Most." [7] The personal qualities or traits mentioned, in the order of their frequency, were cooperativeness and democratic attitude, kindliness, consideration for the individual, patience, a wide variety of interests, general appearance and pleasing manner, fairness and impartiality, a sense of humor, a good disposition and consistent behavior, an interest in pupil's problems, flexibility, use of recognition and praise, and an unusual proficiency in teaching a particular subject. In summarizing his findings Witty concluded that "these boys and girls appear to be grateful to the school in proportion to the degree that it offers security, individual success, shared experience, and opportunities for personal and social adjustments. And these are precisely the factors which promote good learning." [8]

In another study Symonds attempted to list those personality traits that seem to make for effective relationships with children.[9] He found that the three major differences that exist in the personalities of superior and inferior teachers seem to be these: Superior teachers like children; inferior ones dislike them. Superior teachers are personally secure and self-assured; those less efficient are insecure and have feelings of inadequacy. Superior teachers are well adjusted and possess good personality organization; inferior ones have personality disorganization.

Superior teachers, according to Symonds, showed their liking for children in such ways as knowing the names of their pupils and making themselves acquainted with the children's backgrounds and interests. Inferior teachers showed their dislike for children by a cold and unapproachable attitude and by complaining that the students were lazy and troublesome. Negative traits such as scolding, nagging, bullying, threatening, and using sarcasm and ridicule were attributed to the inferior teachers.

Formality or informality seemed to make little difference. Good teachers were found among those who maintained a formal attitude in the classroom and among those who were casual. The basic determinant was the inner personality of the teacher rather than her outward behavior in the classroom. The good teacher liked children and liked to teach.

Helping children to face life in today's complex world requires more, however, than attractive personal qualities. It demands a superior preparation. We

[6] Frank W. Hart, *Teachers and Teaching* (New York: The Macmillan Company, 1934), pp. 6, 250–251.

[7] Paul A. Witty, "The Teacher Who Has Helped Me Most," *NEA Journal*, 36:386, May 1947.

[8] Paul A. Witty, *Mental Hygiene in Modern Education*, Fifty-fourth Yearbook of the National Society for the Study of Education, Part II (Chicago: The University of Chicago Press, 1955), p. 312.

[9] Percival Symonds, *A Study of Teacher Personality* (New York: Bureau of Publications, Teachers College, Columbia University, 1957).

must educate children to meet conditions in a changing world. Margaret Mead warns us to be careful

> . . . lest while we have been rearing happy, well-adjusted, unafraid children, we have lagged behind in creating conditions out of which come first-rate achievement in the sciences, in the arts, and in politics. Children who are always active and occupied, who have lots of friends, and who get on well with the group, become people who work well in big organizations and apply knowledge that is already known. Rarely do they contribute original thinking or unique achievement.[10]

Teaching calls for more than a skilled or semiprofessional training. The idea that less careful selection and training are required than for the practice of medicine, law, engineering, or theology needs careful scrutiny. To be sure, what is honored in a society will be cultivated there, and as standards for teaching certification are raised, it is to be hoped that teaching will become the profession these times demand.

Administrators and parents alike are looking for teachers who are fine people, who like children, who are aware of the dignity and breadth of the profession, and who are sensitive to the moral implications of teaching. They seek teachers who try to express in their lives as teachers and as members of the community great and noble concepts of life, of the destiny of man, and of the profession of teaching.

The Teacher's Preparation

LIBERAL EDUCATION

To be effective, the teacher must have a broad background of knowledge. She must have a liberal education. She needs to understand the physical world and man's place in the world. She must be aware of the interaction among the various phases of life, of the likenesses and differences that exist among peoples, and of the development in our changing civilization. Understanding these things, she can help the child understand, interpret, and accept himself and the society in which he lives.

PROFESSIONAL EDUCATION

Professional education consists of more than the mechanics of "keeping school" — the techniques, methods, or mastery of narrow subject matter. It includes a knowledge of educational foundations, educational psychology, child development, principles of education, curriculum, guidance, special methods of teaching, observation of teaching and learning, and directed student teaching. It includes experiences in planning, in using school and community resources, in organizing the school day. It consists of arranging the classroom environment, directing routines, grouping and evaluating pupils,

[10] Margaret Mead, "Raising Children Who'll Reach for the Moon," *Parents Magazine*, 32:44–45, 183, October 1957.

doing experimental teaching, and maintaining classroom control. It involves working with records and reports, preparing instructional materials, meeting parents, and participating in professional meetings.

There is, currently, a trend toward spreading a prospective teacher's professional learning throughout her college career, on the assumption that time is needed for a teacher to develop professional attitudes, insights, and techniques. Yet teaching is not creative if it is considered as only a set of techniques to be learned and applied. No rule of thumb can solve the problems that challenge the teacher. The prospective teacher owes it to her pupils to obtain the finest background possible in the liberal arts, and then to build upon that background in the professional courses that develop the understanding, skills, and techniques that are required for successful teaching.

Professional and Public Relations of Teachers

Teachers are more than the instruments by which the educative process advances. As one of their many roles, they interpret the school to the community. This they do, consciously or unconsciously, through the children they teach. The child who is happy in school, who is successful, and who likes his teacher is the best press agent the school has.

Parents and administrators look to the teacher not only to deal with the needs of the children; they expect teachers to be contributing members of the community, to represent their profession by being leaders in civic affairs, and in general to display sound motivation and reasonable maturity. They have a right to expect this, but in turn they must be sensitive to an equal degree to the needs of the teacher. Both parents and administrators must be con-

The successful teacher not only understands children but also genuinely likes them.

cerned with making teaching a satisfying experience and restoring it to the place it deserves among the professions. Such a goal is imperative, if for no other reason than the fact that unless it is achieved the children will suffer.

TEACHERS NEED STATUS

Teachers are anxious to participate as members of the community, to succeed on the job, and to grow in the profession. All too frequently, however, they are beset by nagging anxieties that stem from a half-shattered self-esteem and an excessive work-load. In order to attract and maintain teachers of quality, teaching must be restored to the dignity and importance it deserves. Teachers should have status commensurate with the demands of the profession. Dr. Harold G. Urey, Nobel Prize winner, voiced the need for a changed attitude toward teachers:

> The popular attitude toward teachers in our schools has become deplorable. It is my belief that teachers should occupy a social and financial position in the local community equivalent to that of the local doctor and local business man. He should be a member of the country club. When that time comes, we will have no difficulty competing with the U.S.S.R. in satellites.[11]

Social acceptance in the community. Teachers should be free to participate as mature individuals in various aspects of community life, at the local, state, and national levels. Such participation should be rewarded, and is in many school systems throughout the country. It signals the abandonment of the tradition that the teacher should be something less than a human being.

Teachers often join social, civic, service, veteran, and fraternal organizations, though the frequency with which they do so varies with the community. They should feel free not only to join but to aspire to leadership in various types of organizations, whether devoted to the promotion of general welfare, the advancement of the arts and sciences, or to the simple enjoyment of good fellowship. There is, in addition, every reason for a teacher to pursue hobbies of the greatest variety, from hiking to performing in the local symphony and from stamp collecting to growing roses. In recent years, too, as was not always the case, teachers are permitted to marry and rear children without the loss of a position in the school.

Improved working conditions. The teacher should be relieved of excessive demands on his time and energies. Counts makes two suggestions for improving working conditions:

> (1) Reduction of class size and teaching load to enable the teacher to know the pupils individually, to become acquainted with their parents and home surroundings, and to participate effectively in the formulation of school policy.
> (2) The complete abandonment of the tradition that the teacher is merely a

11 Harold C. Urey, "Education's Dilemma," an address given at Eastern Michigan College of Education, Ypsilanti, Michigan, February 28, 1958.

more or less high-grade servant who may be called upon at will by members of the board of education or private persons in the community to perform manifold duties such as driving the school bus or administering an essay contest on the virtues of advertising.[12]

Teachers who have gone into the profession with high hopes and enthusiasm cite various reasons for their gradual, reluctant decision to seek new careers: large classes, the pressures of a full teaching schedule without a coffee break, numerous papers to correct, and extra duties — lunch duties, playground duties, bus supervision, hall duties, committee appointments, and professional meetings.

In an effort to meet this situation, the parents in some communities come into the school and relieve the teachers of the routine chores, so they can have time for relaxation in the middle of the morning and afternoon as well as for planning.

Adequate financial remuneration. Thinking people everywhere are concerned with the problem of sufficient pay for teachers. Salaries should be adequate to assure the teacher normal financial security and to provide an average amount for general cultivation of personal interests. Many schemes have been advanced for meeting the emergencies of sudden expansion in our schools. "But," says Conant, "unless the schools' educational budgets can be very much expanded, all efforts to improve the quality of the staffs of our public schools will come to nothing. The level of salaries must be greatly raised." [13]

Lawrence G. Derthick, United States Commissioner of Education, makes a plea to all citizens everywhere to come out of the bargain basement in their search for qualified teachers. "Throughout the United States," he points out, "we are paying starting salaries approximately $1,000 a year less than the average starting salary for workers in major industrial and business concerns." [14] He goes on to list the duties of a teacher. A teacher is expected to be on duty each morning well before school starts, in addition to teaching classes all day; to supervise lunch rooms, recess activities, or study halls; to go home facing other hours of correcting papers and planning. For the teacher of older children, he goes on to say, "there are night and Saturday duties at football games, band concerts, class plays and a whole series of official meetings to round out the work week." [15]

In short, a teacher is expected to:

(1) Have a college education and continue training on a lifetime basis.
(2) Take charge of 25 to 40 children every school day.

[12] George Counts, *Education and American Civilization* (New York: Bureau of Publications, Teachers College, Columbia University, 1952), p. 467.

[13] James Bryant Conant, *The Citadel of Learning* (New Haven: Yale University Press, 1956), p. 78.

[14] Lawrence G. Derthick, "The Bargain," *School Life.*

[15] *Ibid.*, p. 2.

(3) Be master of both subject matter and teaching techniques.

(4) Dress well.

(5) Be firm, but patient and reasonable.

(6) Preserve our cultural heritage.

(7) Advance the frontiers of knowledge.

(8) Nurture the young genius; improve the average student; discover and assist the pupil with special problems.

(9) Participate in community affairs.

(10) Encourage thrift, hard work, and clear thinking.

(11) Exemplify the ideals of democracy.[16]

All sorts of schemes — everything but the obvious one — have been advanced for mitigating the teacher shortage, as Dr. Carr comments:

> Any kind of makeshift — conscription, television, teacher-aides, larger classes, all-year schools, Saturday schools, double sessions, abolition of professional preparation, or some other patent medicine — is apparently regarded by some as preferable to the simple expedient of paying qualified teachers what they are worth.[17]

A more optimistic note is sounded in a statement by the President of the Board of the Long Beach, New York, schools, George B. Castigan: "The type of teacher we want is the most important single factor in determining the quality of our educational program." [18] To this, Dr. George Salten added:

[16] William Carr, "Qualified Teachers," *NEA Journal*, 45:570, December 1956.

[17] *Ibid.*

[18] "Long Beach Ends Teacher Scarcity," *New York Times*, April 22, 1956.

Teaching in a foreign country through an exchange program broadens the background and interests of a teacher.

The kind of teacher our children need is the kind who can afford to buy a book whenever he wants to, to go to a concert fairly often, take an extended vacation once a year and travel abroad at least once or twice during his career. He should be able to send his children to college without suffering undue financial hardship, and in general should have a standard of living commensurate with his role in the community without having to resort to part-time, after-school and summer jobs to make ends meet.[19]

A promising trend toward attracting and retaining teachers of quality in the profession is this interest, on a nationwide scale, in improving the status of teachers. Of course, teachers who are interested in teaching are not interested in status alone, however important that may be. Today's teacher is a product of the age; she is both practical and idealistic. Convinced that teaching must be restored to a profession, with the ensuing rewards a profession affords, she is convinced, too, that there are rewards beyond the tangible ones.

The Rewards of Teaching

VACATIONS

When asked what she liked best about teaching, a young kindergarten teacher exclaimed enthusiastically, "Why, the vacations, of course." Amid the uproar that followed she went on hurriedly to explain that what she liked about vacations was the opportunity for study, for new experiences, for reading, travel, and general improvement.

TRAVEL

Opportunity for travel has greatly increased within recent years. Teachers and administrators at all levels, from the elementary school through the university, are being offered chances to participate in a wide variety of programs that facilitate travel. Some are sponsored by the federal government, others by private companies, institutions, foundations, and organizations such as the National Education Association, the American Association of University Women, and the Organización Mundial Educación Pre-escolar. Many of these jobs take one to the less well-developed areas of the globe. The teacher who wants to travel may find such an overseas assignment the most rewarding experience of her professional career.

ADVANCED STUDY

Scholarships, fellowships, research grants, and opportunities for exchange are more numerous now than in any other period of educational history. The teacher who is ambitious and who is willing to apply herself has a chance to avail herself of the privilege of advanced study.

[19] *Ibid.*

OTHER BENEFITS

Policies relating to retirement, tenure, and sick leave are improving all the time. Beyond these material benefits, however, the reward that brings the greatest satisfaction is that of seeing individuals develop, of watching a child discover or rekindle the creative spark within him, of challenging each individual to achieve his potential. Henry Adams was thinking of such a reward when he said: "A teacher affects eternity; he never knows where his influence ends." [20]

Perhaps the greatest reward comes in knowing that one's work has no ending — in realizing that because of the teacher's efforts

> . . . the child is the person who will continue what you have begun, who will sit right where you are sitting and witness the things you consider very important, when you have gone. You may take all the measures you like, but the manner in which they are carried out will depend on him. Even though you may sign alliances and treaties, it is he who will execute them. He will take his seat in the assembly and will assume control of cities, nations and empires. It is he who will be in charge of your churches, schools, universities, councils, corporations, and institutions. All your work will be judged, praised or condemned by him. The future and the destiny will be in his hands. . . .[21]

Self-Evaluation

If she expects to obtain and retain the esteem of her colleagues and the community, the teacher is professionally obligated to engage in continuous self-improvement and in self-evaluation. She must be a superior person. She should possess a knowledge of the world in which she lives and understand the cultural context in which all education takes place. Such knowledge involves an understanding of the effects of urbanization, industrialization, economic planning, cultural lag, the effect of the scientific approach to problems, and the characteristics of the contemporary scene, not only in America but in the entire world. The teacher should understand the function of education in its broadest sense, in order to relate it to her task of guiding growth, development, and learning in the classroom. She should be prepared to take her place as a contributing member of the community in which she teaches. She will be conversant with the nature of development and growth in the child and of the learning process in general. She must, above all, possess and develop skill in guiding each child in his particular design for optimum development.

The following self-evaluation scale is designed specifically for individual self-appraisal. An objective analysis should help the individual teacher to become aware of both strengths and weaknesses.

[20] *Childhood Education*, 33:59, October 1956.
[21] Translation of a Christmas card sent out by the Official Children's Agency in Panama, 1944. *Children*, January–February 1957, p. 8.

A Self-Evaluation Scale for the Teacher

Circle One

I. Personal Qualities

A. Considerateness (kindliness, courtesy, tact)	5	4	3	2	1
B. Emotional stability (poise)	5	4	3	2	1
C. Resourcefulness (initiative, drive)	5	4	3	2	1
D. Attractiveness (appearance, dress)	5	4	3	2	1
E. Intelligence (personal, professional)	5	4	3	2	1
F. Cooperativeness	5	4	3	2	1
G. Adaptability	5	4	3	2	1
H. Reliability	5	4	3	2	1
I. Sense of humor	5	4	3	2	1

II. Competencies

A. Creating emotional climate to free children to use their intelligence	5	4	3	2	1
B. Identifying pupil needs and formulation of objectives	5	4	3	2	1
C. Selecting and organizing meaningful experiences	5	4	3	2	1
D. Directing learning experiences	5	4	3	2	1
E. Developing concepts	5	4	3	2	1
F. Regulating tempo of learning activities	5	4	3	2	1
G. Providing for individual differences	5	4	3	2	1
H. Using desirable methods of control	5	4	3	2	1
I. Providing opportunities for creative use of materials and self-expression in the arts	5	4	3	2	1
J. Evaluating pupil growth	5	4	3	2	1
K. Staff planning	5	4	3	2	1

III. Behavior Controls

A. General knowledge

1. Child behavior and development	5	4	3	2	1
2. Educational principles and practice	5	4	3	2	1
3. Subject matter	5	4	3	2	1
4. Cultural background	5	4	3	2	1

B. General skills

1. Human relations	5	4	3	2	1
2. Problem solving	5	4	3	2	1
3. Use of language	5	4	3	2	1

C. Interests, attitudes, ideals

1. Interest in children	5	4	3	2	1
2. Emotional and intellectual acceptance of all children	5	4	3	2	1
3. Professional attitude	5	4	3	2	1

D. Health

1. Physical	5	4	3	2	1
2. Mental	5	4	3	2	1
3. Emotional	5	4	3	2	1

Highest possible score
Sum of all scores
Average score

The nursery-school teacher is one of the first significant outside influences on a child.

Underwood and Underwood

Summary

Teaching in today's world demands a person who looks upon teaching as a profession, not as a set of prescribed rules and techniques. It requires further that the teacher have a frame of reference in terms of the kinds of persons she is helping the children to become. It takes more than knowledge, skill, and insight to become the kind of teacher children remember, parents respect, and administrators hire. We must remember, "knowledge without goodness is dangerous, just as goodness without knowledge is weak and feeble, but both united form the noblest character and lay the surest foundation of usefulness to mankind." [22]

QUESTIONS AND ACTIVITIES

1. Why is teacher welfare essential to pupil welfare? What evidences of concern for teacher welfare do you observe in your community, in your state, and in the nation at large?

2. What personal qualities do you believe made your elemetary-school teachers successful? What qualities characterized the least successful teachers?

3. Talk with teachers whom you admire and discover how they feel about teach-

[22] William Landeen, "An Historian Looks at American Education." Speech presented at American Education Week dinner, Evansville, Indiana, November 11, 1957.

ing as a profession. What satisfaction does teaching bring them? Is there a relationship between teacher effectiveness in the classroom and satisfaction in her work?

4. What are the values of self-evaluation scales for teachers and student teachers? Using the scale on page 76, make as objective an analysis of yourself as possible. What qualities, competencies, and knowledge do you have that will contribute to your success as a teacher of young children? What weaknesses do you find?

5. Consult an elementary-school principal concerning the qualities he looks for in teachers. What weaknesses does he generally find in beginning teachers? In what ways does he help them improve?

6. List the specific personal qualities, understandings, competencies, knowledge, and techniques that in your opinion are essential to success in teaching young children. How does this list differ from one for secondary teachers?

7. Visit two classrooms and try to discover whether the teachers appear to be growing professionally. What evidence have you that professional growth of teachers influences the learning environment in the classroom?

8. Consult your director of teacher education concerning the evaluation form by which you will be evaluated in your student teaching experience. How does this scale compare with the one used by the local school system?

9. What relationship should exist between professional growth and salaries?

10. To what extent should a teacher be expected to participate in the life of the community he serves?

11. How can the status of the teacher be raised to that of other professions in the community?

SELECTED READINGS

Barr, A. S., et al. "The Measurement and Prediction of Teaching Efficiency: A Summary of Investigations," Journal of Experimental Education, 16:203–283, June 1948.

Barr, A. S., et al. "Second Report of the Committee on Criteria of Teacher Effectiveness," Journal of Educational Research, 46:656–657, 1953.

Bernard, Harold W. Mental Hygiene for Classroom Teachers. New York: McGraw-Hill Book Company, Inc., 1952.

Carr, William G. "Values in Teaching," Modern Education and Human Values. Pitcairn-Crabbe Foundation Lecture Series, 4:113–134. Pittsburgh: University of Pittsburgh Press, 1952.

Cottrell, Donald P. (ed.). Teacher Education for a Free People. Oneonta, N.Y.: The American Association of Colleges for Teacher Education, 1956.

Department of Classroom Teachers. Factors Making or Marring Good Teaching. Washington, D.C.: National Education Association, 1950.

Drawhorne, C. L. "Relation Between Pupil and Student: Teacher Interactions and

Teaching Effectiveness," *Educational Administration and Supervision,* 40:283–296, May 1954.

Elsbree, Willard S. *The American Teacher.* New York: American Book Company, 1939.

Hedlund, Paul, and Foster Brown. "Conditions that Lower Teacher Morale," *The Nation's Schools,* 48:40–42, September 1951.

Jersild, Arthur T. *When Teachers Face Themselves.* New York: Bureau of Publications, Teachers College, Columbia University, 1955.

Keener, E. E. "Are You a Good Teacher?" *The Educational Forum,* 19:5–11, November 1954.

Lieberman, Myron. *Education as a Profession.* Englewood Cliffs, N.J.: Prentice-Hall, Inc., 1956.

Morse, William C., and G. Max Wingo. *Psychology and Teaching.* Chicago: Scott, Foresman and Company, 1955.

National Education Association, Research Division. "First Year Teachers in 1954–1955." *Research Bulletin,* No. 34. Washington, D.C.: National Education Association, 1956.

Rogers, Dorothy. "A Study of the Reactions of Forty Men to Teaching in the Elementary School," *Journal of Educational Sociology,* 27:24–35, September 1953.

Terrien, Frederic. "Who Thinks about Educators?" *American Journal of Sociology,* 59:150–158, September 1953.

Tomlinson, Loren R. "Recent Studies in the Evaluation of Teaching," *Educational Research Bulletin,* 34:172–186, October 1955.

Wasson, Margaret. *Teaching is Exciting!* Washington, D.C.: The Association for Childhood Education, 1951.

Witty, Paul A. (ed.). *Mental Health in Modern Education.* Fifty-fourth Yearbook of the National Society for the Study of Education, Part II, pp. 307–333. Chicago: The University of Chicago Press, 1955.

Yauch, Wilbur A., *et al. The Beginning Teacher.* New York: Henry Holt & Company, Inc., 1955.

Zimmerman, Kent A., and Elizabeth Lewton. "Teacher Personality in School Relationships," *Education Leadership,* 8:422–428, April 1951.

DEVELOPING AND

EVALUATING THE

PROGRAM

II

Part I was the prologue to that key task of teachers: organizing, developing, and evaluating learning experiences that will have both value and vitality for young children. The stage is now set, the properties present, but the characters are not yet on stage. Not until Part II do we see the action, as teacher and pupils together select, organize, develop, and evaluate learning experiences that will be significant for them for the age in which they are living and that will enable them to meet the exigencies of a period that is itself dynamic, changing, and unpredictable.

In Part II we will look at a program designed to meet the needs of these children, who come to school to learn. We will discover how to organize a program that will equip children for successful living. We will consider how the teacher selects, organizes, and develops a curriculum with and for a particular group of children. Finally, we will observe how a teacher and her group evaluate their progress, so that they can plan the next step.

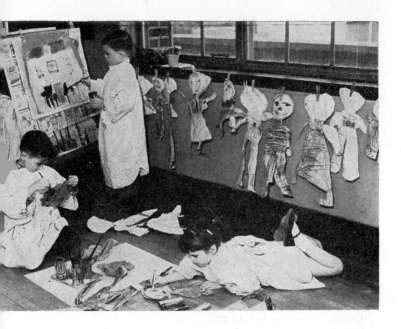

6

Planning the Daily Program

*There are no perfect blueprints — there are only sketches.
Each group develops its own design.*

— Nagol

All teachers need help in planning a daily schedule, in selecting worth-while activities on the basis of objectives that will have meaning and significance for the children. They need a frame of reference within which they can make the best possible decisions dealing with problems of guidance and curriculum. This is one of the most difficult tasks that a teacher faces. For each group of children the problems are different.

This chapter is concerned with planning a daily program so that it will have meaning for children inasmuch as it takes into consideration their needs, abilities, and interests, and is conceived to the end that each child may be encouraged to develop a design for living and learning that is woven according to his particular specifications and that will allow him to develop his own peculiar abilities.

Objectives of Early Childhood

"The child and his needs have long been an important referent for selecting learning experiences of children in programs of elementary education, nursery, kindergarten, and primary grades." [1]

In defining objectives it makes a difference whether the teacher focuses on the child, the aspects of social living, or man's knowledge. The problem is not to determine which is the most important; the question is, rather, which of the three will serve as the initial focus.

The nursery school offers a young child certain opportunities:

1. To gain coordination and control in his bodily activities.
2. To learn to work and play happily and cooperatively with others of approximately the same age.
3. To acquire desirable habits and wholesome attitudes toward helping himself.
4. To think constructively, to use his imagination, and to develop resourcefulness and originality.
5. To broaden his interests and his understanding of the world around him.
6. To enrich his appreciation of simple aesthetic experiences, including music, art, and stories. [2]

The daily program in a nursery school is designed to take advantage of these opportunities. It provides the occasion for dramatic play, for the use of creative materials (blocks, clay, paints, crayons, paste), for experiences with music (listening to records, singing, and rhythms), for stories and puzzles, for vigorous physical activity, and for regular performance of routine tasks (resting, toileting, and eating).

A Good Day in the Nursery School

"When will we have our juice?" "Will we play outdoors after our nap?" "When will Mother come?" Questions such as these show that children are interested in knowing what will happen next and when it will happen. Basically, they like order in living.

Teachers, too, need the security of plans in daily living. Even before school opens, a teacher can organize a tentative plan for the beginning days of school on the basis of what she knows about children: the ways in which children are alike and the ways in which they differ, their needs and interests and the developmental tasks with which they are struggling, the physical facilities of the school, the length of the school day, the number of children in each group, and the number of teachers or assistants.

[1] Virgil Herrick, et al., The Elementary School (Englewood Cliffs, N.J.: Prentice-Hall, Inc., 1956), p. 79.
[2] Objectives of the Union College Preschool, Lincoln, Nebraska, 1953–1954.

How the teacher approaches the task of organizing a daily schedule and planning the program will be determined by various factors, among them her philosophy of education, the referent she uses to define her objectives, and her experience in teaching. The teacher who holds the basic concept of the worth of the individual will respect individual differences and provide for them in her schedule. Flexibility and balance will characterize her program.

DEVELOPMENTAL TASKS IN THE NURSERY SCHOOL

One of the most important responsibilities of the nursery-school teacher centers around helping the twos, threes, fours, and some fives master the tasks basic to satisfactory biological adjustment. These developmental tasks must be considered in planning the schedule. If the child is to become independent, it is essential to establish routines within which he can learn to achieve in such activities as eating, sleeping, washing, dressing, undressing, and toileting. Children vary in the amount of help they need in these tasks. One child who needed a great deal of help bore witness to the importance of the task when, in reply to the question of her grandmother, "What is your teacher's name?" she said in all seriousness, "I don't know *her* name, but Miss King is the 'panty-buttoner.'"

The average child is willing and usually anxious to do things for himself if adults allow him some leeway within the task itself and assume a matter-of-fact attitude toward it. The teacher's responsibility is primarily that of helping the child to help himself. She must gear the responsibility she expects the child to assume to the maturity of the individual child. Some children will accept responsibilities without protest. With others she must be prepared to

The child is eager to learn and to expand the boundaries of his present world.

The child learns to coordinate the larger muscles in free outdoor play.

Afternoon Session
(same for both groups)

11:45–12:00	Clean-up, rest
12:00–12:45	Lunch, preparation for naps
12:45– 2:30	Naps, dressing
2:30– 4:00	Outdoor play

The All-Day Care Center

7:00–10:00	Arrival, health inspection
7:00– 8:20	Rest on cots
8:20– 8:30	Toileting
8:30– 9:00	Cereal for all children
9:00– 9:30	Outdoor play
9:30	Cod-liver oil, juice
9:30–11:30	Choice of indoor or outdoor activities
9:45–10:15	Toileting for two-year-olds
10:15–11:15	Rest on cots for two-year-olds
11:15–11:45	Outdoor play

give more help. Praising a child for progress and maintaining an attitude of confidence helps him gradually assume the responsibility himself.

The importance of these tasks is evident when we examine schedules in the nursery schools. About one-third of the day centers around the activities of eating, sleeping, dressing, undressing, and toileting.

THE DAILY SCHEDULE

An examination of daily schedules in different types of nursery schools reveals their emphasis on creative activity, physical activity, the communication skills needed in social living, and the mastery of developmental tasks. Although variations in the length of day exist, an ample amount of time is given to such activities in each schedule. Some programs cover the child's entire day; others are planned for a briefer period. Eight- and ten-hour nursery schools are usually referred to as day nurseries; the all-day nursery school in research centers and private schools lasts from six to seven hours. Typical schedules of half-day, full-day, day-nursery, and neighborhood play groups follow:

The Half-Day Session

9:00	Health inspection while parent waits
9:00–10:30	Free play — outdoors and indoors
10:30–11:00	Toilet, juice, story
11:00–11:15	Rest on cots
11:15–11:30	Toilet, wraps
11:30–12:00	Outdoor play — ready for parents

The Full-Day Nursery School
Morning session

Younger Children

9:00–10:00	Outdoor play with sand, construction material, bicycles, wagons, jungle gym, swings, teeters
10:00–10:30	Wraps, toilet, midmorning juice or milk
10:30–11:00	Play with materials such as plasticene, blocks, paints, peg boards, trains, dolls
11:00–11:30	Stories, rhythms, music, dance
11:30–11:45	Wraps, outdoor play

Older Children

9:00– 9:45	Free play with materials such as plasticene, clay, blocks, paints, fingerpaint, carpenter materials, paper and crayons, dolls
9:45–10:30	Music, rhythms, literature, conversation, stories, science
10:30–10:50	Rest, toilet
10:50–11:00	Wraps
11:00–11:45	Outdoor play

11:45	Morning children go home
11:45–12:15	Toileting and story for all
12:15–12:45	Lunch for staff and children who stay for lunch
12:45– 3:00	Toileting and naps for all
3:00– 3:30	Toileting for all children
3:15– 3:30	Milk and juice
4:00	Children enrolled from 9:00 to 4:00 go home
3:00– 6:00	Indoor-outdoor activities for those who remain entire day [3]

The Neighborhood Play Group

| 9:30–10:00 | Free play. Children work off their early-in-the-day need for gross motor activity, exploring the pleasures of a new yard and working off energy. Here, too, is their chance for social development, as they learn to play with others. Mother in charge supervises closely, but mostly unseen, from the house. |
| 10:00 | Juice and crackers. Ten-minute rest period — on living-room rug when weather demands it. A craft period follows the rest, then fingers-plays, rhythms, or childhood games. Then a story, and finally free play again until departure.[4] |

WHAT A TYPICAL DAY'S PROGRAM INCLUDES

An examination of the daily schedules shows that the programs are organized around the physical, social, and creative needs of the child.

The day starts with a concern for physical needs — health inspection while the parent waits. Lunch, naps, and out-of-door activities continue the provision for the physical.

Playing out-of-doors is usually the first social activity of the day unless the weather forbids. One of the teachers should be outdoors when the children arrive. She should have the outdoor equipment — the blocks, barrels, ladder, easels, sand toys, packing boxes, and other materials — in readiness. Walks in the immediate neighborhood help the child get acquainted with his expanding world. In season, digging, planting, raking leaves, making a snow man further provide for the child's need for activity.

Creative needs are met through experiences with blocks and art media. Block play offers endless stimulation; blocks become trains, boats, planes, jets, rockets, trucks, garages, and houses. Farms and cities spring up in the course of a morning. Easel and fingerpainting, clay modeling, dancing, playing records, and experimenting with musical instruments (from the piano to water glasses) provide pleasure and afford an outlet for the creative urge.

The skeleton of a daily schedule is a barren and empty shell, but it comes to life as we spend a morning with Debbie and follow her through the sequence of events in the half-day nursery school she attends:

[3] Rhoda Kellogg, *Nursery School Guide* (Boston: Houghton Mifflin Company, 1949), p. 118.

[4] June Johnson, *Home Play for the Preschool Child* (New York: Harper & Brothers, 1957), p. 138.

9:00　Debbie, a three-and-a-half-year-old, arrives at the nursery school with her mother and brother on this wintry morning. After health inspection she runs outdoors and plays in the snow with the outdoor group and Miss Lamson. The snow is deep and Debbie enjoys it. The group plays on the jungle gym and the telephone pole, and they make a snow man. Some of the children revel in the snow with Miss Lamson, who is wearing a ski-suit and stadium boots.

10:00　By 10:00 Debbie is ready to come inside. So are the others, although Ronnie and Jimmie tease Miss Lamson by hiding behind the bushes. They come in laughing and Miss Lamson helps them take off their wraps and hang them in the proper place. Debbie hangs hers up hurriedly, runs to the bathroom, and rushes to the doll house. Her favorite doll is there; Debbie takes her for a walk in the doll buggy. Lyndon, her brother, comes along and tries to help her, but she pushes him away. When she has walked a little, she goes back to the doll house and rocks the doll to sleep. She hurries over to the easel and splashes red and purple strokes on the newsprint. By this time most of the children are ready for juice.

10:40　Today it is tomato juice. As Miss Jenson plays the piano, the children cluster around her waiting for the juice to be served. Miss Jenson suggests they go to the bathroom and wash their hands before they sit at tables and are served tomato juice and crackers. Debbie likes juice better than milk. She drinks it all. Miss Lamson has set up the cots. The children find their places. Debbie goes to hers without protest and after a few wriggles settles down. Miss Lamson lowers the shades, and soon everyone is resting.

11:30　As the children get up from the cots in response to the piano, they go to the bathroom, if they need to, and Miss Lamson and Miss Jenson help the youngsters put on their boots and snow suits. In warm weather the children have a shorter rest and spend the last half hour outdoors playing. Today, however, most of the youngsters spend only about fifteen minutes outdoors waiting for their parents.

11:45　Debbie is dressed and ready to go when her mother arrives. She asks, "Can we play out a while before we go home?" Mother answers, "You can play out tomorrow. I have to go home to get lunch for Daddy." The day at the nursery school is over for Debbie.

But the day is not over for the teachers. They will spend the afternoon planning, working on records, and having conferences. They share with parents the responsibility of providing a favorable environment and a program for learning.

Planning in the Kindergarten

The question that a kindergarten teacher must be prepared to answer at all times is, "What do they learn in kindergarten?" One of the most comprehensible statements of the learning program in kindergarten comes from the pen of Dr. Laura Zirbes:

Habits of personal cleanliness and health should be a part of the daily program.

They don't learn *lessons*, but they *do* learn a great many important things which launch their school lives and give them a good start. The kindergarten "readies" children for good adjustment in school living, for attention to group guidance, for self-reliance in the routines of school living. It broadens the child's outlook and enriches his experience with appropriate stories, songs and group games; it encourages him to explore the possibilities of painting and other forms of creative activity. Those learnings are all developmental, and developmental learnings call for insightful guidance rather than formal instruction on the kindergarten level.[5]

DEVELOPMENTAL TASKS IN THE KINDERGARTEN

Some of the children in kindergarten are still working on the developmental tasks of early childhood. Other kindergarten children are working on the developmental tasks of middle childhood. The period is characterized by three new features: the thrust of the child out of the home and into the peer group, the physical entrance into the world of games and work requiring neuromuscular skills, and the mental thrust into the world of communication, adult ideas, logic, and symbolism. The tasks in which the school specializes are those involving the mental skills. The kindergarten teacher helps the children achieve the tasks at which they are working. She need not ignore any of the developmental tasks of boys and girls in her room; in fact, she may use the developmental tasks in defining her objectives and may organize her program around these learning problems.

[5] Laura Zirbes, "When Critics Ask Questions," *The Association for Childhood Education Journal*, 31:419, May 1955.

THE DAILY SCHEDULE IN THE KINDERGARTEN

Kindergartens concerned with the developmental needs of children differ from nursery schools primarily in providing for the expanding interests, skills, and abilities of the children. The teacher is responsible for organizing and developing learning experiences in harmony with their expanding interests and powers. Some of the objectives a teacher will have in mind as she works with a group of fours and fives are these:

1. To develop happy, well-adjusted, socially responsible children.
2. To have warm, secure teacher-child-parent relationships.
3. To recognize and emphasize the value of the individual as a participating member of the group.
4. To teach children to enjoy association with peers.
5. To encourage creative use of materials.
6. To encourage creative experiences in music, art, rhythms, and dramatics.
7. To provide direct experiences as the basis of the learning program.

According to one popular analysis of curriculum types, curricula are divided into three categories: subject-centered, child-centered, and society-centered.[6] In Chapter 7 we shall discuss these three types of curriculum organization. Meanwhile, we shall examine several daily schedules:

The Half-Day Session

8:30– 9:20	Free play: choose activities, experiment, converse, solve social problems, dramatize
9:20– 9:35	Conversation
9:35– 9:50	Health habits; toilet habits
9:50–10:00	Quiet time
10:00–10:30	Reading readiness
10:30–11:00	Music
11:00–11:30	Stories, games
11:30–11:45	Put on wraps, play outdoors
11:45–12:00	Dismissal

The Three-Hour Session

8:30– 9:00	Arrival, morning inspection, room activities, sharing
9:00– 9:30	Outdoor play, rhythms, excursions, or swimming
9:30– 9:40	Toileting
9:40–10:00	Rest on rugs
10:00–10:15	Fruit juice
10:15–11:00	Work period with clean-up responsibilities
11:00–11:30	Varied activities: singing, dramatization, science and art activities, rhythm band, excursions, and story
11:30	Ready for parents

[6] Herbert C. Rudman, "Patterns of Textbook Use — Key to Curriculum Development," *The Elementary School Journal*, 58:401, April 1958.

The Two-and-a-Half-Hour Session

9:00– 9:30 Social Living
    Arrival, inspection, room interests
    Indoor activities: blocks, Patty Hill blocks, playhouse, books,
      puzzles, apparatus, easel painting, clay modeling
    Clean-up, evaluation, and conversation
9:30–10:00 Swimming
10:00–10:30 Routines
    Bathroom
    Rest, milk, listening to records
10:30–11:00 Outdoor play, excursions, story
11:00–11:30 Creative Activities
    Monday: singing
    Tuesday: rhythms and singing games
    Wednesday: rhythm band
    Thursday: dramatizing stories
    Friday: library
11:30–11:40 Dismissal

The All-Day Session

8:30– 9:25 Arrival, inspection, free play, fruit juice
9:25– 9:50 Group meeting, sharing period, and plans for work
9:50–11:00 Work period, clean-up, story time
11:00–11:30 Music and preparation for lunch
11:30–12:15 Lunch
12:15– 1:15 Outdoor play

If the school building has no adequate rest facilities, the teacher should improvise.

     1:15– 3:00   Rest on cots
                      Preparation for rest
                      Resting
                      Dressing, making beds, bathroom, milk and crackers
     3:00– 3:30   Outdoor play, when weather permits
                      Listening to records or stories in inclement weather
     3:30   Dismissal

In view of the variation in individual programs and the difficulty in allotting time on the basis of the significance of activities in the total day, the following may serve as a tentative plan. Many teachers have found it helpful as a starting point for planning.

     60 minutes   Work period
                      Discussion of work — further plans
                      Clean-up
     60 minutes   Outdoor play
                      Rest
                      Mid-morning juice or milk
     60 minutes   Creative experiences
                      Singing, rhythms, rhythm band
                      Story-telling, dramatization, science

A School Day in the Primary Grades

Children who enter the primary school do not suddenly change because they are first graders. Many of them will still be working at the developmental tasks they were working on in the kindergarten. But now they are first graders! Now some of them are six, and suddenly parents, teachers, and friends become troubled if they do not read. One child expressed the exigent demands of adults when she said in a worried voice, "I liked kindergarten, but I don't like first grade. I don't want to read, but everyone tells me I have to." Another disappointed lad of six, after his first day in the primary school, announced, "I'm not going back to that school. I can't read, I can't write, and my teacher won't let me talk." Fortunately, however, many teachers do understand the pressures on first graders.

Although in any particular class situation the teacher will vary the amounts of time spent on various areas to suit the needs of the children in that class, some general time allotments have been suggested. These are as follows:

Approximate Time Allotments to Subject-Matter Areas

Percentage of Time	Subject Area
50	Language arts: reading, language, spelling, and writing

10	Fine and industrial arts: music, rhythmic play, arts, and crafts
10	Arithmetic
10	Health: physical education, nutrition, health services, recreation
20	Social studies: history, geography, science, citizenship

A suggested schedule for first grade might be:

8:20– 8:35	Attendance check, lunch reports, and plans for day
8:35– 9:35	Reading activities
9:35–10:00	Writing
10:00–10:15	Recess
10:15–11:00	Phonics, workbooks, word study
11:00–12:15	Lunch
12:15–12:40	Number concepts
12:40– 1:00	Music and rhythms
1:00– 2:00	Reading activities
2:00– 3:00	Art, story hour, independent activities

A more detailed program for beginning first grade would be:

8:40– 9:00	Lunch report, attendance, drinks, song, conversation
9:00– 9:30	Reading-readiness book
9:30– 9:40	Rhythms, games, rest
9:40– 9:55	Colors
9:55–10:10	Readiness cards
10:10–10:15	Preparation for recess
10:15–10:25	Recess
10:25–10:35	Drinks
10:35–11:00	Arithmetic
11:00–11:20	English, health, science, social studies
11:20– 1:00	Lunch
1:00– 1:10	Drinks and rest
1:10– 1:25	Music
1:25– 1:55	Reading-readiness book
1:55– 2:10	Writing
2:10– 2:15	Preparation for recess
2:15– 2:30	Recess
2:30– 2:35	Drinks
2:35– 3:00	More readiness lessons
3:00– 3:30	Stories, art, films, free activities
3:30	Dismissal

Another schedule for first grade might be:

| 9:00– 9:50 | Planning and work period. This time usually is devoted to strenuous work: building, playing in the playhouse, and other activities that are related to the unit of work and are difficult to do quietly |

9:50–10:00	Clean-up, ready for recess
10:00–10:30	Outdoor recess, rhythms, games, lunch, and rest
10:30–12:00	Fundamental skills, clean-up, evaluation
12:00–12:45	Lunch
12:45– 2:10	Planning, sharing, reading, and related activities centering around the unit of work
2:10– 2:30	Outdoor play, rhythms, music
2:30– 3:20	Creative activities, group evaluation, and planning
3:20– 3:30	Clean-up and dismissal

The latter program is designed to provide a broader base for learning activities than is the first program. Organizing the daily schedule to allow for unit activity gives the teacher more opportunity to work with children in guiding individual interests. Time is provided, too, for social studies, science, and numbers as well as for reading and related activities. In certain instances, of course, the time for fundamental skills must be extended. Additional activities involving reading are planned for the period from 12:45 to 2:10. During this period children frequently read for information about problems in connection with the unit of work, engage in individual reading, or prepare to share a story with the group. During the last period of the day come the creative activities, to which the children look forward: painting on the easel, reading at the library table, using the arithmetic center, gathering around the science center, or dramatizing a play. Some children listen to records, others use the time for creative writing. The teacher can make use of the time to get around the room and give individual help where it is needed. Thus the end of the day finds motivation high and children eager to come back the next day to continue activities and to attempt new experiences.

Let us go on now to a day in the second and third grades:

Grade Two

8:30– 8:50	Plan day's work
8:50– 9:15	Steps to mastery of words
9:15– 9:45	Reading
9:45–10:15	Arithmetic
10:15–10:30	Recess
10:35–11:00	Reading
11:00–11:20	Checking and completing unfinished work
11:20–11:30	Prepare for lunch
11:30– 1:00	Noon hour
1:00– 1:25	Social studies or health
1:25– 1:50	Think-and-do books
1:50– 2:15	English and writing
2:15– 2:30	Recess
2:30– 2:55	Reading activities
2:55– 3:30	Music, art, or science

Grade Three

8:30– 8:40	Plans for the day, organization, lunch money
8:40– 9:10	Steps to mastery of words
9:10–10:00	Reading groups
10:00–10:15	Recess
10:15–10:45	Arithmetic
10:45–11:45	Reading activities (physical education on Friday)
11:45–12:35	Noon hour
12:35– 1:05	Health and science (music on Tuesday)
1:05– 1:40	Writing or English
1:40– 1:55	Recess
1:55– 2:50	Social studies, art
2:50– 3:10	Evaluation, get ready to go home

Let us see what such a schedule actually looks like when it is translated into practice:

A Day in the Second Grade

8:45– 9:15   Mrs. Sailor's second grade at Fairlawn starts the day with roll-call; 28 of the 33 students enrolled are present. The room is organized into five groups, with a table captain responsible for checking attendance at each table.

The pledge to the flag and a morning prayer are followed by sharing time. Lynn shows her new cut-out book, Jim displays the telescope he got with a new pair of shoes, and David tells about falling from his double-bunk last night.

9:15– 9:55   Sharing time gives way to a period of two drills — penmanship and arithmetic. Each child has clothespins with which to build bridges. Randy tells Donald his Dad is an engineer and that engineers must "know their figures" before they can build bridges. Donald answers by wrecking his bridge.

9:55   Pupils are a little restless waiting for recess. The bell sounds and the children scramble for wraps. For twenty minutes there is unorganized play, and the usual skinned shins result.

10:20   The children dictate to Mrs. Sailor as she writes the daily classroom newspaper on the blackboard. The students copy it on writing paper after dictation to the teacher. They tell of music night and a school play, "The Basket House."

10:30   Mrs. Sailor conducts a scientific experiment. The students plant two pots of beans, one of which will be kept in a closet. The other will be watered daily and exposed to sunlight. "If the beans in the closet do not grow, we will have proved that beans need sunlight," the teacher explains.

There is a brief exchange of words, but no blows are struck, in the rear of the room. Jeannie says Micke has her pencil. Micke denies the allegation but offers to give Jeannie one of his six pencils.

11:00–11:45   Language-arts period is quiet and orderly. A three-ring activity period begins. Group I goes off to work on a story they will drama-tize. Group II gathers in the circle at the front of the room for group reading. Group III works on filling in vowel sounds in their workbooks.

11:45   Lunch time arrives. About half of the youngsters walk home to lunch, a few eat sack lunches, and the rest go to the cafeteria.

12:45– 1:15 Class resumes at 12:45 with roll call. The groups rotate with reading, workbooks, and independent activity for half an hour.

1:15   Mrs. Sailor reads a story, "The Country Bunny." All but three children come up for story-time. John writes a note on the chalk board. Jean prefers to draw pictures at the table. Micke goes to the easel to paint. "It's lots of fun, but a little messy," Micke says confidently after admitting he has "artistic talent." He does.

             Story-telling lasts twenty-five minutes. Then Mrs. Sailor an-nounces a review for a spelling test.

1:40   Recess again for 20 minutes. Today recess is highlighted by the presence of a dog, which is boxed into a corner by the youngsters. One girl is scratched and the principal blows a whistle, calls the children in, and sends the dog home.

2:00   After recess the children sing a few songs, accompanied by a port-able record player. Then it is time for the spelling test, which con-sists of ten words and a sentence. For some students the quiz is too easy. For others it is too difficult; two boys can spell only two of the words.

             Following the tests the children make paper kites, using ideas from a film strip shown the day before. Several unguided missiles sail around the room, but the confusion is kept to a minimum.

2:50   Clean-up committees go to work watering plants, cleaning the turtle bowl, and tidying up.

2:55   The monthly fire-drill is carried out with precision.

3:05   Students pack spelling books and readers under their arms, and begin the trek home.[7]

Obviously, this account of a typical day in the second grade is not complete. During the course of a day a number of problems arise that cannot be solved at the time. The teacher merely notes these problems in her anecdotal records and waits until she has time to map out a plan of attack. It is never easy to settle all the problems of fights, accidents, spilled paint, spilled milk, and hurt feelings that arise in any normal day; it is even more difficult on a day when visitors are present. We merely note the problem here, for this chapter is concerned with planning a program, not with settling difficulties. That will come later.

[7] Fairlawn School, Evansville, Indiana.

Planning a Good Daily Schedule

Examination of daily schedules and descriptions of actual accounts in the classroom give the reader an insight into the planning necessary to ensure a good day for children and for teacher. Working out a tentative schedule at the beginning of the year will help. This can be done on the basis of a knowledge of children in general, the locality, and the teacher's own skills, and it will facilitate the daily classroom living while the teacher is getting better acquainted with the children. Some principles that may be useful in planning a good day for children follow:

1. Plan some time to be the child's own. . . . If there is a time when the child may choose what he wants to do, he will have a more relaxing day.

2. Plan for a balance of activities. A morning that consists of coloring outlined drawings, working on puzzles, and practicing manuscript writing is likely to produce tense children, ready to explode when they hit the door at noon. . . . On the other hand, too many free-choice periods in one day may not give the young child the security that comes from knowing what is going to happen next.

Proper balance of individual, small-group, and whole-group activities is also important. . . . The young child comes to school where the teacher as a mother-substitute must be shared with perhaps thirty peers, each of whom has an equal claim to her affection. . . . The teacher who sees that children have an opportu-

The classroom environment should provide freedom to construct, to explore, and to create.

nity to work individually during the day, and who finds time for a personal remark for each child during that time, is recognizing the young child's need for personal contact with his mother-substitute. . . .

3. Plan for individual children insofar as possible. With forty or more children . . . , the teacher cannot possibly make individual plans for each child. But she can make notes, such as one teacher did: "Joe tardy again. May be mad over the bawling-out I gave him when he spilled paint all over the floor. Must watch myself with Joe. . . . Work on finding a pal for him."

4. Plan to prepare children for the unusual. The coming of the school doctor or nurse can be a terrifying occasion for some young children. . . . A change in juice time or rest time or outdoor play can be taken in stride if they know about it in advance.

5. Plan for some periods during the day when children can work [independently]. . . . But the activity should be of educational value for the child. This criterion would eliminate much busywork, such as workbook exercises, hectographed seatwork, and the like. . . .

6. Plan for wise use of consultants. When consultants or special teachers are available in a school system, a plan needs to be worked out so they can be used advantageously. More and more such specialists are available on call. The music teacher . . . the art teacher, too, is available by invitation. . . .

7. Plan for enough sameness in the daily schedule to give children security. . . . Children find security in knowing what to expect, and a daily schedule that changes too frequently can confuse them. Although a flexible program is desirable, and the same daily schedule month in and month out can make for deadly monotony, a daily schedule needs to have enough fixed points so that children usually know what is going to happen next.[8]

"There are no perfect blueprints; there are only sketches." In planning a daily schedule each teacher may be guided by principles such as we have set forth and the suggested daily schedules. She must be guided also by a consideration of factors peculiar to her own situation, such as size of group, length of session, maturity of group, climate, space, buildings, seasonal changes, times at which services of special teachers and consultants are available, times at which playground, gym, and auditorium are free, and times at which milk or juice may be served.

The First Day

The first day of school is a dramatic event in the life of the child. The younger the child, the more the separation from parents and home will disturb him. Thus, the child who is introduced to school at the nursery-school level is usually too immature to adapt to a new environment without the support of a mother-figure. The nursery-school teacher functions in this role. But the child cannot shift at once to this mother-substitute; he has to learn to

[8] Roma Gans, et al., Teaching Young Children (Yonkers-on-Hudson, N.Y.: World Book Company, 1952), pp. 102–105.

A personal welcome to school helps to build a feeling of security in the child.

know her before he can trust himself to her. On the whole, nursery-school groups are small, and the teacher has time to help the child adjust. Often, however, the kindergarten teacher is faced with a large number of children on the first day, many of whom have not attended nursery school and have not even had the experience of visiting a kindergarten. These children may be worried, tense, and uncertain. How the teacher can help children enjoy the day by taking time to interest them in various activities is suggested here:

Greeting the children	The teacher can put the children at ease by greeting them as they come in and showing them where to hang their wraps.
Time to explore	Help the children become interested in an activity in the room or in seeing what materials are available for them to play with in the various centers of interest.
Freedom to move	Let the children know that they are free to look around the room and play with materials and equipment, and that they are not expected to come and sit down until they hear a signal.
A signal to come	While the children are playing or working at various activities, the teacher may go to the piano and play a chord or strike a triangle to get the attention of the group. This is the signal to come and sit down.
Time for conversation	This can become the signal for children to listen and put their work away and join the group for talking, sharing, or discussing plans.
Time for singing	Frequently the children will suggest singing some songs they know or they will respond to music if the teacher

	plays some lively tunes and then varies the music to something quiet and relaxing.
Time for a story	A story is always enjoyed if it is told well or if the pictures are intriguing.
No midmorning lunch	The excitement that often accompanies the first day makes midmorning lunch and rest impractical.
No rest	Today children can show their rugs, but do not expect them to lie down on cots or rugs and sleep. Let them relax as they need to, but skip the formal rest.
Routines	Show the children where the bathroom is; do not just tell them. If necessary take them by the hand and point out, "This is our bathroom."
Get acquainted	Outdoor play on the first day is difficult if there is only one teacher. One person must be free to take care of a child in case of an accident, an attempted run-away, or other unforeseen experiences. Once children become attached to the kindergarten room, there is little danger of their wanting to run home. Save the outdoor period for later days when school is not so strange and the children are more at home.
A happy dismissal	Be sure you know how each child is going home and who calls for him. Schools vary in dismissal procedure, but permitting the parents to come to the room for the children the first few days avoids the problems that arise when children start home without knowing how, with whom, and where they are going.

Following are some "do's" and "don'ts" that a number of teachers have found useful on the first day:

DO

Plan a staggered enrollment.

Wear your prettiest dress and brightest smile.

Have a flexible daily plan.

Have centers of interest which encourage exploration, experimentation, manipulation, and creation.

Provide a name tag for each child.

Participate in activities.

Recognize the significance of the day.

BUT

Do not plan a formal rest period.

Do not have a midmorning lunch.

Do not ignore the shy child.

Do not lose your perspective or poise.

Do not forget that teaching can be exciting! [9]

9 Lillian Logan, "Everybody Begins," *Journal of the Association for Childhood Education International*, 30:8, 1953.

Summary

Children differ, so do schedules, but certain principles are applicable. We have tried in this chapter to help teachers determine worthwhile objectives, procedures, and learning experiences, and decide, on the basis of the goals of education, the needs of children, and the aspects of social living, how to plan a daily program. Among the principles for the teacher to keep in mind in scheduling a good day for children are the following:

1. Provide blocks of time to allow for developing activities and evaluating progress. Periods shorter than half-an-hour are not recommended, because they cause tension, conflict, and frustration.

2. Balance the active and the quiet activities. A morning that consists of drawing, practicing writing, working on handwork activities, and reading is likely to produce frustrated, unhappy children; on the other hand, too many free periods fail to give security to the children or stability to the program.

3. Plan for some time to be the child's own. There is a need for a child to relax, to choose what he would especially like to do, to make his own choices of activity, materials, and children with whom to work.

4. Vary the program from day to day and week to week, but allow enough stability to give the children the security of knowing when certain activities come. Prepare the children for the unusual.

5. Plan for individual differences, interests, and abilities by giving children opportunity to participate in varied projects.

6. Make use of teacher-pupil planning to provide for continuity in the program, to give children opportunity for developing skills in group discussion and processes and in problem-solving techniques.

7. Plan to use resource people in the program. Use the art teacher, the science teacher, the gym teacher, and the auditorium teacher, if there is one, to enrich the learning experiences of the group.

8. Consider mechanical factors when planning the schedule. Among these are climate, space, building arrangements, size of group, length of session, maturity of group, seasonal changes, times at which you can get services of special teachers, and times the playground and gym facilities are available.

QUESTIONS AND ACTIVITIES

1. In the objectives of early childhood on page 83, determine whether the teacher should be primarily concerned with the child, the subject matter, or the aspects of social living. Justify your answer on the basis of what you have read in this chapter.

2. Under what circumstances might the 60-minute time allotment suggested on page 92 have value for the kindergarten teacher? What criticism would you make of it in terms of what you know about children's needs and development?

3. Plan a daily schedule for a half-day kindergarten based on the activities for a specific-subjects program and for a broad-fields program. The activities to be included in each schedule are listed below:

I. Specific Subjects
   Health activities
   Physical education, outdoor play
   Work period
   Language
   Literature
   Art, music, games, and rhythms
   Science
   Reading readiness
   Industrial art
II. Broad Fields
   Social living
   Science
   Social studies
   Language arts
   Creative arts

4. Suppose the nursery-school teacher or the second-grade teacher, in the accounts given in this chapter, sensed an explosive quality in the atmosphere. Suggest possible changes in the daily schedule that might have relieved or avoided the situation.

5. Keep in mind the suggestions listed on page 99 as you observe how a teacher plans for the first day of school. Why is it unnecessary to state specifically the time allotment for the exact order of activities on the first day?

SELECTED READINGS

The Association for Childhood Education. "Children Differ — So Should Programs," *Childhood Education*, Vol. 29, No. 4, December 1952.

Foster, Josephine, and Neith E. Headley. *Education in the Kindergarten*, Second Edition. New York: American Book Company, 1948.

Foster, Josephine, and Marion Mattson. *Nursery School Education*. New York: Appleton-Century-Crofts, Inc., 1938.

Gans, Roma, *et al. Teaching Young Children*. Yonkers-on-Hudson, N.Y.: World Book Company, 1952.

Green, Marjorie, and Elizabeth Woods. *A Nursery School Handbook for Teachers and Parents*, Revised Edition. Sierra Madre, Cal.: Sierra Madre Community Nursery School Association, 1953.

Heffernan, Helen, *et al. Guiding the Young Child*, Revised Edition. Boston: D. C. Heath & Company, 1959.

Herrick, Virgil, *et al. The Elementary School*. Englewood Cliffs, N.J.: Prentice-Hall, Inc., 1956.

Johnson, June. *Home Play for the Preschool Child*. New York: Harper & Brothers, 1957.

Klausmeier, Herbert, *et al*. *Teaching in the Elementary School*. New York: Harper & Brothers, 1956.

Kyte, George C. *The Elementary School Teacher at Work*. New York: The Dryden Press, Inc., 1957.

Lambert, Helen. *The Kindergarten Child*. New York: Harcourt, Brace & Company, Inc., 1958.

Lee, J. Murray, and Dorris May Lee. *The Child and his Curriculum*. New York: Appleton-Century-Crofts, Inc., 1950.

Lindsey, Margaret. "Children's Time in School," *Childhood Education*, 30:164–168, December 1953.

Otto, Henry J. *Elementary-School Organization and Administration*, Second Edition. New York: Appleton-Century-Crofts, Inc., 1954.

Ragan, W. B. *Modern Elementary Curriculum*, Second Edition. New York: The Dryden Press, Inc., 1953.

Read, Katherine. *The Nursery School*, Second Edition. Philadelphia: W. B. Saunders Company, 1955.

Stendler, B. Celia. *Teaching in the Elementary School*. New York: Harcourt, Brace & Company, Inc., 1958.

Warner, Ruby H. *The Child and his Elementary School World*. Englewood Cliffs, N.J.: Prentice-Hall, Inc., 1957.

Wills, Clarence D., and William H. Stegeman. *Living in the Kindergarten*. Chicago: Follett Publishing Company, 1956.

Wills, Clarence D., and William H. Stegeman. *Living in the Primary Grades*. Chicago: Follett Publishing Company, 1956.

7

Organizing the Curriculum

*The function of organization is to set the stage and to
facilitate the application in the classroom of the kind
of education one desires for children and the method
whereby children may get it.*

— HENRY J. OTTO

Children come to school to learn. They are eager and ready to push back
the boundaries of their small world. They want to know "why" and "how."
The function of the school is to facilitate learning; the function of the
teacher is to set the stage for learning and to organize experiences that
will challenge a child to develop the skills essential for his maximum development. How shall we accomplish this purpose? How shall we set the stage
for effective learning? Who shall determine what is to be taught? How can
we decide what knowledge, what skills, what concepts will prepare a child to
live with confidence not only in today's world but also in tomorrow's?

In this chapter we shall consider the problem of organizing a curriculum in such a way as to provide continuity for children as they progress from nursery school through the primary grades. No curriculum design is effective without good teachers, but even good teachers need a plan.

Organizing the Classroom Environment

The characteristics of the learner, paralleled by the characteristics of a suitable setting for learning, appear below:

The Learner

1. The learner, like all living organisms, is a unitary, integrating whole.

2. The learner, like any other living organism, seeks always to maintain equilibrium or balance.

3. The learner is a goal-seeking organism, pursuing aims to satisfy needs, thus to maintain equilibrium.

4. The learner is an active, behaving, exploratory individual.

5. The learner has a design and rhythm of development peculiar to the individual. Notable differences exist between individuals in rate of learning, energy output, depth of feeling, facility of insight.

6. The learner brings with him a personality, a set of aims, values, social habits.

7. A learner may be immature in relation to one set of standards and experiences and mature in relation to another.

The Setting for Learning

1. The desirable setting for functional learning experiences will provide for natural integration of feeling-doing-thinking.

2. Desirable learning experiences will provide for success in meeting needs and solving problems, but will also give constant challenge to go beyond immediate situations.

3. The desirable setting for learning will be dominated by purposes and goals set up either by the learner or learners themselves, or with appropriate guidance from the total group, including consultants.

4. The setting must provide freedom to explore, to construct, to question, to differ, to make mistakes; freedom to develop creative contributions. The limits of freedom are democratic controls, rights of others, and good taste.

5. Widely varied types of learning experiences should be provided, adaptable to levels of maturity, to different rates, interests, and abilities.

6. The purposes and experiences established should arise out of and be continuous with the life of the learner. The family background and social-class status, as well as the individuality of the learner, must be taken into account.

7. Learners need sympathetic guidance while building an awareness and personality within their own experiences. They need protection from situations

in which they cannot yet act intelligently, protection from fears and anxieties, protection sufficient to insure security and status on various levels, plus the challenge to grow, to conquer problems, to develop self-reliance. The learner needs guidance from consultants who know and understand the problems of a growing personality, and who see learning as a developmental process. Guidance must be free from domination or coercion.

8. The learner is a social being and naturally seeks activities involving other persons.

8. The setting must provide many varied opportunities to work in "we" relationships developing eventually into self-directed group activity. The whole range of interactive human relationships, the co-operative group process, is essential to the development of the mature socialized personality.[1]

What Curriculum Is

To some, curriculum means a course of study to be followed with great care; to others it means a series of units of work. To some it refers to what the school plans for children to learn; to others it designates what the children actually learn as a result of guided experiences set up in the school. Many educators today look upon curriculum as the totality of those learning experiences provided by the school that are essential to the maximum development of the individual as a useful member of society.

Whether curriculum is defined as a "sequence of potential experiences . . . set up in the school for the purpose of disciplining children and youth in group ways of thinking and acting,"[2] or whether it is defined as "existing only in the experiences of children," it is the teacher who must make it work. As one educator says:

The curriculum exists only in the experiences of children; it does not exist in textbooks, in the course of study, or in the plans and intentions of the teachers. . . .

The curriculum does not exist in the content to be learned. The selection of

[1] William H. Burton, "Basic Principles in a Good Teaching–Learning Situation." *Phi Delta Kappan,* 39:248, March 1958.

[2] B. O. Smith, W. O. Stanley, and J. H. Shores, *Fundamentals of Curriculum Development* (Yonkers-on-Hudson, N.Y.: World Book Company, 1950), p. 4.

useful content is a very important responsibility of the teachers, but does not constitute the curriculum until it becomes a part of the experience of the child. . . . The teacher-pupil and pupil-teacher relationships, the methods of teaching and the evaluation procedures are as much a part of curriculum as the content to be learned.[3]

In general, one can say that the curriculum is an enterprise in guided living. The goal is to help children enrich their lives and contribute to the improvement of society through the acquisition of essential information, skills, and attitudes. But the ways in which teachers seek to accomplish this goal differ. The responsibility of the teacher is to understand the tasks involved in any concept of curriculum, to understand the specific concept held in the school in which she teaches, and to recognize that, whatever the approach, the goal is to assure maximum learning.

In a very literal sense the school provides, but the child decides what his curriculum shall be. He designs his own curriculum as he selects what he wants to learn. In this text we shall endeavor to help the teacher narrow the chasm between what the school plans for the child to learn and what he actually chooses to learn. Our starting point obviously will be with the sequence of experiences the school plans for the child.

The degree of responsibility assumed by the teacher in making decisions about the curriculum varies with the type of organization. The persisting problem, however, is that of continuously evaluating teaching under any curriculum. To improve teaching, therefore, it is important that the teacher understand the general characteristics of the principal types of curricula.

In some countries there is a uniform curriculum in use in every school. In our country, on the other hand, there is no uniform curriculum. Despite this autonomy, relatively few types of curriculum designs have evolved. In many schools, the design is based upon a separation of man's knowledge into discrete subjects. In other schools, these subjects are to a certain extent correlated or integrated. Still other schools have moved even farther away from the use of separate subjects and follow a problems approach. Finally, the experience curriculum attempts a completely integrated approach. We shall consider each of these types of designs briefly.

Types of Curriculum Organizations

THE SEPARATE-SUBJECTS CURRICULUM

The unique characteristic of a curriculum based upon separate subjects is that learning activities take place in discrete subject fields without any attempt to relate them to one another. In a school that adopts such a design, the day is devoted to separate periods for reading, writing, spelling, arithmetic, science, music, art, literature, health, and physical education.

[3] W. B. Ragan, *Modern Elementary Curriculum* (New York: The Dryden Press. Inc., 1953) , pp. 4-5.

The choice of curriculum organization influences the method of teaching. The single textbook becomes under this method the most important teaching tool; children read the text, write out answers to questions, and take tests on the text material. Teachers assign written compositions, oral reports, and use illustrative materials and bulletin boards to motivate interest. The tight schedule, the need for multiple class preparations, and the logical organization of the subject matter, all cause the teacher to rely heavily on the text.

THE BROAD-FIELDS CURRICULUM

The basic idea that underlies organization by subject fields — that the logical organization of specified subject matter is the most effective way for the school to help pupils achieve good citizenship — also underlies the broad-fields curriculum. The use of broad fields has the advantage of cutting across disparate subject-matter fields, thus enabling the teacher to organize the school day around five or six areas instead of from nine to fifteen subjects. Such a scheme, based on larger blocks of time, allows the teacher to deal with children's personal and social concerns on a broader basis. Language arts, social studies, science and health, and arts and crafts form the broad divisions of this kind of curriculum. Arithmetic is still largely taught as a separate subject.

THE PROBLEMS-OF-LIVING CURRICULUM

In this type of organization the area of the social studies is expanded and becomes the core of the whole curriculum. Problems in social living are often used as the basic themes for organizing centers, thereby affording children opportunity to move from one cultural region, political division, or geographical area to another with continuity. The underlying assumption is that persistent social problems exist in the lives of both children and

The reading period is an integral part of the second-grade separate-subjects curriculum.

adults, and that if these persistent problems can be examined and dealt with at the child's particular level of maturity, all learning in the subject fields and all intellectual processes can be identified and brought to bear on their solution. Indeed, these persistent problems are considered to be significant enough to constitute the core of the child's educational experience.[4]

Continuity is provided in two ways: (a) the staff defines the areas of living and the related social functions and (b) day-by-day planning is carried on by the teacher and pupils. The teacher plans and prepares resource units in advance. The details are filled in by the teacher and the group as the unit develops.

The criteria listed below will aid in ensuring the selection of a significant problem:

The problem must contribute to the understanding of social functions and processes.

The problem must provide the children with opportunities to practice the social processes.

The problem must come within the area as defined by the staff.

The problem must continue from previous problems that children in our society face.

Instructional programs organized around such persistent problems of living have often taken the second step of defining the area to be covered at each grade level or in the primary and intermediate grades. This definition serves in most cases to limit the sequence in the instructional program. The simplest and most widely used definition in this type of curriculum is that of sequence, as in the expanding community or in the child's expanding world, which is essentially geographic in nature. Thus, the broad problem and the subproblems that are appropriate to it fall within the area or center of interest defined for a grade level.

The Experience, or Activity, Curriculum

This is the most radical departure from the other curricula we have described. Its starting point is in the children's own concerns or interests, which provide centers around which teachers and pupils plan learning experiences. Certain concepts underly this approach:

(1) Any significant curriculum must emerge from the needs of the children who are involved.

(2) If children's needs and interests are explored and identified, a curriculum emerges in day-by-day living in the classroom.

(3) On-the-spot planning instead of preplanning by the teacher is essential to the learning of democratic processes.

[4] A comprehensive discussion of the problems-of-living approach to curriculum is found in Florence Stratemeyer, et al., Developing a Curriculum for Modern Living, Revised Edition (New York: Bureau of Publications, Teachers College, Columbia University, 1957).

Learning centers around the activity or experience. Knowledge and skills are brought in as they are needed in the solution of problems. Since there is no curriculum framework to guide the teacher, her task consists of arranging a permissive environment in which children feel free to define their ends and solve their problems. In the experience curriculum there is no established pattern for the daily program. Teachers and pupils plan the agenda from day to day and from week to week, deciding which problems have priority, which problems will include a number of others, which problems can be postponed, which problems can be worked on simultaneously, and which, if any, are so insignificant that they can be disregarded.

There are several questions that the teacher, the staff, and the community must consider in dealing with such a curriculum design: What is the nature of the child, as a living organism? How can we help the child to identify, select, organize, and evaluate important educational concerns and needs? How can we as a staff and community plan so that the emerging educational program of these children will have adequate significance, breadth, organization, and continuity?

In the hands of a master teacher this type of curriculum can be exciting and worth while. Few elementary teachers, however, have the broad cultural training necessary to ensure the child's access to man's ideas and ways of thinking about the problems the child faces. A program of this type demands

Community trips and visitors to the classroom encourage the child to relate his learning to everyday experiences.

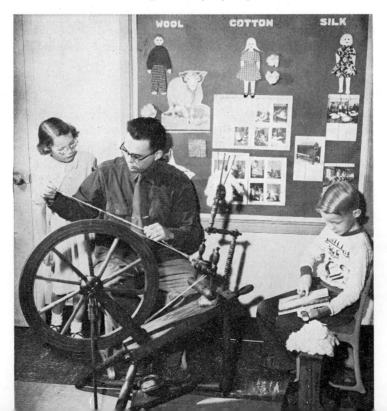

that the teacher be skilled in many ways — in group processes, in cooperative action, in the use of educational resources, and in communication. It is difficult to find teachers who wish to accept the responsibility for the decision-making demanded by such a curriculum.[5] It is even more difficult to find a community or a school organization that wishes to risk the hazards of the unknown.

Teachers frequently do use this type of organization in planning for co-curriculum activities, programs for parents, or recreational programs after school. Some have ventured to try it in such fields as the arts, health and physical education, and the social studies. It does of course make use of children's needs; children are motivated to learn, and preplanning is staff and communal planning. It is the democratic process in action.

The various types of curriculum designs we have examined provide an opportunity for the teacher to see the relationships that exist among the various tasks of teaching. Identifying one's objectives and planning, developing, and evaluating the learning experiences are related to one's beliefs about children, the nature of society, the function of the school, the school organization, and the school policies.

Organizing Learning Experiences

THE CURRICULUM IN THE NURSERY SCHOOL

A good nursery-school curriculum is not a haphazard affair. It is the result of careful planning based on the teacher's knowledge of children and their spontaneous interests and needs. Through firsthand experiences, through the type of equipment she provides, through personal interests and explanations of new ideas, the teacher helps the children develop concepts, organize ideas, and broaden horizons.

ORGANIZING CENTERS IN THE KINDERGARTEN

The younger of the kindergarten children, as is true of nursery-school children, are intensely interested in themselves and their environment and in communicating these interests. Hence, for them the curriculum is child-centered. Creating, manipulating, exploring, and communicating form the core of their curriculum. Observation of young children reveals the personal, short-spanned, fleeting, and individualistic nature of their interests. In the span of a single morning they may build a house, construct a zoo, build a fleet of boats, and take a trip in a rocket to the moon and back. As the year progresses, they become interested in exploring such phases of the environment as the school, the home, the neighborhood, ways of travel, varieties of pets, and other experiences with natural and physical science.

---

[5] A comprehensive discussion of the experience curriculum is found in Thomas Hopkins, *Interaction: The Democratic Process* (Boston: D. C. Heath & Company, 1941).

Older kindergarten children enjoy activities centering around building a doll house, making a home, learning about pets, going to the zoo, taking trips to the corner grocery store and the post office. They enjoy, too, experiences with methods of transportation such as the bus, the train, and the boat.

ORGANIZING CENTERS IN THE PRIMARY GRADES

When kindergarten children enter the primary school, their broadened interests, increased attention span, and pronounced individual differences call for organizing the learning experiences in such a way as to tie children, ideas, materials, and activities together in some meaningful fashion. Herrick suggests that an organizing center is "whatever a teacher and class can get their hands on and their minds around to enrich the quality of classroom living. Visualizing in the center the qualities that make it worthwhile determines its usefulness."[6] Among the organizing centers useful in the primary grades are:

1. *Centers of interest:* For younger children centers of interest such as a science center, a library center, an arithmetic center, a workbench, a doll house, and an art and music center serve to stimulate exploration and creativity.

2. *Problems of living:* Finding out how people travel, how they live, how they communicate, how they transport goods, and how they make a living in the community affords effective organizing centers.

3. *Places:* Places such as the playground, the community, the zoo, the farm, the airport, the harbor, the post office, or the market stimulate children's interests and serve as effective centers.

4. *People:* People can be studied — people in our country and people in other countries — with the idea of developing world understanding through appreciation of cultural differences.

5. *Ideas:* Such concepts as time, space, man, and his place in the universe have traditionally served as organizing centers.

Progressing Through the Year

SCOPE OF THE CURRICULUM

On the whole, the personal-social needs of children help us to determine *what* experiences we should provide; the interests, abilities, and maturity of the children tell us *when* to teach; the objectives of the curriculum tell us primarily *how* to teach and the function of the school tells us *why* to teach.

In dealing with young children the teacher can base the scope of the curriculum on their identifiable and persistent needs. In order to identify these needs she must know their physical, mental, and emotional characteristics and potentialities, the characteristics of the society in which they live, and the demands that society places upon them.

[6] Virgil Herrick, *et al.*, *The Elementary School* (Englewood Cliffs, N.J.: Prentice-Hall, Inc., 1956), p. 111.

Criteria for determining scope. Here are some of the questions the teacher must answer in relation to the scope of the learning experiences she provides for children:

Does the experience meet the personal-social needs of children as defined in the objectives of the school?

Is the experience rich in opportunities for democratic group living?

Does it focus upon real-life situations, thereby offering children opportunities to solve problems inherent in the culture and having meaning for them at their stage of development?

Does the experience provide for continuity of learning experiences so that the children will grow in knowledge, skills, and social understanding, and in their understanding of significant social and scientific concepts?

Will the experience provide for the individual differences in the classroom and at the same time challenge children at all grade levels on a graduated level of depth of understanding?

Does the learning experience offer concrete evidence of relationships between what the child is learning in school and everyday life?

SEQUENCE IN THE CURRICULUM

Sequence refers to the *when* of the curriculum and determines the placing of a particular learning experience. In some schools the scope and sequence pattern applies to the whole curriculum; in others to the social studies program; and in still others it is used to determine what units are to be taught and when they are to be taught. Sequences may be based on experiences proceeding from the immediate to the remote, or they may be based on interests of children in a broader setting.

Criteria for determining sequence. Some questions the teacher may ask in terms of the sequence of learning experience follow:

Is the learning experience suited to the maturity of the children and to their physical and psychological needs?

Is the content appropriate at this grade level?

Does the content allow for pupil-teacher planning?

Does the sequence provide for continuity, integration, and coordination of learning experiences within the grade and between grades?

Is the sequence comprehensive and does it provide balance in long-range planning?

Is the sequence feasible in terms of adequate and appropriate materials and resources and the background of the teacher's knowledge?

Following is an example of sequence in a curriculum:

Kindergarten   The home and the school. Adjustment to school life; making the transition from home to school; relating one's self to the expanded peer group.

Grade 1	The home, school, and neighborhood.
Grade 2	The immediate community.
Grade 3	The human resources of the community. Adjustment of the various culture groups within the community; background and contributions of these groups.
Grade 4	The community in its metropolitan area and geographic region. The manner in which natural and controlled environmental factors influence and contribute to community living.
Grades 5 and 6	The areas of living in the state and their relation to living in the community. The present in relation to the past — Grade 5; living in the United States and its relation to living in our community — Grade 6.[7]

The Course of Study

REPRESENTATIVE TOPICS AND UNITS BY GRADES

From a sampling of curriculum guides and courses of study published by various cities, states, and counties since 1948, a list of typical centers of interest, topics, units, and areas appears on the following page. The tendency to repeat certain topics, with broadened scope, is evident, as is also the tendency to go from the near to the remote.

The topics listed indicate a tendency to consider children's interests and development according to grade placement; they display sequences designed to meet children's needs in various curriculum areas by means of activities that are educationally sound and satisfying to children. The list reveals the influence of the community in the selection of topics and points to the recurrence of certain topics or problems with an expanded scope.

One of the first things a new teacher does when she arrives at the school where she will teach is to see if there is a curriculum guide, an outline, a course of study, a scope and sequence chart, a statement of objectives, or even a plan book, to brief her on the possible organization of learning experiences used in that school. Most teachers in nursery school, kindergarten, and the primary grades will find some such guide available. A statement of objectives serves to orient the teacher to the philosophy of the school and helps her in any preplanning she wishes to do. In this activity as in all others, of course, the cold words in the outline or the statement of objectives or the curriculum guide come alive only as the teacher gives them meaning. It is her mature judgment, her experience in living, her enthusiasm in teaching children that must translate the curriculum guide into challenging learning experiences. All young children are entitled to

---

[7] University of Wisconsin Summer Laboratory School, 1950.

Topics and Units in Curriculum Guides and Courses of Study

Kindergarten	Grade I	Grade II	Grade III
Airplanes	A grocery store	Our community	Living in our community
Boats	Family life at home	Our neighborhood	Living in contrasting cultures
A toy shop	Our school	Transportation	Discovering ways to meet basic
Caring for pets	Community helpers	Communication	needs for food, shelter, cloth-
Creative dramatization	The neighborhood	Food production	ing
Birthday parties	Transportation	The farm	How our community began and
Holidays	The farm	The dairy	grew
Gardening	Safety	The post office	Ways of communicating
Living together at home	Healthful living	Pets	Methods of transportation
Living together at school	Our pets	Health and safety	Life in a primitive community
Our play house	Animals, homes	Planting seeds	Children of other lands
Mother hen and chicks	How plants and animals live	Weather	The grocery store
The zoo	The seasons	People who help us	The school bank
The circus	Puppet shows	Numbers	The city hall
The weather	Our flower garden	Spelling	The post office
The train	Indians	How animals live in winter	A truck-farm neighborhood
The rhythm band	Our circus	The policeman	How nature works for us
Trips to the park	A toy shop	The janitor	Indian life
Writing a letter	Reading experience	A beehive	Why air and water are im-
Reading readiness	Charts	The market	portant
Number readiness	Numbers	The store	Arithmetic
Writing readiness	Writing	Writing	Cursive writing
Rhythms	Rhythm	Dancing	Language and spelling
Thrift	Dramatics	The fire station	Music and art
Safety club	Spelling	Reading	Reading
Outdoor guides	Sharing	Indians	

115

The teacher creates the environment and supplies the materials, thus guiding the child in the selection of the area to study.

such experiences. A five-year-old put it this way. As he enrolled in kindergarten, he was overheard to say, "I hope they teach me to learn; I'm tired of being teached to play."

The curriculum guides offer a teacher guidance in developing and carrying out a suggested topic in an integrated organization in the classroom. But how she organizes the learning experiences to ensure effective learning will have much to do with her success as a teacher.

Summary

In helping to make school experiences significant and educationally as important as possible, the curriculum design planned by teachers, staff, and members of the community should give evidence of objectives.

Every curriculum plan involves children, the material to be learned, and its social application. Each has the goal of enriching the life of the child and helping him develop the skills and knowledge he needs for successful living; they differ, however, as to which of the three referents chosen as a starting point.

Most frequently used of the curriculum types are those based on subjects and broad fields, both of which utilize the same kind of curriculum design. Persistent problems of living or experiences are being used by a few teachers as organizing centers for some phase of the program. Few teachers or schools, however, organize the total school program on either of these bases.

Good curriculum planning requires the teacher and staff to see the relationships between objectives, children, ideas, processes, materials, resources, and organization. Good planning is not a panacea; it is dependent upon the knowledge, ability, and understanding of the teacher. The type of curriculum design is important to the extent that it releases the teacher's creative energies as she works with children and staff.

Good curriculum planning results in desirable learning experiences that have significance, educationally speaking, in breadth and depth, continuity, and integration in a classroom setting conducive to effective learning.

QUESTIONS AND ACTIVITIES

1. Which type of curriculum organization do you think is in keeping with modern objectives of education and modern concepts of child development? Why?

2. Define the kinds of curricula based on separate subjects, broad fields, problems of living, and experience. Describe a classroom you have visited and tell which of the four patterns was used.

3. Under which type of curriculum would you like to do your first teaching in the nursery school? In the kindergarten? In the third grade? Is there a difference? If so, why?

4. How do you define scope and sequence in the broad fields? In the curriculum based on the problems of living? In the experience curriculum?

5. How would you choose a problem to solve in the curriculum based on problems of living? In the experience curriculum?

6. Noting the list of units suggested in courses of study or curriculum guides, discuss to what extent the list is in harmony with children's interests, needs, and abilities.

7. Discuss with the local superintendent or principal the responsibility teachers have in curriculum organization of the school. Read the laws and regulations of your state concerning curriculum requirements. What are the implications for the teacher?

8. Assume that you are to teach the first grade in a school that utilizes a separate-subjects curriculum. A designated course of study is provided for you when you begin teaching. What can you do toward improving the curriculum of your school?

SELECTED READINGS

Adams, Fay. *Educating America's Children: Elementary School Curriculum and Methods.* New York: The Ronald Press Company, 1954.

Beck, R. H., *et al. Curriculum in the Modern Elementary School.* Englewood Cliffs, N.J.: Prentice-Hall, Inc., 1953.

California Journal of Elementary Education, Kindergarten Issue. Vol. 24, August 1955.

Caswell, H. L., and A. W. Foshay. *Education in the Elementary School.* New York: American Book Company, 1950.

Doak, Elizabeth. *What Does the Nursery School Teacher Teach?* Chicago: National Association for Nursery Education, 1951.

Foster, Josephine, and Neith Headley. *Education in the Kindergarten*, Revised Edition. New York: American Book Company, 1948.

Gans, Roma, *et al. Teaching Young Children in Nursery School, Kindergarten, and Primary Grades.* Yonkers-on-Hudson, N.Y.: World Book Company, 1952.

Harap, Henry. *Curriculum Trends at Mid-Century.* Cincinnati: South-Western Publishing Co., 1953.

Headley, Neith. *Foundation Learnings in the Kindergarten.* Washington, D.C.: National Education Association, 1958.

Heffernan, Helen, *et al. Guiding the Young Child*, Revised Edition. Boston: D. C. Heath & Company, 1954.

Herrick, Virgil. *Issues in Elementary Education.* Minneapolis: Burgess Publishing Co., 1952.

Herrick, Virgil, *et al. The Elementary School.* Englewood Cliffs, N.J.: Prentice-Hall, Inc., 1956.

Kelner, Bernard. *How to Teach in the Elementary School.* New York: McGraw-Hill Book Company, Inc., 1958.

Lambert, Hazel. *The Kindergarten Child.* New York: Harcourt, Brace & Company, Inc., 1958.

Leavett, Jerome E. (ed.). *Nursery–Kindergarten Education.* New York: McGraw-Hill Book Company, Inc., 1958.

Lee, J. Murray, and Dorris May Lee. *The Child and His Curriculum.* New York: Appleton-Century-Crofts, Inc., 1950.

Miel, Alice, *et al. Cooperative Procedures in Learning.* New York: Bureau of Publications, Teachers College, Columbia University, 1952.

Northrup, Ann Holmes. *Child Development Principles in Kindergarten Education.* Greenfield, Ind.: Wm. Mitchell Printing Co., 1954.

Ragan, William B. *Modern Elementary Curriculum.* New York: The Dryden Press, Inc., 1953.

Read, Katherine. *The Nursery School*, Second Edition. Philadelphia: W. B. Saunders Company, 1955.

Rudolph, Margareta. *Living and Learning in the Nursery School.* New York: Harper & Brothers, 1954.

Salor, John G. *Curriculum Planning for Better Teaching and Learning.* New York: Rinehart & Company, Inc., 1954.

Sheehy, Emma Dickson. *The Fives and Sixes Go to School.* New York: Henry Holt & Company, Inc., 1954.

Stendler, Celia B. *Teaching in the Elementary School.* New York: Harcourt, Brace & Company, Inc., 1958.

U.S. Department of Health, Education, and Welfare. *Where Children Live Affects the Curriculum.* Bulletin No. 7. Washington, D.C.: Government Printing Office, 1955.

Wills, Clarence D., and William H. Stegeman. *Living in the Primary Grades.* Chicago: Follett Publishing Company, 1956.

8

Developing the Unit of Work

In binding these elements into a . . . fabric of beauty and strength, let us keep the original fibers so intact that the fineness of each will show in the completed handiwork.

— FRANKLIN D. ROOSEVELT

Volumes have been written about organizing learning experiences in such a way that optimum learning is achieved by the maximum number with the minimum amount of frustration. The unit of work, if correctly conceived and carefully used, will accomplish this purpose. But in order to determine the value of the unit of work in the educational process, it is necessary to understand it.

What a Unit of Work Is

A unit of work is an organization of varied learning experiences around a significant central theme, problem, or purpose. The literature designates a variety of types of units, among them resource units, experience units, activity units, center-of-interest units, core units, culture units, topic units, problem units, commercial units, subject-matter units, and teaching units, to name the most common.

Analysis of the units reveals that in general they are of two types: subject-matter units and experience units. The difference between the two is primarily one of emphasis. In the subject-matter unit, the central concern is the acquisition of information; the activities are more formalized and less numerous. In the experience unit, the central concern is the development of desirable behavior traits, and subject matter is used as a means to that end. In a sense all units are experience units, center-of-interest units, and process units if they meet the needs, interests, and purposes of children and teacher.

Despite the variation in nomenclature, certain characteristics are common to all types. Some units are experience-centered, that is, "Building a grocery store"; some are topic-centered, that is, "Water"; some are problem-centered, that is, "How are sewage facilities handled in our town?"; some are concept-centered, that is, "Magnetism"; and some are culture-centered, that is, "Life in Alaska."

A unit of work cuts across subject matter. The core may be selected from the social studies, science, or health, but experiences in literature, art, music, and composition contribute to its development. It is important, however, not to carry the correlation too far.

A unit of work is comprehensive and complex enough to provide for individual differences in the classroom. The maturity of the children, the amount and complexity of the material to be studied, the availability of materials and personnel for carrying out the projects, the time allotted daily for unit activities, the personal interests of children, all these determine the length of the unit. A unit may last only a week, or it may continue for several weeks.

A unit of work is cohesive. The material in the unit should grow out of and be related to other phases of the children's experience; integration is essential. A unit includes many types of activities — not just reading and reciting. Reading to learn is an aspect of the unit of work. Activities such as experiments, excursions, construction, and films provide valuable experiences for the learner.

Value of the unit. The value of the unit of work is dependent upon the extent to which it:

Provides for teacher–pupil planning.
Provides for individual differences.
Offers educationally significant learning opportunities.
Has continuity.
Results in changes of behavior.

Teachers who employ unit teaching agree that it offers rich opportunities for children to satisfy innate drives — to be active, to explore, to experiment, to construct, to create, to communicate, to dramatize, to satisfy curiosity, to satisfy their needs for achievement and acceptance. It gives the teacher and pupils opportunity for democratic living and the practice of the "Three R's" in the classroom.

Planning the Unit of Work

THE DAILY SCHEDULE

Flexibility is an essential characteristic of a curriculum that utilizes the unit. In the self-contained classroom it is possible to adjust the schedule to meet the demands of the day's activities. Although the unit may be scheduled at any time of day, many teachers prefer it in the morning, in order to allow for organization of the classroom, to set the tone for the day, and to begin the work on the unit when the children are rested, refreshed, and eager.

Time should be allotted in the schedule for the practice of needed skills. Certain skills must be taught when the teachable moment arrives. Individual skills, interests, and abilities need time to develop. To ensure a balanced daily program the teacher should include five major phases in the schedule: social living, language arts, creative arts, science, and numbers. From one to two hours a day is usually devoted to the unit.

LONG-RANGE PLANNING

The course of study or curriculum guide provide the teacher with information concerning what is to be taught in each grade. These publications usually include a statement of the philosophy of the school, the objectives, and some information about the developmental characteristics of the children. Scope and sequence are also usually included. Most guides are organized on the broadfields approach to curriculum. Separate sections indicate the curriculum for the language arts, social studies, science and health, arithmetic, art and music. Often illustrative units are given for each grade level.

If the teacher is not provided with a curriculum guide or a scope and sequence chart, she has the sole responsibility for selecting a unit. In order to select a tentative list of problems for study, the teacher should try to find out the interests, needs, and abilities of her group, as well as their experiential background and common interests. She must know the nature of the community in which the children live and which problems have social significance in terms of the community. She must determine the accessibility of resources, background reading, instructional material, and the possibilities for excursions and experiments.

There is no one best way of planning a unit; it varies with the teacher.

The questions that arise during a reading period may provide a starting point for a unit of work.

There is the informal planning of the teacher who jots down a few ideas at random, then writes up the unit on the basis of her memory of materials she has read about and the activities she knows previous groups have used. In addition, she may consult textbooks or ask other teachers for suggestions. For more formal planning she may refer to a resource unit.

Good teaching requires the teacher to plan carefully in advance, to draw up a statement of concepts and generalizations to be taught, to list suitable learning activities, to locate instructional materials, and to determine evaluation procedures. When the preplanning is done, the teacher will want to involve the children in the selection of the specific problem to be studied, so that they may choose from among the various activities possible those that they need to solve the problem.

Below is a general outline for a unit of work. Although any specific unit would probably not include all the suggested activities, many units would necessarily include most of these steps.

1. Heading
    a. Title or topic
    b. Age or grade level
    c. Time allotted
2. Introductory statement clarifying the topic and general purpose
3. Selecting the problem

4. Formulating concepts and generalizations to be taught
    a. Important concepts to be learned
    b. Major social understandings to be gained
    c. Skills to be learned
5. Planning possible learning activities
    a. Initiatory activities required to interest children: instructional materials, resource people, films, excursions
    b. Developmental learning activities required if the pupils are to learn the concepts and understand the generalizations to be taught
    c. Culminating activities to which each pupil can contribute, toward which the class directs its efforts throughout the unit
6. Materials and resources
    a. Printed materials, audio-visual aids, and materials for demonstration, experimentation, or display needed in carrying out the activities
    b. Facilities outside the classroom that can be used
    c. Plans for bringing resource people in and taking pupils on excursions
7. Evaluation procedures
    a. To determine where pupils are at the outset of the unit
    b. To help pupils measure their own progress
    c. To help evaluate pupil growth in concepts, generalizations, and skills

Any design must, of course, be adapted to the particular teacher's purposes and situation.

Selecting a Problem for Study

In the process of selecting a problem for the unit, the teacher's role is that of leader and counselor. As such she must preplan; this she does by drawing up a tentative list of problems for study. She bases her choice on her knowledge of the class, trying to anticipate the areas in which children have erroneous or sketchy concepts.

The teacher must have an extensive background in the subject of the unit. Before the unit begins, she must do research and wide reading. Through experience she will discover the intrinsic value of various units suggested by the curriculum guide in terms of a particular group of children.

A beginning teacher will need to know the children, the community, and the resource units, in order to enhance her background before she begins a unit with her group.

Formulating Concepts and Generalizations

When the tentative list of problems has been selected, the next step is to set down the underlying concepts necessary to answer the questions thus raised. Such preparation ensures that the unit will have intellectual content and social meaning as well as activities interesting in themselves. Hanna states the reason for such a procedure:

> A child may have many worthwhile and enriching experiences during the development of a unit of work but he may miss the underlying, basic social principles. To avoid this the teacher must be ever alert to the concepts, conclusions, and generalizations that are intrinsic in any sound unit of study. In order to be alert to these important basic social principles and insure teaching–learning situations that will make them clear and meaningful to children, the teacher should formulate the most important ones for himself before beginning the unit. If these are kept before him as the unit develops, they will not be neglected.[1]

This idea has significant implications for teachers. Those who plan to teach must realize the importance of knowing as much as possible about the world and the problems that need to be solved. How else can a teacher guide children in selecting learning experiences? For experienced teachers it may even mean throwing away units on such topics as "The Circus."

One of the most satisfying types of units to teach is a cultural unit. There is usually a wealth of material available. A number of resource units have been developed in cultural areas, and the possibilities for dramatic play and construction work, art, music, and dance are unlimited. The cultural unit is especially significant in today's shrinking world. Children need to understand the likenesses and appreciate the differences that exist between their own culture and those of other peoples in the world.

An important outcome of a unit of work is a better understanding of the social and physical world in which we live. Although many facts are forgotten, concepts and generalizations are retained. All this means that the teacher herself must see her goal clearly. Unless she has well in mind the insights she wants the children to get from a unit of study, the development of the unit may well be a series of isolated experiences. Understanding occurs when a child is able to act, feel, or think intelligently with respect to a given situation. Even nursery-school and kindergarten children like to be challenged to analyze and evaluate problems.

Possible Learning Activities

At the beginning of the century the term "learning experience" was not used. The textbooks used such terms as "exercises," "examples," "problems," and "assignments" to designate the learning tasks or homework of the pupil; the word "recitation" was the term used to designate the oral response the pupil made as he came before the class. Today writers on curriculum are using the term "learning experiences."

[1] Lavone A. Hanna, Gladys Potter, and Neva Hagaman, *Unit Teaching in the Elementary School* (New York: Rinehart & Company, Inc., 1955), p. 534.

The school librarian should coordinate her work with that of the classroom teacher in helping children set up a reading center.

The children engaged in a unit of work will be participating in a variety of experiences — planning and conferring in small groups, writing letters for information, interviewing an authority on a specific subject, rehearsing a play, preparing a science exhibit, conducting a science experiment, painting a mural, making costumes for a play, building a greenhouse, planting a garden, reading for information to solve a problem, and a number of other activities. Teaching children the democratic processes of working together to solve problems, taking the responsibility for group action, and settling differences by peaceable methods is possible through this type of organization.

The questions the teacher can ask to determine whether the activity is justifiable are: "What are the pupils learning from this activity? Does this activity really focus on important concepts and generalizations that pupils should learn, or are they just having fun?"

Culminating Activities

One of the problems in the unit of work is to decide when to conclude it. The time will differ with units, schools, and teachers. A rule of thumb might be that a unit should be ended when the interest is still high; it should not be dragged out until it is squeezed dry. The reactions of children are an index to the length of the unit. If the children's interest is lagging, if they cannot be stimulated by new activities, new materials, or subproblems to investigate, if the unit seems to have been poorly chosen, if adequate materials are not available, if the teacher is inexperienced in the ways of unit development, or if the possible experiences appear to be exhausted — it is time to call a halt, no matter how short a time has been spent on the unit. On the other hand, if children's interest remains at a high level and there are many possibilities for meaningful experiences, then the unit may continue for several weeks.

An example comes to mind of a group of children who were working with a student teacher and were tremendously interested in finding out about transportation. The student teacher had herself been much interested in boats and had worked out a transportation unit on boats in a social studies class. The children in this first grade, however, were living in an inland city, where boats meant nothing to them. The father of one of the children, who was connected with the airport a few miles from the city, had invited the group to visit the airport and promised that he would escort them to the control tower. Naturally the children were eager to go, but the student teacher persisted in her effort to initiate and carry out the unit on boats. Despite her attempt to arouse and retain the interest of the children, her efforts were in vain. Fortunately, the term ended, and the next student teacher built upon the interest the children had in air travel and taught a stimulating unit.

It is useful for teachers inexperienced in teaching units to observe the more or less natural intervals in the school calendar. It might be that one unit would terminate at Christmas vacation; another would be studied from January to spring vacation; and the last one from the close of spring vacation until the end of the year. An example of such a sequence might be that the children in a second grade would study "The Farm" from the beginning of the year until Christmas, the "Wholesale Market" from January to March, and the "Bakery" from March until June. A first grade might study "The Home," "The School," "The Community." The third grade might study three phases of transportation, such as "How We Travel by Bus, by Train, and by Plane."

Children in kindergarten, although they do not participate in highly structured units, might progress through the year with a sequence such as the following: "Becoming Acquainted with Our School" from September to December, "Becoming Acquainted with Our Immediate Neighborhood" from January to March, and "What Happens When Spring Comes to Our Town" from March until the end of school.

The culminating experiences of a unit should be the natural outgrowth of the accompanying activities. It is really a time for teachers and pupils to summarize what they have learned and to make evaluations such as these:

> What have we learned in our study?
> What do we know that we did not really know before?
> What new skills have we learned?
> What old skills have we improved?
> What should we try to improve next?
> What did we enjoy most?

The teacher should help children draw generalizations from their experiences. For example, the children who are studying the school should know that many people in the school contribute to their needs; the group studying the community should understand the interdependence of people; children engaged in a study of transportation should know the effects of travel by air on individuals, cities, states, nations, and the world.

Culminating experiences may take various forms — summarizing the information about things learned and plans the class carried through to completion; making a movie; giving a play, based on use of the properties made during the unit; completing a mural or map; evaluating what has been learned; or inviting another class or parents to share some of the experiences most enjoyed.

If another class or parents are invited in, activities that children participate in gladly are dramatizing an experience they particularly enjoyed, such as launching ships, taking the train, or making *refrescos* for the fiesta; dramatizing a favorite television script; explaining a mural or large map; dancing some favorite dances; sharing rhythms, singing songs; serving cookies they themselves have made. It is important to keep the culminating activity simple. If it is not, the result is staged, superficial, and stereotyped.

Teaching Materials

Listing, locating, and collecting all the materials needed for use in teaching the unit is a responsibility not to be discharged lightly. In addition to a basic text, schools today are using such aids as globes, maps, charts, games, models, film strips, movies, lantern slides, tape recorders, and so forth.

The cultural unit develops creative skills as well as understandings.

The use of movies, and especially those with sound tracks, has made it possible to analyze movements and to show relationships of time and space more graphically, to analyze and improve voice quality, and to increase the sense of reality when dealing with subjects requiring vicarious treatment. Television is pushing back the boundaries of the school, and by removing physical barriers is providing experiences as broad as life itself.

Teachers should make use of materials that aid in motivated drill sessions. Certain skills cannot be learned without motivated practice. To catch and hold the interest of a child so that he repeats correctly a response until he has learned it is the objective of these newer teaching aids.

The teacher should begin at the outset of her educational career to build a store of instructional aids and a file of information about them. She should begin early to clip pictures from magazines, order free materials, obtain drill materials, collect materials she can use in science, try to keep up with new materials reviewed in educational journals, and keep records on her use of all these aids.

The determining factor as to which instructional materials have value should be the needs and developmental level of the group. The teacher may well ask the question, "Will this contribute to concept or skill development, or is it just a gimmick?"

In this phase of teaching as in all others it is the teacher who makes the difference; it takes a wise individual to select well from the variety of instructional materials available, and it takes both wisdom and experience to use the materials effectively once they are chosen.

Evaluation

Evaluation is a continuing process. It does not consist merely of testing children at the end of the unit, nor is it synonymous with marking report cards. It is used for determining the extent to which the objectives are being realized; it helps each child determine his own progress; and it is useful in conferences with parents. Since principles of evaluation apply to other phases of the educational program as well as to unit teaching, however, they will be discussed in Chapter 9.

A Sample Unit

An example of the way in which one school used a cultural unit at the third grade level is presented as it was first organized by the teacher. The story of how it developed day by day in a class of third graders is told in a log written by the teacher and pupils as the unit progressed. Third graders were unanimous in reporting growth in knowledge, understanding, skill, and insight, as they literally turned their classroom into a primary school in Mexico for several weeks.

A Mexican Unit

I. Introduction

Motivation. A child's aunt visited Mexico, and the trip was reviewed one morning by the child. Enthusiastic reception resulted in the unit on Mexico.

II. Objectives

A. General.

1. To learn more about our southern neighbor, because a good-neighbor policy is worth while. Up to now a large gap has existed between Mexico and the United States; misleading information in geography books, economic pressures, and conflicts over ownership of oil resources have put distance between the two countries.

2. To gain understanding of the customs, background, and beliefs of the people of Mexico.

B. Specific.

1. To appreciate beauty in art, music, and literature.

2. To participate as a group in thinking and mutual understanding.

3. To learn to share.

4. To gain in creative expression through verses, stories, and plays.

5. To read better, to scan, and to choose outstanding information.

6. To construct better sentences.

7. To develop vocabulary.

III. Development

A. History.

1. Aztecs.

2. Spanish conquerors and Cortez.

3. Revolt of the peasants.

Questions:

1. How did the Indians become slaves?

2. What happened when Mexico won its independence from Spain?

3. Why did the peasants revolt?

B. Geography.

1. Mountains.

2. Rivers.

3. Climate.

4. Cities.

5. Soil.

6. Material resources.

Questions:

1. Where are the mountains and rivers?

2. What is the climate?

3. Where are the large cities?

4. What kinds of soils are found?

5. What are the natural resources?

C. Industries.

1. Pottery making.

2. Weaving.

    3. Farming.

    4. Jewelry making.

    5. Mining.

    6. Glass blowing.

Questions:

    1. What do the Mexicans raise on their farms?

    2. How do they weave, make pottery, and make their jewelry?

    3. How important is mining?

D. Peoples and their origins.

    1. Peasants.

    2. Mexican children.

    3. Social structure.

    4. Various nationalities.

Questions:

    1. How is a peon different from a man of society?

    2. How are Mexican children different from American children?

    3. How are they alike?

E. Clothing.

    1. Work clothes.

    2. Dress-up clothes.

    3. How clothes are made.

Questions:

    1. What do the Indian women wear?

    2. How do Mexican children dress?

    3. What is the difference between owning a peon's hat and a hat belonging to a society man?

F. Homes.

    1. Structure.

    2. Size.

    3. Interiors.

Questions:

    1. What are the differences between homes in the city and a Mexican hacienda?

    2. What is an adobe house like?

    3. Who builds most of the homes?

    4. How do Mexicans light their homes?

G. Food and drink.

    1. Number of meals per day.

    2. Kinds of food.

    3. Preparation of food.

    4. Beverages.

Questions:

    1. What do Mexicans eat?

    2. Do they raise everything they eat?

    3. What do they drink?

H. Utensils and farm implements.

    1. Kinds.

    2. Materials.

Questions:
1. Of what are water jugs made?
2. Are Mexican tools modern?
3. How do Mexicans plow?

I. Religion, churches, and shrines.
1. Dominant religion.
2. Other beliefs.
3. Description of churches.
4. Shrine of the nation.

Questions:
1. Why did Catholicism become the general religion?
2. Describe the churches and the decorations found in them.
3. Where is the national shrine?
4. How did the shrine happen to be built?

J. Language.
1. Dominant language.
2. Other languages.

Questions:
1. What is the dominant language?
2. Why is it the dominant language?
3. What other languages are spoken?

K. Recreation.
1. Dances.
2. Games.
3. Fiestas.
4. Bullfights.

Questions:
1. What kind of dances do Mexicans enjoy?
2. Can you describe a fiesta?
3. In bullfighting, who are the toreadors, picadors, and matadors?

L. Education.
1. Kinds of schools.
2. Comparison with ours.

Questions:
1. What language is used in the schools?
2. How did the Mexican Revolution influence education?

M. Travel.
1. Difficulty in transportation.
2. Vehicles and animals.
3. Railroads, river transportation, and airlines.

Questions:
1. Why do the mountain ranges hinder transportation?
2. Why are there few railroads?
3. How do deserts and a tropical climate retard communication?

N. Government.
1. Leaders.
2. How chosen.
3. Kinds.

Questions:
  1. For how long a term is a president elected?
  2. Is there a congress?
  3. How many states, territories, and federal districts are there?
O. Literature.
  1. Stories.
  2. Poems.
  3. Legends.
Questions:
  1. How do the stories illustrate the customs of Mexico?
  2. Can you tell briefly one of the legends?
P. Art.
  1. Museums.
  2. Art in everyday life.
  3. Indian and Spanish influence.
  4. Artists.
Questions:
  1. What kinds of folk art exist?
  2. Who is Diego Rivera?
  3. What does the "Mexican Peasant," by Aguirre, show?
  4. What media are used in Mexican art?
Q. Music and dances.
  1. Musicians.
  2. Types of musical instruments.
  3. Kinds of dances.
Questions:
  1. Who is Carlos Chávez?
  2. Why is "La Paloma" a well-loved song?
  3. What musical instruments are much used in Mexico?
  4. Can you describe difficult Mexican dances — for example, "The Hat Dance"?
IV. Suggested Activities
    The nature of the unit should be easily recognized by observation of bulletin boards, walls, and so forth. Attractiveness is important; therefore, careful planning is essential. Committee work may be used to good advantage here.
  A. Room decorations (collections).
    1. Pictures.
    2. Books (library corner).
    3. Drawings.
    4. Dolls.
    5. Embroidery.
    6. Vases.
    7. Baskets.
    8. Clothes and hats.
    9. Rugs.
    10. Charm strings.
    11. Painted plates.

Children enjoy using imagination and creativity in learning.

      12. Shadow boxes.
      13. Murals.
      14. Coins.
      15. Gourds.
      16. Maps.
      17. Scrapbooks.
      18. Designs.
      19. Flag.
      20. Guitars.
  B. Literature.
      1. Famous stories — for example, *Pablo and Petra*, by M. Lee.
      2. Legends — for example, *Popo, the Smoking Mountain*.
      3. Poems.
      4. Writers and poets.
  C. Creative Writing.
      1. Stories on markets, home life, animals, farming.
      2. Original poems.
  D. Dramatic Play.
    Act out loading a burro, living in a peon's house, and so forth.
  E. Experience with numbers.
      1. Compare a peso with a dollar.
      2. Measure maps.
      3. Buy articles with Mexican money at play markets.
  F. Arts.
      1. Crafts.
      2. Drawings and designs.

    3. Murals.

    4. Pictures of artists.

    5. Famous pictures.

G. Music.

    1. Songs (*canción* — ballad).

    2. Records.

    3. Dances — for example, the "Jarabe."

    4. Lives of musicians.

    5. Making musical instruments.

H. Science.

    1. Weather maps.

    2. Seasons and climate.

I. Food.

    1. Kinds of food.

    2. Value of corn.

    3. Average meal.

J. Plants, flowers, and trees.

    1. Kinds.

    2. Colors.

    3. Quantity.

    4. Make paper flowers.

    5. Bring in cactus.

K. Animals and birds.

    1. Kinds.

    2. Uses.

L. Physical play and sports.

    1. Games — for example, "Hanging Judas."

    2. Bullfighting.

    3. Jai alai (something like tennis and handball).

    4. Baseball.

M. Audio-visual aids.

    1. Slides.

    2. Black-and-white pictures.

    3. Colored pictures.

N. Vocabulary

adiós	*buenas tardes*	*dos*
adobe	*buenas noches*	*tres*
fiesta	*Montezuma*	*mamá*
hacienda	*Diego Rivera*	*papá*
piñata	*Carlos Chávez*	*matador*
señorita	*Guadelupe*	*toreador*
señor	*amigo*	*picador*
señora	*burro*	*tierra caliente*
Ixtaccihuatl	*gracias*	*tierra fría*
Orizaba	*mestizos*	*tierra templada*
Popocatépetl	*rebozo*	*cacao*
Hasta mañana	*sarape*	*maguey*

buenos días	*sí*	*patio*
uno	*Rio Grande*	*peón*
siesta	*Sierra Madre*	*peso*
sombrero	*centavos*	*frijoles*
tamales	*Cortéz*	*pulque*
tortilla	*Aztec*	*Xochimilco*
corrido	*charro*	

V. Culminating activities
  A. Children bring together their new information in a notebook.
  B. A fiesta for the parents may be planned.
  C. A test may be given.
    1. Matching test items.
    2. Outlined map study.
    3. Locating and indicating places on map.
    4. Multiple-choice questions.
    5. Completion questions.
    6. Essay questions.

VI. Outcomes
  A. Appreciation of beauty and color of another country.
  B. Appreciation of art, music, literature, and history of a different country.
  C. Curiosity aroused in investigation of the country.
  D. Improvement in cooperation, responsibility, and leadership.
  E. Stimulation toward clearer thinking.
  F. Improvement in orderliness, neatness, and accuracy.
  G. Improvement in personality traits.
  H. Introduction to Spanish language.
  I. A better pupil-teacher relationship.
  J. Addition of new words and new skills.

VII. Bibliography
  A. Books for the teacher.
    1. *Compton's Pictured Encyclopedia.* Chicago: F. E. Compton & Co.. 1951.
    2. Franck, Harry A. *Mexico and Central America.* New York: F. A. Owen Publishing Co., 1927.
    3. Goetz, Delia. *Neighbors to the South.* New York: Harcourt, Brace & Company, 1941.
    4. Gruening, Ernest. In *The Encyclopedia Americana,* Vol. 18, pp. 739–838. New York: Americana Corporation, 1954.
    5. MacRae, Margit. *Teaching Spanish in the Grades.* Boston: Houghton Mifflin Company, 1957.
    6. Parkes, Henry B. *History of Mexico.* Boston: Houghton Mifflin Company, 1950.
  B. Music Books.
    1. Chase, Gilbert. *The Music of Spain.* New York: W. W. Norton & Company, Inc., 1941. Pp. 257–272.
    2. Chávez, Carlos. *Toward a New Music.* New York: Herbert Weinstock, 1937.

C. Records.
  1. Chávez, Carlos. "Sones Mariachi"
     "La Paloma"
     "Xychipili-Macuilxochitl"
     "Yaqui Music"
  2. Kostelanetz, Andre. "Jarabe Tapatio"
     "Cielito Lindo"
     "La Golondrina"

D. Songs.
  1. "Feliz Cumplianos"
  2. "Fray Felipe"
  3. "La Cucaracha"

E. Dances.
  1. "Chiapanecas"
  2. "Hat Dance"

F. Games.
  1. "Hanging Judas"
  2. "Piñata"
  3. "Sí, Non"
  4. For older people
     a. Baseball
     b. Basketball
     c. Bullfighting
     d. Football
     e. Jai alai

G. Story materials for the children.
  1. Brandeis, Madeline. *The Little Mexican Donkey Boy.* Chicago: A. Flanagan Co., 1931.
  2. Busoni, Rafaello. *Mexico and the Inca's Lands.* New York: Holiday House, 1942.
  3. Cordon, Priscilla. *The Vanilla Village.* New York: Ariel Books, 1952.
  4. Durfee, Burr. *Mateo and Lolita.* Boston: Houghton Mifflin Company, 1939.
  5. Eberle, Irmengarde. *The Very Good Neighbors.* Philadelphia: J. B. Lippincott Co., 1945.
  6. Grumbine, E. Evalyn. *Patsy's Mexican Adventure.* New York: Dodd, Mead & Co., 1953.
  7. Henry, Marguerite. *Mexico.* Chicago: Albert Whitman & Co., 1941.
  8. Hildreth, Gertrude. *Today and Tomorrow.* Philadelphia: The John C. Winston Company, 1948.
  9. Hogner, Dorothy. *Children of Mexico.* Boston: D. C. Heath & Company, 1942.
  10. Holmes, Burton. *Mexico.* Chicago: Wheeler Publishing Company, 1939.
  11. McDonald, E. A., and J. Dalrymple. *Manuel in Mexico.* Boston: Little, Brown & Company, 1927.

12. McNally, E. Evalyn. *This is Mexico*. New York: Dodd, Mead & Co., 1947.
13. Perkins, Lucy. *The Mexican Twins*. Boston: Houghton Mifflin Company, 1951.
14. Quinn, Vernon. *Picture Map Geography*. Philadelphia: J. B. Lippincott Co., 1943.
15. Ross, Patricia F. *Let's Read about Mexico*. Grand Rapids: The Fideler Co., 1955.
16. Ross, Patricia F. *The Hungry Moon.* New York: Alfred A. Knopf, Inc., 1946.
17. Smith, Susan. *Made in Mexico*. New York: Alfred A. Knopf, Inc., 1930.

VIII. Log on Mexico

October 1: We decided to take an imaginary trip into Mexico after hearing the report of Bobby about his aunt's travels.

October 2: Mrs. Ballman gave us a bookcase in one corner for exhibits. We brought in and arranged on the shelves silver earrings, salt and pepper shakers, necklaces, bracelets, pins, vases, baskets, plates, dolls, hats, gourds, coins, and mats.

On the library table in the back of the room, Mrs. Ballman placed a box containing books and pictures from the library. We arranged the pictures and maps on five bulletin boards and placed the books on the library table.

During the rest of the day, when other subjects were completed, we looked at the books.

October 3: Today we decided to decorate our sixth bulletin board, located above one of our blackboards. The girls made pink paper flowers, while the boys made butterflies.

October 4: Someone suggested keeping a scrapbook of our trip to Mexico. We made an outline map, which was to appear first in our book. As time went on, we planned to put in the mountain ranges, cities, and so forth.

During the rest of our period of study we discussed the early Indian tribes, Spanish conquerors and Cortez, and the revolt of the peasants.

October 5: We made the flag of Mexico. This took care of our second page in our scrapbook.

Next we decided what we must have to enter Mexico, how careful we must be on the highways, the worth of pesos in our American money, what we should drink, and how well we should know the Spanish language. The last brought on an interesting discussion that ended with the gracious proposal of a high-school junior and her teacher to help us with the language. Now we are really enthusiastic!

October 8: Today we had our first Spanish lesson. We are no longer Larry, Anna, or Robert, but Lorenzo, Ana, and Roberto. We learned the Spanish way of saying "Good morning," "Good-by," "Thank you," and many more words that seemed easy. We even learned to sing the Spanish words to "Are You Sleeping?"

October 9: Today we discussed the Mexican country, climate, people, and products. We even "visited" Maria, a Mexican girl, for a day.

Some sort of culminating activity is necessary to give the children a focal point for evaluation.

October 10: Some of us made reports on Mexican homes in the cities, a Mexican hacienda, and the kinds of foods available.

October 11: After we discussed the kind of dishes used in Mexico, each of us decorated and shellacked an unfinished plate.

October 12: While finishing our plates, we listened to Spanish music. Our favorite record is "La Paloma." We liked it even better after Mrs. Ballman told us the story connected with the music. We were interested in Emperor Maximilian and Empress Carlotta.

October 15: Plates are dry and on display around the room. While boys were at gym, the girls started their embroidery work on Mexican designs. This is to be continued every Monday.

October 16: Shadow boxes were started today. They will be seen on display by the end of the week.

A story on the shrine of the nation was read and a colored slidefilm called "Mexico" was seen. On one slide was a picture of Our Lady of Guadeloupe.

October 17: Our Spanish teacher taught us more Spanish phrases, two Mexican games, the alphabet, the numbers from 1 to 20, and the Spanish words for "Happy Birthday."

We put in our scrapbooks information about the shrine of the nation, the mountains, floating gardens, and pottery.

We listened to more Spanish music, and started three murals.

October 18: Our murals were the center of interest today. Everyone added a little. We learned how to share and cooperate.

October 19: Today we filled in our outline map at the beginning of our scrapbook with cities, mountain ranges, and so forth.

We wrote letters to Mexican children telling them about our country and the things we do.

The girls stayed in at recess and we started a Mexican dance, "Chiapanecas." The music teacher lent us the record.

October 22: Some of the children dressed as Mexicans today, and Mrs. Ballman took their picture outside our school. Two of the girls held a tablecloth made from the century plant. They hoped to call the picture "Outdoor Market."

The Spanish teacher came again today to help us with our Spanish. We had a Spanish contest, more Spanish phrases, and a short test.

The music teacher taught us "La Cucaracha" and one of our teachers gave us the painting she found on the front cover of a magazine to be placed on one of our bulletin boards.

October 23: The murals, shadow boxes, and embroidery designs were finished today.

We discussed the animals, flowers, trees, and birds of Mexico. Art pictures were made, some very original.

October 24: We saw the movie "Rural Life in Mexico" and the slidefilms "Mexico" and "Mexican Children."

At recess, we practiced the Hat Dance for a little while.

One teacher asked to let her room see our display. We enjoyed their visit.

October 29: Today we learned the Spanish words for the colors and months of the year. We reviewed our songs and played a new game called "Sí, Non." The Spanish teacher ended her class period by telling us about Pan-American Day, to be held sometime in the future at the high school.

October 30: One of our teachers offered to take us to the bullfight today. Another room wished to be present, so we really had an audience. The visiting teacher dressed as a Mexican, and Lorenzo was the bull. He carried the horns above his head.

October 31: We wrote plays today. Some were read and acted.

We discussed the streets, stores, and markets. Since the markets are so artistic, it was a good time to emphasize the art of Mexico.

November 1: We have some interesting clippings added to our bulletin boards. One is a menu from one of the hotels in Mexico. It states in one place —

Tenderloin of Beef — 13.00

Someone thought it meant $13.00. (13.00 pesos = $1.04)

A mother sent us one of her original drawings for our bulletin board.

November 2: Today we wrote original poems about Mexico, and some of us read them aloud.

We learned to play "Hanging Judas," a Mexican game.

November 5: Music arranged by Carlos Chávez was played and discussed today. "La Paloma" remains the favorite.

November 6: The Spanish teacher reviewed all that had been taught during her weekly visits. A short test was given, and a promise was made to teach us once a week from now on.

November 7: A photographer from the Sunday paper visited us today and took some pictures. Those who were dressed as Mexicans were in the pictures.

November 8: Scrapbook covers were made, and the books were put together.

November 9: We reviewed our project and agreed we had become better acquainted with one another during the weeks of traveling in Mexico. We had a little feeling of regret in having to leave the country.

November 12: We worked hard today getting our room ready for open house.

November 13: Open house tonight ended our Mexican project. We won a $5.00 attendance award. More important, we now understand the Mexicans better.[2]

Summary

The unit of work represents one of the best methods for achieving the broader objectives of education in the primary grades. It offers opportunities for rich experiences in a desirable learning environment.

The major essentials in unit planning involve selecting worthwhile problems for study based on defined objectives, deciding on the important concepts, generalizations, and skills to be learned, organizing and developing experiences that will contribute to the understanding of such concepts, generalizations, and skills, locating materials and resources that are needed to make the learning activities meaningful to the child, planning significant culminating activities, and devising effective evaluation procedures.

The terminology used in describing the program of unit teaching is not the most important consideration for the teacher. The important concern is that significant and varied experiences be provided, that emphasis be placed on pupil participation in planning, developing, and evaluating the work, and that experiences be selected in terms of worthwhile purposes that are meaningful to children and that adults in their mature judgment deem essential to maximum development of the child.

QUESTIONS AND ACTIVITIES

1. What types of units have you discovered in your reading? What are the distinguishing characteristics of each?

2. What are the main characteristics of a teaching unit? How does a teaching unit for the kindergarten differ from one for the third grade?

3. Plan a teaching unit for a grade of your choice.

4. Observe in a primary grade and see to what extent the children are involved in deciding class activities. To what extent are they involved in planning on the nursery-school level?

5. What is the meaning of initiatory, developmental, and culminating activities? Evaluate the activities illustrated in the unit on Mexico.

6. How does daily planning differ from unit planning? What evidence of daily planning have you observed in the schools you visit? Of unit planning? Of other long-range planning?

7. Visit a primary grade and time the number of minutes the teacher uses in directing activities, discussing, demonstrating, and evaluating; also the number of minutes the children work individually, in groups, and as an entire class.

[2] From material submitted by Mrs. Mildred Ballman, Highland School, Evansville, Ind.

8. Organize a role-playing situation in which you are initiating a unit of work. Set up an hypothetical class level and discuss the first steps in the unit activity.

9. Why is it important to give children responsibility in choosing and planning a unit cooperatively?

10. Should a teacher ever interrupt an ongoing unit of work for a study of current interest? What criteria can you set up that will help in making such a decision?

11. If the unit of work offers so many advantages for growth, why is it not used in the nursery school?

12. As you examine the design for a unit of work presented on pages 129–140, decide at what point you should make provision for the pupils to share in the planning. How might such a design be used in planning a resource unit?

13. Evaluate the following activities in terms of what you know about children's developmental needs and the nature of effective learning: (a) First-grade children visit a steel mill to learn how steel is produced. (b) Third-graders dramatize a story, "The Health King," about the proper care of health. (c) Kindergarten children take an all-day bus trip to a zoo. (d) Second-graders build an airport in the sandbox. What principles are implied in these activities? Can you suggest additional principles for evaluating activities?

SELECTED READINGS

Association for Supervision and Curriculum Development. *Using Free Materials in the Classroom.* Washington, D.C.: National Education Association, 1953.

Burton, William H. *The Guidance of Learning Activities.* New York: Appleton-Century-Crofts, Inc., 1952.

Caswell, Hollis I., and A. Wesley Foshay. *Education in the Elementary School.* New York: American Book Company, 1950.

Gwynn, J. Minor. *Curriculum Guidance and Social Trends.* New York: The Macmillan Company, 1950.

Hanna, Lavone, Gladys Potter, and Neva Hagaman. *Unit Teaching in the Elementary School.* New York: Rinehart & Company, Inc., 1955.

Jones, Arthur, *et al. Principles of Unit Construction.* New York: McGraw-Hill Book Company, Inc., 1939.

Kinney, Lucien, and Katherine Dresden. *Better Learning Through Current Materials.* Stanford: Stanford University Press, 1952.

Krug, Edward A. *Curriculum Planning,* Revised Edition. New York: Harper & Brothers, 1957.

Macomber, Freeman G. *Guiding Child Development.* New York: American Book Company, 1941.

Macomber, Freeman G. *Principles of Teaching in the Elementary School.* New York: American Book Company, 1954.

Miel, Alice, and Peggy Brogan. *More than Social Studies.* Englewood Cliffs, N.J.: Prentice-Hall, Inc., 1957.

Nelson, Leslie. *Instructional Aids.* Dubuque, Iowa: Wm. C. Brown Company, 1958.

Preston, Ralph C. *Teaching Social Studies in the Elementary School,* Revised Edition. New York: Rinehart & Company, Inc., 1958.

Price, Roy A. (ed.). "New Viewpoints in the Social Sciences." *Twenty-eighth Yearbook,* National Council for Social Studies. Washington, D.C.: National Education Association, 1958.

Ragan, William B. *Modern Elementary Curriculum.* New York: The Dryden Press, Inc., 1953.

Shane, Harold G., and Eldridge T. McSwain. *Evaluation and the Elementary Curriculum,* Revised Edition. New York: Henry Holt & Company, Inc., 1958.

Strickland, Ruby. *How to Build a Unit of Work.* U.S. Office of Education, Bulletin No. 5. Washington, D.C.: Government Printing Office, 1946.

Thralls, Zoe A. *The Teaching of Geography.* New York: Appleton-Century-Crofts, Inc., 1958.

Tyler, Ralph. "The Curriculum — Then and Now," *The Elementary School Journal,* 57:364–374, April 1957.

9

Evaluating Progress

One cannot hurry the growth that has its origin deep within the child, nor can this growth be measured at a stated, inflexible time, for it is a continuous process in which the teacher helps the child select the threads which will be woven into the design for development which is his alone.

— LILLIAN LOGAN

Evaluating progress has always been the task of teachers. Formerly the emphasis was on measurement alone, an appraisal of pupil mastery of information and skills. As the base of evaluation broadened, as new techniques and methods for measuring interests, attitudes, critical thinking, and personal adjustment were developed and refined in response to insights obtained about growth and development, the emphasis shifted to broad personality changes as major objectives of the educational curriculum. The current emphasis is upon selection of objectives which will underlie the learning activities themselves and upon which evaluation will eventually be based. In short, one begins with the kind of learning that requires the intellectual skills needed to reach the highest level of competence.

Is evaluation an appraisal of the over-all program of the school — the voice of the principal and supervisor setting up a program to determine the adequacy of the curriculum? Is it the instruments used in measuring specific aspects of the child's behavior? Is it the voice of the teacher-counselor reporting progress or failure to parents? Evaluation is all these and more. It is concerned with the effect of school experience on the total growth of the child. Evaluation is a continuous process of inquiry, based upon objectives developed cooperatively in the school community and concerned with the study and guidance of desirable learning changes of children.

Evaluation includes measurement, but it is more than measurement. Two extreme viewpoints have made themselves felt and should be made clear at this point. One completely overlooks the need for instruments by which adequate evaluation can be made; the other refuses to accept any kind of subjective evidence on the assumption that evaluation and measurement are synonymous. In terms of children's educational experiences both are important. Measurement may be considered less significant than analysis and interpretation, but rarely, if ever, can any worthwhile appraisal be made unless it is based upon reasonably objective evidence. A third concept of evaluation, which is becoming more prevalent, requires that evaluation appraise not only pupil mastery of information, intellectual skills, and concepts, but also pupil growth in areas such as critical thinking, creative expression, and social learning and behavior. All three are essential. Schools today accept as a major responsibility the selection of objectives that harmonize with the need for learning experiences of a high order — the kind of learning that involves important intellectual skills and the social learning needed for successful living in a world that assigns increasing importance to the educated individual.

An Adequate Program of Evaluation

The design of the evaluation program should be comprehensive. We have pointed out the need for a broad base, to cover not only personal and social adjustment but knowledge, skills and concepts, attitudes, appreciation, interests, and critical thinking as well. A comprehensive evaluation program involves the whole school and embraces the objectives set up by the school. The teacher must take responsibility for guiding growth not only in academic achievement but also in the less tangible areas of interests and attitudes, and social and emotional adaptability.

The evaluation program should be continuous and interrelated with the curriculum. If evaluation is sporadic or set for a specific date, the sampling of behavior may come at a time when the child is ill, disturbed, or simply "out of sorts." Wrightstone suggests that day-by-day observations, ratings, and tests should furnish the data by which the teacher evaluates and guides the child's growth and should serve as the basis for judging the changes that may be needed to improve teaching practices.[1]

Evaluation should focus on the individual. Teachers should be concerned with the total behavior of the individual in every learning situation. If the child is bored by too easy tasks, or if he is frustrated by too difficult tasks, his learning will be adversely affected. Also, the learner's progress should be measured against objectives that have been defined and made known to him. For example, the following criteria for oral reports should be known to the learner and used in the evaluation:

He speaks in a conversational tone.
His voice is loud enough to be heard.
He looks at his audience as he speaks.
He has worthwhile content.
He has his report organized and presents it clearly.

When the performance of the pupil is judged according to these characteristics, the desired behavior becomes the criterion for evaluation.

The results of evaluation should be summarized into a meaningful interpretation. Synthesis into a pattern of scores that is readable is essential. Moreover, the statistical, graphic, and verbal scores should make up a behavior profile that allows comparison of an individual's present progress with previous progress. The directions and areas of growth and the rate of development should be indicated. Such relationships speed the process of guiding the child's learning wisely. A teacher should keep in mind as she looks at a child that "to measure you by your smallest deed is to reckon the power of the ocean by the fraility of its foam. To judge you by your failures is to cast blame upon the seasons for their inconstancy."[2]

Evaluation should be a cooperative enterprise. The entire school staff as well as the parents and the community should be concerned with evaluation. The need for or better use of specialists in child guidance may be indicated as a result of evaluation. Parents, teachers, and children must find a way to improve communication. To this end, children can have a part in setting up goals, in working together to achieve them, and finally in evaluating progress. When the child knows where he is going, what he is expected to do when he gets there, and how to judge whether he has accomplished what he set out to do, he is well on the way to effective learning.

[1] Jacob Wrightstone, *et al.*, *Evaluation in Modern Education* (New York: American Book Company, 1956), p. 24.
[2] Kahil Gibran, *The Prophet* (New York: Alfred A. Knopf, Inc., 1923), p. 6.

The child's lack of interest may be the result of the teacher's inability to evaluate his needs and abilities.

Evaluation involves the appraisal of pupil progress in achieving defined goals. Reporting pupil progress is generally understood to mean the process by which the teacher tells the parent where the pupil stands in terms of the child's own goals, in comparison with his previous achievements, in comparison with his classmates, and in terms of the standards of achievement set up by the school. A more limited approach to reporting often results in anxieties, frustrations, misunderstandings, and confusion for teacher, child, and parent. As schools make more use of such practices as teacher-pupil conferences, as teachers and parents cooperate to determine what is best for the child, in terms of standards already agreed on, and as the interdependence of academic achievement and behavior goals is understood, reporting will improve. As it is at present, to promote or not to promote remains a problem that plagues teachers, principals, parents, and children.

The Role of the Teacher in Evaluation

In order to discharge her responsibilities, the teacher must view evaluation as a process in three dimensions. As a staff member she must work to carry out the over-all evaluation program for the improvement of instruction in the entire school. As a teacher in the classroom she must use the actual instruments and techniques of evaluation to diagnose strengths and weakness in order to guide growth and learning effectively. As a teacher-counselor she must know her students individually, appraise progress, and keep records that will be useful when she reports to parents on the adequacy of the child's progress.

As a Member of the Staff

It is the teacher who carries out the over-all evaluation program of the school. She conceives of it as a cooperative enterprise in continuous improvement and appraisal of instruction for the purposes of modifying the program to ensure more effective learning experiences for the child. Such an evaluation is useful, particularly if the effort to improve the quality of teaching focuses on the individual child rather than on an effort to determine how this school system compares with other school systems. In the in-service program, there must be cooperation among members of the staff in their task of judging the adequacy of the effect of the instructional program on the child. There are many questions to be considered. What is our school trying to accomplish? What should we try to accomplish? What criteria should we use in deciding to what extent we are achieving our objectives? Where in the instructional program should we make improvements? Where should planning and action take place? Have we utilized our resources as efficiently as possible?

As a member of the staff the teacher should help keep the focal point of the evaluation program where it belongs — on the effect of instruction on the learning and growth of the individual child.

As a Teacher in the Classroom

In the classroom the teacher is continuously involved in making judgments about the progress of children, whether as a group or as individuals. On the basis of those judgments she decides what guidance to offer and what experiences to plan next. In the classroom, indeed, the teacher plays the crucial role in evaluating individual children. Her insights will operate in the guidance and motivation she provides for the children. It is she who will plan the learning experiences; it is she who will use many of the evaluative techniques and instruments.

If the teacher stresses the instruments and techniques of evaluation at the expense of the understanding to be derived from their use, she may well become a robot — endlessly administering, recording, and filing without making any impression on the child. At the other extreme is the teacher who provides a permissive environment and effective growing and learning experiences without making any provision for evaluation. For such a person, teaching has crystallized at the level of the techniques; she works now largely on the basis of hunch.

Somewhere between the two extremes is the kind of teaching in which evaluation plays its part. In such a curriculum evaluative procedures are used for the purposes of knowing what each child is like, why he is as he is, and what teachers and parents can do to help him improve in his learning. In the classroom, in short, the focus is on the child and his progress, not on the techniques of evaluation.

Evaluative Techniques

Techniques that the teacher can use to obtain information for determining adequacy of progress include observation, anecdotal records, inventories and interviews, attitude and personality tests, projective techniques and media, tests of ability, cumulative records, and case studies. Sociometric methods may be used for group appraisal.

Observation, anecdotal records, check lists, and interviews are particularly successful in getting information on personal and social adjustment. The teacher may use the results of these techniques in three ways: (1) to identify those pupils who are well adjusted and those who are poorly adjusted, (2) to diagnose factors contributing to maladjustment, and (3) to set up conditions contributing to individual and group adjustment.

Interest inventories may be used for identifying pupils' interests in reading and other activities. Armed with such information the teacher can find materials best suited to motivate each student toward improving his skills in reading, and can better adapt the curriculum to his needs.

The sociometric techniques are used by the teacher to understand and direct group behavior in the classroom. Cumulative records should be made to provide a picture of continuous growth in the individual.

OBSERVATION

Observation is a basic technique in evaluation, particularly valuable in teaching the youngest children. By observing the child both in informal groups and in classes, the teacher learns the child's interests, his reactions to others, and his reactions to failure and success. Although observation may take several forms, the three forms most widely used are:

Puzzles can be used to test a child's ability to see special relationships.

(1) Unrecorded observation, used in helping individual children adjust to the immediate situation more effectively.

(2) Anecdotal records, written snapshots of typical or exceptional behavior, reports of significant episodes in the life of the child.

(3) Observation of an individual in a particular class, club, or other group. This type of record deals with a number of samples of behavior in relation to that of other members of the group.

UNRECORDED OBSERVATION

The teacher observes children all the time — in the classroom, on the playground, during routines, in the lunch room, on excursions, in group organizations, and in testing situations. For the most part, her observation is never recorded; she uses it immediately. Some behavior, however, is so significant that the teacher should describe the behavior in written form and file it in her cumulative record folder. The observed behavior in written form becomes the anecdotal record.

THE ANECDOTAL RECORD

To the extent that anecdotal records are usable and possible in terms of time and effort, they are a real aid to the teacher and staff. Minimum information includes date of entry, statement of the situation in which the incident occurred, a factual description of the incident, what the child said, what the child did, an objective report of any pertinent related information, and an adequate number and sequence of anecdotal records upon which to base judgment. Three suggestions to remember are: delay the interpretation, keep the method of reporting simple, and record more than negative behavior.

Use of anecdotal records. Teachers use anecdotal records as a means of getting to know individual children within a group situation. A teacher faced with thirty or forty children on the first day of school is apt to react with a feeling of inadequacy as she looks into the sea of faces in front of her.

As the teacher looks down the long list of names at the end of the first day and tries to recall in each case the child who belongs to the name, some stand out clearly, but many blanks remain. It will help if she jots down a few names with a few identifying characteristics, such as:

Marjorie: A perfect doll, would not play outdoors though, dresses too well.
Ellen: Much too fat, wonder about her diet.
Peter: Not too bright, wonder what he can do.
Rachel: Fragile and growing too fast.
Betty: Just sits and giggles, must test her, wonder what her I.Q. is.
Ronald: Clumsy, trips over the aisle when he walks.
Jack: Sound substitution, hope the speech therapist is nice.
Glen: Constantly mumbling.
Tommy: Hides under the desk.

This, she may well decide, is the best she can do at this point: "I will get to know them, though, as fast as I can. I have to know them to teach them. Tomorrow I'll start keeping an anecdotal record about Tommy; he spent most of the morning and afternoon under my desk."

Such an anecdotal record kept for four months about Tommy, a first grader, appears below:

September 8. Tommy was crawling under my desk this morning when his group came up for reading-readiness activity. He left the group to go to the bathroom. He had been to the bathroom ten minutes before. When he came back, he went to his desk and scribbled on drawing paper. When I asked him to come up with his group, he ignored me and went on scribbling. I did not insist.

September 15. Tommy still won't come up for reading-readiness activity. Today he asked to give out the coloring paper, to sharpen a pencil, and to hold the door open for Betty, who is too short to open it. He did not crawl under the desk today. He wanted to be the leader when it was time to form the lines to go home.

September 29. Tommy still doesn't come up for reading-readiness activity. He participates in everything else. Today we went to the gym. All the children cooperated in following the directions the gym teacher gave. Tommy wouldn't stay. He said, "My room, my room." I took him upstairs. He said, "I'll paint a pretty picture for you when the others go to the gym." I noticed that on his kindergarten report card the teacher repeatedly emphasized the fact that Tommy could not skip and that he'd better learn how. This is probably one of the things that is bothering him.

December 4. Today Tommy asked if he could go to the gym when we did. I was anxious to see why. He had learned to skip. He said, "Tomorrow I want to read with my group." He had not been coming up for reading, although he read for me alone and was reading at the level of the second group.

December 5. Today Tommy came up for reading. The children said, "Let's name it Tommy's group instead of Rachael's group." Tommy beamed and said, "I know how to skip and I know how to read; now I wonder what I'll learn next."

There were no more anecdotal notes about Tommy. He no longer crawled under the table, remained at his desk, or painted during the gym period. One day he said, "I don't need to stay under the desk any more."

Some people feel that anecdotal records are too time-consuming, too subjective, too dependent upon the teacher's knowledge of children and her philosophy of education, and thus can have no place in evaluation. Despite these limitations, the anecdotal record accurately made and wisely interpreted is considered by many to be the basic evaluative device for early childhood. For the observation of social development and personality growth, it is more effective with young children than with older children. As the teacher works with older boys and girls, she needs a broader base for evaluation than the anecdotal record supplies.

INVENTORIES AND INTERVIEWS

If the teacher needs more detailed information on a particular aspect of the child's living — for example, what he does in his leisure time, what his hobbies are, or what books he has read — she may use an inventory or interview. Such questionnaires are valuable aids to the teacher and may be easily obtained.[3] The "Interest Finder" devised by Jersild and Tasch is an example of a technique for finding out about children's interests.[4] If the child is unable to read, the inventory may be conducted as a personal interview.

Perhaps the most important single factor in guiding growth is the rapport the teacher establishes with the child. Her insights and skills in understanding the child's story are at the heart of guidance and at the root of evaluation in any form. In interviews, guided conversation is the method, informality is the means, and understanding is the end.

ATTITUDE AND PERSONALITY TESTS

Numerous attitude and personality tests are available. In most cases, however, the teacher of young children will find that her most satisfying experiences are based on insights obtained through a happy relationship with the child himself. What is sought by the teacher is an understanding of the child's problems, his attitudes and activities, and an interpretation of his point of view. Not everyone is capable of establishing the kind of rapport that is essential to an understanding of the child. Sympathy, tact, caution, genuineness, and objectivity of mind are not innate traits; they must be cultivated. Children, especially young children, prefer talking with an adult whom they regard as a friend, counselor, and guide, to taking a test, however disguised in phrases such as "Let's play an interesting game," or "You tell me how you feel about Peter." The latter, for example, is followed by a question asking the child whether he is just like Peter or wishes to be; this demands a degree of concentration and realistic judgment that many first graders have not as yet achieved.

PROJECTIVE TECHNIQUES

Because the major projective tests are primarily clinical devices, they are not suitable for use by the classroom teacher. The Thematic Apperception Test, however, has been adapted and may be used if desired. A child is shown pictures of specific situations and reacts to them. The purpose of the test is to determine the child's own problems through his response to problem situations.

[3] See Claudia Wannamaker, *Child Guidance Procedures* (New York: D. Appleton-Century Co., 1937) ; and H. Lehman and Paul Witty, *Psychology of Play Activities* (New York: A. S. Barnes & Co., 1927).

[4] Arthur Jersild and Ruth Tasch, *Children's Interests and What They Suggest for Education* (New York: Teachers College, Columbia University, 1949). Quoted in Arthur T. Jersild, *Child Psychology*, Fourth Edition (Englewood Cliffs, N.J.: Prentice-Hall, Inc., 1954), pp. 508–510.

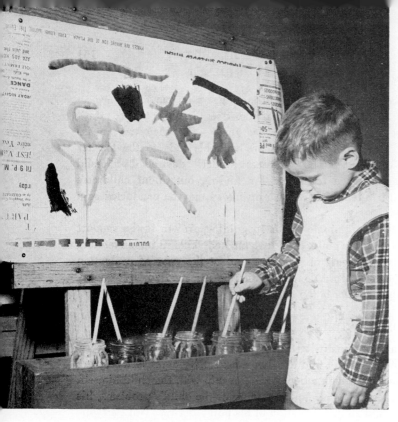

Through studying a child's art work, the teacher can learn much about his emotional environment.

Many teachers use art media as projective tests. Any material that allows creative expression may be used by a child as an outlet for his feelings and to show how he views life. In a research project involving kindergarten children, the writer was able to identify emotionally disturbed children through their use of specific patterns and colors, and through a tendency to muddy or destroy a beautiful picture they had just painted. Conditions in the home — separation of parents, divorce, or the presence of a new baby — account for most of the emotional disturbances expressed in art. When studied in the light of previous experiences, art products afford considerable insight into the child's personal concerns and inner feelings.

Tests of Ability

The teacher is responsible, too, for knowing what the child is capable of doing, so that she may accurately judge his performance.

The younger the child at the time of testing, the less accurate will be the prediction of later status from early status. After the child begins to talk, the tests begin to have predictive value, although the amount of confidence one can place in the results as indices of the child's ultimate level of development is small up to the age of four or five years. The value of intelligence tests for preschool children is greatly dependent upon the skill of the examiner in getting the child's attention and cooperation. Since reliability and validity ordinarily increase with age, tests given toward the end of the preschool period form a better basis for predicting later intelligence than do the tests given during infancy.

The Stanford-Binet intelligence test correctly administered and interpreted may be regarded as a useful tool.[5] It gives a picture of what a child can do under specific conditions. Although as a measure of ability it has its place, it can be considered only as one aid in knowing the child's potential capacity. The examiner records not only the score of the child's intelligence test but his behavior during the test. Some children, although young, are stimulated by taking the test; others react differently. The Stanford-Binet test must be administered individually by a trained examiner.

One adapted form of the Wechsler-Bellevue Intelligence Scale has been used for children from the ages of four to thirteen.[6] Both the Binet and the Wechsler tests make use of performance as well as verbal responses to estimate intelligence. The advantage of the individual intelligence test is that it allows opportunity for observing the behavior, interest, adjustment, motivation, and working habits of the child as they relate to his general intelligence. The disadvantage is that some children are reluctant to be singled out of the group to take the test.

Group tests. Group tests of intelligence are administered to an entire class or group of individuals, and prepared responses of the questions are checked by the examinee.

In addition to verbal tests there are performance tests of mental ability for children unable to read or write. Among these are the Goodenough Draw-A-Man Test and the Lorge-Thorndike Intelligence tests, which have very high reliability. Most of these do not have as high reliability as do the verbal tests.

CHECK LISTS OF AREAS OF BEHAVIOR

Short lists of types of behavior, by which the teacher judges a child in terms of a three-to-five point scale, are also useful. Such check lists include intellectual, social, emotional, aesthetic, and physical behavior.

ACHIEVEMENT TESTS

In view of the statement that evaluation takes into consideration those goals appropriate to the individual child and his group, the question may well arise as to whether there are no standards that obtain for all the children in a given grade. To suggest that standards or norms are useless would be ridiculous. The

---

[5] Stanford-Binet Scale, Revised. L. M. Terman and M. A. Merrill (Boston: Houghton Mifflin Company, 1960).

[6] Wechsler, David, *Wechsler Intelligence Scale for Children: Manual* (New York: The Psychological Corporation, 1949).

question is how to measure them. If measures appropriate to early childhood could be developed, they might well prove useful to nursery schools and junior and senior kindergartens, as well as to primary grades.

The meaning of a norm must be understood in order to evaluate it in relation to learning. A norm is the average test performance of given groups, obtained in the process of standardizing a test. A standardized test is a sample of the performance of an individual group obtained under prescribed conditions, scored according to prescribed rules, and interpreted by reference to normative data.

To be a real criterion of what a child has learned, the test ought to be based on and related to the things he has been taught and experienced in living. For this reason a well-constructed test made by his own teacher or a test that accompanies a textbook series may be fairer indication of what the child has learned than a standardized achievement test. Particularly is this true at the first-grade level. As children mature, they enjoy the challenge of competition, and comparison is not always unwelcome. Standardized achievement tests have their place in the evaluation program as long as the term "average" in relation to the child is understood. The tests serve a purpose if the teacher uses them to discover weaknesses and strengths, and then studies the results with the child to determine a remedy for the weaknesses disclosed.

SOCIOMETRIC DEVICES

Within recent years, research has brought to our attention evidence that there are dynamics not only of individual behavior but also of the group. Teachers should know how children act in groups compared to their behavior

The Rorschach ink-spot test reveals the problems of the disturbed child.

as individuals. Children try different roles. Some attract favorable attention of others; others irritate children and cause an unsettled atmosphere in the room. Certain children work and play well together until a volatile child enters the group. Children frequently sense this. The teacher will do well to study the structure of her group in order to determine the causative factors of group disruption and disintegration.

An experienced teacher is so well able to detect signs of a storm brewing that, as if by magic, she is there to suggest, to cajole, to engage in conversation, to apply oil to the troubled waters. With young children, emotions are so near the surface that it is possible to keep tabs on the temperature of the room through observation. It is easy to see who gets along with whom, who fights with whom, which children seem to disturb the others, and which combinations of youngsters attract and repel. As children mature, they learn to conceal their feelings, and some of the obvious signs no longer are evident. Long practice in observation of children, however, will reveal such signs as the arched back, the drawn line around the mouth, the quick intake of breath, the sudden pout, the defensive reddening of the ears, and the undercurrent of muttering that seems to come from nowhere.

Observation may not always be sufficient or feasible. In that case sociometric techniques such as the sociogram, the friendship test, the guess-who test, in which children indicate who in the group fits the description of a particular role, may be used. To the extent that the teacher understands the purpose and use of the various subjective and objective techniques for understanding behavior, tests are valuable. If the teacher understands the group attitude toward certain children, she may be able to restructure the group and so modify group or personal goals as to improve the learning environment.

What Makes a Good Year?

In Chapter 6 we saw what makes a good day for young children from the nursery school through the primary grades. A more difficult problem, and one of the persistent problems a teacher must solve, is that of establishing criteria for a good year. A subjective way of solving the problem is to leave it to the feelings of relief and regret that a teacher experiences on that final day in June. To evaluate the year then, however, is not realistic. If evaluation is an on-going process, it is necessary to come to grips with questions such as those raised by the following questionnaire for kindergarten teachers:

Questionnaire I
(To be checked at the end of three months)
I. What kind of administrative procedure did you follow in orienting the children and introducing them to school?
II. What did you do to help your children adjust to group living?
    1. To feel at ease and welcome.

  2. To become oriented to the room.

  3. To use materials.

  4. To put materials away.

  5. To drink milk or juice at midmorning lunch.

  6. To adjust to toilet routines.

  7. To take care of belongings.

  8. To adjust to rest period.

  9. To follow group directions.

III. What kind of experiences did the children have the first month?

  1. In language arts.

  2. In outdoor play.

  3. In using creative materials.

  4. In problem-solving.

  5. In dramatic play, music, and rhythms.

IV. What experiences have the children had in social living? In social studies? In science?

V. What readiness for reading has developed as a result of these experiences?

Questionnaire II
(To be checked at the end of the first semester)

I. How do you provide for individual differences? How much nonconformity do you allow?

II. What activities are children free to choose?

III. What activities are teacher-directed?

IV. What new experiences have you provided in social studies?

V. What readiness for learning has developed as a result of these activities?

Questionnaire III
(To be checked the last month of school)

I. How much nonconformity do you allow? More or less than previously?

II. What activities are children free to choose? How much time is allowed for these?

III. What activities are teacher-directed?

IV. What additional experiences have you provided in social studies? In science?

V. What readiness for reading has developed as a result of these activities? Can you give descriptive illustrations?

VI. How do you define readiness for first grade?

VII. How do you decide on promotion to first grade?

VIII. What method of reporting to parents do you use?

IX. What additional contacts with parents do you have?

X. What contacts have your children had to acquaint them with their first grade? How are the children assigned to first grade?

CLASS INVENTORY

Another very useful way of evaluating group progress is measuring classroom behavior with a pupil reaction inventory. It is possible to construct an instrument in which pupils' responses to questions about the activities in the classroom can yield information not only about the pupil's feelings toward the teacher and other children but also toward what actually goes on in the classroom, so long as items can be checked against an independent measure. After all, the pupils know more about what goes on in the classroom than an observer can hope to know. "My Class" inventory is an example.[7] It purports to measure feelings (halo) toward the teacher, behavior (disorder) of the children, supportive behavior of the teacher, and traditionalism (the discrimination between the "lock-step" classroom and the permissive, democratic one) in grades three, four, five, six.

Items from each of the scales are given here as an illustration of the way in which such devices can be used:

The Halo Scale

Do you ever feel like staying away from school?
Do you like to be in this class?
Do you have much fun in this class?
Do you learn a lot in this class?
Are you proud to be in this class?
Do you always do your best in this class?
Do most of the pupils like the teacher?
Does the teacher help enough?

Disorder Scale (Pupil Behavior)

Are the children in class polite to each other?
Do pupils like to tease the teacher?
Do you ever feel the class is making fun of you?
Do pupils often make so much noise it is hard for you to work?
Do the children usually stay in line?
Do children break class rules a lot?
Do children often fight or say mean things to each other?
Are the children usually quiet in your room?
Are some children always showing off?
Do pupils ever waste time?
Do some pupils in your class tattle?

The Supportive Scale

Is your work usually good enough?
Do some pupils get scolded a lot?
Are you often behind in your work?
Are some of the pupils pretty dumb?
Are you called on when you raise your hand?
Does your teacher laugh when something funny happens?
In this class do you get plenty of chances to do what you like to do?
Does somebody ever get the blame for what someone else did in your class?

[7] Donald M. Medley and Alix A. Klein, "Measuring Classroom Behavior with a Pupil-Reaction Inventory," *The Elementary School Journal,* 58:316–318, March 1957.

Do you sometimes do more school work than you have to?

Do you often bring something to school to show the whole class?

When your teacher asks questions, do you usually know the answers?

Do the pupils ask a lot of questions?

The Traditionalism Scale

Do the pupils in your class usually work in groups?

Do you ever wonder why you have to do what you are doing in school?

Are there some pupils in your class nobody likes?

Do you have lots of things to do in school that you don't want to do?

Do you leave your seat without asking?

Are you always told what to do and when to do it?

Do all the pupils in the class use the same books at the same time?

Did the pupils in the class help make up the class rules they are supposed to obey?

Do you help plan what the class is going to do?

Do you have a class period almost every day when you can do anything you like?

Do you often get a chance to talk to the whole class?

Do the same pupils always try to answer the teacher's questions?

Do you get much homework?

Do you have to stand up to answer a question?

Does the teacher let you do work that no one else in the class is doing?

Although this particular inventory was used with children in grades three through six, it is possible to use some such instrument for measuring the various types of behavior at earlier grade levels. It is particularly useful for the teacher to use as a guide in evaluating some of her own practices in the classroom.

Parents in Evaluation

In the traditional school the parents felt they were not needed except as they were invited to talk over a problem, to attend a program, or just to visit. A parent's major means of communication with the school was the monthly report card. From this report he learned how his child stood in each of the academic subjects and in relation to his classmates; he also learned whether he had good deportment.

Nursery schools have done much to involve parents in the educational scene. There they are welcome as part of the school organization. Teachers need parents to help them understand the child, and parents need teachers to help interpret the report card. It is not unusual to overhear a parent say, "What in the world does this mean? Here's a check under reading where it says 'Needs improvement,' and here's one that is checked satisfactory for 'Helps himself with new words'; but 'Needs improvement' under 'Masters new words on his reading level.' I know he reads better than Jane, and she got satisfactory on 'Masters new words on his reading level.' Why don't

Teachers today welcome parental visits and participation in the classroom.

they stick to A, B, C, D, or even numbers, like they had when I went to school?" It is in the area of reporting to parents that the teacher plays a significant role as a counselor.

THE TEACHER AS A COUNSELOR

Getting to know the pupils, learning to keep records and reports that will be useful in understanding progress, and working cooperatively with parents, all are parts of the evaluation program. Here, too, the focus must be on the child. As one child said to his teacher, "Do you know my mother? Then how can the two of you bring me up right?" Since much of the information the teacher needs to know about the child can come only from the parent, it is well for the teacher to think in terms of getting to know parents and finding ways to talk with them about the child's development. Through conferences with parents, teachers can get information about the physical and cultural set-up of the home and about the attitudes, values, and interests of the family — both vitally important in affecting the child's behavior.

Initial interview. One of the problems in getting to know individual children is the fact that there are so many; frequently thirty-five, forty, or even sixty children are assigned to a teacher. The teacher who tries to learn something by which to identify each child is at a loss as to where to begin.

Kindergarten teachers particularly are faced with the problem of getting to know so many and must make some effort to give them individual time and attention. Working with the administrative staff, the teacher may be able to develop a program whereby she can learn to know the group with whom she is to work. A systematic plan is useful. One school has solved the problem this way:

In a special effort to improve the relationship between the home and the school, a three-fold approach to enrollment in kindergarten is used. One of these is the initial interview the teacher has with the parent in the spring preceding the child's enrollment in kindergarten. The summer round-up committee of the P.T.A. is responsible for identifying the prospective kindergarten child. The teacher schedules the initial interview in the spring preceding the child's entrance into school.

The second phase of the program is the physical examination conducted by the school doctor and arranged to precede actual school entrance. Again, the summer round-up committee goes into action and notifies the parents.

The third and perhaps most enjoyable aspect of the program is the initial visit to the kindergarten classroom by mother and child. This may be combined with the parent interview if there are two teachers; while one teacher talks with the mother, the other introduces the child to one of the play materials in the room. If the oncoming class of kindergartners is too large to arrange for individual interviews, the mother and child are invited to a program given by the kindergarten, at which time the child meets his teacher, sees his room, plays with toys, and has cookies and punch.

From the information the teacher has gained through the enrollment process and initial interview, she is in possession of tentative answers to some of the following questions:

1. What are this child's favorite games, interests, and abilities? Such information gives the teacher an opening which does not disturb the parent. The teacher will find both child and parent ready to talk about the child's interests. In fact, the child may decide to go and play with the blocks as they are discussed.

2. What are this child's physical resources? These will be apparent from the general vigor discovered in the physical examination, the history of illness, the evident rate of growth, and state of health. At this time the teacher may discover whether the child has any unusual difficulties with his heart, motor coordination, routines, or developmental tasks.

3. What are his social and emotional characteristics? Has he had any socializing experiences, or is he still in need of being weaned from mother? How does he respond to correction? What type of control do the parents use?

4. What is his feeling about himself and his family? Does he appear to accept himself and the other members of his family?

5. What is his optimum stress level? What is his frustration level? What seems to precipitate his behavior from satisfaction to frustration? The answers will be apparent in part from his reaction to the physical examination, in his visit to the classroom, and from the parent's description of his behavior.

The teacher does not, of course, ask such questions in a one, two, three order. General principles for working with parents will be discussed in a later chapter, but at this point it is well to state that the focus of the interview remains on the child. The success of the interview depends upon the skill of the teacher in finding answers to this tentative outline without letting the structure show. A genuine interest in people — both parents and child — will aid the teacher in learning what she needs to know.

The report card. There are several ways of reporting progress to parents, but the most widely used is still the report that is sent to parents periodically and reports on many aspects of the child's learning activities, social habits, work habits, and health habits. It defines school subjects, health goals, and social and emotional development in order to explain to the parent what is regarded as important to satisfactory progress. The teacher checks the items according to the school's evaluation system and writes a brief note, leaving space for the parent to write in return. Report cards are sent out at regular times, from once a month to three or four times a year. If the check list is long, parents feel it takes too much time to read; teachers, too, prefer short ones, particularly if they have one hundred or more report cards to write out.

Letters. Form letters vary in type, but in general there is space for a teacher to write a report concerning physical factors, social factors, emotional factors, and intellectual factors. An alternative type of letter form has two headings for the teacher's evaluation: report on academic progress and report on attitudes and behavior. In either case the teacher will touch on many of the habits, skills, attitudes, growths, and achievements found on the report form. Considerable skill and effort are required to make these reports; in cases where the class numbers over fifty, the letter is too time-consuming to be practicable. When used, the letter should be sincere, concise, and based on an understanding of the child. It is a good idea to start writing the letters early if they are to show sincerity, originality, and spontaneity. Just recently a mother said, "I don't know where teachers find the form letters they use for reporting. I have three children and each teacher says the same thing. Do they memorize a form?"

Some suggestions to the teacher may be useful in avoiding the stereotyped letter about which the mother complained:

(1) Visualize the child as you write.
(2) Start by thinking of the most encouraging news about the child.
(3) Close on a note of optimism.
(4) If there is a problem — social, physical, academic, emotional — ask the parent to help you with it.
(5) Deal with each of the aspects of development.
(6) Write in plain language; avoid jargon.

(7) Compare the child's current effort with his own previous efforts and with the objectives set up by the school, not with the progress of the boy who sits next to him.

(8) Speak of his achievement in terms of his ability to do school work and of his perseverance in applying himself. Try to suggest possible reasons for lack of progress — absence, poor hearing, poor sight, lack of application, lack of motivation. Ask the mother to suggest other reasons.

(9) If advice is needed in terms of improvement of the child's health, his need of an eye examination or a general health examination, suggest that the mother visit the school nurse for information regarding the aid the school can give.

The personal conference. The most extensive use of the personal conference has been made at the preschool level. In a number of schools it has been combined with or has replaced the report card or the letter in reporting progress to parents. In order for the conference to be successful, the teacher must be skillful as well as genuinely interested in children. Although not all teachers have the same tact and understanding, the ability to listen and to see the other person's viewpoint, there are some guiding principles of human relationships that should help in improving the quality of parent conferences.

The teacher should establish rapport with the parent. She can do this by putting the parent at ease in the strange environment of the classroom and treating her as she would a guest in her home. It is neither necessary nor desirable for the teacher to be seated behind the desk. A face-to-face relationship results in better communication.

The teacher should have some concrete evidences of the child's work available to discuss with the parent. Achievement in terms of actual products rather than vague generalities makes for a more successful conference. She should use common terms that are understood by the parent. Much of the tension that parents feel in talking to teachers is caused by the terminology teachers use — in and out of the classroom — which is meant for other educators, not for parents. She should also be a good listener and let the parent tell her story, particularly if there is a problem or misunderstanding. She should not interrupt, but be ready to contribute at the appropriate time.

A feeling that time is not of the essence, but rather that the child and his interests take precedence over other considerations, will be possible only if the teacher is relaxed and does not appear to be in a hurry.

After the conference, the teacher may wish to record the most significant points, but she should not take notes during the interview.

A combination of methods. Some schools use a combination of the three methods described. A comprehensive interview with the parent comes near the beginning of school in the fall; a second report, which may be a conference, letter, or form, is scheduled during the middle of the year; and a final report at the end of the year is issued by means of a standard form. The emphasis is upon all phases of the child's progress from the standpoint of growth, in terms of his ability. Many schools require a notification of the child's lack of progress or failure before the last grading period.

Reporting to parents is not the teacher's problem alone; it is an administrative problem as well. The teacher must be freed of other duties to devote the required time to them if personal conferences are to be part of the school's plan. She must not be overburdened with committee assignments, teaching duties, and co-curriculum activities during the period for conferences. In some schools parents are invited to confer with the teacher on a planned schedule, consisting of twenty to thirty minutes for each during the regular school day. The children are dismissed in order to free the teacher for personal conferences with parents. Unless some such plan is provided, the conference, one of the best methods of reporting to parents, can become a source of irritation, low morale, and discouragement to an already overburdened teacher. The end of the day, when the teacher is worn out and the parent harassed, is not the best time to test the success of the parent-teacher conference as a method of reporting.

It is in this sphere of reporting to parents on the adequacy of a child's growth and of involving parents in the diagnosis of weaknesses and the programs for improvement that the teacher's skill as a counselor has an opportunity to reveal itself.

To Promote or Not to Promote

Promotion is an evaluation problem. To make a wise decision as to whether or not a child is ready to move on to the next level of learning, the teacher must look at the whole process of evaluation. She must consider the over-all effects of promotion or nonpromotion in terms of their effects on the child's development rather than in terms of progress in individual subject areas.

If a child is not promoted to a higher grade at the end of the year, his parents, his classmates, and his neighbors may consider him a failure. He, too, may feel that he has failed. In making a decision whether or not to promote, the teacher must consider whether the stigma attached to failing a grade would result in negative factors in the child's growth, or whether an opportunity at the same level a second year would build self-confidence. The decision is often made under pressure in terms of the way a child or his parents feel about it rather than in terms of what is best for the child. But every busy teacher must face this problem again and again. As long as schools are organized by grade classification where children move from step to step, as long as courses of study and textbooks and even teachers are organized around the grade concept, as long as there are such great variations in any group of thirty or more children — just so long the question of retaining those who deviate from the rest will be raised and have to be answered.

In the light of research that has turned up evidence to the effect that children do not necessarily profit (particularly in social adjustment) from nonpromotion, the teacher should ask herself this question: "Knowing this child as I do, will the chances for successful school experiences in the years to follow be greater if I retain him?" If the answer is "No," the teacher is advised to give the child the benefit of the doubt and promote him. If, on the other hand, the answer is "Yes," then the teacher should in consultation with the parent and the principal recommend nonpromotion. The school must do something about challenging the repeater, however; simply to go over the material that he failed to do last year is not enough. His being in a room with children who are younger must be filled with exciting challenges and opportunity for leadership, not dulled with repetition.

To promote the slow learner to tasks in which he cannot possibly succeed is not kindness either. Whether children who are slow learners are promoted regularly or irregularly, adequate provision must be made for their needs. Schools should be reorganized on a continuous plan, free from the limitations of grade barriers which have fostered the idea that each child should arrive at the given norm each June.

An example of how one teacher worked out the problem of promotion may be encouraging to teachers with similar problems. Howard came into the

The teacher gains a broader understanding of the child through the parent-teacher conference.

first grade in November; he was eight years old, having been in the first grade for two years. His parents were in a low-income bracket. He sulked, he fought, he wouldn't get his lessons. "I had all that stuff for two years," he said. The teacher felt that if she could get to know Howard and find his interests, she might not have to retain him the following year. One day she discovered he liked to paint. Each day she asked him to paint a picture; she made a frame and displayed Howard's picture proudly as soon as it was ready for framing. With thirty-three other first graders, all this took time, but she did it. She went to the library and got books for him to read — books that were easy, but different from the basic texts used by the reading groups. She asked Howard to get a story ready to read to the class. He became used to the idea of "reading to learn." The months went by, until one day Howard asked if he could join the second reading group. The next day he invited his mother to come to visit and hear him read. He read with real satisfaction and only a few misunderstood words. By the third week in February Howard was reading with the group every day. He remarked to his teacher, "This is the best first grade I've been in. I've been in first grade two years before I came here. That's why I'm eight. I like it here. I get to paint and play games. I like to read and play stories. If I didn't want to be in second grade so badly, I'd stay here another year."

Howard was promoted to second grade, thanks to a teacher who understood children, one who knew that evaluation involves knowing a child, using the tools of evaluation to discover his strengths and weaknesses, and then getting him and his parents to do something about it.

Summary

Evaluation in today's school is a three-dimensional process. The teacher has a responsibility in each. As a member of the staff she helps carry out the over-all evaluation of the instructional program. As a teacher in the classroom she uses the instruments and techniques of evaluation as a basis for planning and for guiding further learning. As a teacher-counselor she prepares diagnostic reports on the progress of the child in such a way that communication between the school, the home, and the community is improved.

An adequate program of appraisal of pupil progress must be comprehensive, continuous, and integrated; it must be a cooperative effort of parent and teacher; and it must focus on the child.

Major factors of pupil growth that need to be evaluated include personal-social adjustment, interests and attitudes, mental ability or aptitude, achievement in curriculum areas, critical thinking, creative self-expression, and ability to work in groups.

Skill in reporting progress, in consulting with parents, and in making decisions on promotion requires an understanding of child development and of techniques in counseling, and an interest in the child's welfare.

QUESTIONS AND ACTIVITIES

1. In writing anecdotal records, what kinds of behavior might a teacher observe on the playground? Before school in the hall? In the room? During the work period? During music and art? What are the minimum essentials she should include in an anecdotal record?

2. In some schools the teachers report to parents by the conference method, supplemented by a written letter three times a year. Here is a letter written by a third-grade teacher:

> Dear Mrs. Edwards,
>   Billy is not getting along as well this year as I had hoped. I had his sister Betty in my room last year and was expecting some fine things of him. So far, he has been a disappointment. His behavior is very erratic; at times he shows a glimmer of promise, but almost at once he reverts. He doesn't listen and sits day-dreaming and looking out the window where the kindergarten children are playing. He doesn't seem to be able to follow directions. I wonder if a hearing test would help; or maybe a physical check-up. Does he look at television late at night? I want you to come for a conference so I can discuss his progress with you in greater detail. Come at your convenience.
>
> Sincerely,

Evaluate this letter in terms of the criteria in the chapter. Compose a letter that would be more meaningful in terms of helping the mother to see the problem or problems that the letter implies.

3. Four-year-old Chuckie's I.Q. as measured by Stanford-Binet Test of Intelligence was 140. His vocabulary was typical of a second grader. His nursery-school teacher insisted that he play with other children for his social adjustment. He rebelled, saying, "I don't belong in nursery school. I want to learn, not play." What use of the examiner's test has the teacher made? What might she do with the results of the report?

4. Cumulative records are individual folders into which records of achievement and dated samples of work are placed, along with letters or notes from home. In what ways might the teacher make use of such folders?

5. By interview and observation in a school, try to determine the uses made of intelligence and achievement tests and of observational data by the teacher, the principal, and the guidance counselor.

6. Using the list of evaluation techniques cited in the chapter, check with the teachers in one of the schools you visited to determine which techniques are used most frequently.

7. What are the major differences between measurement and evaluation?

SELECTED READINGS

Ayer, Fred. *Practical Child Accounting*, Revised Edition. Austin, Texas: The Steck Company, 1953.

Cook, Walter W. *Grouping and Promotion in the Elementary Schools.* Minneapolis: University of Minnesota Press, 1941.

Corey, Stephen. *Action Research to Improve School Practices.* New York: Bureau of Publications, Teachers College, Columbia University, 1953.

Foster, Charles R. *Guidance for Today's School.* Boston: Ginn & Company, 1957.

Goodlad, John. "To Promote or Not to Promote," *Childhood Education,* 30:212–215, January 1954.

Harris, Fred E. *Three Persistent Educational Problems: Grading, Promoting and Reporting to Parents.* Lexington, Ky.: Bureau of School Service, College of Education, University of Kentucky, 1953.

Mortyn, Kenneth. "The Parent Conference: Progress Report, Not Psychotherapy," *Elementary School Journal,* 57:42–44, October 1956.

Noll, Victor H. *Introduction to Educational Measurement.* Boston: Houghton Mifflin Company. 1957.

Ross, Clay C., and Julian C. Stanley. *Measurement in Today's Schools,* Third Edition. Englewood Cliffs, N.J.: Prentice-Hall, Inc., 1954.

Shane, Harold G., and Edward T. McSwain. *Evaluation and the Elementary Curriculum.* New York: Henry Holt & Company, Inc., 1951.

Shane, Harold G., and Wilbur A. Yauch. *Creative School Administration.* New York: Henry Holt & Company, Inc., 1954.

Strang, Ruth. "Do Children Grow by Time Tables?" *National Parent-Teacher,* 51:12–14, September 1956.

Strang, Ruth. *How to Report Pupil Progress.* Chicago: Science Research Associates, Inc., 1955.

Strang, Ruth. *Reporting to Parents.* New York: Bureau of Publications, Teachers College, Columbia University, 1952.

Thomas, Robert Murray. *Judging Student Progress.* New York: Longmans, Green & Company, 1951.

Torgerson, Theodore L., and Georgia Sachs Adams. *Measurement and Evaluation for the Elementary School Teacher.* New York: The Dryden Press, Inc., 1954.

Wiles, Kimball. *Supervision for Better Schools,* Second Edition. Englewood Cliffs, N.J.: Prentice-Hall, Inc., 1955.

Wrightstone, Jacob, Joseph Justman, and Irving Robbins. *Evaluation in Modern Education.* New York: American Book Company, 1956.

Wrinkle, William L. *Improving Marking and Reporting Practices in Elementary and Secondary Schools.* New York: Rinehart & Company, Inc., 1947.

CURRICULUM AREAS

III

In Part III we take a closer look at the curriculum areas in programs of childhood education. What do children really learn when they come to school and progress from nursery school through the primary grades? How do they learn to communicate, to expand their horizons, and to grow in understanding of their social and physical environment? How do they extend their concepts about the world in which they live, the world of people, places, and things, the world of numbers, arts, and literature? We see these curriculum areas not as separate subjects to be taught in discrete fields but as integrated learning experiences to be woven into the design for development that offers the teacher and her group the best possible way of preserving the individuality and uniqueness of each child while at the same time contributing to the maximum development of the group. We are concerned not alone with what learning experiences children should have, but with how these learning experiences may best be selected, organized, developed, and evaluated in the classroom setting — a setting in which children are challenged to their best efforts, teachers are dedicated to a high quality of teaching, and administrators, staff, parents, and children work cooperatively to achieve the goal of helping each child reach his maximum potential.

10

Communication Skills

*We must gather from all words taken together the sense
in which each is to be interpreted.*

— FRANCIS BACON

The power to think, to express, to interpret, and to evaluate ideas distinguishes man from the beasts of the field and the creatures of the jungle. "Speech," wrote Thomas Mann, "is civilization." It is through speech and the other communication skills that man discusses with his fellows the problems that confront them; it is by such skills that they come to some common understanding. Through listening, reading, speaking, and writing, men can understand one another's ideas and influence the course of action.

Never before has the significance of communication been more generally recognized. Never before has such emphasis been placed on the need for providing experiences in learning, practicing, and using all the skills of communication in the classroom. Listening, reading, speaking, and writing are interrelated skills; they are woven throughout the life of an individual, from infancy through adult life. They must be woven, too, throughout the daily life of the child. They must be the very foundation of his educational experience.

"Words are the threads of line and sound from which the fabric of language is loomed. And in the weaving of it there are patterns." [1] As the child develops in his understanding of the words, as he brings meaning to the symbols through experiences that make words come alive, and as he learns that words are symbols for things and ideas and processes, he will develop a sensitivity to patterns. He will enjoy exploring patterns unlike those he already knows, and he will learn to relate the spoken word to the written symbol. He will come to comprehend and interpret the symbols that relate to ideas grounded in experiences. These ideas, these things, these processes lie behind the symbol whether it is oral or written.

Because reading and writing are both modes of symbolic functioning, the process in each requires that the child have a broad background of experience upon which he can draw in bringing meaning to the printed symbols he is to interpret. Reading is something we do, not so much "with our eyes as such, as with our knowledge and interests and enthusiasms, . . . our fondnesses and fears, our evaluations in all their forms and aspects." [2] Not until the child has developed an oral vocabulary and has become fluent in expressing his ideas orally is he ready to approach the complex process of interpreting the printed symbols used in reading and writing.

Listening, experiencing, and interpreting the world about him are essential prerequisites for the child who would become skillful in the arts as well as the skills of communication. How the child develops his ability to use the skills of communication for purposes that are vital to him will be considered in this chapter. How he develops from an infant who is too young to know what words mean to an individual who can use all the skills of communication effectively is a fascinating study that challenges all who work with boys and girls in this vital area. Theirs is the responsibility for instilling within the child a desire for understanding and interpreting words. Theirs is the responsibility for guiding the child as he weaves the fabric of language, as he makes the exciting discovery that there are patterns in the weaving, and that these patterns are altered by the quality of experiences he has had that help him clothe the words with meaning. The teacher guides as the child learns to associate symbols with ideas, as he develops a vocabulary that expresses more adequately what it is he is trying to communicate through the other language arts.

Such guidance requires a profound conviction that in the arts of language lies the key to an understanding of one's fellow men, a belief that such understanding will grow to the degree that we listen to others speak, respect their point of view, and acknowledge their contribution.

[1] Wendell Johnson, *Your Most Enchanted Listener* (New York: Harper & Brothers, 1956), p. 132.
[2] *Ibid.*, p. 123.

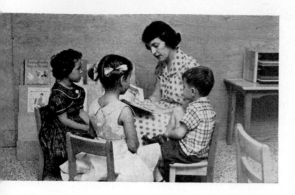

In our society, reading and listening constitute the basic tools of learning as well as the prime media of social intercourse. In the fulfillment of these roles, the importance of reading has never been questioned. More recently ... the significance of listening is receiving increased attention.

— HARRY GOLDSTEIN

COMMUNICATION SKILLS

Listening

Listening is a combination of what we hear, what we comprehend, and what we remember; it is the assimilation of aural plus visual cues. Reading is the assimilation of visual cues alone. Usually listening is a group activity, and reading an individual activity. Listening demands that the hearer adjust to the pace of the speaker; reading requires adjustment to the reader's pace alone. Listening and reading are the two great media through which most of us do nearly all our learning. They are definitely related skills:

> Studies of their relationship usually show a co-efficient correlation of about .70 and when the factor of intelligence is held, of about .50. Very probably the same cortical area of the brain which interprets visual symbols, relating the facts and ideas they carry to others previously learned, operates in about the same way when aural symbols carry the bulk of the message.[3]

Listening and reading are known as the assimilative skills; speaking and writing as the expressive skills. Proficiency in the skills of assimilation should precede or be closely integrated with the expressive skills of speaking and writing.

Skills in listening are essential to success in learning to read. Research has revealed several important interrelationships between reading and listening. Because instruction in reading is given through oral language, the pupils' ability to comprehend is vital. Listening is the chief means of verbalized learning during the primary grades. Until pupils reach the upper grades, lis-

[3] Ralph G. Nichols and Thomas R. Lewis, *Listening and Speaking* (Dubuque, Iowa: William C. Brown Company, Publishers, 1954), p. 1.

tening comprehension is superior to reading comprehension. Retarded readers continue to learn more by listening than by reading. Although listening comprehension is superior to reading comprehension, research indicates that there is only 25 per cent recall with untrained listening. Pupils do not learn effective listening merely by being told by the teacher, "Now listen, boys and girls, do you hear me?" They need specific, guided, graded exercises as a part of the instructional program. Children who have a limited listening vocabulary have difficulties in learning to read well. Correlation between reading vocabulary and listening vocabulary runs high — possibly .80 or higher. Poor auditory discrimination is often associated with poor reading and may be a causative factor. Discriminative listening helps children get main ideas rather than minute details. What a child hears and comprehends may stay with him longer than what he reads.

Thus listening and reading skills are closely related. Yet it is a mistake to assume that improvement in one will automatically ensure corresponding improvement in the other. Training in one does not result in a significant carry-over. When teachers understand the importance of listening to learn, many of the random efforts to teach children to listen will give way to systematic effort. Too frequently when children are passive and quiet the teacher is satisfied, not realizing that children can turn their ears "off" and "on."

Listening should be taught through graded exercises. When mental age is taken into consideration, primary children are the best listeners; the level of listening decreases as age increases. Adults listen least well of all groups. Tests show that skills in listening can be increased as much as skills in reading.

Assumptions About Listening

Why is it, then, that much more emphasis has been placed on teaching the other phases of communication — that is, reading, speaking, writing, and spelling — than on listening? One of the reasons is that people have had, in general, certain assumptions about listening that have stood in the way of specific instruction in the skill. Many of these ideas have no basis in fact. For example, teachers take it for granted that children are listening; it apparently never occurs to them that the child wearies of listening to the teacher's voice and that after a while he simply stops listening.

Listening is not largely a matter of intelligence. We listen with our experience, not with our intelligence. The relationship between listening and intelligence does not prove to be close. Neither is listening related closely to hearing acuity. Only three to six per cent of children in school suffer hearing defects severe enough to impair learning in the classroom. What is regarded as a hearing loss is often merely a lack of attention. Studies show that individual listening comprehension varies at any single grade level as much as reading comprehension. Developing skills in listening is a curriculum problem.

Learning to listen is at least as important as learning to read. We listen three times as much as we read. In addition, tests show that listening has a greater effect on our behavior.

Factors That Influence Listening

Among the considerations that help determine the effectiveness and quality of listening are those concerned with physical, psychological, and experiential factors.

PHYSICAL FACTORS

Physical conditions within the listener may impair his listening. For example, he may be hard of hearing, hungry, or merely fatigued; he may be chronically ill. A person in excellent condition is potentially a better listener than a person in poor physical condition.

The physical environment also influences the quality of listening. Good ventilation and an even temperature aid in keeping the listening level high. Distracting noises in the street, in another part of the room, or in an adjoining room make listening difficult. The members of the audience have a responsibility to be courteous to a speaker, but occasionally the speaker is so ill-prepared or so lacking in the skills of communication that the audience is unwilling to hear.

The conditions for teaching listening skills may not be ideal. Many teachers hold forth from one to two hours a day above the din of gym classes, of the outdoor playground directly under the window, and above the sound of street workers, construction projects, and children passing to and from classes.

PSYCHOLOGICAL FACTORS

Psychological factors involving personality traits and attitudes may also contribute to poor listening. Psychological deaf-spots are areas of sensitivity; when the speaker uses words that are emotion-laden, we cease listening and merely feel. Poor listeners are, on the whole, more biased than good listeners. The poor listener has less emotional control, broods about what is happening to his pet theory, stops listening to the speaker, and organizes a speech of his own. The good listener, on the other hand, waits until he has heard the speaker out before he makes up his mind.

EXPERIENTIAL FACTORS

The experiential background is an important factor in listening. The child who has had rich and varied experiences will be interested in many facets of living. As he enjoys these new experiences, he will add to his vocabulary the words necessary to explain them.

Encouraging Good Listening

PHYSICAL ARRANGEMENT

The teacher should make sure that the arrangement of the room is conducive to good listening. If the children are seated in rows, the child in the back of the room has very little contact with the speaker. Informal seating arrangements, with desks or tables placed close together so children can work in groups, encourages good listening. Too great a distance between the speaker and the listener is often a barrier to communication.

ATMOSPHERE OF THE CLASS

The classroom climate should motivate listening. There should be a permissive atmosphere in which children are free to express their ideas; they should feel that their contribution will be accepted and respected. The teacher should take advantage of opportunities for teaching listening and plan specific activities to promote it.

In this connection the teacher should allow for individual differences and should provide for the maturity of the children. Youngsters in nursery school and kindergarten have a short attention span, those in the upper elementary grades a considerably longer one. The teacher should set standards for good listening in terms of the abilities and maturity of the children.

Types and Levels of Listening

Generally speaking, listening may be said to be of three types: appreciative listening to any kind of stimuli pleasing to the sense of the listener; dis-

Listening to musical instruments helps the child learn to distinguish differences in tonal quality.

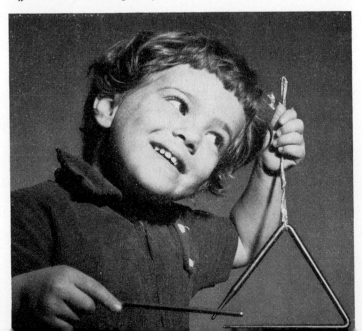

criminative listening to informative speech for the purpose of comprehension; critical listening to persuasive speech for the purpose of evaluating the speaker's argument and evidence.

If the teacher understands the developmental process of listening, she can direct learning through the experiences she provides in the classroom. Though goals may be similar from nursery school through high school, each year the children should be nearer the highest level of listening as a communication skill. The development of listening skills and behavior is outlined below:

1. Little conscious listening on the part of the child and then only when he is the center of interest; easily distracted by people and things.

2. Half-listening; the child more interested in his own ideas, waiting to "break in."

3. Passive listening; the child just sitting there, with little or no reaction.

4. Sporadic listening; the child showing interest if the conversation is closely related to his own experience, but shutting off the current when the conversation turns away from him.

5. Listening; some reaction shown through comments or questions.

6. Listening; indication of sincere emotional and intellectual response.

7. Highest level of listening; complete understanding of what is being said.

Children listen at one or more of these levels throughout the day. Young children vary in their ability to listen. The youngest ones do very little conscious listening. As they begin to react to what they hear, they ask questions. Finally, real communication occurs when the child understands what is being said.

Activities to Improve Listening

SETTING GOALS

Children enjoy setting standards for desirable behavior. Even young children can learn basic listening skills as a part of the speech situation. For instance, a group of kindergarteners set up the following criteria for good listening:

1. We listen to the speaker to understand other people's ideas.
2. We wait for the children who are noisy.
3. We stop what we are doing. We look at the speaker. We keep very quiet.
4. We think before we speak, so we have something interesting to say.
5. We listen to the teacher when she talks.
6. We do not interrupt when someone is talking.
7. We stop what we are doing and listen when the teacher gives a signal.
8. We listen to the whole thing.
9. We give a signal for silence if someone talks to us when we are listening.
10. We listen when someone reads to us.

A Good Listening Program

The school day should offer many opportunities for practicing communication skills. In the preschool and kindergarten the only time children are not permitted to talk is during rest period and the story. The following activities are suggested for a good listening program:

1. Conversation and telephoning (a real phone if possible, otherwise a toy one)
2. Sharing experiences
3. Discussing, planning, and evaluating
4. Directions and announcements, as in carrying out specific instructions
5. Story-telling and dramatization
6. Poetry and choral speaking
7. Listening to music at rest period and during the self-chosen activities
8. Reporting on excursions or science experiments
9. Oral reading in order to share what one has prepared
10. Introducing parents when they visit school
11. Having programs and assemblies in the gym
12. Listening to sound films, recordings, transcriptions, radio and television programs in school and home
13. Listening to sounds around us — birds, wind, rain, and so forth
14. Listening creatively for imaginary sensory experiences

Teachers should keep in mind the types of listening skills they wish pupils to develop and plan activities that involve a specific kind. A number of suggestions follow. Some may be used as they are presented; others may need to be modified and adapted to the needs of a particular teacher and group.

Conversation. Conversation requires listening skills that the child will need during his entire life. The child who has been the center of attention at home finds a shift of emphasis as he enters nursery school, kindergarten, or first grade. He will need to be taught that speech is a two-way process. He should listen to others not only for information but as an act of courtesy. He must learn that there is a time for talking and a time for listening. To be sure, children should be given numerous opportunities for talking as well as for listening. Sharing interesting happenings with the entire group, perhaps by way of a show-and-tell or sharing period, promotes good listening.

Telephoning. Telephoning is an activity that promotes good listening. It is particularly appropriate to use in the preschool and kindergarten. If no telephone is available it is possible to use a role-playing technique. Children frequently engage in such conversations as the following, which was recorded in a kindergarten:

Mrs. Jones? Good morning. No, you're not interrupting me. I just sent my husband off to work. Yes, he has his job back. The plant opened again. I'm glad to have him out from under. What did you say? Just a moment. I hear Janie outside. She wants a drink. Pardon me. How is your little girl? I'm so glad. I hear she was pretty bad. By the way, what did you say? No! You don't say! I think that's my doorbell. Well, come over and see me; then we can talk. Good-bye.

Children can set up standards for telephone behavior such as these, thought out by a group in a self-contained classroom:

1. Answer the phone correctly; say, "This is the preschool, Roberta Johnson speaking."
2. Listen attentively to the person on the end of the line.
3. If someone is called to the phone, answer, "Just a moment. I'll call him."
4. Talk for a brief time; others may want the line.
5. Say good-bye before you hang up.

Discussion and planning. Discussion, planning, and evaluating periods call for purposeful listening so that group decisions are carefully made. Children should set the standards. Careful attention is necessary if discussion is to be worth while. Since there are usually great differences in the ability of children to express themselves clearly and to listen effectively, the best solution is to let the children work in small groups, and then come back to the group as a whole with a report from the various subcommittees.

Directions and announcements. Directions and announcements can provide the type of listening that any directions require. The child can use the "who, when, where, what" techniques of listening. This skill can be improved by games in the classroom, especially those that require concentration.

Dramatic activities and story-telling. Dramatic activities and story-telling offer numerous opportunities for listening. Puppet shows, plays, creative dramatics, flannel-board demonstrations, television and radio programs, choral speaking, and poetry reading are excellent avenues of appreciative listening.

Musical activities. Musical activities, such as listening to various instruments or to water glasses, chimes, or bells, as well as to recordings and radio programs, improve the child's listening skills and his appreciation of music as an art. Listening to music during rest periods is always relaxing.

Listening for central ideas. This grows out of activities related to reports and speeches. Children can begin early to listen for the central idea. When they listen to a speech, for instance, they should try to recall the main idea. This technique can also be used in a story situation.

Taking notes on lectures, trips, interviews. Taking notes is a part of the child's experience in listening. Finding the main idea and evaluating the talk give the child experience in critical listening. Radio and television programs likewise provide opportunity to exercise discriminating listening. Teachers can help children develop standards by which they will benefit from such media; children should listen for enjoyment but use evaluative techniques to distinguish between fact and fiction.

Listening to programs. Listening to programs in the gym or assembly hall should help the children in developing standards of discriminating and appreciative listening. Children should listen to programs and evaluate them in terms of previously agreed upon criteria. Activities designed thus to develop critical listening should begin early. Even the young child should learn to evaluate emotion-laden words, facts without proof, high-pressure selling techniques, and propaganda when he hears them.

Listening to reports. Listening to reports of excursions, science experiments, and other activities interests the class as a whole. Once again, they listen for the central idea, following the sequence of the speaker and evaluating the content of the report.

Listening to a story. Listening to a story prepared by a child is important in teaching listening skills, for it serves as a source of motivation for children as they prepare the story for an audience.

Sounds all around us. When children are highly stimulated and interesting outside noises distract them, the teacher can ask them to listen to quiet sounds in the midst of a noisy environment — the ticking of the clock, perhaps, or the whisper of the teacher, or the sound of the triangle.

Games for Developing Listening Skill

"What Did I Do?" Children sit in a semicircle. One child goes behind the semicircle and performs some action such as skipping, running, hopping, sliding, jumping, or clapping. He then goes before the group and asks, "What did I do?" The child who answers correctly performs the next action.

"Do This." Teacher initiates game by tapping on table or toy drum and asking children to imitate her. For example, the teacher may say, "Do this," and then she may make one long and two short taps. Chosen child imitates these taps. After some practice a child can be leader. Variation: "Patterns of sound" may be made by clapping.

"Tick! Tock! Where Is the Clock?" Hide a loudly ticking clock while children cover eyes. Then ask children, "Tick, tock, where is the clock?" Choose two or three children to hunt. Child who finds clock hides it next.

Listening implies an active effort on the part of the listener to comprehend what he is hearing.

"*Finding the Bell.*" One child leaves the room. Another child is given a small bell to be held loosely. When the child enters the room, all children wave hands until the child locates the bell.

"*Listen and Tell.*" Children close eyes and listen and then tell what they hear.

"*Mother Cat and Kittens.*" This is a familiar game. The child who is mother cat chooses three kittens. Mother cat covers her eyes, and then kittens hide in room. Mother cat locates kittens by listening to their "meows."

"*What Is This?*" Child imitates a noise such as an animal or a machine noise and asks, "What is this?"

"*Add-a-Word.*" Teacher names two or three words that begin alike, such as fish, farmer. The child must add a word beginning with the same letter, for example, father.

Below is a check list for evaluating listening opportunities:

Did I give children opportunities to develop listening skills in the following areas:

1. Personal experiences.
   Telling about weekend experiences, parties, new baby, trip.
   Showing and telling about a possession, toy, clothing, pet, science specimen.
   Listening to directions and messages.
   Listening to telephone conversations.

Listening to original stories and rhymes.

Listening to a story read by the teacher or other children.

2. Group experiences.

Planning a group activity.

Discussing experiences such as a new game, holidays, a celebration.

Planning an experience chart based on an excursion, movie, science experiment, standards.

Being a member of a committee to plan a party.

Planning and reporting an interview with people in the community.

Evaluating an excursion, movie, television or radio program, the day's work.

Dramatic play and creative dramatization.

Cooperating in teacher-pupil planning for units of work and general routines.

3. Observing acceptable social courtesies.

Listening attentively when anyone is speaking.

Taking a share of responsibility for conversation.

Sensing occasions when it is not appropriate to talk, such as during rest, during programs, when the teacher or another adult is speaking, in libraries, in theaters, or during the prayer and in church.

By using such a check list and by keeping before her the specific objectives for teaching listening skills, the teacher can help the children in developing skills vital to them in social intercourse in daily living, gathering information to solve problems, appreciation, relaxation, enjoyment, and critical evaluation of what they hear and read.

QUESTIONS AND ACTIVITIES

1. What is the relationship between listening and reading?

2. What obstacles get in the way of effective listening?

3. List the types of skills needed for effective listening. Evaluate your own listening in terms of these skills.

4. In what types of listening have you engaged today? Throughout the week?

5. Observe in a nursery school or in a primary grade. List the occasions that require listening. How would you evaluate the effectiveness of the listening?

6. Does the teacher whom you observed seem to sense the relationship between listening and reading. Why do you think so?

SELECTED READINGS

Adams, Harlem M. "Learning to be Discriminating Listeners," *The English Journal,* 36:11–15, 1947.

Berry, Althea. "Listening Activities in the Elementary Schools," *Elementary English Review,* 23:69–79, February 1946.

Dale, Edgar. *Audio-Visual Methods in Teaching,* Revised Edition. New York: The Dryden Press, Inc., 1954.

Deas, Earl J. "Three Levels of Listening," *The English Journal*, 36:252–254, January 1957.

Elliff, Gertrude. "A Direct Approach to the Study of Listening," *The English Journal*, 46:20–27, 1957.

Herrick, Virgil E., and Leland Jacobs (eds.). *Children and the Language Arts.* Englewood Cliffs, N.J.: Prentice-Hall, Inc., 1955.

Morkovin, Boris V. "Growth through Speaking and Listening," *Elementary English Review*, 26:129–130, March 1949.

Murphy, G. "We Also Learn by Listening," *Elementary English Review*, 26:256–260, March 1949.

Nichols, Ralph G. *Are You Listening?* New York: McGraw-Hill Book Company, Inc., 1954.

Nichols, Ralph G., and Thomas R. Lewis. *Listening and Speaking.* Dubuque, Ia.: William C. Brown Company, 1954.

Ogilvie, Mardel. *Speech in the Elementary School.* New York: McGraw-Hill Book Company, Inc., 1957.

Parkes, M. B. "Children's Ways of Talking and Listening," *Childhood Education*, 29:223–230, 1953.

Pratt, Edward. "Experimental Evaluation of a Program for the Improvement of Listening," *The Elementary School Journal*, 56:315–320, March 1956.

"The Status of Teaching Listening," *The Elementary School Journal*, 56:151, January 1957.

Strickland, Ruth. *Language Arts in the Elementary School.* Boston: D. C. Heath & Company, 1957.

. . . And I opened it and turned pages and held it near a window and had my wondering about how those black marks on white paper could be words your eyes would pick off into words your tongue would speak.

— CARL SANDBURG

Reading

The wonder that the child feels when he first realizes that those black marks on white paper can open a hitherto closed door is surpassed only by the wonder of the teacher who understands what opening the magic door can do to influence the destiny of the child. Fortunate is the child who, faced with the interpretation of symbols or with the desire to translate into meaning those symbols on the printed page, has the guidance of a teacher who will turn the desire into a permanent interest in reading.

If all teachers and parents of young children in the nursery school, kindergarten, and primary grades fully appreciated the significance of the introduction of a child to reading — the art of choosing what to read, what to know, what to think about, what to enjoy — they would treat the phenomenon as one of the highest gifts accessible to the human mind. As a result, children would receive more encouragement and more practical aids in unlocking the door. They would learn with greater ease and with a promise of an ever-broadening experience as they continue to learn about life through the great books men have been writing for thousands of years, building up the resources on which the individual can draw.

Words are the symbols of man's ideas and man's reactions to the world in which he lives; they are not the ideas or the things. Words merely serve to convey the ideas and to clothe them; they serve as cues for the association of things. They come to life only as they are associated with experience, with meaning. To the degree that the reader brings meaning and experience to the printed page, to the degree that the printed symbol is associated with the meaning, to that extent only the recognition process is effective in communicating ideas.

Up to this point in the child's life he has read symbols other than the printed word. He has read the expressions on the faces of people around him, he has read the symbols in nature; he has read oral symbols. He has learned to "read" the spoken word; now he will read the printed word.

It is necessary to note the importance of the child's desire to know what the symbols mean, for this is an essential element in the process of reading to learn. There is a distinction between teaching a child to learn to read and teaching a child to read to learn. In the former, the emphasis is on the "how," the process. In the latter, the emphasis is on the "why" and the "what." This calls for an understanding of the purposes of reading. When children are motivated to read, when they have a desire to read, and when they indicate a wish to read for a purpose, the process of teaching is free of many of the difficulties that exist in teaching a child who is not eager.

Purposes of Reading

The child needs a reason for reading. Research relating to child development has indicated that children differ widely in their readiness for reading. A child may be ready to read anywhere between the chronological ages of three and eight, or even later. First he must know why people read and believe that the reasons are worth while. He must be shown that people who read learn many things that are vital to them and that they have exciting adventures denied to others. The values of reading should be made clear not by talking about them but by demonstrating them. The child who is surrounded by adults who value reading is likely to enjoy reading, too.

Reading, in the life of an adult, serves four purposes: reading for information, reading for enjoyment, reading for problem solving, and reading for evaluation. Reading to learn stimulates thinking, creates broadened interests, and contributes to personal and social adjustment. The child's reasons for reading are exactly the same as the adult's.

The Reading Program in the Primary School

In harmony with the thesis that a child should read to learn, it is vital that the school create an environment in which the invitation to read is clearly sensed. A wide selection of reading materials related to the children's interests, varying abilities, and maturity should be provided. Every classroom needs an extensive collection of the good, attractive, worthwhile, and inexpensive books available today. The school library and the city or county library offer additional materials for supplementary, individual reading.

To meet the needs of children with widely differing potentialities, interests, needs, and backgrounds, the teacher must plan a definite program for determining the readiness of a child for reading. Nothing is gained by forcing a child to read before he evidences readiness; in fact, permanent damage may be done. On the other hand, since the purpose of instruction is to aid the process of maturation, the teacher must offer every opportunity for the child who is ready. Some children are ready to read earlier than others. Girls tend to be ready to read before boys of the same chronological age; remedial classes in reading have, in general, many more boys than girls. To lessen the number of unhappy children who fill such remedial classes, the teacher of the youngest must provide adequate readiness programs. The influence of kindergarten on the development of the child and on his achievement in reading tests in the first grade has been the subject of research since the beginning of the century. "The results of investigations show that children with kindergarten experience advance more rapidly in reading, arithmetic, and are generally more advanced throughout the elementary school." [4]

GENERAL READINESS

The rich experiences children have in kindergarten, in which they learn to adjust to group living, to experience success in working with others, to engage in creative experiences, to solve problems, to listen with comprehension, to express themselves with increasing clarity and fluency, and to develop a desire to read, contribute much to their success in the primary grades.

General readiness is not confined to kindergarten and early first grade. It is a concept that applies to every level of reading development. It refers to the factors that determine the probable success of an individual for a particular experience. These factors are frequently classified under four headings: physical, mental, social, and psychological. The factors that are of significance for readiness in reading at the first-grade level are important at every other level of development.

Physical readiness. The physical readiness of the child is dependent upon his physical development, his general health, and lack of any defects. Such aspects of development as hearing, vision, speech, physical control, muscular coordination, effects of childhood diseases, and present health should be ascertained by the teacher through the school nurse or the teacher's interview with the parent. It is essential for a teacher to check on each of these aspects in order to meet individual needs.

There was the case of Susan, for instance. Susan, a bright, attractive five-year-old, had been in kindergarten several weeks before the fire alarm sounded. The children, having been instructed in advance on the procedure during a fire drill, promptly marched to the door. Since the kindergarten was located on the second floor, leaving the building meant going down the stairs. In the process of going down in a hurry, Susan came down like the three-year-olds; under the stress of the experience she seemed to revert in her motor skills. The children were rather critical of her performance, because she had slowed them down. Susan, who had been such a happy child, was sensitive to the criticism. When her mother came to see the teacher about Susan's changed

---

[4] Irene Fast, "Kindergarten Training and Grade I Reading," *The Journal of Educational Psychology*, 48:52, January 1957.

attitude toward school, she reported that Susan had fallen arches and was unable to go down the stairs easily. Had this fact been made known to the teacher at the beginning of the year, some effort could have been made to help Susan. What the teacher did now was to choose Susan to be the leader to go down the stairs, and walked with her until she learned to go down the steps as the others did. The next month Susan was the leader for fire drill. This time the children were delighted. "She walks like the rest of us now," they said.

Mental readiness. The child's mental readiness may be determined by teacher observation, a reading-readiness test, and an intelligence test.

The most significant kind of evaluation is teacher observation of the pupil to discover the extent of the child's desire to read, his interest in books, his ability to listen to stories, and his fluency in oral expression and comprehension. The readiness test purports to test proficiency in skills such as following directions, interpreting illustrations, seeing likenesses and differences between words, discriminating between word forms, recognizing sound elements, forms of objects, numbers, and words, and comprehending common words and common things.

The intelligence test is an invaluable aid in understanding the child's potential as well as his actual performance. When tests are used, certain things must be considered: They must be administered with care. The children should be adjusted to school and have confidence in the administrator. The physical needs of the children should be considered when they are taking the test. The tests should not be administered too early in the fall. Usually they should be given in first grade rather than in kindergarten.

The results of tests must not be taken as completely reliable or indicative of the child's ability to read. The stress of the situation, fatigue, illness, and emotional reactions result in unreliable scores for some children.

Many schools prepare check lists to be used by kindergarten and first-grade teachers to make periodic and systematic observations relating to various factors in reading readiness. Check lists are also used to help the teacher determine what prereading skills the child needs.

Social and emotional readiness. The social and emotional readiness of the child depends upon his contacts with other people, places, and things, upon his ability to be content away from his mother, and upon his willingness to be part of a group. The child who is not thus adjusted but who is unhappy or shy and lacking in confidence has difficulty in reading with a group. The answer to his problem is not necessarily to delay the reading program. He may profit from a program of individual instruction.

Experiential background. Children differ widely in experience. In the same kindergarten, for example, were Fifi, who had traveled from Iran and enrolled in a preschool group, Selma, who had lived in Africa, Chuckie, who had traveled to Europe with his family, and Douglas, who had lived all his life in his own neighborhood. There are six-year-olds who have been halfway around the world and who have attended both nursery school and kindergarten. There are others who have not traveled as far as the capital of their own state. Some children have parents who read to them; others never see anything more of books than a slick-paper magazine. In a recent survey of 150 kindergarten children it was discovered that the parents of only 14 of the children read to them at bedtime. Many of them said their mothers watched television at that time. A teacher must know her boys and girls well to determine the supplementary experiences needed before reading will be meaningful to them.

Psychological readiness. Psychological readiness is closely interwoven with aspects of physical, mental, and social development. Many first-grade children are psychologically unequipped to meet the demands of reading. Evidences of withdrawal, hostility, restlessness, lack of concentration, negative reaction to others, negative reaction to new experiences, unwillingness to read, all indicate a lack of readiness. Parental rejection, a broken home, maladjustment to relationships in the home, all contribute to feelings of insecurity that may result in a psychological unreadiness for first grade in general and for reading in particular.

Some children are disturbed by the thought that, now they are in the first grade, they are expected to read. These children respond much more enthusiastically to a first-grade situation where the emphasis is on the activities that invite a child to learn about the world in which he lives, and where reading is regarded simply as one way in which he can accomplish this objective.

Activities for Developing Readiness

Teachers who have taught kindergarten or first grade know that, although the kindergarten child is interested in learning to play with other children, he is also interested in academic achievement before the year is over. The expression, "But what are we going to learn?" is common. Each day is rich with opportunities for learning many things that later give meaning to the printed page. The child does not get meaning from the printed word; he brings meaning to it. Watch a child react to the word "giraffe" if he has seen a giraffe at the zoo. Everything a child sees, smells, hears, feels, and tastes, he interprets in terms of his own experience, and draws upon it to bring meaning to the printed symbols. The wider experience he has, the more opportunities to work with others, to talk, to make things, to experiment, to manipulate, to create, to solve problems, the more anxious he will be to add yet another method of extending his knowledge of life.

Some specific ways in which teachers help children expand their horizons include bringing in objects for show-and-tell time, taking care of and talking about pets, taking walks around the school and community, taking trips and excursions, enjoying stories and movies, dramatizing stories, planning, evaluating, and talking about experiences, looking at pictures and discussing them, drawing, painting, modeling, and working with other art media, engaging in matching games of all sorts, doing creative rhythms, dictating stories to the teacher, and carrying on scientific experiments.

SPECIFIC PREREADING SKILLS

We have pointed out that reading in the primary grades begins with a readiness program. Such a program teaches the child the specific prereading skills essential to success in beginning reading. These skills include:

1. A capacity for critical and sustained listening.
2. Auditory discrimination: the ability to hear, reproduce, and recall sounds accurately.
3. Visual discrimination: the ability to recognize likenesses and differences in color, size, shape, and so forth; the ability to discriminate between words and letter forms.
4. Comprehension of words.
5. An adequate speaking vocabulary.

Juxtaposition of pictures and words helps the child to relate the appearance of the letter to its sound.

6. Mechanics of reading: reading from left to right with proper eye movement, reading from top to bottom, turning pages, and handling books properly.

To make sure the teacher knows when each child has acquired the necessary general and specific prereading skills, she may want to use a check list similar to the one presented here:

Name of child		
	Comments	Date
1. He looks at picture books.		
2. He listens to stories read.		
3. He asks questions about the story.		
4. He asks about certain words, labels, and so forth.		
5. He understands the story and asks for another.		
6. He knows the titles of many of the books.		
7. He memorizes poems and songs readily.		
8. He works at a job for 15 to 20 minutes.		
9. He likes to paint, draw, and "write letters."		
10. He holds books correctly.		
11. He speaks with considerable ease. He uses sentences and good enunciation.		
12. He sees similarity between spoken and written words.		
13. He can identify a unit in print or on a chart.		
14. He goes from left to right with the pointer and his eyes.		
15. He can tell a story in sequence.		
16. He understands that words have meaning for him.		
17. He has a desire to read.		

McKee suggests that the kindergarten and first-grade teachers accept the responsibility for helping children develop readiness for beginning reading by a systematic program including the following six instructional jobs:

(1) providing training in visual discrimination, (2) providing training in auditory discrimination, (3) developing the understanding that reading matter is to be observed from left to right, (4) providing training in listening, (5) creating a desire to learn to read, and (6) *if necessary,* constructing concepts and developing listening vocabulary needed for beginning reading.[5]

Beginning Reading

In the early phase of the primary reading program, the activities of reading readiness merge with initial experiences in reading. As the teacher observes that children show evidence of readiness for reading and are eager to begin, she groups them according to their ability. Groups are kept flexible; children move from one group to another as their progress warrants; they are free also to organize temporary reading groups of their own in free reading time.

Children continue to create their own stories as a language activity and read them from experience charts and from the chalkboard. The socializing and exploratory activities of the readiness period continue throughout the year, even though the children are now reading. The teacher, too, must continue to provide an atmosphere in which children are eager to read, to plan, and to evaluate experiences. It is important that children find reasons for reading that have meaning for them.

The teacher should be familiar with several methods of teaching reading. No matter what methods are adopted for teaching beginners, the teacher must provide for differences in rates of learning, varying levels of interest in reading, and various types of reading material.

READING FROM BOOKS

Children are gradually introduced to books. There is no sharp line of demarcation, no sudden and world-shaking shift from the readiness program to a formal reading program. As the teacher and pupils work together and as she notes their proficiency in the essential prereading skills, she groups them according to their ability to profit from working in certain groups. Different groups begin reading at different times. Some of the children who are ready to read when school begins will be organizing a reading group as early as the third or fourth day. Some need time to become adjusted to the first grade, time to work and talk with the children and the teacher, time to plan and participate in the many challenging activities. Through observation and the use of readiness tests and intelligence tests, the teacher will come to know when children are ready to read from books.

5 Paul McKee, *The Teaching of Reading in the Elementary School* (Boston: Houghton Mifflin Company, 1948), p. 145.

The Preprimer. The most exciting day in the life of many a first-grade youngster is the day he starts to read in the preprimer. The objective of this period is to build a basic sight vocabulary that will help the child read simple stories. The teacher allows the children to examine the preprimer carefully before she discusses the characters in the story and the plot as revealed by the pictures. The children are learning to use picture clues as they read silently. Following the silent reading, they read orally to answer questions. The teacher should use a sense of the dramatic in her teaching. After the children and teacher have discussed the story, the children read it silently and then there is a discussion in relation to the questions asked. The children will participate in follow-up or related activities, which may lead to rereading, dramatization, choral speaking, art expression, and so forth.

In beginning primary reading, the stories are short, limited to a few selected words and brief sentences. They involve getting the meaning of sentences, phrases, and words, and learning to distingush one form from the other. Related activities are an integral part of the program. The basic aim is to comprehend the printed page and to enjoy reading.

Oral reading for enjoyment and sharing with the group is an important part of the program. Usually the silent reading is for the purpose of getting information and the oral is for sharing materials with others, either to give pleasure to the audience or to participate in dramatization. The teacher evaluates continually to see if her grouping may be made more effective. Each child should be encouraged to progress at his own rate but each child should be motivated to do his very best.

Phonetic analysis is one method of teaching children new words.

The role of basal readers. Proper use of basal reading materials, supplemented by a variety of other instructional materials and aids, appears to help most teachers in integrating reading as one of the communication skills. Making use of the basal series, beginning with the first little preprimers in the reading series, gives security to teachers and satisfaction to children in initial reading as the foundation of reading instruction. The preprimers and the basal readers are used in a variety of ways: for experience in group reading, for practice in specific skills in reading, for individual library reading in connection with individual projects or unit activities, and for study.

Although there are those who use individualized reading methods — experience charts, library-table reading of simple story material, booklets, and film-strips in connection with workbooks — as the basis of reading activities or various combinations of these approaches, the use of a basal series has a number of definite values in initial reading instruction. The group situation involved in reading from a basal reader is a satisfying experience to many children. The vocabulary is controlled in such a way that children need to learn only a common core of words, and there is sufficient repetition and overlapping of words within the books of a particular series of readers. The sequentially graded difficulty of the stories within a series is conducive to success in reading, and success leads to further success. From the teacher's point of view, the manuals that accompany the better series prove to be a source of support, giving her practical suggestions that can form a point of departure for her instruction. The basal series is a time-saver for the teacher. In this day of large classes teachers need effective material that is easy to read, colorful, and well-organized in terms of identified difficulty. The better series organize the reading material and accompanying practice material and workbooks in such a way that attention is given to all the basic reading skills from the very beginning. The controlled vocabulary and the separate book units also make it possible to use the basal series to provide for individual differences.

The supplementary materials should be of a wide variety to meet the needs of children of varying ability and maturity. Schools are making a greater effort to vary the reading fare and to provide for individual differences. The child with reading skills beyond his grade level, too, is provided with challenging material. If a workbook is used, it must be carefully motivated, checked, and supervised, in order that it does not deteriorate into mere busy work. In a typical first grade, by the end of the year, some children will be reading at third-grade level, and some will still be in the preprimer.

Independent Reading

At the earliest possible moment, the child is encouraged to read independently. By the time he is in the third grade, he will be faced with reading in the content areas, and he must comprehend the vocabulary of such fields.

The teacher should therefore check the child's progress both in comprehension and in word recognition.

One of the basic aims in reading is word recognition. There are a number of ways in which this process may be facilitated. The clues to "unlock" new words make use of visual perception, association, and analysis. Context, picture clues, and structural and phonetic analysis help children read independently. Since the problem of word recognition is such a persistent one, we will discuss each of the clues briefly.

Picture clues and context clues are widely used in recognition of basic sight words; that is, the unknown word is associated with a picture. At first children see words such as *toy, dog, cat,* the object itself being depicted in story pictures. Later the words are printed on pages showing the pictures. Thus, association leads to recognition. Association of a word with the context involves a series of words in a phrase in which all but one word is known. The children figure out the meaning of the new word from the context.

Another way of unlocking new words that may be useful is that of *analysis.* Two methods of analysis may be used — phonetics and structural. Phonetic analysis is used as an integrated activity in reading, not as an isolated drill. Structural analysis includes attention to prefixes, suffixes, root forms and compound words, contractions, and so forth.

Word form clues are used by some children; they look at the word and try to remember any distinguishing characteristics, such as length, tall letters, and so forth. Although this type of clue is considered effective by many educators, others feel that, because of the errors and confusion that can occur as a result of dissimilar words having similar configurations, the method should not be used.

Aids to word recognition, such as picture clues and context clues, phonetic and structural analysis, and configuration, give the child an integrated approach to the learning of a new word. After he has developed a basic sight vocabulary, new words appear rapidly. It is at this point that the clues that use visual perception, association, and analysis are useful to the child. The teacher should remember that the techniques are a means to an end, not an end in themselves; there is no one best method of unlocking new words. Children who are motivated to read usually select the type of word recognition that fits their particular need at any particular time. The use of the dictionary is generally taught to advanced third graders as an additional clue to word recognition.

Throughout the reading program in the primary grades the child is reading to learn what he wants to know about the world in which he lives. By the time he has progressed through the primary grades, he should be able to read and understand some materials published for adults. He is still reading for the same purposes that motivated him in first grade and that will motivate him as an adult; to learn, to be entertained, to evaluate facts, and to solve problems. After this point, he is mainly concerned with improving his skill.

QUESTIONS AND ACTIVITIES

1. What are the aspects of the reading-readiness program? What are the differences between general and specific prereading skills?

2. What are the advantages of using experience charts in teaching beginning reading? What are the limitations?

3. Why is it essential that the child be ready for the first experience in reading from a book? How can the teacher tell when he is ready? Observe in a primary grade and try to see on what basis the teacher determines readiness.

4. When should formal instruction in using structural and phonetic analysis for independent word recognition begin?

5. Identify and discuss the major purposes for reading in the primary grades. In what way are they similar to an adult's purposes for reading? How do they differ?

6. Observe in a primary grade and note the ways in which children are being motivated to read. Can you think of opportunities for motivation that the teacher has overlooked?

7. Describe some ways in which you could determine a child's interests in order to provide him with material that will motivate him to read.

SELECTED READINGS

Artley, A. Sterl. *Your Child Learns to Read.* Chicago: Scott, Foresman and Company, 1953.

Bond, Guy, and Eva Bond Wagner. *Teaching the Child to Read.* New York: The Macmillan Company, 1950.

Burton, William H., Clara Belle Baker, and Kracek Kemp. *Reading in Child Development.* New York: The Bobbs-Merrill Company, 1956.

Carter, Homer L., and Dorothy McGinnis. *Learning to Read.* New York: McGraw-Hill Book Company, Inc., 1953.

Dawson, Mildred A., and Henry A. Bamman. *Fundamentals of Basic Reading Instruction.* New York: Longmans, Green & Company, 1959.

Dawson, Mildred A., and Morida Zollwiger. *Guiding Language Learning.* Yonkers-on-Hudson, N.Y.: World Book Company, 1957.

Dolch, Edward W., *Psychology and Teaching of Reading.* Champaign, Ill.: The Garrard Press, 1951.

Dolch, Edward W. *Teaching Primary Reading.* Champaign, Ill.: The Garrard Press, 1951.

Durrell, Donald. *Improving Reading Instruction.* Yonkers-on-Hudson, N.Y.: World Book Company, 1956.

Gates, Arthur L. *The Improvement of Reading.* New York: The Macmillan Company, 1950.

Harris, Albert J. *How to Increase Reading Ability,* Third Edition. New York: Longmans, Green & Company, 1956.

Hildreth, Gertrude. *Readiness for School Beginners.* Yonkers-on-Hudson, N.Y.: World Book Company, 1950.

Hildreth, Gertrude. *Teaching Reading.* New York: Henry Holt & Company, Inc., 1958.

Larrick, Nancy. "How Children Learn to Read," *NEA Journal,* 47:160–161, March 1958.

McCullough, Constance. "Individualized Reading," *NEA Journal,* 47:163, March 1958.

McKee, Paul. *The Teaching of Reading in the Elementary School.* Boston: Houghton Mifflin Company, 1948.

McKim, Margaret G. *Guiding Growth in Reading in the Modern Elementary School.* New York: The Macmillan Company, 1955.

Monroe, Marion. *Growing into Reading.* Chicago: Scott, Foresman and Company, 1951.

Parsons, Arthur J. "The Teachers Need to Read," *NEA Journal,* 47:168–169, March 1958.

Russell, David C. *Children Learn to Read.* Boston: Ginn and Company, 1949.

Strang, Ruth. *Making Better Readers.* Boston: D. C. Heath & Company, 1957.

Strang, Ruth, *et al. Problems in the Improvement of Reading.* New York: McGraw-Hill Book Company, Inc., 1955.

Strickland, Ruth G. "Children's Reading and Creativity," *Elementary English,* 34:234–241, April 1957.

Tinker, Miles. *Teaching Elementary Reading.* New York: Appleton-Century-Crofts, Inc., 1952.

Wingo, Charles, and Julie Hay. *Reading with Phonics.* Philadelphia: J. P. Lippincott Company, 1954.

Woolf, Maurice, and Jeanne Woolf. *Remedial Reading.* New York: McGraw-Hill Book Company, Inc., 1957.

One day you will write a poem which everyone will read, but first you must learn how to handle the material from which poems are created.

— NAGOL

COMMUNICATION SKILLS

Functional Writing

Writing is for communicating. Whether it is functional or creative, the goal is to write so that what is written can be read. This means that teachers must strive continually to find better ways of teaching handwriting that combine legibility with speed, motor skill with social purpose, and basic principles with individual variation.

The misunderstanding that comes in the teaching of handwriting lies in the fact that the public conceives of it merely as the ability to form letters correctly and join them into words. The school, on the other hand, thinks of writing in a broader sense, as a means of communication, a phase of the language arts in which the skills of communication are taught. The concept of writing to communicate puts a new emphasis on the tool.

Handwriting is a developmental process. Even the preschool child is interested in this tool of communication. Because children vary in muscular coordination, however, many of them are not ready for formal writing until some time in the first grade. If they indicate interest, the teacher should have materials ready for them to use. By the third grade children have, for the most part, developed enough skill in handwriting so that they are ready to write their own stories.

ARRANGING THE ENVIRONMENT

Children learn to write well when:

1. They are comfortable and have proper materials with which to work.
2. Provision is made for individual differences in handedness, style of writing, and method of forming letters.

3. They have systematic, thorough teaching, followed by sufficient time for motivated drills.
4. They have a strong incentive to improve their writing skills.
5. They are given individualized instruction.
6. They are allowed to advance as soon as they show readiness.
7. They are constantly encouraged to evaluate their writing in terms of previous accomplishments and present needs.
8. They are encouraged to do their best work, keeping in mind that writing as a tool of communication requires the habit of craftsmanship.

Procedures

Handwriting should be taught systematically. The words that children practice in class should be chosen according to a graduated scale of difficulty. In addition to the general list, the child may have his personal word list.

If children have difficulty writing a word, the teacher demonstrates how to form each letter and gives them a correct copy; she encourages them to practice both at the board and at the tables, and teaches them how to apply the basic principles of manuscript or cursive writing.

Manuscript writing is generally taught first. Children find it easier to print, and the printed page of the reader is more closely related to manuscript than to cursive writing. Most children are ready for cursive writing by the third grade, but some are not ready until later. In case of serious handwriting problems, children may be allowed to continue manuscript writing indefinitely. Since cursive writing is required for legal purposes and in business, it should eventually be taught.

The time alloted to the teaching of handwriting varies according to the purpose of the writing and the abilities of the children. In general, young children do not profit from more than 15-minute periods. Sixty to 75 minutes a week are sufficient. The planned instruction period varies according to needs, and time is given to individual instruction.

The urge to write well comes more spontaneously if the child gets satisfaction from the product. He will not be motivated merely by being told to write well. Motivation, an appropriate attitude, a readiness for the mechanical problem involved, systematic teaching, and continuous analysis of the writing, all are essential to success. Principles of handwriting should be taught, examples given, diagnostic charts that show levels of perfection provided. Pupils should use such charts to evaluate their progress toward the next level of legibility rather than their distance from perfection.

Activities to Develop Writing Skills

In kindergarten. Kindergarten children enjoy dictating stories to the teacher. These she writes on the board and later transfers to a chart. They are

When the child has learned to write legibly, he should learn to use this skill to communicate ideas.

pleased to discover that writing is "talk written down," and they like to see their own ideas take shape as the teacher writes.

No formal writing is taught in kindergarten. Many authorities believe that writing should not be attempted before a seven-year level of maturity. Children who are ready, however, should be guided in writing on an individual basis.

In the primary grades. Opportunities for writing in the primary grades come in such ways as these:

A. Personal experiences
　　1. Printing name
　　2. Writing captions and labels
　　　　a. Single words
　　　　b. Phrases and sentences
　　3. Writing tags for gifts
　　4. Writing brief notes, cards, and letters
　　5. Observing and recording daily temperature
　　6. Keeping memoranda to take home
　　7. Keeping a diary of a trip or everyday events
　　8. Writing stories for school newspaper
　　9. Recording results of daily planning
　　10. Copying recipes for mother
　　11. Keeping records of lunch money, attendance, date, library books read
　　12. Writing numbers for pages of booklets and for playing number games
　　13. Writing questions to be used in interviews with neighborhood and school personnel
　　14. Keeping a word list
　　15. Making a dictionary
　　16. Writing creatively — poems, songs, riddles, and stories
B. Group experiences
　　1. Developing stories for experience charts
　　2. Selecting captions for pictures

3. Writing letters, invitations, thank-you notes
4. Planning and listing questions to be asked concerning an excursion, initiating a unit of work, selecting characters for dramatization, room duties, books to be read, games to be played, rules of behavior

Evaluation of Writing Ability

Giving a child an opportunity to see growth in his writing skills is a source of motivation. Many teachers keep a file in which they gather samples of the child's work. Perhaps a sample at the beginning of the year in first grade looks very discouraging. Within a few weeks, however, a child will be able to copy from the board a story dictated by the children and written by the teacher, and he may use this as a yardstick by which to measure growth. If the teacher keeps in mind the skills she wishes to help children develop in the primary grades, evaluation will be facilitated.

Teachers feel more secure if they have an idea of what the child should accomplish in each of the primary grades. The following outline provides such a guide:

A. Writing in the first grade
   I. Writing skills
      a. Use correct manuscript form
         1. Head paper in correct form
         2. Make letters clear and neat
      b. Use capitalization correctly
         1. Form capitals and small letters correctly
         2. Capitalize the first word in a sentence
         3. Capitalize special names
         4. Capitalize greeting and closing of letter
         5. Capitalize Mr., Mrs., Miss, Dr.
         6. Capitalize the word "I"
         7. Use capital in first word of each line of verse
      c. Use correct punctuation
         1. Use a period at end of sentence
         2. Use a question mark at end of sentence
         3. Use exclamation marks
B. Writing in the second grade
   I. Writing skills
      a. Use correct manuscript form
         1. Head papers correctly
         2. Leave prescribed margins
         3. Write neatly
      b. Use capital letters correctly
         1. Review items for first grade
         2. Capitalize titles of books, stories, pictures
      c. Use correct punctuation
      d. Spell correctly with teacher's help

Writing on the blackboard can be used both for individual practice and for group demonstration.

    II. Major activities
- a. Copying from the blackboard
  1. Experience chart or personal letter
  2. Announcement
  3. List or agenda
  4. Poem, rhyme, or joke
- b. Copying from teacher's notepad
  1. Label or picture story
  2. Individual or personal writing
- c. Independent writing
  1. Creative stories, experience stories
  2. Thank-you notes, letters of invitation to parents
  3. Letters to parents reporting on activities of the school
- d. Library cards
- e. Evaluation
  1. Self-evaluation of activities and skills listed
  2. Use of model in order to locate errors or weak spots
  3. Practice on trouble spots under teacher's guidance

C. Writing in the third grade
    I. Writing skills
- a. Use correct manuscript form the first half of the year; begin cursive writing during the second half
  1. Review skills for second grade
  2. Use correct form in writing personal note
- b. Use capital letters correctly
  1. Review rules learned in first and second grade
  2. Use capitals in sequence, such as *R.F.D.*
- c. Use correct punctuation

      1. Review items listed for second grade

      2. Master the skills in using the apostrophe — contraction, possessive singular

      3. Use a period after Mr., Mrs., Dr., Rev.

    d. Spell correctly through the use of aids given by the teacher

      1. Begin the dictionary habit

      2. Use other aids such as a notebook list, a spelling list, a textbook

      3. Progress in mastering contractions and homonyms

  II. Major activities

    a. Review filling out simple forms such as library cards

    b. Compose and write class standards on the blackboard or on note-paper

    c. Write an announcement on the bulletin board

    d. Write a news story for the school paper

    e. List questions to be answered in reading a story

    f. List the names of the children in your reading group

    g. Make a class directory

    h. Write a report about a trip or science experiment

D. Other skills related to writing

  I. Vocabulary development

    a. Use words in writing vocabulary

    b. Use descriptive words, recognize rhyming qualities of words

    c. Use such technical terms as sentence, capital letter, period, question mark, comma, greeting, closing, margin, heading, indent, paragraph, apostrophe, contraction, command

  II. Experience with sentences

    a. Recognize a sentence

    b. Express ideas in interesting, clear, and concise sentences

    c. Realize that a sentence tells or asks something

    d. Recognize the earmarks of a sentence

    e. Begin to discriminate against the run-on sentence and particularly against the "and" habit

    f. Compose correct and interesting sentences

  III. Organization of ideas

    a. Stick to the point in dictating stories

    b. Tell stories in proper time sequence

    c. Restrict a paragraph to a single topic

    d. Relate the events of a story in sequence

    e. Revise work to be sure that it is correct

The responsibility for developing skill in writing lies almost entirely with the teacher. In all but a few cases children start writing in school. At their own level of maturity, kindergarten and primary children have a need to write. Their first writing experiences should be directed toward goals that stress the importance of thoughtful, legible, and interesting writing, making correct statements, finding words that express what they mean, and giving clear explanations.

QUESTIONS AND ACTIVITIES

1. Discuss the pros and cons of teaching manuscript writing throughout the primary grades.

2. What should be the guiding factor in determining the adequacy of a child's handwriting?

3. What procedures should a teacher use to motivate a child to write more clearly? To motivate a child to write with greater speed?

4. Suggest ways in which you would provide for individual differences in handwriting?

5. Observe a primary grade. Try to get samples of the best writing and the poorest writing in the class. Determine reasons for the difference. What information do you need?

SELECTED READINGS

Ames, Louise, and Frances Ilg. "Developmental Trends in Writing Behavior," *Pedagogical Seminary and Journal of Genetic Psychology*, 79:29–46, September 1951.

Cole, Luella. "Reflections on the Teaching of Handwriting," *The Elementary School Journal*, 52:95–99, November 1956.

Freeman, Frank. "The Transition from Manuscript to Cursive Writing," *Elementary English*, 40:366–373, October 1958.

Freeman, Frank. *What Research Says to the Teacher: Teaching Handwriting*. Washington, D.C.: National Education Association, 1954.

Furness, Edna L. "Diagnosis and Remediation of Handwriting Defects," *Elementary English Review*, 32:224–228, April 1955.

Hendricks, Archie H. "Manuscript and Cursive Writing in Brookline," *Elementary School Journal*, 55:447–452, April 1955.

Leavitt, Jerome S., and Isabel B. Lewis. "Handwriting Dilemma," *Childhood Education*, 29:281–283, February 1953.

McIntosh, Helen K., and Wilhelmina Hill. *How Children Learn to Write*. Bulletin No. 2. Washington, D.C.: U.S. Office of Education, 1953.

Quant, Leslie. "Factors Affecting the Legibility of Handwriting," *Journal of Experimental Education*, 14:297–316, June 1946.

Stewart, Dorothy. "Handwriting up to Date," *Elementary English Review*, 29:407–410, February 1953.

Sullivan, Mary. "Functional Handwriting Program," *Elementary English Review*, 30:85–89, February 1953.

Wagner, Rosemary. "Writing is for Reading," *NEA Journal*, 45:555–557, December 1956.

Who does not remember the enlivening effects of the spelling matches of his boyhood? So intensely was their attention concentrated upon the subject in hand, that grown men remember distinctly the very words missed by themselves and others in some remarkable contests.

— J. L. HUGHES

COMMUNICATION SKILLS

Spelling

Methods of teaching spelling have changed since the days when our grandfathers "spelled down" in the little country schoolhouse. Today we look upon spelling as a tool of communication, a utilitarian activity. But have we not lost something of the enjoyment that was our grandfathers'? Many pupils enjoy the challenge such an activity brings. There are children who cannot succeed in other activities more academic in nature, but who can, by motivated practice, achieve status and success in activities requiring drill.

A child must have a desire to spell, and this means that he must be motivated to spell correctly. A functional approach to spelling is the answer for some children. Others enjoy the stimulation of the drill, the competition, the challenge a different activity can bring. Children differ in their reactions to learning and their motivation. The teacher has the task of discovering the key to unlock the child's interest in learning what he needs to know. She must provide a wide variety of interesting projects that will give each child a purpose in spelling correctly.

Teachers frequently ask what makes a spelling program good. Typical questions are:

What is a good study plan for teaching spelling?
How can children be helped to improve in spelling and written expression?
How can children's individual needs be met?
What are the best ways of building good spelling habits?
What words are most often met in writing?
What are some ways to help children fix words in their minds?
What methods can be used to diagnose spelling problems of slow learners?
How can children evaluate their work in spelling?

Objectives of a Spelling Program

In order to plan an effective spelling program, the teacher must determine her objectives. These should be based on the concept of spelling as a tool for communication and should be correlated with the entire school program. Because individuals differ greatly in maturity and ability, differences should be considered in planning the core words. Each child should have two lists of words on which to work: a basic word list useful in writing at his grade level and a list that grows out of his personal needs.

Although drill and systematic review are vital, the teacher should provide activities that integrate life experiences with school instruction.

The teacher should check misspelled words on the child's written work in all his subjects. Correct spelling must become habitual not only in spelling classes but in all work. In addition, the child should be encouraged to check his own work for incorrect spelling.

Whether the teacher uses the textbook plan or not, she must make weekly lists that include the words needed by individuals in the class. To ensure that these are complete, teachers may use lists of words established by research.

Methods of Teaching Spelling

Though much has been written about the irregularity of the English language — and it is true that a large percentage of English words are not wholly phonetic — many words are either wholly or partially phonetic. Hanna and Moore analyzed a 3,000-word spelling vocabulary and discovered that approximately 85 per cent of the phonemes were represented by spelling that was regular as far as sound-letter associations were concerned.[6] They also found that about 82 per cent of the consonant blends had only one spelling.

The teacher should make use of such aids as auditory training. By selecting from the child's speaking vocabulary words that begin and end with identical sounds, and by calling attention to the fact that the same symbol is used to write the sound, she can help the child arrive at a useful generalization for translating and relating the spoken sound to the written symbol.

In the early stages children should be taught words that are consistently phonetic. Principles of spelling should be emphasized at the beginning of each weekly spelling lesson and reviewed as needed. The child must form the habit of looking not only at the familiar patterns he recognizes in a word but also at anything in the word he does not expect to see.

The teacher of spelling must herself understand the relationships of communication skills. She must know not only phonetics but the principles of

[6] Paul R. Hanna and James T. Moore, "Spelling from Spoken Word to Written Symbol," *Elementary School Journal*, 53:329–337, February 1953.

learning, ways of helping children reason, generalize, and find relationships in word patterns. Phonetic techniques that aid children in spelling are learning the groups of words and syllables that are found in certain phonic categories, identifying phonograms, developing the ability to say the letter equivalent for common sounds, acquiring correct pronunciation and articulation, and some skill in syllabizing.

It is commonly agreed that a time must be set aside during the regular school day for teaching spelling. There should be a definite plan of instruction. There are many ways to teach spelling, and the following plan is merely a suggestion. It permits easy administration to the class, allowing individuals not only to participate in discussion of principles but also to proceed at their own rate and to work with individualized lists as the need arises.

Direct the attention of the children to the new unit of words on Friday before the work begins on the following Monday.

Monday
1. Discussion of spelling principles that will be useful in the week's work. Children should learn principles that will facilitate study of words.
2. Understanding of principles and meanings of words. This may be accomplished by:
    a. Matching words and meanings.
    b. Using dictionary to find and study words.
    c. Discussing principles and definition of words.
3. After listening to the correct pronunciation, the children should pronounce the words in unison.

Tuesday
1. Dictation of the words by the teacher as a pretest.
2. Each child makes up his own list of those he needs to study for the week. He should use the new words in writing word units, stories, and descriptions.

Wednesday
1. Supervised study of new and review words. Children should be directed to study word meaning and usage in exercises.
2. Review of spelling rules, nonphonetic spelling, hard spots, use of homonyms, and so forth.

Thursday
1. Misspelled and illegible words graded by teacher.
2. Misspelled words written in child's "hard-word" or "demon" list.

Friday
1. The final test of the week dictated by teacher.
2. Child should be motivated to use his newly mastered words in:
    a. Dictation.
    b. News items.
    c. Letters.
    d. Announcements.

Some games and activities that may be used in spelling are:

1. Crossword puzzles.
2. Missing-letter puzzles.

3. Spelling battles.
4. Spelling matches.
5. Making up riddles.
6. Anagrams.
7. Matching words and meanings.
8. Using the dictionary.

SUGGESTED GAMES FOR SPELLING

"Card Game." Make up a book of related words on cards, such as *like, likes, liking, liked, talk, talked, talks, talking.* The children may use these as a card game in a group or underline known parts of new words.

"Bingo Spelling Game." Children fold paper into sixteen squares. They call out sixteen words, which the teacher writes on the board. A child who mentions a word for the teacher to write must spell it. The children write these words on their papers in the sixteen squares in any order. A child comes to the front of the room and turns his back to the board, and the teacher calls out one of the words for him to spell. Each child puts a disc on that word on his paper. When a row or diagonal is filled, the child calls, "Bingo."

"Alphabet Game." A boy whose name begins with *A* writes it on the blackboard, then a girl whose name begins with *B,* and so on through the alphabet. This game is varied by using other categories such as fruits, vegetables, or animals for each letter of the alphabet.

Correct spelling can be encouraged by a variety of classroom activities.

"Tea Kettle." One player leaves the room. The group chooses a word. The player is called back and members of the group use the word in sentences, substituting "tea kettle" for the correct word; for example, I have a new "tea kettle" (pair) of shoes. The player is to guess the word and spell it correctly.

"Can You Guess the Word?" A list of words to be reviewed is written on the board. A child stands near the list and silently chooses a word. Children raise hands, and the child calls on someone. This child says, "Judy, are you thinking of the word *climb*, C–L–I–M–B?" Judy answers, "No, I am not thinking of *climb*." Continue until the word is guessed.

"Take-a-Chance." Words written on separate slips are placed in a box. The pupil draws a slip but does not look at it. He hands it to the leader, who pronounces the word for the pupil to write on the board. The pupil keeps the slip if the word is spelled incorrectly. Pupils who have no slips at the end are the winners.

"Erase the Word and Spell." The teacher places review words on several blackboard spaces. Then she asks, "Who can find, erase, and spell *neighbor?*" A variation is, "Who can pick out and spell the word that means something to wear, to eat, to do?"

INDEPENDENT STUDY PLAN

Children learn through the senses. Dr. Maria Montessori made much use of the senses in teaching children to read, write, and spell.[7] Some suggestions for self-study that make use of sense imagery are:

1. Look carefully at the word written on the board.
2. Notice anything in the word you did not expect to see there.
3. Pronounce the word slowly and distinctly.
4. Close your eyes and visualize the word.
5. Look at the word again. Did you see it right in your mind's eye?
6. Write the word in the air without looking at the board.
7. Trace the letters on the top of your desk or table.
8. Check with the word on the board or the copy in your notebook.
9. Write the word again three ways: in the air, on the desk, and in the book.
10. Write a sentence using the word.

QUESTIONS AND ACTIVITIES

1. Look over a set of spelling papers. Compare the misspelled words with a graded list. Which words would you stress in practice with the slow learners? Which would you stress with the proficient spellers?

[7] See Maria Montessori, *The Montessori Method*, translated by Anne George (New York: Frederick Stokes Co., 1912).

2. Observe a spelling class to determine whether the teacher is using a planned program or teaching spelling incidentally. Are the children learning to spell?

3. How would you go about helping the children you observed learn the difficult words they misspelled?

4. Make out a spelling program for a two-week period for a grade of your choice. What is the advantage of planned spelling instruction? Are there disadvantages?

SELECTED READINGS

Artley, A. Sterl. "Principles Applying to Improvement of Spelling Ability," *Elementary School Journal*, 49:137–148, November 1948.

Bryan, Fred E. "How Large Are Children's Vocabularies?" *Elementary School Journal*, 54:210–216, December 1953.

Delacato, Carl H. "Spelling — a Five-Year Study," *Elementary English*, 32:296–298, May 1955.

Dolch, Edward W. *Modern Teaching of Spelling*. Champaign, Ill.: Garrard Press, 1950.

Fitzgerald, James A. *A Basic Spelling Vocabulary*. Milwaukee: The Bruce Publishing Co., 1951.

Fitzgerald, James A. *The Teaching of Spelling*. Milwaukee: The Bruce Publishing Co., 1951.

Furness, Edna, and Gertrude Boyd. "335 Real Spelling Demons," *College English*, 20:292–297, March 1959.

Hanna, Paul R., and James T. Moore. "Spelling from Spoken Word to Written Symbol," *Elementary School Journal*, 53:329–337, February 1953.

Hatchett, Ethel, and Donald Hughes. *Teaching Language Arts in Elementary School*. New York: The Ronald Press Company, 1956.

Herrick, Virgil E., and Leland Jacobs (eds.). *Children and the Language Arts*. Englewood Cliffs, N.J.: Prentice-Hall, Inc., 1955.

Hildreth, Gertrude. *Teaching Spelling*. New York: Henry Holt & Company, Inc., 1955.

Horn, Ernest. "What Research Says to the Teacher: Teaching Spelling," *NEA Journal*, 47:277–285.

McIntire, Alta. "Spelling Can Be Fun," *Elementary English*, 22:271–272, November 1945.

National Council of Teachers of English. *Language Arts for Today's Children*. New York: Appleton-Century-Crofts, Inc., 1954.

Russell, David H. "A Diagnostic Study of Spelling Readiness," *Journal of Educational Research*, 37:276–283, December 1943.

Russell, David H. "A Second Study of Characteristics of Good and Poor Spellers," *Journal of Educational Research*, 46:129–141, March 1955.

Strickland, Ruth G. "Utilizing Spelling Research," *The Education Digest*, 21:40–43, February 1956.

Wilson, Louise Ada. "Children's Spelling Needs and Their Implications for Classroom Procedure," *Elementary School Journal*, 47:98–102, October 1946.

Words used by the tale-teller are as colors used by the painter. Forms grow out of the materials of the tale and the teller's reaction to them.

— SHERWOOD ANDERSON

COMMUNICATION SKILLS

Expressive Writing

Children create when they are stirred to say something. They create when they are happy and when they know that their product will be accepted. They write from that sense of urgency that Santayana calls the "itch to write." "Neither theme nor method of treatment may come from the teacher. . . . Theme and treatment are the business of the artist, never the teacher." [8] Expression of ideas must be the result of some inner emotional reaction to an experience or an impression that the writer has felt deeply and that he is compelled to express spontaneously. It is the teacher's task to provide a permissive atmosphere.

Chagall clearly expresses the close relationship of the artist and the writer when he says, "You listen silently and the sacred power that is within you dictates and you obey; and that is what is called creation. Art doesn't set out to reproduce anything." [9] All the arts are related; the creative arts belong together. Children must be free to say what they think and feel through whatever medium they choose. Children are waiting for someone to kindle the flame, to ignite the spark that is within them. Whether that spark is expressed in the dance, drama, music, art, or writing is not important. What is important is that the child be helped to discover and use the tremendous power within him.

It is the teacher who, in the words of Winifred Ward, "deliberately plants in likely souls a faith in the possibilities of creative ability even when they

[8] Hughes Mearns, *Creative Youth* (New York: Doubleday Page and Co., 1925), p. 37.
[9] Carleton Lake, "Color As Love, A Portrait of Chagall," *The Atlantic Monthly*, 201:73, June 1958.

give no outward sign of having any. . . . You have something to say. Find out what it is. That is the beginning." [10]

This is the opportunity awaiting the teacher — not only to foster the few who reveal their abilities at the outset but to work with all children to bring each to his highest potential.

Encouraging Creativity

How does the teacher go about the process of encouraging children to write creatively? Is the environment so different from that she provides for the artist who chooses the palette or the one who chooses the dance? Is it different for the gifted from what it is for the average child?

There are certain essential requirements in an environment without which creativeness in children cannot flourish. The teacher must consciously arrange a classroom environment in which creativity can flourish. Before the child will feel free to express himself he must be in the presence of another creative individual — one who "takes off the lid, as it were, where an unimaginative teacher claps the lid on." [11] An occasional poem, a song or story to be shared, a new rhythm or a painting makes the teacher, too, a creative person.

Secondly, the teacher must provide opportunities rich for experiencing: pictures that stir the imagination, movies, excursions, rhythm band instruments, a costume box, a wide variety of art media, a doll corner or playhouse, blocks, tools, and other materials having creative potential. The use of bulletin boards to display creative writing is good only if products of all children who contribute are occasionally displayed. Creative writing must be handled with care. Children who are encouraged by someone who believes in them will reach surprising heights of expression.

The atmosphere in which creativity flourishes is not an accident. The teacher plans for it. The children should have a balanced program in which there is time for individual creative effort. Time should be provided for sharing stories. This occasion can be made the high point of the week, where children and teacher participate in a relationship permeated with the magic of understanding. Appreciation is the keynote in shared creativity.

Teachers who have worked with children in creative experiences agree that the role of the teacher in guiding expressive writing, as in guiding all creative activities, consists in giving children opportunity to experience widely — to see, feel, smell, hear, taste, and express their inner feelings.

Having arranged the kind of environment in which children can create, the teacher does not sit idly by. She is ever alert to encourage, to guide, to give help as it is needed. She may find that some children have not yet learned to use the tools for writing. Still, they have something to say. They can dictate to the teacher.

[10] Hughes Mearns, *Creative Power* (New York: Doubleday & Co., Inc., 1929), p. ix.
[11] *Ibid.*, p. 7.

Imaginative Writing

Children who sing at their work or chant at their play often say some lovely bits of verse; there is no effort involved. An example of this type of writing happened one day when Tom, a five-year-old, was painting a beautiful boat at the easel. He was completely absorbed in his work, and this is what he was saying:

> All the blue blue water all over,
> And the green green boat sailing through.
> All the blue blue water all over,
> Where is my boat going home again to?

When the day has been rich with experiences such as a new-fallen snow or a make-believe trip over the ocean, children express themselves in poetry. Here is such a poem by a second grader:

> I went to Spain once in the rain,
> There was a bullfight and there was a rain,
> I went alone and I'll go back again,
> But next time I go it won't be to Spain.

Children have a natural sense of rhythm, which tells them when the poem or the story is right. The poetry of the child is spontaneous, as seen by examples of children's writing when they are not forced to write or when no emphasis has been placed on form. Sometimes the child feels a poem

A child cannot in the beginning create by himself, but pressure will cause frustration.

must rhyme. At that point the verse is likely to become forced and lose its charm. Here is an example:

> When I was big I wore a wig,
> You said, "You are a prig."
> When you were big you used to dig,
> And I don't give a fig.

This child had written a charming poem a few months earlier. He had been at the seashore for his vacation and was full of talk about shells and the ocean. This is what he wrote then:

> There were miles and miles of water along the coast down there
> I wondered if I'd get to wherever it went to.
> The waves were blue and oh so fast — and sometimes — they were slow
> And oh the shells I found the day I went to where it went.

Workshop in Creative Writing

The following examples were the results of a workshop on creative writing in which a group of teachers entered into the spirit of creativity with boys and girls in the primary grades.[12] It would be difficult to say who gained the most from the experience — the children or their teachers.

GRADE 1

Motivation: imagery. Sounds are mysterious. Children love to listen and express the sound in words. For instance, thumb tacks falling into a pan make interesting sounds. The children were challenged to tell what they heard. They said:

Popcorn popping	Big hail balls
Tiny rocks falling	Pumpkin seeds falling in a pan
Beads breaking	Money
Tacks bouncing	Shotgun shells
Marbles falling	Pencils dropping
Buttons dropping	Crayons
Electrons going all over	Chalk

Motivation: sense of touch. After the children had defined and discussed touch, they felt various articles and told what they liked to touch.

Motivation: animals. From pets brought to school by children came the material for dictating stories. The teacher copied stories on the board.

---

12 Workshop on Creative Writing in the Primary Grades. Evansville Public Schools, Evansville, Ind., 1958. Martha Stinson, Harwood School, Chairman.

Motivation: filmstrips. Filmstrips provided another source of story material. The children saw the filmstrips without comment. Then they told their own stories. Here are two examples of such stories:

Once upon a time there was a little Japanese boy. He had a dog. He went to a palace. He saw three old men talking to children. He went to see the swans. It was raining. He went to the store. His puppy knocked over the onions and things. The puppy jumped on a table and jumped down. The little boy came and his puppy wasn't there. He sat by the pond and started to think. He said, "H-m-m-m-m." He went to the store. He saw another little boy. He picked up what he wanted. The little boy "shuck" his head. The boy went outside and walked away.

A little baby was floating in the ocean. She started flying. A face was looking at her. She yelled; the face looked mean. She flew on. She went up to the sky and stayed there for a long time. A farmer and little boy were on the ground making corn. It started to rain. The cloud was mean. It had things like lightning. The baby ran from the cloud and hid around a big old hill. The lightning went on. A white cloud helped. It was big and strong and had a funny face. It went way up in the sky and got the rain. The sun got the crop ugly looking. The cloud saw it needed rain and then he got all the stuff he needed. The rain poured down so the crop looked straighter. The farmer saw the rainbow. They lived happily ever after.

GRADE 2

Motivation: senses. The class talked about their chart entitled "The Senses." Then we asked, "What would you like to hear? What would you like to see?" Two interesting responses were:

I like to see an apple tree in bloom;
It looks like a ball of pink cotton candy.

I like to hear the thunder;
It sounds like the devil beating the drum.

Motivation: pictures. Photographs of any sort provide inspiration. After seeing pictures and newspaper articles, the children discussed the new baby hippopotamus at the zoo:

The Hippos
Hippos, hippos, hippos,
What if they had to jump
Like bunny rabbits?

Motivation: lead sentences. Lead sentences taken from their stories invite further story writing:

Tonight was Ringtail's chance . . .
He walked bravely into the stream . . .
Ringtail was in a great hurry . . .
Peeping through the tall weeds and bushes . . .
Just as the round moon began to shine . . .

Ringtail's Adventure

Just as the big round moon began to shine, Ringtail went down the tree slowly. Around the bush, through a hole in the fence and around to the front yard he went. Then on the porch he jumped. He stepped on a squeaky board and the noise scared him. He jumped off the porch and ran home.

GRADE 3

Motivation: imagery based on a winter scene. What teacher hasn't wondered how to liven up an old school room for January and at the same time provide a good learning situation? A winter scene furnishes beauty and motivation for writing. While constructing the scene, the children had fun writing stories, poems, and riddles. Here are some examples:

Snow, snow everywhere,
Snow on the ground but I don't care.
Snow on the pond, snow on the hill,
So come and play with us if you will.

Snow, snow soft and white
Falling, falling pretty and bright.
Snow, snow everywhere
Snow in my hair — but I don't care.

Motivation: let's pretend. Another idea was to let the children choose something they would like to be and tell something that might happen to them "if they were. . . ." One response was the following:

A Broom
I am a broom. I sweeps the
floor. I sweeps the water off the
porch. I sweeps the spider webs
off the seeling. I sweeps the rug.
I always sweeps the ground.

Motivation: using a phrase as a stimulus. Two lines were supplied to the children:

I knew the snow fell;
I heard the wind blow.

I knew the snow fell;	I knew the snow fell
I heard the wind blow.	I heard the wind blow;
I saw three little dogs,	I saw little fairies
Playing in the snow.	Dancing in the snow.

Motivation: pictures. The children viewed a photograph of a rabbit wearing a napkin and eating spaghetti. After discussing this unusual situation, several children wrote stories that expressed their individual interpretations:

Pink Ears, The Bunny

My name is Pink Ears. I am 3 years old. My mistress's name is Micki Ann Allen. She is 8½ years old. My master gave me some spaghetti and a dish towel. I love spaghetti. You don't love spaghetti as much as I do. I love, love, love spaghetti.

Using the Arts as Stimulus

MUSIC

Many children have oral contributions to make about what they hear in music. Saint-Saëns' *Carnival of the Animals* was played, after a statement that the music was written to remind us of different animals. The music was then replayed, and the children wrote as they listened. Most of the writing consisted of disconnected sentences. Some of the results follow:

The ostrich with a beautiful tailfeather is dancing. A baby duck and a mother duck are lost. A butterfly flying in the air. A little blue bird. A mad tiger hunting food. A beautiful swan that is as white as snow. A little red squirrel jumping from tree to tree.

On another occasion, Debussy's *Afternoon of a Faun* brought out the following story:

Once upon a time there was a husband and wife robin. Mother robin was waiting impatiently for her eggs to hatch. One sunshiny day they did hatch, that is, all except one. Mother Robin worried and worried and waited and waited.

After about four days the last egg finally hatched. Now the family was really worried for the baby did not look like a robin at all. The more Mother Robin looked at him the madder she became. Finally she could stand it no longer and she kicked him right out of the nest.

Soon it was almost time for fall and the robin couldn't fly yet so he sadly watched the others fly by overhead. A solid red bird was up in the tree watching and when he saw how sad the little bird was he chirped a shrill "Hello!"

Little Robin was glad to find someone to talk to and when he told the bright red bird his story the other bird laughed harder and harder. Soon Little Robin was so bothered by the strange actions of his friend that he stopped talking and started crying.

"There is no need to cry," chirped the bright bird. "You are very lucky, really. I could have told you right away that you are not a robin at all but a cardinal, so there!"

The story spread and other cardinals came to help Ugly Robin learn to fly. He was so happy and he learned quickly. Before the really cold days came, he joined his kinfolks and flew quickly away.

The music that will inspire creativity is plentiful. The following is merely a selection:

Debussy	*Afternoon of a Faun*
	Cathédrale Engloutie
Elgar	*Pomp and Circumstance*
Gershwin	*Rhapsody in Blue*
Gounod	*Funeral March of a Marionette*
Grieg	*Ase's Death* from *Peer Gynt Suite*
Haydn	*The Toy Symphony*
	Andante from *The Surprise Symphony*
Herbert	*March of the Toys*
MacDowell	*Woodland Sketches*
Mendelssohn	*Spring Song*
Pierne	*March of the Little Lead Soldiers*
Poldini	*The Waltzing Doll*
Ponchielli	*Dance of the Hours*
Ravel	*Pavanne for a Dead Princess*
Saint-Saëns	*Carnival of the Animals*
	Danse Macabre
Schumann	*Papillon*
	The Wild Horseman
Strauss	*Pizzicato Polka*
	Blue Danube Waltz
Stravinsky	*Firebird Suite*
Wagner	*Ride of the Valkyries*

The Group Method of Writing Creatively

Some children gain confidence in writing by beginning to write as part of a group. It is easier to contribute when the composition is created by the class than it is to assume responsibility for the whole enterprise.

A unit of work may stimulate the child to write not only reports but also stories and poems.

The teacher might ask, "Is this a good day to write a poem as a group project?" If the answer is favorable, the teacher and the children decide what to write. As each child makes his contribution, the teacher writes it on the board. "Who will give me the first line?" In the first example that follows you will see how the group contributed sentence by sentence and how the individual phrases were put together to form the poem:

> It's raining flowers.
> I think they look like white stars.
> They are pieces from the sky.
> Like Christmas.
> Ivory Flakes.
> Little white sticks flying in the air.
> White feathers coming out of a pillow.
> Milkweed seeds coming out a pod.
> Snowy white popcorn.
> Little bits of white cloud.
> Suds; bubbles; a white sheet; Christmas trees.

Putting these together they wrote:

> Snow! Snow! like tiny white feathers,
> Or milkweed seeds coming out of a pod.
>
> Snow! Snow! soap suds flying;
> Little pieces out of the sky.

Snow! Snow! It's raining white flowers.
Sometimes I think white stars are falling.

Snow! Snow! A White Christmas!
But it's too late, for Christmas is past!

On the second occasion the children contributed individual stories but did not put them together to form a poem:

The snow looked like millions and millions of bugs up in the sky. It made me think of a ferris wheel going round.

You know that the snow was so little and white that it looked like little pieces of bread for birds.

The snow looks like burned popcorn way up in the sky but as it falls it looks like white popcorn for you and I.

The snow is white and when it flies it looks like stars falling. All at once it is snow you know. It always snows when you want it to snow.

Snow looks like atoms up in the sky.

The snow looks like hundreds and hundreds of bumble bees flying in the sky.

Evaluation

Children should not evaluate the creative products of others, for negative criticism is anathema to the urge to create. A child should evaluate his own work. He needs to know when he has done his best and when he needs new skills in order to express his ideas adequately. It is helpful, too, for him to know that his teacher is interested enough in him to hold him to his highest level of expression. Thus the child and the teacher work together. The child grows in creativity by sharing his products in such continuous evaluation and by improving the skills needed for expression of his ideas.

Encouraging Expressive Writing

As children gain confidence and independence in writing creatively the teacher can encourage them in the following ways:

1. By waiting for a child to bring in a product that he wishes to share with the group. Creativity does not flow from a production line. Rhymes, poems, or prose are not turned out in units at the rate of a poem a week or a composition a day. When the child is ready, he will bring in a poem.

2. By welcoming as a gift the verse, poem, story, or song entrusted to her by the child. She must regard his work as a finished product and never

write on his copy. Experience shows that publicly criticizing creative writing results in imitation or in curtailment of writing. Either is unfortunate.

3. By correcting functional writing such as notices, memoranda, letters, captions, reports, and handwriting to provide compelling motives for neatness, accuracy of information, correct spelling, punctuation, and learning the mechanics of grammar and usage. Achievement in functional writing helps a child maintain standards of correct form that enable him to express his ideas with clarity and that give him a sense of pride. Achievement of this sort, together with the satisfaction he receives from creative writing, provides the inner satisfaction that every individual needs.

4. By providing a special place in the room for depositing one's writing until the group can get together to share the writing they have been doing.

The teacher will discover that children's dancing, dramatics, music, painting, design, and writing all spring from the same creative source. Confidence and faith on the part of the teacher are all that are needed to set it free. Once the teacher has helped the child discover and release this creativity, the child is ready to go forward on his own. He himself has the drive to express what he feels and the confidence to go ahead and say it. Once he knows what he wants to say and loves to do it, the road is clear.

In the beginning, the child cannot do this for himself. Only as the teacher builds the child's faith in himself through expressing her belief in him is she developing his creative expression.

QUESTIONS AND ACTIVITIES

1. What is the relation between communication and expressive writing?

2. Teachers have often interpreted the goal of democratic education as identical opportunities for all pupils. In what sense might this prove to be undemocratic?

3. What is the teacher's role in expressive writing?

4. Visit a third-grade class and try to see samples of writing. What is the attitude of the children toward sharing their products?

5. Make a case study of a child who is exceptionally creative in writing. Try to determine the factors that contribute to his creativity.

6. Do you see any evidence of a relationship between expressive writing ability and academic achievement?

7. There are two points of view on creative writing. One holds that the province of creativity is the child's own, that neither theme nor method of treatment may come from the teacher, that only a spontaneous expression of a reaction to a strong emotion unsolicited by the teacher constitutes creative expression. The other view holds that although this type of expression is desirable, many forms of functional writing could also be considered creative. With which view do you agree? Why? Defend your position on the basis of your knowledge of art, creativity, and children.

SELECTED READINGS

Applegate, Mauree. *Helping Children Write.* Scranton, Pa.: International Text-book Co., 1949.

Applegate, Mauree. "Learning to Associate with the High and the Beautiful," *Grade Teacher*, 74:34–35, April 1957.

Applegate, Mauree. "To Write Imaginatively," *Grade Teacher*, 74:26, March 1957.

Belt, Estelle. "Creative Writing," *Grade Teacher*, 70:40, April 1953.

Bracken, Kathryn A. "My First Graders Write Original Stories," *The Instructor*, 66:81, 90, February 1957.

Buckley, Helen. "Children Communicate through Writing," *Childhood Education*, 33:162–164, December 1956.

Burrows, Alvina, *et al. They All Want to Write.* Englewood Cliffs, N.J.: Prentice-Hall, Inc., 1952.

Cole, Natalie. "Creative Writing for Therapy," *Elementary English*, 22:124, April 1945.

Devon, Getrude. "Creative Writing," *The Instructor*, 66:81, December 1957.

Green, Arthur S. "Children Create Pictures and Stories," *Grade Teacher*, 73:66, October 1956.

Hall, Robert D. "Creative Writing, a Psychological Tool," *Elementary English*, 31:25–29, January 1954.

Hall, Robert D. "Motivation for Creative Writing," *Elementary English*, 32:154–156, March 1955.

Herrick, Virgil, and Leland B. Jacob (eds.). *Children and the Language Arts.* Englewood Cliffs, N.J.: Prentice-Hall, Inc., 1955.

Hutchenson, Eleanor J. "Improve Reading by Writing," *Grade Teacher*, 74:44, January 1956.

Johnson, Gladys O. "Poetry Study Then and Now," *Grade Teacher*, 40:72, September 1957.

Kyte, George C. *The Elementary School Teacher at Work.* New York: The Dryden Press, Inc., 1957.

McKee, Paul. *Language in the Elementary School.* Boston: Houghton Mifflin Company, 1939.

Meltzer, Ida S. "Writing Poetry is Fun," *Grade Teacher*, 74:117, April 1956.

National Council of Teachers of English. *Language Arts for Today's Children.* New York: Appleton-Century-Crofts, Inc., 1954.

Peavy, Katherine B. "Get Them to Write," *The Instructor*, 66:5, January 1957.

Roach, Bonita Marie. "The Cartoon Story," *The Instructor*, 67:34, October 1957.

Shane, Harold G. "Research Helps in Teaching the Language Arts," *Childhood Education*, 31:67, March 1954.

Sollars, Sophia. "Poems for Children by Children," *Grade Teacher*, 70:8, May 1953.

Strickland, Ruth. *Language Arts in the Elementary School.* Boston: D. C. Heath & Company, 1957.

Wagner, David. "Why Indifference or Hatred toward Poetry," *Education Digest*, 20:64, March 1954.

Zollinger, Marian. "Children Don't Just Express," *The Instructor*, 67:41, May 1958.

The power to speak well and think right will reward the man who approaches the art of discourse with the love of wisdom and love of honour.

— ISOCRATES

COMMUNICATION SKILLS

Speech

Speech is the apex of the language arts. To become effective in communication it is necessary for the child to assume his place in the group. In order to do this he must know how to think critically and to express his ideas clearly and accurately. He must be able to gather information from others by careful, critical, and respectful listening. He must be able to phrase his questions clearly and concisely. All these things he must be able to do in order to get along well with others.

Realizing that speech is so important, the school is placing increasingly more emphasis on the language arts — listening, reading, writing, and speaking. Increased recognition is being given to teaching speech even in the preschool and primary grades.

The child's speech has, of course, been established before he comes to school. Many children are handicapped because they come to school poorly equipped in their habits of speech. There is now, however, general recognition of the fact that, although children have begun to talk when they enter school, they go right on learning to talk better or worse well into adult life. Thus, an adequate speech program will ensure their talking better. The school that provides an adequate program is meeting the needs both of the child and of society.

In order for the child to improve in his skills of communication, the school must help him develop language facility. The child must become increasingly able to use language easily and satisfactorily. He must know how to select the right word without doubt and how to use it without hesitation.

The Responsibility of the Teacher

It is important for the teacher to have a clear concept of the inter-dependence of thought and speech. When the child says to the teacher: "I know what I mean, but I can't say it," the teacher recognizes that the child is not yet "at home" with the language; he has not had enough experiences in thinking and speaking to have the "feel" of it. The task of the teacher, at whatever level, is to help children attain basic language facility. To accomplish this, guided practice is essential.

Before the teacher can be considered qualified to guide this phase of the child's education, she must have an awareness of the importance of the "what" as well as the "how" of what is being said. Only then can she assume responsibility for helping the child attain the command of oral language essential to satisfying his needs for communication. The teacher who recognizes her task and assumes the responsibility must keep in mind the following minimum essentials of a good learning environment in which to develop the speech program:

1. The teacher must help each child to achieve a basic language facility.
2. The teacher must help each child to develop appropriate speech habits.
3. The teacher must provide daily opportunity for practice in meaningful speech situations.
4. The oral language program should stimulate participation in the creative arts.
5. The oral language program should afford opportunity to practice the democratic process in the classroom.

Guides for Teaching Speech

The child must have something important to say. Even the young child can learn that the speaker has a responsibility to tell something important to the group. The contribution must, however, be judged in terms of the child's level of ability, maturity, language skills, and need for recognition. The goal is to help the child improve his language skills. In nursery school and kindergarten the timid child may not be able to give all the information he has because of timidity. But as soon as it is feasible, the child should learn that a person must have something worthwhile to say to the group and that he must know what he is talking about.

The child must communicate. The good speaker makes a conscious effort to interest the group in what he is saying. He watches their reactions; he notices whether or not they are responding. By entering into the experience about which he is telling, he recreates the thoughts and feelings to which the children respond. The teacher can check on the quality of the communication by looking for two essentials: an understanding of the content of words as they are spoken, and sense of the circular reciprocal quality of communication.

The child must organize his ideas.   He must make his listeners understand what he is saying as well as be interested in it. His thoughts should be ordered in a logical sequence. Whether a child tells a story, gives a report, or makes an announcement, he should have his material organized.

The child's voice and diction should not hinder communication.   The child in nursery school and kindergarten is learning so many new things and is so eager to express the ideas that are bubbling over within him that he tends to block in his speech. Many mothers become unduly disturbed and accentuate the problem. If the child suffers from blocking or other speech problems, the teacher, speech therapist, or counselor should work with the parents to understand the best way of helping the child with his difficulty.

The child should use speech to take care of his social needs.   Young children in general are interested in themselves. They soon, however, like to work and play with another person. Later they broaden the circle to include a few more children. By the time they are in the intermediate school they enjoy gangs and work well in large groups. To live effectively in a group the child can adapt to his social world through speech, and through group discussion he can participate in group decisions. Speech is a two-way process, a social activity. One does not talk to oneself. Parents and inexperienced teachers may think a nursery-school or kindergarten child is talking to himself, but in reality he is talking to a "friend." The fact that the friend is invisible to all other eyes is not important.

As a child matures, he should learn to adapt to the social group through speech. He can be taught the skills of the group processes even in kindergarten and the primary grades. In some classes, all questions involving decisions are settled by the teacher; in others they are settled by a show of hands. With the good teachers, however, children are taught to make decisions through the use of language in problem-solving. It is better for children to reach decisions by defining the problem, examining it, finding possible solutions, evaluating them, and finally deciding on the best solution.

Grade Placement of Activities

To guide the teacher in planning an adequate speech program, a chart listing the aims of speech education appears on pages 224–231. The characteristics of language growth in children and a list of speaking activities are presented. The activities have been organized for three levels — the nursery school, the kindergarten, and the primary grades.

How soon such learning can be accomplished differs with individuals, with groups, and with teachers. The attainment of speaking skills is a developmental process. As children mature, they investigate, share ideas, think, and discuss in group situations with increasing proficiency. How much each child

Speech Development

Aims in Teaching Communication	Language Growth of Children Two to Nine Years Old	Speaking Activities
	IN THE NURSERY SCHOOL	
To use speech as a means of self-expression.	"No" expresses the two's attitude. He begins to express feelings through words instead of through blows.	"Talking it out" when he feels hostile. Expressing inner feelings in rhythm and play.
To speak freely and listen to others.	The twos recite nursery rhymes and use short sentences. The threes and fours invent new words. The threes and fours boast. The threes respond to verbal guidance. The threes listen to adult words. Fours carry on conversation with adults.	Conversation with other children. Listening to others. Conversation with visitors about home, pets, weather, toys, new baby.
To listen to stories appreciatively.	Twos, threes, fours all enjoy nursery rhymes. Threes like simple stories. Fours listen raptly to stories and rhymes.	Listening to teacher tell stories or read them. Watching illustrations.
To use language to create a story.	Fours create stories.	Making up original stories. Repeating rhymes with teacher.
To take advantage of a large number of activities.	The threes and fours can carry a tune. The fours repeat entire verses of songs.	Retelling a short story or reporting an excursion.

To express oneself in dramatic play.	Threes like being simple animals and acting nursery rhymes. Fours like imaginative play.	Dramatic play in doll house, with blocks, and so forth.
To participate in group expression.	Threes and fours chant coined words with rhythmic swing.	Repeating a chant.
To acquire a larger and more meaningful vocabulary.	Children at nursery school age want to know what words mean.	Talking with teacher.
To seek answers to questions.	Threes begin to ask questions.	Learning to use inquiry.
To use language to explain one's actions.	Fours like to explain.	Explaining why he did something a certain way. Explaining how to do something.

IN THE KINDERGARTEN

To talk fluently about experiences. To listen appreciatively to others.	Fives like to talk. Conversation is ego-centered — pets, hobbies, and arguments. They like to tell what happened at home, on trips.	Conversation about items of interest to the child, such as home activities, family, birthdays, holidays, play activities, weather, pets, trips, visits, new clothes, new experiences.
To use speech as a tool to adjust to social situations. To take advantage of opportunities for developing language through a variety of experiences.	Fives greet friends, say "Please," "Thank you," "I beg your pardon," "Excuse me." They introduce mother or friend, acknowledge introductions, invite visitors to come in.	Greeting each other and strangers. Introducing parents or friends. Serving as hosts or hostesses to mothers or children from other grades. Saying "Thank you," "Please," and other forms of the social amenities.

Language Growth of Children Two to Nine Years Old

Aims in Teaching Communication	Language Growth of Children Two to Nine Years Old	Speaking Activities
		Dictating a letter to the parent who went with the children to the zoo, or to the firemen who showed them around the fire-station, or to a child who is in the hospital.
To listen to stories appreciatively. To tell a short, simple story. To participate in choral speaking of favorite poems. To tell the story ending when the teacher asks them to do this.	Fives like to listen to stories. Some like to read. Children of five can narrate a complete occurrence and repeat a familiar story in sequence.	Listening to the teacher tell and read stories. Listening to children tell stories. Creating stories and dictating to the teacher. "Reading" the stories from the chart. Repeating with the teacher favorite refrains of nursery rhymes or stories. Retelling a simple story to the group. Participating in choral speaking.
To contribute information to the class.	Fives seek information. They ask innumerable questions. Fives are interested in using new, large and colorful words.	Explaining the work accomplished during the work period. Explaining how to do a certain task or how to get to a particular place. Explaining standards of behavior on trips. Explaining and interpreting the picture painted during the work period. Telling why they did work as they did.

To begin to take part in group planning.	Fives like to make decisions. They exhibit increasing willingness to share and are beginning to be interested in the welfare of others.	Planning the work of the class. Planning the work of small groups. Planning the standards of the group. Planning activities for entertaining parents. Discussing the work the group has done. Making plans for tomorrow. Evaluating the work done. Discussing the behavior of the group during the fire drill or trip.
To express oneself in dramatic play.	Children of five are highly dramatic. They like to imitate adults. Both girls and boys play in the doll house and take the roles of adults. Boys and girls choose the same activities in the kindergarten. Fives are highly imaginative, but some are beginning to distinguish fact from fancy.	Dramatic play in the doll house. Role playing of events such as going to the dentist. Dramatizing stories. Dramatizing nursery rhymes. Using hand or stick puppets to tell nursery rhymes and stories.

IN THE PRIMARY GRADES

To talk freely and easily about new experiences. To listen with increasing ability to get other's point of view. To increase fund of ideas through listening to literature, listening to music, looking at and "reading" pictures, taking trips, listening to people who come in to talk to the group.	Children of six, seven, and eight are interested in almost everything. Sixes use language aggressively. Sevens are more introspective. They like to talk about themselves. They are likely to use language to complain.	Conversation about topics of mutual interest or class activities. Relating personal experiences. Talking over the trip on returning from an excursion.

227

Aims in Teaching Communication	Language Growth of Children Two to Nine Years Old	Speaking Activities
	Eights talk a great deal. They tell tales, boast, exaggerate. Some prefer to talk to adults and engage in real social conversation with adults. Nines talk things over with adults.	Using the telephone to give and receive invitations. Using the telephone to deliver simple messages. Ordering supplies. Taking simple messages.
To use the telephone correctly.	Sixes use the telephone with ease. Sevens do considerable phoning. They call home to see about lunch money or after-school plans. They use the phone for helping mother with grocery list. They receive and send messages.	
To respond easily to simple social situations.	Sixes enjoy offering and receiving hospitality from their peers. Some sevens like to introduce their mothers to their friends. Eights use language fluently. Nines are more cooperative and make plans far in advance, without adult direction.	Giving and receiving invitations. Making introductions. Responding to introductions. Serving as host and hostess to visitors. Greeting guests. Showing visitors around the room. Carrying on an interesting conversation with visitors.
To tell stories for others. To listen appreciatively to stories.	Primary children respond to humor. Primary children can listen to stories for twenty minutes with courtesy and obvious enjoyment.	Listening to stories read or told by the teacher. Telling stories to the group.

Sixes like legends and fables as well as stories about themselves and the activities of other children.

Sevens have wider interests; they are interested in stories about nature, animals, space ships and rockets, children of other countries. They like myths, legends, some fanciful tales, and stories about grown-up occupations.

Eights show interest in primitive cultures. They also are turning to stories of adventure and humor. They still enjoy stories of children, animals, and wee folk.

Nines love adventure stories.

Telling stories the children have created.
Listening to a story the teacher reads and making up the ending.

To tell an experience.
To report an event or activity in an orderly manner.
To stick to the main point and develop the point by means of a simple sequence of ideas.

Sixes show a marked interest in construction, transportation, and science.

Sevens want to acquire knowledge of natural and social sciences, through excursions, projects, and celebration of holidays.

Eights show a greater interest in people of foreign lands and like to read about strange and distant places. They are extremely interested in nature and science and they have numerous hobbies.

Participating in a sharing period.
Reporting materials read.
Explaining pictures they have painted or colored.
Explaining a game or process.
Reporting on events, seen or heard.
Reporting on individual or group activities.

To read aloud a simple poem or story and share it with the group.

Sixes, sevens, and eights like to read aloud to the group.

Reading a story or poem aloud.
Reading reports aloud.

[*Speech Development, continued*]

Aims in Teaching Communication	Language Growth of Children Two to Nine Years Old	Speaking Activities
	Nines are getting to be avid readers. Some nines also like choral speaking.	Choral speaking with children selecting the poem and deciding on the interpretation.
To select a topic for discussion. To share information by means of group discussion. To settle issues through group discussion.	Children cannot plan far in advance. Sixes need help in making choices. They should not be confronted with too many alternatives. Sevens find it easier to make up their minds but harder to change. They engage in genuine argument in which they put forth reasons in support of the assertions they make. Sevens are methodical and like to plan their day. Sevens are very critical. Eights make up their minds easily but they listen to reason and are willing to change their minds. Eights verbalize ideas and concerns. They begin to understand relationships of cause and effect. Eights take criticism if it is sincerely given. They want to improve in what they do. Nines listen to others.	Planning activities (both of the class as a whole and sub-groups). Planning and preparing for trips and excursions. Talking about the trips. Talking about the benefits gained from the trips. Discussing the work of the members of the class. Evaluating work. Settling an issue through group discussion.

To engage in dramatic play.

To dramatize a story so that the listeners can follow it readily and enjoy it.

Children from six to nine enjoy dressing up and playing appropriate roles, which they not only play but live. Several children will make up a play, work on it by themselves, and present it to the group.

Sixes increase in ability to tell fact from fantasy. They like spontaneous dramatic play and creative dramatics, not a formal play. They pretend to be a pony, an airplane, or a space ship. For them, a block or piece of furniture can be anything they want it to be. They play school, house, library, grocery store, traveling by boat, train, bus, or plane. Outdoors they choose more active games.

Sevens want realism in their play. They play transportation activities, community helpers such as postman, fireman, policeman, grocery man. Outdoor games are active. Girls tend to be dancers and prima donnas; boys tend toward television stars and gun play.

Sevens, eights, and nines all enjoy putting on a show or playing a dramatic role.

Each age group participates in dramatizing events and activities. They impersonate things and people as well as animals.

Nines enjoy dramatization and creative play.

Dramatizing every-day occurrences.

Pantomiming.

Playing a story or poem with stick or hand puppets.

Dramatic play in the room using doll house and later building post offices, florist shops, markets, stations, airports, in the room.

Dramatizing puppet plays.

Choral speaking.

achieves depends upon his ability, his rate of growth, his previous experiences, and the characteristics and dynamics of the group to which he belongs.

Pertinent items about growth in language arts, collected by the writer from various authoritative sources and by observation, are listed to give the reader an idea of trends of growth at the various age levels. The reader must remember that these items are only approximate averages of many children observed under similar conditions. Because each child is an individual, he develops in his own pattern. Thus the individual may not fit the norm; even some whole age groups will not fit the pattern, for groups differ even more widely than individuals.

The speaking activities listed are by no means exhaustive; they are merely suggestive. The major role of the teacher is to guide the development of the communication skills. Knowing that children differ greatly in innate ability, she must select the activities that will best help each child as an individual and as a member of the group. While dramatic play in the doll house will challenge one kindergarten child, another will be challenged by talking to the policeman who takes him across the street. The teacher should provide a variety of experiences from which children may choose. As W. C. Olson and B. L. Hughes say, "The child . . . reacts selectively to the surroundings that are supplied and creates his own world of experience within them. He tends to reject the experience for which he is not ready." [13]

The teacher should keep constantly in mind the interrelatedness of growth. In considering the chart, she must remember that ability to speak is but one phase of the child's development. Her job is to build on all the strengths of the child, including those in language.

Evaluating the Speech Program

The objectives of teaching speech naturally form the basis for evaluation. Thus, the teacher who keeps specific objectives in mind is more likely not only to plan an adequate curriculum but also to have a basis for evaluation already at hand. The objectives serve as useful criteria for judging the adequacy of the program:

1. To communicate with others.
2. To express thoughts and feelings.
3. To make friends with others.
4. To talk out problems together and arrive at solutions which represent the best thought of the group.[14]

---

[13] W. C. Olson and B. L. Hughes, "Concepts of Growth: Their Significance to Teachers," *Childhood Education*, 21:1, October 1944.

[14] Letitia Raubicheck, *Your Voice and Your Speech*, Englewood Cliffs, N.J.: Prentice-Hall, Inc., 1953), pp. 6–7.

Summary

The communication skills are among the most important for the growing child. Through them he learns to understand and interact with the outside world. A child's initial learning comes through listening. Just as he listens to learn, so does he later read to learn. His reading readiness program prepares him by relating reading to the things he already knows. When he has learned to receive communication from others, he must learn to express his own ideas. Writing therefore includes not only the techniques but also the skills of expression and creation. At the apex of all the communication arts is speech, without which no child can communicate effectively with the people in his environment. A curriculum must include all these skills if it is to meet the needs of the child and prepare him to live in a democratic society.

QUESTIONS AND ACTIVITIES

1. Record a conversation, a poem, or a song that you hear during an observation in a preschool or kindergarten. Note the circumstances under which it occurred.

2. What are some of the most serious consequences of allowing a child to persist in "baby talk?" What can the teacher do to discourage this type of speaking?

3. What is your idea of the relative importance of form and content in oral communication in the first grade?

4. How may the teacher motivate children in the second and third grades so that they will practice the correct forms of expression?

5. How may instruction in all the language arts be integrated with other areas of instruction in the kindergarten and primary grades? In the nursery school?

6. Make a list of stories and poems well suited to listening by five-year-olds. Which are best told? Which best read? Experiment with a group of kindergarten children to help you determine the answer.

SELECTED READINGS

Akin, Johnnye. *And So We Speak*. Englewood Cliffs, N.J.: Prentice-Hall, Inc., 1958.

Anderson, Virgil G. *Improving the Child's Speech*. New York: Oxford University Press, 1953.

Eisenson, Jon. *The Improvement of Voice and Diction*. New York: The Macmillan Company, 1958.

Fessenden, Seth Arthur. *The Teacher Speaks*. Englewood Cliffs, N.J.: Prentice-Hall, Inc., 1954.

Long, Charles. *Will Your Child Learn to Talk Correctly?* Albuquerque, N.M.: The New Mexico Publishing Co., 1957.

National Education Association, Department of Elementary School Principals. *Role of Speech in the Elementary School*. Washington, D. C.: The Association, 1947.

Newby, Hayes A. *Audiology*. New York: Appleton-Century-Crofts, Inc., 1958.

Ogilvie, Mardel. *Speech in the Elementary School*. New York: McGraw-Hill Book Company, Inc., 1954.

Pronovost, W. L. *Speaking and Listening in the Elementary School*. New York: Longmans, Green and Company, 1959.

Pruiz, John J. "General Speech Training in the Elementary School," *Quarterly Journal of Speech*, 36: 520–523, December 1950.

Rassmussen, Carrie. *Speech Methods in the Elementary School*. New York: The Ronald Press Company, 1949.

Schreiber, Flora Rheta. *Your Child's Speech*. New York: G. P. Putnam's Sons, 1956.

Templin, Mildred C. *Certain Language Skills in Children*. Minneapolis: University of Minnesota Press, 1957.

Van Riper, Charles, and Katherine Butler. *Speech in the Elementary Classroom*. New York: Harper & Brothers, 1955.

Walsh, Gertrude. *Sing your Way to Better Speech*. New York: E. P. Dutton & Company, Inc., 1948.

Ward, Winifred. *Playmaking with Children*, Second Edition. New York: Appleton-Century-Crofts, Inc., 1957.

11

Social Studies

. . . Most, if not all, human problems can be solved by human beings working together cooperatively rather than in conflict with one another.

— WALTER STARKE

Social studies start with social living, but social studies are more than social living. What we call social studies is content as well as process. Although the process is the initial referent, it is not the entire program; a unified program includes both process and content. It is on just this point that many teachers are confused. They read descriptions of programs for social studies in which emphasis is on the "how" and in which the "what" is ignored.

In Chapter 10 we studied the process by which problems are solved. Note the similarity between the objectives in the speech program and the objectives of the social-living program. The speech objectives are:

1. To communicate with others.
2. To express our thoughts and feelings.

3. To make friendly contacts with others.
4. To discuss problems and arrive at solutions that represent the best thinking of the group.

The aims of classes in social living are:

1. To help pupils work together, understand, and get along with others.
2. To improve the pupils' ability to listen and to communicate orally and in writing.
3. To develop useful skills.[1]

The objectives, as one can readily see, are essentially the same for both. Activities in the social-living program are permeated by the necessity for oral communication in groups. Conversation, discussion, interview, and many other speech skills are used. Since these skills are already being learned as language arts, the social studies curriculum should concern itself primarily with the content, not with the process.

What We Mean by Social Studies

Preston defines the social studies as "those portions of the social sciences that are selected for use in teaching."[2] The social sciences include those fields of knowledge that are concerned with man's social behavior, his social life, and his social institutions. The fields that are drawn upon by the program of social studies in the elementary school and that serve as content are history, sociology, economics, geography, political science, government, anthropology, and psychology. The better the teacher's command of these fields, the better her ability to guide children in the social studies.

Social studies are concerned with people — how they solve the problems relating to their physical needs for food, clothing, and shelter and how they solve the problems of getting along together in small and in large groups.

The Nature of the Social Studies Program

There are three distinguishing characteristics of the social studies program: (1) it is social; (2) its content can be drawn from any one or more of a number of subject fields; (3) it can be organized in any of several ways.

PLACE IN THE CURRICULUM

Notice that the curriculum includes both social living and social studies:

Social living — in which the child learns the process of getting along in the group.

[1] Board of Education of the City of New York, "Suggestions to Teachers of Experimental Core Classes," *Curriculum Bulletin Series*, No. 2, 1951.
[2] Ralph C. Preston, *Teaching Social Studies in the Elementary Schools*, Revised Edition (New York: Rinehart & Company, Inc., 1958), p. 4.

Language arts or communication skills — in which the child acquires the basic tools for listening, reading, writing, spelling, and speaking.

Social studies — in which the child learns the facts, skills, and attitudes essential to an understanding of the relationship of man to his social environment.

Science and mathematics — in which the child learns the facts, processes, and skills related to reasoning and an understanding of the world of nature and of quantitative relationships.

Creative arts — in which the child experiences both release and that discipline that the true enjoyment of an art demands and affords.

It is evident that the social studies, like the language arts, can serve as the core or organizing center of a curriculum.

BOTH PROCESS AND CONTENT

There are, as has been pointed out, two aspects in the teaching of social studies. One concerns the process — the process of getting along with people, working, planning, and developing a curriculum; and the other concerns the content — drawn from the social science fields. The younger the child, the more the emphasis should be on the former, on the various personal relationships experienced in everyday social living in the classroom.

The Purposes of the Social Studies

The purpose of teaching social studies is twofold: (1) to help the child develop the skills, insights, and moral qualities that are essential to effective citizenship in a democratic society, and (2) to understand the concepts that

Cooperation is one of the democratic skills that can be learned in the preschool and kindergarten.

describe and explain human society, to the end that better human understanding may be achieved.

The teacher will be more likely to provide appropriate situations for learning in the social studies if she defines her objectives and keeps them before her. Such basic objectives prescribe that she promote the development of:

1. Attitudes and behavior necessary for good citizenship in our society.
2. Skill in problem-solving and in group processes.
3. Knowledge and understanding of society.
4. Skill in using appropriate tools to solve problems. These include the study skills, the creative arts, and critical thinking.

Sequence in the Social Studies Program

Sequence in this sphere has been based largely on the idea of the expanding community. Theoretically, the child is interested in people in the home, in the school, and in the community. Children study the agencies within the community that help the family meet its basic needs; they study basic social functions. But throughout the primary grades the child does not need to go beyond his neighborhood or his community to find the area for his social studies. He progresses from the home to the school, then to the community. Later, in the intermediate grades, he moves on to the city, the state, the region, the nation, and the community of nations.

This concept of a sequence of learning experiences based on the expanding community stems from the belief that social studies should start with the ordinary affairs of school and home life. From participation in the solution of problems found in the immediate environment, children extend their horizons gradually but surely to include the whole earth. Note, for example, the stand taken in the recommendations by the Commission of the Social Studies in 1934:

> That experiences in the grades need to be carefully selected and wisely directed towards major concepts to be built up gradually is likewise a conception gaining rapidly in consequence.[3]

In a study undertaken in 1934 an overlapping of certain topics was revealed, and efforts were made to map out certain areas for specific grade levels in order to prevent such duplication. The explanation was that

> . . . there is little objective evidence to indicate that young children are interested in people of other lands. . . . It is doubtful whether the study of foreign lands should come below the fifth grade. Perhaps the study of nations from the standpoint of geography and history may be postponed until the junior high.[4]

[3] American Historical Association, Commission of the Social Studies, *Conclusions and Recommendations* (New York: Charles Scribner's Sons, 1934).

[4] Joy M. Lacey, *Teaching Social Studies in the Elementary School* (Minneapolis, Minn.: Burgess Publishing Co., 1941), p. 49.

It is in harmony with this theory that many of the programs in the social studies have been organized. The kindergarten and first three grades are thus to concern themselves with living in the home, the family group, and the school, the neighborhood, and the larger immediate community. The intermediate grades broaden the information about the community by a study of the geography of the state in which the child lives and its historical background, leading on to a study of the various sections of the United States and eventually to world history and world geography.

On the basis of such trends in planning the curriculum, the question arises, do the social studies stand in need of modification to meet the challenge of today's world?

The Challenge of Social Studies

In general, thinking about the social studies has not undergone much change. In an article entitled "Social Studies for Today," [5] for instance, the author makes use of the various communities of men as a sequence of grade emphases. Beginning at the kindergarten or first-grade level with a study of the family, he advocates studying each of the communities in terms of nine activities that people everywhere and throughout history have always carried on.[6] Multiple membership in expanding communities is the basis for allocating emphasis to various grades. The emphasis is first on the home. Within this area a wide range of experiences related to the nine social functions can be planned for the fives and sixes. For example, transporting people and goods suggests that transportation in one's own family includes roller skates, the family car, or a baby carriage. The second-grade child, building on those concepts he has learned, goes forth into the school and neighborhood. The neighborhood helps children anticipate the larger community in which their school is located. By the time the child is in third grade, he is ready for the local community. Here the child is free to explore the nine basic activities. Not until the child reaches the fifth grade does he study Inter-America; not until then may he turn his attention to cultures other than his own. Though all this is good in its way, it is not enough. It presents no challenge to the children. And we prepare them to live only in yesterday's world when we restrict their experiences to the sequence merely of home, school, and community.

Today's child cannot remember when there was no television, when there were no airplanes, no atom bombs, no rockets and space ships, no United Nations, no exciting events halfway across the world. For today's child the

5 Paul Hanna, "Social Studies for Today," *NEA Journal*, 45:36–38, April 1956.
6 These activities include (1) protecting and conserving life, health, resources and properties; (2) producing, distributing, and consuming food, clothing, shelter; (3) creating and producing tools; (4) transporting people and goods; (5) communicating; (6) providing education; (7) providing recreation; (8) organizing and governing; and (9) expressing esthetic impulses.

world has shrunk. The child attends school with children from across the ocean — displaced children from all parts of the world. He rubs shoulders with them; he learns their language. In order to understand them, he must know the cultures whence they came. This thought is succinctly stated in the words of Dr. Harold Flensmark, President of the *Organización de Mundial Educación Preescolar*: "To be truly able to help a person I must be able to understand more than he understands. But first I must understand all that he understands." [7]

The child must be taught to appreciate the differences that exist in people and cultures, not merely to accept or tolerate them. Today's child cannot look for the stabilized world for which his parents were prepared. In order to live in this changing society he must be equipped to meet the future courageously, with wisdom born of meeting and solving problems that are significant and vital to him.

The Role of the Teacher in Guiding Social Studies

The teacher of today must help the child improve the skills essential to living and surviving in this changing, shrinking world. She must first teach him the tools with which to work; she must then provide opportunities for a broader base of experiences and learning experiences that place a premium on hard work and study. She must help the child learn the essential facts and develop the attitudes by which he can understand and cooperate with other peoples. How can she go about such a task?

The learning experiences should of course be appropriate to his level of development. Such experiences include working and playing together, working alone to develop creative abilities and inner resources, taking increasing

[7] Lecture at The Association for Childhood Education, International Study Conference. Washington, D.C. April, 1957.

Visits to nearby places of interest lead the child toward exploration of the broader community.

responsibility for desirable behavior, developing feelings of security and adequacy, developing social skills, practicing democratic living in the classroom, developing skill in group processes, developing critical thinking, understanding one's fellow man through a study of cultures, and developing real world understanding.

From Nursery School Through the Primary Grades

IN THE NURSERY SCHOOL

The world of the nursery-school child can be expanded through excursions to the farm, the fire station, the grocery store, and so forth. In fact, any trip that is not too tiring for children or too difficult to plan and that provides opportunity for learning what the community is really like is worth while.

The teacher must know her children, know the resources of the community, and have two or three adults along to take care of any emergencies. She must plan ahead for transportation and toilet facilities as well as for permission from the parents of the children. Parents are frequently willing to help with the transportation; before taking the responsibility, however, parents and teacher should check on the possible indemnity factors in case of accidents.

Excursions bring rewards in the form of new ideas expressed in dramatic play class projects. Children who attended a school near a chicken hatchery, for example, brought baby chicks back with them and fed and cared for them until Easter.

IN THE KINDERGARTEN AND PRIMARY GRADES

Social studies are also concerned with the development of an understanding of human relationships. The child adjusts to society while he adjusts to the group with whom he works and plays at school. He makes a beginning in understanding the world. He learns ways of working with others to solve problems. The experiences of young children in social living form the basis for the more organized social studies curriculum later on.

Working and playing together. To think of the other person is something that children have to learn. Sharing and carrying on work in a cooperative manner require both understanding and the skills of communication. Before he has learned to share, if a child wants another's toy, he grabs. Here the teacher has a responsibility to teach the difference between what is "mine" and what is "yours." She must teach the child to take turns, to share, and to give someone else the limelight. It is not easy for a child who has been the center of attention at home for some three, four, or five years to share the stage with many others.

Working alone to develop creative abilities and inner resources. The teacher will not insist, however, that the child always engage in group ac-

Learning to obey the rules and to give everyone a chance to participate is a social-living skill.

tivity. There are times when children need to work alone. Living calls not only for skills in group processes but for skills that are developed through creative thinking. Creative thinking is not the product of group participation or constant group living.

Developing socially approved behavior. Children are eager for order; they do not want chaos, even when they are responsible for it.

Children need the security that grows out of a knowledge that the teacher accepts them, that she is their friend and has a real affection for them, but that she expects them to take increasing responsibility for desirable behavior. Teacher and pupils should set standards of behavior together and then abide by the rules they have formulated. Although using a suggestive approach to behavior is good, it will not always work. Some children are so constituted or have been so conditioned that they do not understand this approach.

Behavior responses are learned. Although the teacher is responsible for finding the cause of individual behavior problems and working on it, she is also responsible to the group. When the behavior of any child endangers the physical or mental well-being of another, the teacher should step in and isolate the aggressive youngster. One of the reasons for his problem may be that he is overstimulated. If a child is asked to rest for a while, he usually feels better. Rest must be a privilege, however, not a punishment. The teacher varies her methods of guidance according to the needs of the child. Some children need more, some need less guidance. All of them need a teacher who with patience, kindness, and insight guides them from external discipline to self-discipline.

Developing feelings of security and adequacy in school. All children need the sense of security and adequacy that stems from a knowledge that one is wanted, loved, and valued. Though a teacher may find it more difficult to feel affection for a child who is ungainly, unkempt, and unscrubbed, this child probably needs acceptance and affection far more than the child of the golden curls, the sparkling eyes, and the pretty clothes. One important essential in teaching children is to be able emotionally to accept and value each child. Children intuitively sense when they are accepted intellectually rather than emotionally, and they react unfavorably toward the individual who feels no empathy with them.

Self-confidence is a by-product of such acceptance. Children need to know they are accepted by the teacher. She in turn can do much to help others accept the child, not by telling them to "be friends with Kathy" but by being friends with Kathy herself. Children are quick to follow the teacher's lead in this respect. The child who is helped to participate and engage in tasks in which he can succeed is likely to develop self-confidence. It is thus important for a teacher to study children to determine their special abilities and those areas in which they can achieve.

Developing social skills in the program. The daily living in the nursery school lends itself to the development of essential social skills. Opportunities for developing these skills are:

Opening. Sharing experiences, taking turns talking, listening to others.

Planning. Planning the day's activities in such a way that both the interests of the group and the interests of the individual are met, sharing materials, equipment, teacher, working in such a way as not to disturb those who are concentrating on other projects, thinking of the needs of others, caring for room responsibilities.

Clean-up time. Assuming responsibility for putting materials away, leaving the room in order for an afternoon group.

Evaluation and sharing. Listening courteously when others speak, taking turns, appreciating efforts of others, giving best judgment on solution of problems.

Outdoor period. Playing together as a group, taking turns, trying new activities, abiding by the rules, respecting physical prowess of others, taking turns in leadership, coming in at the designated time without protest.

Bathroom. Understanding the importance of washing hands after toileting, keeping bathroom clean, flushing toilets.

Midmorning juice. Washing hands before eating, showing courteous behavior at table, helping set table, passing food, and cleaning up after lunch.

Rest. Resting quietly so others can sleep, allowing children who are sleeping to rest until they wake up.

Group sharing experiences. Participating as a group in music, games, dramatics, and science.

Story time.   Building concepts of social living in story time, learning about other places and people as well as about people in the home and community.

PRACTICING DEMOCRATIC PRINCIPLES IN THE CLASSROOM

Such activities as taking turns, cooperating on a project, listening to and respecting the other person's point of view, recognizing that differences in color of skin do not mean inferiority — all these are a part of social studies in the preschool and primary grades as children learn to live together. No child is too young to learn such social relationships.

The classroom is ideal for the practice of skills essential in a democratic society. In the relatively protected atmosphere of the self-contained classroom, teacher and pupils propose and plan work, make decisions, and evaluate.

DEVELOPING SKILLS IN GROUP PROCESSES

With specific instruction children learn the skills of problem-solving. They learn to define a problem, then find an appropriate course of action, test its validity, think through the problem, and finally arrive at its best solution. These steps in problem-solving can be learned if the teacher knows them and is willing to teach them. Some of the most important aspects of democratic action are determining the objectives, formulating plans for realizing them, devising methods for putting these plans into action, evaluating the results in terms of improved social living, and selecting new purposes for continued cooperative action.

In engaging in such activities, the child improves his thinking; and as each child improves in the ability to think, the thinking of the group improves. The skills that the child learns in other spheres, such as the language arts — exploring, interviewing, creating, sharing, evaluating, listening, delegating, prac-

The child must learn tolerance and understanding in the classroom.

ticing, accepting, leading — are all brought to bear on the solution of problems in the social studies. In all preschool and primary-grade activities there is an opportunity for social living; the teacher should be continually aware of the opportunities for group planning in a democracy.

DEVELOPING SKILL IN CRITICAL THINKING

Preschool, kindergarten, and primary children should be encouraged to think. The child should learn to make decisions on the basis of reasoning rather than on purely emotional bases, on the basis of facts, not prejudice.

DEVELOPING ATTITUDES OF UNDERSTANDING

Through an understanding of good personal relationships in the classroom, children can learn to understand people of other cultures; indeed, love and understanding of one's fellow man begins in the classroom at the level of personal relationships. Appreciation of members of the group, and later appreciation of those outside the little circle of the classroom, should extend finally even beyond the community to those far from the world in which the child lives. Children are very much interested in learning about the countries from which their new-found playmates come. They are not worried about differences. Children are not born with prejudices; they learn them.

There is no place for racial, economic, ethnic, or religious prejudice in a classroom. Nor need one stop at mere tolerance; understanding goes far beyond tolerance. Understanding calls for a knowledge of various cultures.

One of the effective units for developing understanding is the intercultural unit. Experiments with this type of unit at different grade levels show evidence of growth in understanding of other peoples. The social studies program should not be crystallized at any level or type of organization. It should be the result of continuous study of children's needs and interests.

Evaluation

Check List for Evaluating the Social Studies Program

_____ 1. Opportunities are provided for children to expand their world beyond the home, school, and community in response to their needs, interests, and abilities.

_____ 2. Children learn the skills of the group process in planning and executing the program in social studies.

_____ 3. Individuals and groups are expected to assume increasing responsibility for behavior, for making decisions, and for abiding by the decisions of the group.

_____ 4. As the children mature, the program is organized around significant units of work cooperatively planned by children and teacher.

_____ 5. Children learn through the program that man lives in an ever-changing environment.

_____ 6. Emphasis is placed on the cultural, social, and educational factors of a problem.

_____ 7. Children learn to compare their environment with those of other regions and countries.

_____ 8. Teachers and pupils have made a survey of the resources which the community has to offer in studying and solving problems.

_____ 9. Learning experiences are varied and provide for individual differences in children.

_____10. The sequence of learning experiences provides for continuous growth through over-all cooperative planning among staff, principal, and supervisors.

_____11. The program is flexible. Teachers are free to select learning experiences from a number of suggested possibilities.

_____12. Evaluation is continuous on the basis of known objectives.

_____13. Learning experiences are sufficiently varied so every child can participate with satisfaction.

_____14. Children learn about the home, school, community, and the interdependence of people in the various communities and cultures.

_____15. Children learn about the social functions and institutions of society.

_____16. Children learn to use a variety of instructional materials in solving problems.

_____17. Special teachers correlate the arts with the social studies program.

Summary

Social studies begin with social living. Without losing sight of the need for acquiring useful information, the modern social studies program must enable each child to grow continuously in the abilities and skills needed for effective participation in a democratic society.

In addition to learning the processes for group living, the children should have a content drawn from the social sciences, organized around a significant problem. The quality of the social studies program is determined in the final analysis by whether or not the experiences are meaningful and useful to children.

In the past, the sequence of units in the social studies has been organized on an expanding community basis: the child moves from the immediate environment toward places, events, and peoples far removed in time and space. In view of the shrunken world in which children live today, however, the technological and scientific advances, the new media of communication, this is no longer the most realistic method of determining the sequence of experiences. Even small children are interested in other peoples far across the world; they are interested in knowing how they live, their customs and languages. Newer emphasis in social studies must include inter-cultural education, greater emphasis on historical backgrounds, and the study of communities from the standpoint of improvement.

QUESTIONS AND ACTIVITIES

1. Outline a social studies unit you would like to teach in a primary grade. Indicate how you would make use of the services of special teachers.

2. Analyze the program of social studies in a course of study and indicate in what way it meets and fails to meet the interests and needs of children.

3. Construct a simple interview test for primary grades dealing with foreign cultures. Administer it to one primary-grade child. Pool your results with those of other members of your class and draw conclusions as to the information possessed by primary children. Discuss the implications for the social studies program.

4. Discuss the differences in units that emphasize the community, the past, the social processes, and regions and cultures. Find one unit representative of each of these types and evaluate it.

5. Give several suggestions as to how the study of the community may be broadened to bring in relationships with the outside world. What is the value of units emphasizing the community?

6. Visit a playground and try to determine children's interests, social concepts, gaps of knowledge, and needs. What evidence do you have that children are interested primarily in the "here and now"? What evidence did you find to the contrary?

7. Start a social studies card file. When you see new instructional materials, make cards for them, with description, grade level, source, and your evaluation. Include such things as sources of free or inexpensive materials, films, filmstrips, slides, movies, flat mounts, texts, supplementary reading lists, and reference books for teacher and children.

SELECTED READINGS

The Association for Childhood Education. *Social Studies for Children.* Bulletin No. 97. Washington, D.C.: Government Printing Office, 1956.

Campbell, Doris. *How a Child Feels about Entering a Nursery Center.* New York: Committee on Mental Hygiene, 1948.

Cunningham, Ruth, *et al. Understanding Group Behavior of Boys and Girls.* New York: Bureau of Publications, Teachers College, Columbia University, 1954.

Foshay, Arthur W., *et al. Children's Social Values.* New York: Bureau of Publications, Teachers College, Columbia University, 1954.

Heffernan, Helen (ed.). *Guiding the Young Child.* Boston: D. C. Heath & Company, 1951.

Hilliard, Pauline. *Improving Social Learnings in the Elementary School.* New York: Bureau of Publications, Teachers College, Columbia University, 1954.

Horwich, Frances. "Orienting the Threes and Fours," *Childhood Education,* 26:10–13, September 1949.

Jarolimek, John. *Social Studies in Elementary Education.* New York: The Macmillan Company, 1959.

Johnson, Earl. *Theory and Practice of the Social Studies.* New York: The Macmillan Company, 1951.

Lacey, Joy M. *Teaching Social Studies in the Elementary School*. Minneapolis: Burgess Publishing Company, 1948.

Michaelis, John U. *Social Studies for Children in a Democracy*. Englewood Cliffs, N.J.: Prentice-Hall, Inc., 1950.

Miel, Alice. *Cooperative Procedures in Learning*. New York: Bureau of Publications, Teachers College, Columbia University, 1952.

Miel, Alice, and Peggy Brogan. *More Than Social Studies*. Englewood Cliffs, N.J.: Prentice-Hall, Inc., 1957.

Moffat, Maurice, and Hazel W. Howell. *Elementary Social Studies Instruction*. New York: Longmans, Green & Company, Inc., 1952.

National Society for the Study of Education. *Social Studies in the Elementary School*. Fifty-Sixth Yearbook, Part II. Chicago: The University of Chicago Press, 1957.

Preston, Ralph C. *Teaching Social Studies in the Elementary Schools*, Revised Edition. New York: Rinehart & Company, Inc., 1958.

Rehage, Kenneth J. "On Re-thinking the Social Studies Program," *Elementary School Journal*, 62:10–15, October 1956.

Rudolph, Marguerite. *Living and Learning in Nursery School*. New York: Harper & Brothers, 1954.

Stanley, William O., *et al*. (eds.). *Social Foundations of Education*. New York: The Dryden Press, Inc., 1956.

Stephens, Ada. *Providing Developmental Experiences for Young Children*. New York: Bureau of Publications, Teachers College, Columbia University, 1952.

Wesley, Edgar R., and Mary A. Adams. *Teaching Social Studies in the Elementary School*, Revised Edition. Boston: D. C. Heath & Company, 1952.

Wilcockson, Mary. *Social Education of Young Children*. Washington, D.C.: National Education Association, 1950.

Wills, Clarice D., and William H. Stegeman. *Living in the Kindergarten*, Revised Edition. Chicago: Follett Publishing Company, 1956.

Wills, Clarice D., and William H. Stegeman. *Living in the Primary Grades*. Chicago: Follett Publishing Company, 1956.

12

Science

Never tell a child anything he can discover for himself.

PESTALOZZI

"What makes it rain? Why does the sun set? What's in a cloud? What makes grass grow? Why does the wind blow? What keeps the airplane from falling? What will happen if . . . ?"

Children are scientists. They want answers to these questions, but they want to find the answers themselves. Helping children find answers makes teaching science a challenging responsibility. Science is everywhere: in the home, in the school, in the community.

The adult who is not interested in helping the child find the answers will not succeed in directing the child's insatiable curiosity about his environment. Young children are eager to experience and experiment. Because they want to find answers to their questions, their very eagerness and natural curiosity will force the teacher, whether she wants to or not, to deal with science in one way or another.

Suppose Jimmie comes rushing into the classroom one rainy morning with an earthworm dangling from his grubby hand, holding it out to his teacher for all to see. He is bringing a treasure to share with her. Does she respond in order to motivate his interest in nature or, not sharing his feelings, does she say to herself, "Ugh. A dirty, earthy, old worm that I don't know anything about and care less"? As she goes to the cupboard to get a glass container for the worm, she perhaps says in her "company" voice, "So you found a worm on the doorstep." She may even really try to put some enthusiasm in her voice, but it is a pretty feeble effort and it does not delude Jimmie. He turns away with a vague feeling of disappointment, and Miss Dart, too, has a feeling of uneasiness as she thinks, "He won't bother me again about a worm. But I should have been interested. Maybe I should do something about science."

Here was an opportunity missed. Jimmy might have learned that when it rains the worms that come out are fascinating to watch. Instead, he learned that Miss Dart did not like him to bring worms to school.

Miss Dart is not alone in her attitude. As a teacher, however, she has a responsibility for encouraging the child to learn. She is there to teach him, just as he is there to learn. How easily she might have turned the episode of the worm into a learning experience, not alone for Jimmie but for the group! She lost an opportunity for teaching a way of exploring the environment and a way of solving problems.

Objectives of Science Education

Children, as we have seen, are interested in the physical world as it relates to them. In order to guide their natural curiosity the teacher must have clear objectives on which to base learning. Blough, Schwartz, and Huggett have stated the objectives of elementary science as follows:

> 1. . . . The study of science should help boys and girls come to know some generalizations or big meanings of science principles that they can use in solving problems in their environment.
> 2. . . . A study of science should help children grow in ability to solve problems effectively.
> 3. . . . The study of science should develop in children a scientific attitude.
> 4. Science is, furthermore, supposed to create in children an interest in and appreciation for the world in which they live.[1]

Science is concerned with the study of the physical environment and of the concepts that help man control that environment. Science is tested experience. We teach science not only to help boys and girls know some of the significant principles that they can use in understanding their environment but also to help them learn to use the scientific method in solving problems.

[1] Glenn O. Blough, Julius Schwartz, and Albert J. Huggett, *Elementary School Science and How to Teach It*, Revised Edition (New York: The Dryden Press, Inc., 1958), pp. 12, 13, 17, 21.

THE SCIENTIFIC METHOD

We have discussed the scientific method in the two previous chapters, where we referred to it as problem-solving. We pointed out that children find a problem, define it clearly, suggest and consider various possible solutions, gather data concerning it, weigh the data, test the data, retest if necessary, and draw conclusions based on the findings. Even then, the conclusions are not to be regarded as final, because it might be necessary to modify or throw out the conclusions in the light of further investigation or future study.

Obviously, teaching children a method of solving problems is worth while. Why then is science not taught in more schools? Why is it not taught more effectively in all schools?

Teaching Science

For many teachers the problem is "how." The young child is not concerned with the technical terms, the formulas, and the detailed explanations. Those will come later. But whether he is four, six, eight, or ten, he needs to satisfy his curiosity about his surroundings. He needs someone to help him broaden his curiosity, to nurture his already stimulated interests, and to encourage his enthusiasm. What he does not need, but too often finds, is someone — parent or teacher — who will stifle, ignore, or divert his interest.

Recently a group of elementary teachers were discussing the problem of teaching science. Only two out of some thirty teachers were doing anything about it. As one teacher expressed it, "They can learn all they need after they leave my room." The typical elementary teacher feels inadequately trained in science, and she does not want the youngsters to find out that there are many things she does not know. In addition, even if she has overcome this problem by taking courses to supplement her background in the physical sciences, she finds little time for it.

If we waited until all primary teachers were completely ready to teach science, we would never get started. The teacher who is willing to start without knowing everything can be successful if she approaches teaching science with confidence instead of fear and is willing to learn with the children. The teacher is the guide, but the children make the plans for finding answers to their problems. In order to be a guide, the teacher needs to know general subject matter, but she does not need to be a specialist. The following suggestions may help the teacher:

(a) When you and the group have decided upon an area of science or a problem to investigate, read some of the basic science textbooks on the level of the children and then read good general science or biology textbooks. This will give you a feeling of confidence as you extend your own information.

(b) Try out some simple science experiments suggested in these books so you feel less awkward with the apparatus.

(c) Do some of the activities suggested in the book — try them alone first and later you will be able to guide children in similar activities — trips to observe specific phenomena, observations to make and record, experiments to perform, and collections to make. It is easier to engender enthusiasm for things you yourself are excited about.

(d) Get help from the high school science teacher. He may loan you material to use, give you suggestions for teaching it, and, if it can be arranged, he may come in and teach a science lesson for you.

(e) Let children help you find materials needed for the science program. They will bring everything from magnets to magnifying glasses if you enlist their aid.

(f) Let the children experiment. Use the more able pupils to help you "set up" the experiment. This is a good motivating device and takes some of the responsibility off your shoulders.

(g) Start your science program by teaching a unit about something you are vitally interested in and with which you feel most at home. Don't be concerned by the belief of some persons that all leads must come from children. What is a teacher for if not to guide? If butterflies have been a great interest, if you are interested in magnets, in pulleys or birds, — start with something you know best; then later if you wish, follow the children's needs and some of their interests. They can help with the planning even when they did not initiate the original idea.

(h) Study the teacher's manuals that come with the science textbooks. They have been written with the specific idea of helping you teach more effectively.

(i) Keep track of your notes on teaching, your plans and activities and the science materials you use, in case you repeat the unit with another group of children. The second time you teach the unit you will be pleased with your competence.

(j) Share your experiences in teaching science with other teachers. Get ideas from them and be willing to share your ideas with them. Don't, however, take an attitude of superiority because you are teaching science and some other teacher still hasn't gotten up enough courage to start.[2]

Factors Influencing the Teaching of Science

The science program has been influenced by what we know about the needs of children and by a recognition of the fact that the solution of many of our social problems involves the use of scientific information and procedures.

Using what we know about children. Based on the research about the characteristics of young children and their interests in science, a science program can be developed by the staff in harmony with the principles of child development. Such a program should recognize the basic needs to explore, to satisfy motor needs, to associate with other children, to create, to be

[2] Glenn O. Blough and Albert J. Huggett, *Elementary School Science and How to Teach It* (New York: The Dryden Press, Inc., 1951), p. 5.

Even though a teacher is not trained in science, there are many ways she can stimulate an interest in it.

recognized as an individual. In order to be of real value, all science teaching must be grounded in a knowledge of the child and in the experiences of the child and must result in a genuine clarification of concepts that will be useful as well as interesting.

Social need and the science program. Since the curriculum designer is interested in problems of living, the science program must be closely related to effective individual living and to the solution of the persistent problems that must be dealt with by man in our society. Many of the problems that involve health, safety, and the elimination of superstitions require an understanding of scientific principles.

Health

Probably the most important aspect of living that young children must learn is that of health. Health is not only the concern of the individual; it is the concern of the entire community. Control of communicable diseases, understanding of basic health principles, practice of healthful living in and out of the classroom, habits of good eating, and adequate resting habits, all these form a part of the young child's experiences in school. As children grow older, they become involved with community problems, such as water supply, proper protection of food supply, and sewage disposal, to mention a few.

THE HEALTH PROGRAM

By providing a healthful environment, by teaching children and sometimes parents the principles of healthful living, by giving children opportunity to practice good health habits in the school, by identifying children who have health deficiencies, the school tries to lay a foundation for the continued well-being of its pupils.

The role of the teacher. A child who is ill cannot learn effectively. The teacher of young children has constantly the job of keeping the health of the children uppermost in mind as she guides them, in and out of the classroom. It is the teacher who most frequently has charge of morning inspection. Even where there is a nurse available, teachers often do the initial screening for general health and for vision and hearing defects. In some schools teachers still weigh and measure the children each month, recording such health information on report cards or cumulative records. This practice is no longer rigidly followed, however, as parents are assuming the responsibility for certain phases of children's health needs; indeed, the size of classes makes it impractical.

The teacher does look the children over in an informal manner as they come into the room in the morning, and if she observes any unusual symptom she refers the child to the school nurse or requests the office to contact the parent. Teachers need to recognize the importance of the child's health, from the standpoint of both the individual child and the protection of the group. It is as important for the teacher in the primary grades to be conscientious about observing children's well-being as it is for the teachers of nursery and kindergarten children. Occasionally first-grade teachers feel that it is essential for a child to be in school at all costs, so that he will not get behind in his reading.

The child who is a nutrition problem, or who may not be receiving an adequate supply of vitamins in his diet, may be helped through the school lunch program. Many kindergartens and first grades and all nursery schools provide a mid-morning lunch of juice or milk and crackers. Young children need this boost in the middle of the morning because they are not heavy eaters, especially at breakfast, and they cannot eat enough to last through the entire morning. Teachers need it, too. Children in the primary grades have an opportunity in many cases to eat in the school cafeteria, where nutritious meals are provided at a minimum cost. Increasingly, parents are taking advantage of this service.

The rest period in the nursery school and kindergarten helps take care of at least part of the rest needs of young children. The nursery school is better equipped in this respect than the primary grades; however, even in a crowded classroom it is possible to permit children to continue sleep after others have gotten up.[3] The teacher in any of the primary grades can help children by

[3] Lillian M. Logan, "Successful Rest Periods," *The Instructor*, 68:36, September 1958.

planning a flexible and balanced program, which permits children the privilege of resting when they are tired and provides a balance of active and quiet experiences. During conferences with the parents, teachers can enlist the cooperation of the parent in encouraging children to practice habits of good health, both at home and at school.

Children can be taught principles of health. Children can be taught the principles of good health by practicing them at school. Fundamental rules include keeping clean, washing hands before and after eating, covering the mouth when coughing, resting when tired, staying home when ill, getting sufficient exercise, eating the proper food, wearing the proper clothing, going to see the nurse, doctor, or dentist if the need arises, and having the necessary inoculations. For this last item, it is easy to prepare the children in advance by role-playing the situation. One child can be the doctor, another the nurse, and a third the patient.

Providing health service. A useful program takes more than knowing what to do and practicing health rules. The child who knows that milk is essential in the diet can "drink milk until the cows come home without having a single decayed tooth restored to health. No amount of sneezing into a handkerchief is going to cure Johnny's cold. . . . No waiting for the green light will set Mary's leg." [4] But the teacher can help to prevent children from suffering the after-effects of the communicable diseases if she watches carefully to prevent a child's "coming down" with something at school.

[4] George Wheatley and Grace Hallock, *Health Observation of School Children* (New York: McGraw-Hill Book Company, Inc., 1951), p. 10.

The mid-morning lunch program provides an opportunity to teach rules for good health.

Any of the common symptoms of illness can be observed by the teacher during the day while she goes about her other duties. Indeed, it is not necessary, according to some authorities, to set aside a specific time for inspection; as each child enters the room, the teacher may speak to him and casually notice any signs of illness before the activities get under way.

A good school health program is a planned program; nothing is left to chance. Teacher, health service staff, administrative staff, and parents work together for the continuous evaluation of the health program. Thus, health is an integral part of the curriculum. The quality of its functioning is determined by the results as evidenced in improved living for the child, his family, and the community.

A unit of work that was planned and developed by a third grade will illustrate how health instruction can be an integral part of daily living in the classroom and how scientific concepts may be learned in the process.

Better Breakfasts for Better Children: A Nutrition Unit

Introduction of the Problem.

Today educators accept the teaching of nutrition as an integral part of the school curriculum. Good health depends in large measure upon the right attitude toward health practices. We seek to establish in each child the desire to build a strong, healthy body through eating a good breakfast. We hope to plan experiences that will develop in a child a set of good habits that he will apply at home and in school.

We hope to show the child that food affects his rate of growth, his size, his vigor, his appearance, and that indirectly food affects his attitudes, ability for achievement, and happiness.

We hope to show the child that a poor start for the day will find him less alert and that he will make more mistakes than if he had eaten a good breakfast. Breakfast skimpers and skippers have served as "guinea pigs" in scientific studies. The reactions of these persons were slower, their ability to concentrate poorer, and their work less accurate than those who had breakfasted. We hope to show that food does make a difference and that a good breakfast is the right beginning for the day.

We have planned this unit thinking in terms of an average third-grade child from a family of average income. The exact way in which the unit develops will be determined by the class and the teacher, working together.

We planned for activities to cover about a month's study.

I. *General Purposes*
   A. To help give children a better basic understanding of nutrition — especially related to the need for better breakfasts.
   B. To develop in school a favorable attitude toward certain practices of health, and to instill in children the resolve to go home and carry them out.
   C. To build recognition of the fact that growth is an indication of good health and that good health is a source of strength and ability.

D. To develop good habits as the result of knowing why they are important to health and happiness.

E. To emphasize that proper consideration for others at mealtime helps make meals more enjoyable.

II. *Specific Purposes*

A. To encourage children to eat a better breakfast every day.

B. To establish good eating habits generally.

C. To teach the five basic foods that comprise a good breakfast.

D. To promote the child's desire to encourage his family to realize the importance of better breakfasts.

E. To emphasize the importance of cleanliness in handling and preparing as well as in eating food.

F. To urge the children to share the responsibility of meal planning, preparation, and serving.

G. To teach that proper foods are necessary for good posture and strong teeth.

H. To reveal that good eating habits aid the process of digestion.

 I. To attempt to eliminate mid-morning fatigue and certain behavior problems of children.

III. *Initiation*

A. Arranged environment.

1. Pictures of breakfast foods.

2. Posters showing the basic foods, with captions that are eye-catching.

3. Charts showing why certain foods are necessary.

4. Books attractively arranged in a library corner.
   Your Breakfast and the People Who Made It, Let's Cook, Manners Can Be Fun, Food America Gives the World, The Story Book of Food, etc.

B. A written answer from each child to the question, "What did you have for breakfast this morning?" This is to be kept by the teacher until the end of the unit.

C. Reading of the story "Get off the Ground with a Good Breakfast," on page 171, *The Ladies' Home Journal,* September, 1956.

D. Making a chart, "What We Need to Know About a Good Breakfast."

E. Discussion and planning of the unit with the children.

IV. *Experiences and Activities*

A. Finding out about foods.

1. Discussion of the good breakfast foods.

a. Some fruit or fruit juice.

b. Hot or ready-to-eat cereal.

c. Enriched or whole-grain toast, or rolls or bread, with butter or margarine.

d. An egg.

e. Milk.

2. Discussion of reasons why some children come to school with no breakfast or a very skimpy breakfast.

3. Discussion of how children can help at home to provide themselves with a good breakfast.

4. Asking children to check home cupboards and write menus for their own breakfasts, using the supplies on hand.

5. Study of books, pamphlets, magazine and newspaper articles, and other sources suggested by the children to find out more about proper breakfast foods.

6. Construction of a chart with the group listing the pertinent questions pertaining to a good breakfast.

B. Finding out about each kind of breakfast food.

   1. Each child studies about one food at a time.

   2. Each child makes a scrapbook with information about all the foods.

     a. Pictures.

     b. Production information.

     c. People necessary to the production.

     d. How food is marketed.

     e. Preparation for the table.

     f. How food should be properly served.

C. Finding out about the preparation of breakfast foods.

   1. Discussion of what children know about the preparation of food.

   2. Discussion of how they can find out how to prepare foods.

   3. Collection of recipes, or directions for preparation, to be used in a cook book the class will make for their families to use.

   4. Demonstrations of the preparation of foods in the classroom.

     a. A cooking corner can be set up, with a hot plate, cooking utensils, paper cups, and so forth.

     b. Children can give the demonstrations, if proper time has been provided for study and experimentation.

D. Finding out how other people help us have good food.

   1. Invite a nutrition expert to speak on the importance of breakfasts.

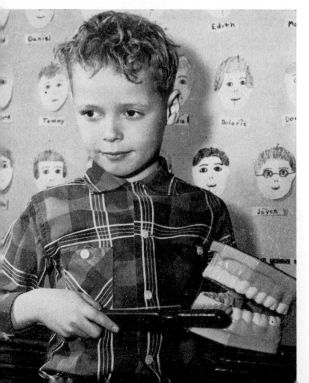

There are many interesting and meaningful ways in which to present the principles of good health.

2. Plan a trip through a dairy to see how milk is processed.

3. Visit a flour mill to learn about the milling of flour.

4. Organize trips by small groups of children to a market, to see how the breakfast foods are grouped and marketed.

5. Show and discuss a film that presents nutritional problems.

6. Make pictorial maps of the United States showing:

   a. Where fruits are grown.

   b. Where grains are raised.

   c. Dairy farms.

   d. Poultry farms.

E. Finding out how food is properly served.

1. The correct way to set a table, with demonstrations.

2. The importance of cleanliness in handling food and dishes.

3. Ways in which the table may be made more attractive; division of children into groups to plan original and interesting table settings.

4. A talk by each child to the class, reporting on a breakfast at an interesting place, such as:

   a. A wayside inn.

   b. Historic eating place.

   c. Modern restaurant.

   d. A boat, plane, or train.

   e. Any other unusual situation where food was served.

F. Finding out about correct table manners.

1. Discussion of the necessity for a pleasant, congenial atmosphere at the table.

   a. Family should be calm and relaxed.

   b. Mealtime is a good time to chat about play and school, to discuss things of mutual interest to all members of the family.

   c. It is important to pray before eating.

2. Reading to find out about correct table manners.

3. Creative dramatics by children divided into groups to portray the correct manners at the table.

   a. Ideal breakfast situations.

   b. Unsatisfactory situations at a family breakfast.

   c. Breakfast in a restaurant.

   d. Serving breakfast to one's family.

   e. Eating in the school cafeteria.

G. Finding out how we can help persuade others to have better breakfasts.

1. How the children can help their mothers prepare breakfast.

   a. Discuss with mothers the basic breakfast foods.

   b. Help with the marketing.

   c. Set the table.

   d. Help with the preparation of the food.

   e. Help keep a happy attitude at the table.

   f. Clear the table and help with the dishes.

2. Plan a "Good Breakfast Parade."

   a. Have each child draw one food included in a good breakfast for an individual poster.

   b. Led by two children carrying the chart the class has made, have the pupils with their drawings go into another classroom to tell what they have learned.

   c. Emphasize foods in each group, nutrients provided by each group, importance of the group to the total diet.

  3. Show concern for others.

   a. For one dollar 22 pounds of surplus food can be sent to any needy country.

   b. Perhaps the children will suggest that each child bring about two cents (purposely keep the amount low) to send to CARE. Have an exhibit of foods, a large bank for donations. (Designate country or not.)

 V. *Culminating Activity*

  A. Preparing and serving breakfast at school.

   1. Form committees for:

    a. Making menus.

    b. Making place mats.

    c. Making napkins and decorations.

    d. Preparing food.

    e. Serving food.

    f. Cleaning up.

 VI. *Evaluation*

  A. Observation by the teacher.

  B. Keeping a log.

  C. Self-evaluation by children — questionnaires.

   1. Charts kept by children showing types of breakfasts eaten.

   2. A "before" and "after" breakfast.

  D. Sociometric techniques.

 VII. *Materials Used*

  A. Children's books.

   1. Clark, Garel. *Let's Start Cooking.* New York: William R. Scott, Inc., 1951.

   2. Girl Scouts of the U.S.A. *Cooking Out-of-Doors.* New York: Girl Scouts of the U.S.A., 1953.

   3. Green, M. M. *Everybody Eats.* New York: William R. Scott, Inc., n.d.

   4. Lach, A. S. *Child's First Cookbook.* New York: Hart Publishing Co., 1950.

   5. Leaf, Munro. *Manners Can Be Fun.* Philadelphia: J. B. Lippincott, Co., 1951.

   6. Petersham, Maud, and Miska Petersham. *The Story Book of Food.* Eau Claire, Wis.: E. M. Hale and Company, n. d.

   7. Riedman, Sarah R. *Food for People.* New York: Abelard-Schuman, Limited, 1954.

   8. Riedman, Sarah R. *Water for People.* New York: Abelard-Schuman, Limited, 1952.

   9. Rombauer, Irma S. *A Cook Book for Boys and Girls.* Indianapolis: The Bobbs-Merrill Company, Inc., 1946.

10. Scheib, Ida. *The First Book of Food*. New York: Franklin Watts, Inc., 1956.

11. Schloat, G. Warren. *Milk for You*. New York: Charles Scribner's Sons, 1949.

12. Schloat, G. Warren. *The Wonderful Egg*. New York: Charles Scribner's Sons, 1949.

B. Informative booklets from the American Red Cross.

C. Pamphlets, booklets, and posters from Dairy Council.

D. Charts from cereal companies.

E. Books for the teacher.

1. Bogert, L. Jean. *Nutrition and Physical Fitness*, Sixth Edition. Philadelphia: W. B. Saunders Company, 1949.

2. Chaney, Margaret Stella. *Nutrition*, Fifth Edition. Boston: Houghton Mifflin Company, 1954.

3. Evansville Public Schools. *Program of Studies for Elementary School*. Evansville, Ind., August 1953.

4. Evansville Public Schools. *Guide for Social Studies in the Primary Grades*. Evansville, Ind., September 1956.

5. *Food and Nutrition*. Towson, Md.: Board of Education of Baltimore County, 1953.

6. "Get off the Ground with a Good Breakfast," *Ladies' Home Journal*, 73:171, September 1956.

7. Heffernan, Helen. "Good Health in the Kindergarten," *Grade Teacher*, 75:14, November 1957.

8. Justin, Margaret M., Lucile O. Rust, and Gladys E. Vail. *Foods: An Introductory Course*, Fourth Edition. Boston: Houghton Mifflin Company, 1956.

9. McCollum, E. V. *A History of Nutrition*. Boston: Houghton Mifflin Company, 1957.

10. *Meal Planning Guide*. St. Louis, Mo.: Home Economics Dept., Pet Milk, 1954.

11. Michaelis, J. U. *Social Studies for Children in a Democracy*, Second Edition. Englewood Cliffs, N.J.: Prentice-Hall, Inc., 1956.

12. Scott, Christine. "Toward Better Breakfasts," *The Instructor*, 68: 73, September 1958.

13. *Social Studies Units*. Instructor Series of 87 Resource Units for All Grades. Chicago: Beckley-Cardy Company, n. d.

14. *Teachers' Activity Book*. Minneapolis: Education Dept., General Mills, n.d.[5]

Safety Education

Like education for health, education for safety grows out of the child's experiences. Children have to learn many things about safety: to play safely, to use apparatus and equipment safely, to keep things out of mouth, nose, ears, and eyes, to walk rather than run as they go to the play area, to

[5] Henrietta Euler, Barbara Harris, Thelma Blemker, and Nancy Allen, Project in Social Studies E 223, Evansville College, Evansville, Indiana, 1957.

walk in the halls and in the room, to look where they are going, to handle toys with sharp edges carefully, to look both ways before crossing the street, to watch the traffic light, to look for cars before running to meet mother.

In the nursery school and kindergarten themselves, the environment must be planned so that the essentials of health and safety are assured and the teacher need not constantly call attention to the hazards. In any setting, positive teaching is good. Rules appropriate to the age level should be developed and consistently employed.

It has been estimated by the National Safety Council that during every year of World War II more lives were lost as a result of preventable accidents than were lost on the battlefields. This problem is primarily an educational one, and education in science can contribute much toward its solution. An understanding of scientific principles is closely related to the prevention of fires, household injuries, reckless driving, and elimination of hazards. Safety education represents an important area in present-day living in which scientific principles need to be made available to children to help them adjust to the environment in which they live and to help them survive in that environment.

Each school can set up a list of objectives that apply to safety education in that particular setting. Such a list, which may be used to guide the teacher and children, follows:

1. To help boys and girls recognize situations involving hazards.
2. To help children develop habits that will enable them to meet situations of daily life with minimum danger to themselves and others.
3. To develop habits of caution, obedience, and observation of safety rules applicable in the home, on the streets, in school, or at play.

Through actual experience children learn desirable safety habits.

4. To teach children early to read, understand, and obey safety regulations.
5. To teach children safe conduct in cars, buses, and street cars.
6. To help children take care of tools, equipment, toys, common articles of the home and school.
7. To teach children caution in the use of fire.
8. To teach children to cooperate to prevent accidents and to avoid taking foolish or unnecessary risks.
9. To help children practice desirable safety behavior at all times.
10. To develop wholesome attitudes concerning safety rules at school and toward law and law enforcement officers.
11. To develop alertness, agility, and muscular control through rhythmic exercises, games, and other physical activities.
12. To teach children what to do in case of fire.

The teacher of even the youngest can do much to help children develop right attitudes toward rules, law, and order, and to practice desirable behavior both in the classroom and on the playground. Children need to recognize the hazards of playing with matches, glass, rusty nails, or tin cans. They can learn to recognize signs even before they actually read them; they can learn to be careful in going down the stairs or crossing streets. They can learn, too, to respect and obey such people as the safety patrol boys, the policeman, and the fireman.

In one kindergarten in which the enrollment is large, there has consistently been at least one parent on the police force or in the fire department. Each year, in the first month of school, the children are given an opportunity to interview the policeman. They are thrilled to find out that the man with the badge is not only a policeman but someone's father. Then they visit the fire station, where someone else's father lets them slide down the pole and helps them climb up and sit in the driver's seat of the fire engine. The unreasonable fear that some children feel toward policemen and firemen is alleviated by finding that the policeman is someone's father and that the fireman is a helper.

Centers of interest or units that grow out of the children's needs are valuable aids in making good safety practices permanent. Children must learn good safety practices on the playground. There should, of course, be a minimum of danger inherent in the playground equipment, area, and in the situation itself. Adequate supervision is essential. If there are more children than one teacher can effectively supervise, then some provision for a teacher's aide or a child from an upper grade should be made. The teacher of small children needs an assistant who will be free to leave the group in case of an emergency. In cases where young children do not have their own playground, play areas should be fenced in. If possible, play periods should be arranged at a time when the older children are indoors. The use of heavy and potentially dangerous equipment should be avoided. Swings in the kindergarten, for instance, are likely to cause accidents if the group is large, supervision limited, and the play area crowded. Equipment should be checked periodically for splinters; the rungs of a wooden jungle gym should be firmly braced; and the castle tower should not be set in concrete. There should be a fence around the ball area in order not to endanger the small children who may be walking in that vicinity. The usefulness of a safety patrol cannot be overestimated, both from the aspect of the training the boys receive in taking responsibility and also in the practical aid they give in teaching children to cross the street safely.

The role of the teacher in safety education. The teacher has to act as a guide, a referee, an interested observer, and as an example. Hers is not a single role; neither is it a simple role. Only through understanding, insight, knowledge, and real interest in children can she effectively discharge her duties in teaching boys and girls practices of health and safety that make for effective living. It should perhaps be taken for granted that teachers will set children a good example in both regards. Teachers who expect children to stay home when they are ill should show the children the same consideration. Teachers who expect children to cross the street at intersections or to observe other safety rules should not violate these rules themselves. Indeed, teachers are expected by the public to set good examples for children. Teachers who are alert to the safety of children will find many ways in which to emphasize the importance of safety in the lives of the children.

One teacher effectively used what might have been an unfortunate situation existing in the school to teach her children the importance of safety and built a unit of work around safety problems. An addition was being built onto the school. Though supposed to be finished by the opening of school, its completion had been delayed by heavy rains. When the children arrived in the fall to enter the second grade, there was no playground for them; outside their door was nothing but gravel, glass, and broken pieces of brick. Several children were injured by falling on the glass. The teacher was at a loss to know what to do when one of the children suggested that they find ways to use the playground safely and learn which things they could and which things they could not safely do. The children and teacher then planned and developed a unit together. By the time it was completed, they had found many safe ways of playing and had learned much about safety at home, on the street, and in the school, as well as on the playground.

A Safety Unit

I. *General Objective*

    To teach children those things they must know in order to live safely.

II. *Instructional Objectives*

    A. To provide many opportunities for developing habits of safety, along with the skills and attitudes that promote it.

    B. To teach children behavior patterns that contribute to their safety and to the safety of others in school, at play, and at home.

C. To teach children to react quickly and correctly in hazardous situations.

III. *Specific Objectives*

A. Safety at School.
1. To learn the safe areas in which to play.
2. To learn the safe way to use play equipment.
3. To learn the safe way to carry a chair and to sit on the chair.
4. To learn to distinguish between right and left.
5. To recognize what constitutes an accident and to report it promptly.
6. To understand the duties of the boys on safety patrol and how they add to safety.
7. To learn the proper way to behave during a fire drill.

B. Safety at Home.
1. To keep toys off walking areas.
2. To keep away from bottles marked poison.
3. To keep away from all bottles in the medicine cabinet.
4. To learn the dangers of playing with matches.
5. To learn the dangers of touching electrical outlets and worn cords.
6. To know how to report a fire and how to protect oneself against fire.

C. Safety on the Street.
1. To know the proper place to cross a street.
2. To learn to look both ways before crossing a street.
3. To learn the meaning of the red and green traffic lights and the words "walk" and "wait" which appear under some traffic signals.
4. To know that the policeman is a friend.
5. To form the habit of walking on the right side and to look in the direction in which one is going.
6. To know one's full name, parents' names, address, and telephone number.
7. To realize that traffic signs and traffic rules are for safety.

IV. *Plan of Approach*

A. Situation at hand, which necessitated a unit of safety.
B. Fire Prevention Week, which gave it the final impetus.
C. Setting the stage.
1. Safety pictures.
2. Exhibit of a safety street showing signs, lights, and policeman.
3. Books with safety stories.
4. Large safety book brought by child.
5. Discussion.

V. *Activities*

A. Excursions.
1. Tour of playground to find areas safe for play.
2. Excursion to neighboring school's playground to observe safe ways of playing on equipment.
3. Tour of school building to become familiar with exit signs.
4. Visit from patrol boys to tell of their duties and behavior expected from the children.

B. Language Arts.
  1. Writing a letter asking permission to visit neighboring playground.
  2. Making a list of standards to follow on excursion.
  3. Writing a thank-you letter to neighboring school.
  4. Making a list of play standards.
  5. Writing a poem together on safety.
  6. Writing a story about a safety picture.
  7. Making a list of questions to ask the patrol boys.
  8. Keeping a list of words for a safety vocabulary.

C. Art.
  1. Making safety pictures with crayon, chalk, and paints.
  2. Constructing a traffic light.
  3. Making safety signs.

D. Dramatic Play.
  1. Small children crossing street.
  2. Accident on playground.
  3. Discovering a fire.
  4. Getting lost.

E. Demonstrations.
  1. Walking on the right side of the hall.
  2. Handling scissors the correct way.
  3. Carrying chairs and sitting on them properly.
  4. Entering door on right side.
  5. Using play equipment correctly.

F. Poems
  1. Fyleman, Rose, *My Policeman.*
  2. Watts, Marjorie, *The Policeman.*

G. Music
  1. Beattie, J. W. *The Traffic Officer.*
  2. *Sing a Song of Safety, Remember Your Name and Address.*

VI. *Culminating Activity*
A. A Safety lesson given to first grade by means of:
  1. Reading charts.
  2. Showing pictures.
  3. Demonstrations.
  4. Music.
  5. Reading safety stories.

VII. *Evaluation*
A. Were the activities important to the child?
B. Was necessary information available?
C. Were the activities at the child's level of interest?
D. Has the child acquired an attitude of responsibility for his own safety and for the safety of others in forming lines, waiting turns, and keeping to the right?
E. Does he have a knowledge of safety terms, such as "exit," "wait," and "walk"?

F. Does he know how to choose a safe area for play?

G. Does the child understand and practice correct precautions in the use of equipment?

H. Does the child recognize a fire alarm and other emergency signals?

I. Does he follow directions quickly in time of emergency?

J. Does the child know simple street signs?

K. Does he know how to cross the street safely?

L. Can he tell his name, parents' names, address, and telephone number?

M. Does he regard the policeman as his friend?

N. Has he a knowledge of the safe crossings in the neighborhood?

O. Has he developed an attitude of willing obedience to the rules of the school and to safety regulations in general?

VIII. *Books*

A. For children.

1. Bauer, W., Dorothy Baruch, and Elizabeth R. Montgomery. *The Basic Health and Safety Program.* Chicago: Scott, Foresman & Company, 1957.

2. Brown, Margaret. *The Little Fireman.* New York: William R. Scott, Inc., 1952.

3. Buckley, H. M., *et al. The Road to Safety.* Vol. 4. New York: American Book Company, 1938.

4. Hefflefinger, Jane, and Elaine Hoffman. *Firemen.* Los Angeles: Melmont Publishers, Inc., 1957.

5. Higgins, Loyta. *Stop and Go.* New York: Simon and Schuster, Inc., 1957.

6. Leaf, Munro. *Safety Can Be Fun.* Philadelphia: J. B. Lippincott Company, 1938.

7. Mitchell, Lucy Sprague. "A City Street," *Told Under the Blue Umbrella.* New York: The Macmillan Company, 1948, p. 87.

8. Schmidt, Anita. "The Big Red Bus," *The Instructor,* 67:87, October 1957.

9. Sherman, Elizabeth. *Let's Look Ahead.* Chicago: Children's Press, Inc., 1950.

10. Stack, Herbert James. *It's Fun to be Safe.* Chicago: Beckley-Cardy Company, 1942.

11. Stack, Herbert James. *Safety Challenges You.* Chicago: Beckley-Cardy Company, 1953.

B. For the teacher.

1. Dieh, Harold, and Anita Laton Sheely. *Health and Safety for You.* New York: McGraw-Hill Book Company, Inc., 1954.

2. Evans, W. A., *et al. Everyday Safety.* Chicago: Lyons & Carnahan, 1952.

3. Floris, A. E., and G. T. Stafford. *Safety Education.* New York: McGraw-Hill Book Company, Inc., 1956.

4. Gentles, Harry, *et al. Habits for Safety.* Indianapolis: The Bobbs-Merrill Company, Inc., 1937.

5. Hodges, Elizabeth F. "Why Safety Rules," *Grade Teacher,* 75:32, 1957.

6. Hyde, Florence, *et al. Safety in the World of Today.* Chicago: Beckley-Cardy Company, 1941.

7. Texas Education Agency. *The Elementary Teacher and Safety Education: An Influence from School to Home.* Bulletin No. 532. Austin, Texas: Texas Education Agency, 1952.[6]

How Children Learn Science

Children learn science in a number of ways. They learn through observation, excursions, experiments, visual aids, reading, radio, and television. We will examine each of these briefly.

OBSERVATION

Children become interested in the world about them at an early age, for the small child learns about life through his senses. He touches, smells, tastes, sees, and hears. Feeling the texture of velvet or the heat from an electric wire attached to a dry cell, smelling the chemicals used in an experiment, seeing the clouds in the sky and the lightning as it flashes, hearing the soft rain or the song of the cardinal, feeling the wind — these are all learning experiences. Children learn not merely to look with a passing glance, but to stop and observe. They observe for a reason: to see the changes in the bulbs they planted, to learn the habits of animals they care for, to see how the experiment turns out. The ability to observe accurately and to report the observation is one that must be developed.

EXCURSIONS

Trips or excursions to solve problems, to get information, or to enjoy the changes that come with the season all have a place in the science program. Children gain much from such a trip if they know in advance its purpose, if they have specific questions they want answered, if the trip is planned and well motivated, if the teacher has help in caring for the children, if the person who is acting as a guide knows beforehand what the youngsters want to see, and if the teacher is familiar with the place, and if evaluation is a part of the excursion. A successful excursion requires a purpose, a plan, a guide, and evaluation.

EXPERIMENTS

Nothing delights children more than to have the teacher or the special science teacher walk into the room with something for an experiment. Teachers should keep the experiments simple, use common materials for the project, encourage children to bring materials from home, and give them a chance to

[6] From Mrs. Ruth Hanshoe, second-grade teacher at West Terrace School, Evansville, Indiana.

The microscope, through showing the child an entirely new world, presents a great challenge to him.

perform the experiments. It is through the experiments that children can learn the important lesson of not jumping to conclusions. When children become scientists, they will discover information that is new; at this point they experiment to understand scientific ideas more clearly and to develop a scientific attitude toward problems.

AUDIO-VISUAL AIDS

Children have learned science through the use of visual aids for many years. A number of media may be used, such as movies, filmstrips, slides, models, pictures, collections. If movies are used, the selection should be made on the basis of the level of teaching for which they are intended. Nothing is more boring to children than to see a film designed for younger children, and nothing can be more disappointing than to be all set for a movie and find it is planned for the upper grades. If the teacher previews the film, if children know what to look for, and if there is a follow-up discussion, the film is a valuable aid in teaching science. The significance of the evaluation cannot be overestimated. During this discussion children may answer questions to the problems raised, ask new questions, clarify hazy concepts, and plan follow-up activities to discover additional information if this is necessary.

More recently, the media of radio and television have made a powerful impact on the lives of children and adults. Some good science programs are available, and children can learn much from them. They must learn to evaluate them carefully, however, to determine which are based on facts and which are fictitious and which mix fact and fiction. Television is being used more frequently now as a teaching medium. The more ways children have of learning, the more numerous the sources of information are, the more important it is that the teacher of young children avail herself of every opportunity to develop a broad background herself, so that she may teach her children to evaluate the information they receive.

READING

Unfortunately, reading has been abused in the teaching of science. For some teachers, who use this method exclusively, science becomes a reading course instead of a science course. Used correctly, reading is an excellent way of learning science, but it should be carefully planned. A wide variety of accurate reading material adapted to the reading abilities of the children must be available. It is in science that children learn to discriminate between fact and fancy in their reading. They learn to check different sources in order to evaluate various points of view. In science they can learn to do research of an elementary nature. Reading is only one way to learn science, but it is an important way.

Approaches to Teaching Science

Teachers should first familiarize themselves with the ways in which children develop their interests in science. Then they may consider methods of teaching science in the school. Here, too, they find a variety of approaches: incidental, integrated, and science-centered.

THE INCIDENTAL APPROACH

As the term suggests, this approach leaves the responsibility for initiating the activity in the science program largely to the child's interests, the teacher merely being on the alert to satisfy the child's curiosity. A child brings a turtle to school. When the child's curiosity is satisfied, his enthusiasm is kept alive by further study and research. These spontaneous and voluntary offerings receive either momentary attention or more prolonged attention, depending on the interest of the children.

THE INTEGRATED APPROACH

Another approach uses science as a part of the social-living program of the school. The processes of group living and the objectives of the core curriculum may be used. According to this plan children explore the problems or areas of living in each grade as defined by the staff: communication, transportation, recreation, education, procurement of food, clothing, and shelter. Other schools may use the unit of work or center of interest, in which children solve the problems raised. In finding the answers science contributes some of the data, but other subjects also contribute to the solution of the problem.

THE SCIENCE-CENTERED APPROACH

This approach to science outlines a developmental sequence of experiences and scientific activities. Such a sequence is related to the child's needs, interests, ability, and level of maturity. The approach is based on the belief that simple scientific concepts are necessary to the understanding of more

Science becomes a part of the social-living program through the integrated approach.

complex ones. Simple experiences with magnets, for example, precede the study of more complicated concepts such as, say, gravitation. Science is regarded as an attitude, a viewpoint, a method that permeates teaching of all kinds. Children use the scientific method in solving problems in school and out of school.

Most teachers will make use of all three approaches — the incidental, the integrated, and the science-centered. Each one has something to offer. The ready-made interest of the incidental approach, the unity and interrelatedness of the integrated approach, and the sequential learnings of the science-centered approach are all important.

The three methods may overlap. The unit that starts spontaneously may before long cut across subject-matter lines and follow sequential steps in its development. One unit may combine the advantages of all three approaches. In the final analysis, evaluation of the science program depends upon selection of worthwhile experiences that meet the developmental needs of the child.

What to Teach in Science

The growth of scientific concepts, interests, appreciation, and understanding is a gradual process. What a child is taught in the primary grades should be based upon knowledge he has acquired before he comes to school. The teacher should take him where he is and broaden his experiences. Even the young child builds up important concepts through which he gradually learns to search further, to discover more, and to relate new concepts to old ones.

SCOPE OF THE SCIENCE PROGRAM

Although the teacher has a responsibility for planning science in the class-room, the over-all plan of the curriculum — its scope and sequence — should be planned by the staff as a whole. It is the principal's responsibility to provide leadership for the entire staff as it studies and plans in relation to the science program. The scope of the learning in science should be considered in terms of the child's growth and development. The child seeks an interpretation of objects in the sky, of the phenomena in the atmosphere, of the earth beneath him, of other living things, of the work of human beings, of evidences of energy and movement, and of social phenomena. A chart such as the one that follows will serve to help the teacher provide a balanced view of the environment insofar as its scientific aspects are concerned. These are topics with which the young child is naturally concerned.

The Science Curriculum

Conditions Necessary to Life

How plants and animals make use of gravity, warmth, light, water, food, and air.

What happens when these conditions are changed.

How some kinds of life are fitted to deserts, swamps, polar regions, etc.

Changes of weather.

The interrelationships of living things and their physical environment.

Past climatic changes.

Struggle for existence.

Balance of nature; relation to health and safety.

How man can change and improve living conditions.

Living Things

Prehistoric life.
Effect of seasonal changes.
Animal homes.
Variety of living things.
Prehistoric animals.
How animals are protected.
Social life of animals.
Animals of today.
How animals become extinct today.
How animals have become extinct in the past.
Struggle for existence.

How living things get their food.
Seed dispersal.
How living things grow up.
Metamorphosis.
Balance of nature.
Economic value.
Man's influence upon nature.
Conservation.
Relation to health.
Wise utilization of other living things.
Wise development of human resources.
The interrelationships of living things.

The Earth

Weathering of rocks.

Erosion.

How rocks are made.
How soil is made.
How mountains are made.
Earthquakes, volcanoes, geysers, caves.
Structure of the earth.
How the earth came to be as it is.
Forces operating on the earth.

Changes in appearance, climates, elevation, plants, and animals.
Changes in the local vicinity.
Gravity and weight.
Variety of earth materials.
Wise utilization of natural resources.
Age of the earth.

Beyond the Earth

The earth in relation to the universe.
Movements of earth.
Effects of sun on earth.
Cause of day and night.
Cause of seasonal change.
Relation of earth and moon.
Cause of tides, eclipses, phases.
Earth a part of solar system.

Our own Milky Way galaxy.
Other galaxies.
Stars, comets, meteors.
Gravitation.
The vastness of space.
Variety of matter and energy in the universe.
Possibilities of space travel.

Physical and Chemical Forces

Heat: changing solids to gases and gases to solids.
Light.
Sound.
Gravity.
Magnetism.
Electricity.
Cause of wind.
Atmosphere.
Different forms of energy.

Sun as a source of energy.
Chemical changes: rusting, breathing.
Where we get our energy.
Relation to health and safety.
Wise utilization of energy.
Elements, compounds, and mixtures.
Man-made substances.
New sources for materials.
Prevention of pollution of air and water.

Man's Attempt to Utilize His Environment

Man's inventions and discoveries.
Man's use of energy.
Man's use of minerals.
How man measures.
Wise utilization of human resources.
How man studies places he cannot reach, i.e., interstellar space and core of the earth.
Man's dominance over other living things.
Man's errors and successes.
Attempts to control pests.

Conservation: a feeling of responsibility for the environment.
Importance of scientific attitude and method to society.
Relation to health and safety.
Wise operation of forces and objects of environment for sake of man's welfare.
Changes in man's way of living created by man's discoveries in science.[7]

[7] Quoted from *Science for the Elementary School Teacher*, New Edition, 1958, by Gerald S. Craig, by permission of Ginn and Company.

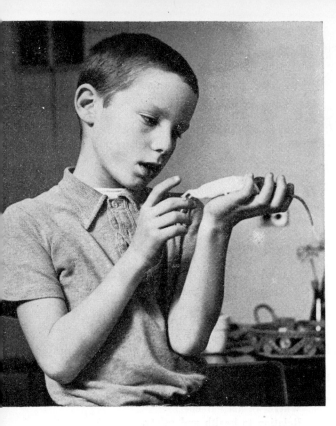

*A science lesson can often be ini-
tiated through the spontaneous
questions raised about a new pet.*

SEQUENCE IN SCIENCE

In organizing the sequence in science, as in the social studies, the school staff must participate in the planning and in the continuous evaluation of the over-all design of the science program. The individual teacher must then adapt this plan to the abilities, interests, maturity, and background of the children and her own ability in the field.

The sequence of scientific experiences need not be rigidly planned or completely incidental. What is needed is continuous, cooperative planning by the entire staff to keep the sequence in harmony with the developmental needs of children. As the young child grows, he meets new problems in his environment. New problems require solutions at his own level of development.

The sequence of scientific experiences must provide for continuity in learning. As can be seen from the chart on pages 272–273, the child's experiences in science will be in terms of problems and meanings. They follow the spiral system of grade placement rather than the ladder system. This means that, since identical problems are explored at different levels of development, children may study any area at all grade levels. In a sense, these are persistent problems that children will face at each level of development. For example, conservation is such a problem, one that will concern the child well into adult life. Instead of taking up the study of living things in kindergarten and then forgetting this study, the child will go on with such study each year on the basis of new learning, new problems, and new solutions. This is much the same idea suggested earlier in this book for the sequence of the program in social studies.

The sequence of scientific experiences must be flexible. Teachers frequently ask for an outline of what subjects to teach in a certain grade. Such outlines can of course be useful, but only if the teacher adapts them to her particular situation. She need not expect each child to evidence the same zeal or ability in each of the topics studied. Children differ not only in their capacity to learn but also in their interest in a given topic. Sometimes teachers squeeze a topic until they have wrung it dry. Since the child will meet the topic again at a later period, such a procedure is unnecessary and may even result in destroying any future challenge the topic might have had for the child.

In science a topic is never mastered; it is never finished. In that respect science is an art. We can begin even in the nursery school to teach children important concepts in science. We can begin there to arouse their interest and to instill in them a desire to learn much more about everything, because there is always more to learn. It is the responsibility of the nursery-school teacher to develop a readiness for learning, and of the kindergarten and primary teachers to expand that interest.

Again, as in social studies, children's interests do not reflect any artificial boundaries, such as the physical or biological sciences. They can be equally enthusiastic about gardening, caring for a pet, or setting up a wire telephone service in the room. There is no advantage to be gained by arbitrarily assigning certain problems relating to the biological sciences to one grade level and those relating to the physical sciences to another. The interests, maturity, and backgrounds of the children will serve as more effective clues to the teacher than will any artificial allocation. Although the teacher's own background may help to determine the topics she will elaborate, lack of knowledge on a specific topic should not hinder her from developing this topic with the children. As soon as she is sufficiently at home with the idea of teaching science and has taught a few units, she will begin to see that science is a challenge that demands endless study. It is her responsibility to inform herself on a topic so she can take her place in working with children for the solution of problems vital to the group.

Although there is some agreement on the scope of the science curriculum, there is less on sequence. Some authorities believe in teaching in every grade concepts from every major scientific area. Such a sequence merely suggests the activities and concepts to which young children react in their everyday environment. If the teacher understands the concepts and has some ideas about how she can teach the children about the scientific phenomena in their own environment, it is likely that more science will be effectively taught and that more children will retain their original enthusiasm for it.

Suggested Scientific Areas

ELECTRICITY

Units on electricity are particularly fascinating to boys. Such units develop an appreciation of the contribution of electricity in improved daily living and speed of communication. Children learn that electricity is a form of energy, that electric current is produced by generators and cells, that electrical energy can be changed into other forms of energy, that lightning is the discharge of static electricity, that electric current is a stream of electrons flowing through a conductor, that some materials are good and others poor conductors of electricity.

WATER

Nursery-school children especially are very much interested in water. There are a number of concepts that children of this age can learn: Some materials float in water, others do not. A siphon can be used to transport water. Water is necessary for life.

ENERGY

A unit on various kinds of energy will develop the following generalizations: The sun is the source of nearly all energy, although energy exists in different forms. Energy cannot be destroyed. Energy is required for growth.

MAGNETS

In a study of magnets the child is primarily interested in knowing what magnets can do. He learns that magnets attract and hold everything made of iron or steel, that they are of different shapes and strength, that they will attract through most substances, that they are stronger at the poles and that like poles repel and unlike poles attract, that they are used in motors, telephones, telegraph, radio, and television.

SEASONAL CHANGES

All children, from nursery school through the primary grades, are extremely interested in seasonal changes. Spring, summer, fall, winter, each provides many topics for study, such as changes in the weather, feeding habits of birds, growing plants, changes in the length of days.

LIVING THINGS

In the area of living things children learn, among other things, that there are many animals in the neighborhood that make good pets. They learn that animals are different in many ways and that they are alike in some respects. They learn that nonliving things have very few characteristics of living things. They learn that living things are either plants or animals. They learn that plants and animals are dependent upon each other.

The child's natural curiosity about his world makes science an obvious part of the curriculum.

Plant life. In this area children learn that plants are adapted to their environment. Plants cannot grow without sunlight, air, water, and food. In studying the life cycle of the mulberry silk worm, for instance, the children discover that the worm needs to feed on the mulberry tree in order to complete its life cycle. They learn that man depends on plants either directly or indirectly for food. Because both plants and animals are important in the scheme of things, children must learn to conserve both.

Animals. Another persistent interest of young children is animals. Preschool, kindergarten, and primary children gain profit and enjoyment from bringing pets to school, observing insects on walks, visiting a farm, studying the ways in which animals benefit man.

An account of how a first-grade group developed an interest in the zoo follows to indicate the way in which one teacher took one activity in which the children were interested and developed it. The unit shows how the learning activities were organized so that each child had an opportunity to make important discoveries for himself.

The Zoo

Sustained enthusiasm for stories of wild animals shown by boys and girls of all ages indicates a genuine interest in those animals. The first graders expressed such an interest when one of the children discovered a book in the library entitled, *What Animal Is It?* Group discussion revealed that, in spite of their interest, many of the children really knew very little about the animals. All this led to the formulation of questions the children wanted answered. In their attempt to answer the questions, the children clarified concepts, extended their information, and broadened their horizons. Among the questions asked were these:

1. Where do these animals live?
2. How do they live in their natural habitat?
3. How do they procure food?
4. How do they rear their young?
5. How long do they live?
6. Where might one go to see these animals?

So we began. Stories about animals were read to the children. Some of the questions were answered through the stories; some stories invited further questions and discussion. Books were displayed on the reading table as a continuing source for finding the answers to the questions. Pictures of animals were arranged on the bulletin boards to aid the children in clarifying concepts and stimulating discussion. A movie of a zoo was shown to the group, and finally a trip to the municipal zoo was planned to integrate information and formulate new concepts concerning these wild animals.

While at the zoo the children saw many animals about which they had been reading. Some were in cages; others were swimming about in moats. The mountain goats made a picturesque sight against the rocks. The tigers were sleeping and refused to answer the cries of the children to "wake up!" The giraffes were in the giraffe house. The elephants remained out of view because of light showers. In spite of temporary disappointment at not seeing the elephants, the children enjoyed the antics of the monkeys, the bears, and the seals.

On the following day plans were made to construct a zoo in the school room. Children were free to choose committees on which they wished to serve. After procedures had been formulated, the groups began to function. Among the committees organized were those for building cages, writing stories, constructing animals, painting scenery, constructing trees, and painting water and birds.

Cages were made from wrapping paper and crates. Animals were painted on paper or made of papîer-maché. Stories were composed and printed below the respective animals in the cages. A background consisting of a large tree, birds, monkeys, and insects was painted. The water committee painted many water animals that they had observed at the zoo.

When the zoo in the room had been completed to the children's satisfaction, they invited the second grade in for a visit. Each child had previously decided what contribution he would make. A report of the entire project was given. The chairman introduced each speaker, who either reported on information he had found in books or talked about his impressions of the trip or read from the experience charts. Songs and rhythms about the zoo and its animals were an important part of the program. Before returning to their room, the second-grade children took a tour of the "grounds" of the zoo and were served peanuts and candy by their first-grade hosts.

All this, of course, in an indirect way benefited the development of regular school subjects. In the language arts, for example, oral language was used to discuss problems that arose in connection with the unit, to dictate a letter to the principal requesting permission to make the trip, to discuss plans for the trip, and to discuss the program for the second grade. Written language was used to write stories about the animals at the zoo, to write letters to mothers requesting permission to make the trip, to write invitations to friends in the second grade to visit the first-grade zoo, and to make captions for the cages.

Reading, too, was useful for finding information in books to answer questions formulated by the group and for enjoying stories about the zoo. The children also listened to stories of animals read by the teacher, and they made experience charts.

In the creative arts, the children made original drawings to illustrate their stories; they painted, drew, made models of and constructed the zoo animals; they constructed their zoo and its cages; they made up songs about the animals and sang others they already knew; and they composed poems and stories about the animals in the zoo. They also made a movie of the story, *Where is Christopher?* [8] and they responded creatively to music representing the animals they had seen.

Evaluation of this unit involved continuous appraisal as the project developed. Numerous opportunities presented themselves for improving skills in communication, problem-solving, critical thinking, group cooperation, and aesthetic experience. Resource personnel in the community, specialists in science, music, and art, contributed to make the project a worthwhile enterprise.

Parents, teachers, and children alike demonstrated a willingness to cooperate and share in the planning. Participation on several committees enabled the children to follow their interests and abilities both in group and in individual enterprises.[9]

Planned Sequence in Teaching Science

When a school staff has determined the concepts to be taught, it arranges a teaching sequence so that the simple scientific concepts will be learned first. An appreciation for and understanding of science develops gradually. Thus, the primary teacher builds upon the experiences the child has had in the nursery school and kindergarten.

An example of concepts learned in the preschool through the primary grades is presented in the following outline of the development of concepts of animal life at each of the grade levels. Although there appears to be some repetition, it must be remembered that with each grade level comes expansion of earlier concepts or development of differences.

8 Anne Lawrence, *Where is Christopher?* (Grand Rapids, Mich.: The Fideler Co., 1950).
9 Lillian M. Logan, "The Zoo," *The Grade Teacher*, 73:18, May 1956.

The presence of a real animal makes a lesson interesting and vital to children.

Developing Concepts of Animal Life

Nursery school and kindergarten.
1. There are many kinds of animals.
2. Not all animals eat the same food.
3. Animals vary in size, shape, body, and covering.
4. Animals need water, food, and air.
5. Most animals have homes.
6. Some baby animals resemble their parents; others do not.
7. Some animals help man.
8. Animals change in size as they grow older.

First grade.
1. Some animals are born alive, some from eggs.
2. Some animals depend on their parents at birth; others do not.
3. Some change when they grow up.
4. Fish, birds, insects, and men are all animals.
5. Animals of the same kind are alike in various ways.
6. Some animals live together all the time; others, only part of the time; some live apart most of the time.
7. Animals care for their young in different ways.
8. Animals change in appearance, size, and ability as they grow older.
9. Animals have many ways to catch food.
10. Animals move in different ways — they crawl, walk, jump, swim, fly, float.

Second grade.
1. Domestic animals (tame animals) need man's care.
2. Plants furnish food for animals.
3. Some animals help farmers; others do not.
4. Young mammals are fed by their mothers.
5. Some animals have one baby at a time; some have many.
6. Living animals give man food — milk, eggs, meat, honey.
7. Animals prepare for winter; some store food, some hibernate.
8. The coats of wild animals are heavier in winter.
9. There are not many babies in the fall.
10. Some animals hibernate all winter.
11. Some animals change color as the seasons change.
12. Some animals shed their skin, their fur, or their feathers from time to time.
13. Some insects are helpful; others are not.

Third grade.
1. Some animals live longer than others.
2. Some animals grow up quickly; others take a long time.
3. Some animals store food all winter.
4. Some animals hunt food all winter.
5. Some animals build special homes for the winter.
6. Physical environment greatly influences animal life.
7. Animals make their homes from many different materials and in many different ways.
8. Some animals can change their color to fit the environment.
9. Many birds migrate in spring and fall.
10. Some birds migrate thousands of miles.
11. Storms and winds hamper migrating birds.
12. The speed of flying depends upon the kind of bird and the weather.
13. Some birds stop to feed and rest as they migrate; others catch insects as they fly and stop only to rest.
14. Birds build their nests where they live in summer.
15. Many birds spend the winter where it is warm and where they have food.
16. Some birds stay in the same locality all winter.

A sample unit worked out by a group of primary children as they studied about the winter birds indicates how some of the concepts might be developed in selected study areas in the first and second grades.

A Study of Winter Birds

Soon after the first snowfall, several pairs of cardinals were seen in our school yard. Some of the children noticed and were delighted by the whistle of these birds. At the beginning of the science class the teacher gave one of the calls of the cardinal and asked the children whether they knew which bird made such a call. This led the children to tell their experiences with cardinals and other birds. Out of this discussion grew an interest in studying winter birds.

Problems and procedure.   Some of the questions to which they wanted answers were these:

1. Which birds stay in the North in the winter?
2. Where have we seen them?
3. What foods do they eat?
4. How are they fitted to get food?
5. What kinds of bird food can they find out-of-doors in winter?
6. How can one tell what kinds of foods birds eat?
7. What can one do to help them?
8. Why should one help them?
9. What are the enemies of winter birds?
10. How can scientists tell which birds are helpful and which are harmful?

A few of the main problems grew out of the approach. Others arose as the unit developed. After the class had discussed possible methods of solving the problems, the following were selected as the most usable methods in a science unit:

1. *Reading to find information.*
2. *Watching birds at home.*   Some questions were answered by groups of children who observed birds at home. Their observations were checked for accuracy by other pupils.
3. *Asking someone who knows.*   The children discussed some of the problems at home and reported their findings to the group.
4. *Experimenting.*   Several pupils set up feeding stations and experimented with different foods to see which kinds the birds ate.

Activities.   In the field of science itself the children engaged in the following activities:

1. Making an excursion to see winter birds and to find different kinds of food that winter birds eat.
2. Making an exhibit of the natural food of winter birds, such as seeds, insects from the bark of trees, berries, and insect eggs.
3. Making an exhibit of food that children can put out for birds in winter, such as suet, grains, nuts, and bread crumbs.
4. Using an evergreen tree in the school yard as a feeding place.
5. Identifying birds through the use of mounted specimens and pictures.

In the way of art and handicrafts, some children drew pictures for a frieze showing winter birds in their natural habitat; others constructed a feeding station to be placed in the school yard. They learned songs about the winter birds and during story hour dramatized legends and poems about them.

Their use of the language arts covered the following activities:

1. Discussing and composing a set of rules for making and maintaining a feeding station.

2. Showing finished feeding station, and discussing the plans used in making it.

3. Explaining, by use of drawings, how birds' bills and claws help them in obtaining food.

4. Showing and telling about food that birds can find and food that children can supply.

5. Discussing some reasons for helping winter birds.

6. Conducting a discussion about winter birds that might come to a feeding station, using pictures and mounted specimens as illustrations.

7. Memorizing poems about winter birds.

8. Writing original stories.

9. Composing original poems.

10. Dramatizing fables, legends, and myths.

Outcomes. The accomplishments of such a project cover the following range:

1. In science itself, an interest in and appreciation of habits of winter birds; skill in making accurate observations and interpreting them; desire to learn about other living creatures; growth of scientific attitude.

2. In art, an ability to express ideas through the medium of art materials.

3. In language, an ability to express opinions and offer helpful criticism; experience in dramatization; and an ability to present science material to an audience in an interesting way. In addition, there was added interest in reading stories and encyclopedia articles about birds.[10]

A Setting Conducive to the Study of Science

Science in the primary grades has moved from the science corner to the entire room and beyond it. Children want to share their discoveries. They want to see what others have brought; they want things labeled and put where they can be seen and used for experimental purposes. The teacher who would provide the right opportunities for a study of science should check on the following activities, typical of scientific experiences young children enjoy and can carry out profitably.

THE INTEREST AREA

No science program is complete without a large interest area in which treasures are labeled and placed after they have been shared. A large burlap hanging may cover the wall behind a table for objects that can be hung up. Some of the things children bring in are magnets, wasps' nests, stuffed animals and birds, and shell collections.

EXHIBITS

Closely related to the interest center are the exhibits that pupils and teacher set up together. Attractive exhibits can be arranged: wildflowers in

[10] Lillian M. Logan, "A Study of Winter Birds," *Guide for Primary Grades* (Evansville Ind.: Evansville Public Schools, 1956), pp. 24–27.

the spring, fossils and rocks, collections of butterflies, all furnish the raw materials for exploration and research. Place the exhibits where children can examine them more than once.

BULLETIN BOARDS

Exhibits usually contain objects, whereas bulletin boards display pictures, charts, and stories the children have written. Weather maps, moths, butterflies, and spring flowers make an attractive bulletin board. Finding poems appropriate to the pictures is another activity children enjoy.

SCIENCE BOOKSHELF

Children should be taught early to go to books for information — not just to one book, but to several for verification. There should be a specific shelf for worthwhile books in science for pupils and teachers to use for independent reading.

FIELD TRIPS

Many schools have an outdoor area in which children can explore the environment. Such a spot yields such alluring things as snails, a turtle, pollywogs, crayfish, plants for a terrarium or aquarium. Each trip to this spot must have a definite purpose and must be carefully planned and evaluated.

EXPERIMENTS

Children can begin early to experiment to learn about such things as magnetism, sound, air pressure, plant life, and animal life. The children help set up the experiments. The classroom takes on the look of a laboratory and children take on the characteristics of scientists as they go about carrying out

Children have a natural curiosity about their world that can serve as a starting point for scientific investigation.

the steps of problem solving. Magnets, tuning forks, tin-can telephones, all should be left where children may experiment further.

SHARED INTERESTS OF OLDER CHILDREN

Children from the intermediate grades bring science materials to school. They should be encouraged to stop in the kindergarten to show them. Pets, a moth, insects, and other animals are interesting to younger children. Children are happy to be invited to share materials of other grades.

FILMSTRIPS AND MOVIES

Audio-visual aids are becoming an increasingly useful teaching tool. They are a means of bringing to children much scientific information that they would otherwise not notice. If the teacher selects the material wisely and plans the experience carefully, the children can benefit greatly.

UNITS

In addition to the incidental experiences with science initiated by the children's interests, the teacher should plan units that are carefully developed in the manner in which the units in the social studies are developed. The units on the winter birds and the zoo indicate that children enjoy developing a unit in science as well as in social studies. As a matter of fact, the two are so closely related that some teachers classify them as science-social-studies units. The units require preplanning, collecting materials, gaining accurate information, and planning procedures in harmony with the scientific method. In developing a unit it is desirable to adapt it to the needs and interests of the children as well as to their ability and maturity. In addition, children should be taught to use correct terminology and develop scientific attitudes toward research.

Evaluating the Science Program

In evaluating the science program in a classroom, the teacher may think in terms of her original objectives and ask the following questions:

1. Did I give the children an opportunity to suggest problems of their own interest?

2. Did I allow them to state the problem in their own words?

3. Did the children suggest possible solutions?

4. Did they gather data in a variety of ways?

5. Did they help provide the needed equipment and materials, set up the apparatus, and take care of the equipment?

6. Did they analyze the information to determine what was worth while and related to the problem?

7. Did they test and retest?

8. Did they come to some conclusions?

9. Did they form such generalizations on the basis of the data or of opinion?

10. Did they apply these generalizations?

11. Do they realize that in science many conclusions must be tentative because future discoveries might change them?

12. Did the children grow under my guidance in planning, experimenting, and evaluating?

13. Did I allow for individual differences among the children?

14. Was there a balance between physical and biological sciences?

15. Were the units that were selected and developed related to the needs, interests, and abilities of the children?

16. Are children broadening their knowledge, skills, and attitudes of important concepts in science?

17. Are the units selected significant in terms of social values?

18. Did the children learn to observe more accurately, report on the basis of their findings, and give evidence of having a scientific attitude by their speech and actions?

19. What science skills have they learned?

20. Have they grown in their concern for the common welfare?

21. Do they look forward with enthusiasm to further experiences with science?

Summary

The major purpose of science education for the young child is to help him to learn such concepts as he will need in order to understand his environment, to develop skills in problem solving, to adopt a scientific attitude toward the interpretation of natural phenomena, and to become more interested in and appreciative of his world.

An adequate science program also provides opportunities for children to understand the contribution of science to the welfare of society. The program is based on what we know about needs and characteristics of children and the needs of society. It has a two-fold concern: to develop the child's understanding of the role of science in the personal and social life of the individual and to discover children who have exceptional ability in science.

Adequate scope and sequence in the science program may be provided by the selection of skills and attitudes that are the most significant in promoting satisfactory adjustment to the environment; the maintenance of a balance between what is significant and what is interesting to the children; and the selection of the most important resources, including books, other sources of written information, adequate equipment, and the local community resources.

Progress in science may be checked in a number of ways, such as observation of pupil behavior, problem-situation tests, and objective tests. The quality of the science program in the school as a whole may be checked by a continuous evaluation of the program.

QUESTIONS AND ACTIVITIES

1. How would you develop a science lesson around a child's question, "What is rain?" What materials would you use to help children understand this phenomenon?

2. Three approaches to teaching science have been presented in the chapter. Explain each and tell which one you would use in your teaching.

3. Plan a lesson for an experience with magnets at the kindergarten level. Include the objectives, activities, and evaluation.

4. What would you include in three to four centers of interest related to science in a grade you would like to teach?

5. Compare the equipment used for science in a self-contained classroom with that used in a room especially equipped as a science laboratory.

6. How may children's interests in science be integrated with instruction in the language arts, the social studies, the creative arts, arithmetic?

7. Observe a group of children at recess and list the questions that might give a teacher a lead on a science experience for the group.

8. State possible differences in the health and safety programs of two first grades composed of totally opposite types of children — from privileged homes and from underprivileged homes.

9. Observe dismissal of a nursery school and of a primary grade. How does the procedure for teaching safety vary between the two?

SELECTED READINGS

Blough, Glenn, and Paul Blackwood. *Teaching Elementary Science.* Washington, D.C.: Government Printing Office, 1948.

Blough, Glenn, and Marjorie Campbell. *Making and Using Classroom Science Materials.* New York: The Dryden Press, Inc., 1954.

Blough, Glenn, and Allan L. Dodd. "Children Are Their Own Resources," *Childhood Education*, 34:21, September 1957.

Blough, Glenn, Julian Schwartz, and Albert J. Huggett. *Elementary School Science and How to Teach It*, Revised Edition. New York: The Dryden Press, Inc., 1958.

Brandwein, Paul F. *The Gifted Students as Future Scientists.* New York: Harcourt, Brace & Co., 1955.

Brink, Ida. "Science in the Kindergarten," *The Instructor*, 47:44, March 1958.

Burnett, Raymond W. *Teaching Science in the Elementary School*, Fifth Edition. New York: Rinehart & Company, 1957.

Craig, Gerald S. *Science for the Elementary School Teacher*, New Edition. Boston: Ginn and Company, 1958.

Freeman, Kenneth, *et al. Helping Children Understand Science.* Philadelphia: The John C. Winston Co., 1954.

Greenlee, Julian. *Teaching Science to Children.* Dubuque, Ia.: William C. Brown Company, Publishers, 1951.

Hubler, Clark. *Working with Children in Science.* Boston: Houghton Mifflin Company, 1956.

Nelson, Leslie W. *Science Activities for Elementary School Children.* Dubuque, Ia.: William C. Brown Company, Publishers, 1952.

Oakes, M. E. *Children's Explanations of Natural Phenomena.* New York: Bureau of Publications, Teachers College, Columbia University, 1947.

Warner, Ruby H. *The Child and his Elementary School World.* Englewood Cliffs, N. J.: Prentice-Hall, Inc., 1957.

Wells, Harrington. *Elementary Science Education in American Public Schools.* New York: McGraw-Hill Book Company, Inc., 1951.

Yates, R. *Science with Simple Things.* New York: Appleton-Century-Crofts, Inc., 1940.

Zim, Herbert S. *This is Science.* Washington, D.C.: The Association for Childhood Education, 1945.

Books on Health and Safety

American Association of Colleges for Teacher Education. *Health Needs of Children.* Oneonta, N. Y.: The Association, 1954.

Anderson, C. L. *School Health Practices.* St. Louis: C. V. Mosby Co., 1956.

The Association for Childhood Education. *Health Education.* Washington, D.C.: Association for Childhood Education International, 1944.

Bauer, W. "It May Be Catching," *NEA Journal,* 45:17–19, January 1956.

Denver Public Schools. *Health Interest of Children.* Denver, Colo.: School District No. 1 in the City and County of Denver, 1947.

Florio, A. E. and G. T. Stafford. *Safety Education.* New York: McGraw-Hill Book Company, Inc., 1959.

Grout, Ruth. *Health Teaching in Schools,* Second Edition. Philadelphia: W. B. Saunders Company, 1953.

Haag, Jessie Helen. *School Health Program.* New York: Henry Holt & Co., Inc., 1958.

Lockwood, E. A. *Activities in Nutrition Education for Kindergarten through Sixth Grade.* New York: Nutrition Foundation, Inc., 1948.

National Education Association. *Health Education.* Washington, D.C.: National Education Association, 1948.

Oberteuffer, Delbert. *School Health Education.* New York: Harper & Brothers, 1949.

Potgieter, M., and V. Everett. "A Study of Children's Eating Habits," *Journal of Home Economics,* 42:363–66, 1950.

Redl, Fritz, and William W. Wattenberg. *Mental Hygiene Unit Teaching.* New York: Harcourt, Brace & Co., 1951.

Schlesinger, Edward R. *Health Services for the Child.* New York: McGraw-Hill Book Company, Inc., 1953.

Schneider, Elsa, and Simon McNeely. *Teachers Contribute to Child Health.* Washington, D.C.: Government Printing Office, 1951.

Turner, C. E. *School Health and Health Education.* St. Louis: C. V. Mosby Co., 1952.

Wheatley, George M., and Grace T. Hallock. *Health Observation of School Children.* New York: McGraw-Hill Book Company, Inc., 1951.

13

Arithmetic

Now I am six, I'm as clever as clever. So I think I'll be six now for ever and ever.

— A. A. MILNE

Children are intensely interested in numbers. Finding the answers to their questions involves for them the excitement of discovery, the thrill that comes with seeing relationships for the first time and then moving on to more challenging experiences. Arithmetic *can* be fascinating and satisfying for children. There is a need, however, for teachers who understand the responsibilities for preserving that spontaneity with which the child approaches his first experience with numbers. The teacher must realize that an understanding of number concepts, quantitative relationships, and decimal notation lays the basis for computational skills. Before children are ready to benefit from drill and practice in the processes of addition, subtraction, multiplication, and division, they must understand the concepts involved in these processes. So must the teacher.

Furthermore, the teacher has the responsibility of meeting the child where he is with respect to ability with numbers and of motivating him to extend his preschool learning. She must teach children what they are ready to learn. Often that is far more than the teacher assumes is possible with or characteristic of a particular age; at times it is less than she expects. Most children like arithmetic if they understand it. If the teacher provides real learning experiences for them and meets their curiosity simply, directly, and intelligently, they will have learned some basic concepts in arithmetic by the time they are six.

Beginnings in Arithmetic

Much important knowledge is acquired by the child before he enters kindergarten or even nursery school. He learns that when he is with someone else, there are two. Many of his first experiences with numbers come from wanting "one more ride." By such means he takes his first steps in addition — the process of adding on, of making more. He learns about subtraction in a similar manner when he finds that if he has five and one is taken away, he has fewer than when he started. All this frequently happens before he gets to nursery school. He begins to acquire, too, a meaningful vocabulary that he can use in forming concepts about numbers. Even before he is in kindergarten a child has an idea of the meaning of more-less, long-short, big-little, near-far, length-width, full-empty, and wide-narrow. Division is easily learned. Every child has been dividing the cookies, dividing the candy, long before he comes to school. These daily experiences with the nomenclature of arithmetic are powerful factors in learning. Concrete experiences in number situations are essential if the child is to begin to understand the meaning and use of numbers. Many children learn to count and enumerate before they come to school. They like to count from one to one hundred by ones and by fives.

Age is an important concept to children, and through this interest they acquire more number relationships. "I was five last week, but I wish I were six like my sister; then I could be in the first grade and read." "I wish I were six. When I get to be six, I'm going to stay six as long as I can." "Six might be as long as a year or forever."

Children are interested in numbers, in concepts of time and space, in relationships. Even young children like numbers. They want you to listen while they count and to commend them when they finish. They are quick to use numbers to compare pieces of candy, pencils, books, and marbles. They chant number rhythms and enjoy number games. For most children, therefore, arithmetic is fun. For only a few is it a frustrating subject. What happens to the spontaneous interest young children have in numbers?

If the teacher who is responsible for teaching arithmetic understood the subject she teaches as well as she understands the child, perhaps there would be fewer unhappy experiences with arithmetic. Attitudes of children are more caught than taught. The pupils of the teacher who likes arithmetic usually agree that arithmetic can be fun; more often than not they regard arithmetic as a stimulating, worthwhile, and highly satisfying activity.

Of course, to achieve this objective the teacher must bring with her to the classroom far more than favorable attitudes and an understanding of children. She should be familiar with applications of mathematics on the technical and scientific level; she should appreciate the importance of mathematics in our culture; and she should know how to teach the concepts to children in a logical, meaningful order.

Aspects of Teaching Arithmetic

The important thing in teaching arithmetic is the quality of the teacher and her preparation. One of the principal needs is for teachers to learn more about their subject in order to teach children effectively and to build on the enthusiasm the children already have for arithmetic when they come to school. To meet the needs of our changing society, leaders in mathematics are emphasizing two important aspects of arithmetic: the mathematical aspect and the social aspect. The first refers to the measurement, properties, and relations of quantities, and the second refers to mathematics as used in daily life in and out of the classroom.

THE MATHEMATICAL ASPECT

The first aspect takes cognizance of the fact that mathematics provides us with a language in which to express, with progressively more subtlety in reasoning, our quantitative ideas. It recognizes that there is a logical sequence to be followed in the development of these quantitative ideas and the skills needed in applying them.

It recognizes, too, that the skills are learned through motivated drill. A child learns to walk by walking; he learns to talk by talking; he learns to figure by figuring. But the drill must be motivated, it must fit his needs; it must be based on his readiness to profit from the experience. Because the teacher knows that drill is necessary to help fix certain processes in a child's mind, she must provide opportunity for drill. She realizes not only that drill is essential in helping a child learn what he needs to know, but that it must be geared to his developmental abilities and needs. Likewise, it must be spaced to fit his attention span, and it must produce results he can see. Such drill is vital to a good arithmetic program. It can take place as children work alone, or as they work in small groups, or as several children work independently on similar materials.

Teachers should remember that number names are symbolic of quantities of things. These numerals are not the numbers themselves; they are merely symbols. The young child does not always distinguish between the mark he puts on the blackboard, "3" for example, and the number itself. But "3" is merely the symbol for the number. It refers to any group possessing the quality of threeness. There are other symbols for the same number or quantity — for example, III, $1 + 2$, $5 - 2$, or $12 \div 4$. When children under-

A grocery-store unit consistently reminds the child that numbers are only symbols for real objects.

stand that the symbols mean things, that they are not themselves the numbers but only the names for numbers, many new approaches to solving problems can be made.

THE SOCIAL ASPECT

The concept of emphasis on the social aspect of arithmetic is not new. As early as 1903 the suggestion was made that

> ... in the study of figures the work should be made practical. Let every child be taught, not merely to solve imaginary problems, but to keep an accurate account of his own income and outgoes. Let him learn the right use of money by using it. Whether supplied by their parents or by their own earnings, let boys and girls learn to select and purchase their own clothing, their books and other necessities; and by keeping an account of their expenses they will learn, as they could in no other way, the value and the use of money.[1]

The social aspect of arithmetic is reflected in the problems as they appear in the arithmetic books. For example, Roman numerals are still taught today, but there is less time spent upon them.

The social aspect of arithmetic is emphasized as children are given opportunities to take care of class business, such as counting Junior Red Cross money, money from ticket sales, lunch money, milk money, the party fund, book rentals, and their bank funds. Children can help the teacher with these projects by relieving her of some of the work of counting money and recording it. They can also help with taking the attendance and keeping a record of

[1] Ellen G. White, *Education* (Mountain View, Calif.: Pacific Press Publishing Assn., 1903), pp. 238–239.

the finances and the budget if there is one. All this gives the children the opportunity for learning. Such learning is referred to as incidental learning, because the primary objective of the activity is not to teach arithmetic, even when arithmetic instruction is introduced to help pupils achieve a social goal, such as in baking cookies, where recipes call for halves and thirds, and the need arises for learning fractions. Mailing a package to an absent child necessitates finding the cost of postage; buying graham crackers for lunch or counting the money to see if there is enough left after the Christmas party to buy a new doll both require the use of arithmetic. The teacher must make sure that learning is expedited through the use of any activities she plans with the pupils in the classroom.

Some teachers, in their zeal to provide children with opportunities for the social application of arithmetic, initiate artificial situations, such as play stores or miniature post offices, in which to practice arithmetic. And indeed children have a wonderful time in kindergarten and the first grade playing store and post office, riding on the train they have built, collecting tickets from the passengers, and dramatizing the activities connected with these situations. Units can be planned in which arithmetic is a prominent part of the activities. The fun of building, painting, stocking, selling, and carrying on the necessary business transactions is fully appreciated by the young children. In addition, those children who have neither the maturity nor the interest to do real arithmetic benefit from such units.

If the primary goal is to teach arithmetic, however, there are more effective ways of doing it than by setting up elaborate play situations. Real situations in which the children buy needed supplies at the grocery store or the school supply store are more meaningful than the activities in connection with such units of work as cited above. If the arithmetic curriculum is given consideration, the incidental learning in connection with such situations will do no harm; but damage comes when mature children are provided with a curriculum in which only incidental learning is possible. There are those who believe that all arithmetic should be taught in social situations. This, unfortunately, has been carried to such an extreme in practice that some children have been taught arithmetic only as an aid to carrying out some classroom activity. Adding, subtracting, dividing, and measuring are taught only in connection with projects. Although the situational method can be valuable in teaching arithmetic processes, it must be used wisely and with discrimination. To the extent that it provides pupils with motivation to learn new processes in numbers, introduces the new arithmetical principles and concepts, and gives an opportunity to the pupil to practice what he has learned in a meaningful situation, it can be useful.

The weakness of the social emphasis is easily discernible. It must be supplemented with drill if it is to have any value. It cannot teach the mathematical theory needed by the child to solve problems that the school cannot foresee, and it cannot provide the repetition that is needed to fix the correct response in the mind of the child. Moreover, it bores the child who is eager to push ahead.

Even in the kindergarten there are children who are ready to move from a situational approach to an organized logical body of subject matter. For example, in one kindergarten there were two children who, early in the year, were interested in playing train, grocery store, and post office. They made tickets, used toy money, collected the money, and had a good learning experience. Then, after Christmas, they made it very clear that they were ready now for some problems written on paper that they could work out during the work period. The teacher accepted their own estimate of their abilities, and taught them the arithmetical concepts for which they were ready.

The good teacher does not minimize the value of the social aspect of arithmetic; neither, however, does she overestimate the value of this aspect. Above all, she does not limit the child, at whatever age, who is ready for the next step in learning arithmetic.

The Approach Through Meaning

The approach that a good many teachers take in teaching arithmetic at present is based on the theory of meaning. This theory recognizes both the mathematical and the social aspects of arithmetic. It holds that both aims can be accomplished only if children understand the meaning of what they learn as they go along. This approach conceives of arithmetic as a closely knit, logically structured system of understandable ideas, principles, and processes. It presents number concepts as part of a system, not as isolated

The alert teacher recognizes and exploits the learning possibilities in the social experiences of the child.

facts. It emphasizes the building of concepts through the use of concrete materials and the recognition of relationships in arithmetic.

Scope and Sequence

The teacher should be familiar with the scope and sequence of the mathematical concepts that young children generally learn before they enter the intermediate grades. As she studies her group and becomes familiar with the curriculum of the school in which she teaches, she will be able to fill in the details of the outline presented below.

Rote counting. The fundamental number experience of young children is counting. They have had experience in this activity before they come to school. Many children know how to count to one hundred by rote before they enter school, but not all of them understand the principle that the number names, "1," "2," "3," and so on, correspond to something that is being counted. The child may merely recite the names of the numbers in rapid order without having a real understanding of the meaning of the number.

Number names of groups: the concept of cardinal numbers. Before he can grasp this concept the child must understand one-to-one correspondence. As he matches books and children in passing out materials to his classmates, he learns that the two (books and children) are equivalent in number. He learns that the number "2" refers to two objects.

Rational counting. Rational counting is the skill of counting objects or people rather than merely reciting number names in order. Counting chairs for the group, counting the number of children at the table, counting the numbers of cakes to serve, all fall into this category.

Grouping experience. As soon as children have some skill in counting, they should be encouraged to compare one group of objects with another. Using groups of concrete objects, the child quickly sees that a group of five is two more than a group of three, and that a group of three is two less than five. Children enjoy having a chance to count groups, to match groups, and to determine the numerical differences between groups. They can use various objects, materials, and blocks to work on these number concepts.

The next step is the recognition of groups without counting their component units. Children in a kindergarten become fascinated with the idea of trying to recognize groups without counting, especially when the teacher tells them she can tell by the "feel" of the room whether there are twenty-five, thirty, or sixty children present. The teacher can use flash cards with large red dots and group them in various arrangements that facilitate the recognition of units. The children should be encouraged to study and use these cards at their leisure. The child must learn not only to identify groups but also to reproduce them.

The process of counting is basic in arithmetic. Children enjoy it. The variety of activities that teach children to count is limited only by the teacher's imagination. It is in counting that the child gains his first concept of quantity. As soon as he is able to discard the crutch of counting on his fingers, counting each individual object, he is ready for the next phase. To recognize, identify, and form groups gives the child an understanding of the number system and teaches him quantitative thinking.

The number system as based on ten. The child who is taught early in his career that the number system is based on ten has made a wonderful discovery. One day he holds up five fingers and then adds five more to show us that his birthday is just ten days away. He has learned that the number "10" represents five objects and five more objects, making a total of ten. In this case it is ten days — ten days until his birthday.

Reading-and-writing-numbers games. By the end of the second grade many children can write as well as read the numbers to 100, read the number names from one to fifty, and understand and use the ordinals through thirty-first. Children learn the first two skills by association. As soon as they grasp the meaning of a number symbol, the teacher shows them what it looks like in symbol form on the board and, later, what it looks like when written out as a word. Some children can write both the number symbol and the word by the time they have completed kindergarten.

One of the more difficult concepts to teach young children is the meaning of ordinal number names. Although they are not taught the terms, they must learn the relationship between "1" and "first," "2" and "second," and so on. The teacher may make this clear by presenting the ordinal number names as those that answer the question "which one?" and the cardinal number names as those that usually tell "how many." Children learn the uses of these number names as they work with the class calendar and with the daily weather chart.

The four fundamental processes. By the end of the primary grades the basic processes of addition and subtraction have been taught. These include addition with carrying and subtraction with borrowing. Some multiplication and division are also taught, but the amount varies from school to school. The concept of multiplication is developed by a one-place number only. There are great differences in programs for teaching arithmetic. One third-grade teacher said, "I think they do well if they recognize subgroups and subtract. I ask eight children to go to the front of the room. Then I ask four to take their seats. If a child can tell how many are left, he is doing pretty well."

Measurement. The learning of measurement begins in nursery school and continues throughout adult life. Early experiences with measurement are aimed at making the child familiar with the vocabulary. Thus he learns that we use such words as "wide" and "narrow," "thick" and "thin," to describe width; or "heavy" and "light" to describe weight. He learns the names of standard units in some systems of measurement: yard, foot, inch; quart, pint; hour, minute; and so on. Only as he is given opportunity to use these instruments of measurement will he be able to incorporate the learning into his own experience.

Most young children are intensely interested in relationships of time and space. Many teachers make use of clocks that point to significant times of the day; one clock denotes the time school opens, another points to the recess hour, others have hands pointing to the hour for lunch time, for a favorite activity, for free activity period, and finally for dismissal. Children should be able also to manipulate clocks that are provided for the specific purpose of teaching them to tell time. The kindergarten children are interested in relationships of time as shown by the hands of the clock. They observe time relationships, such as the fact that after recess comes rest — when the big hand is on twelve and the small one on ten. Often they can arrange the hands of the clock to show how "bed time" or "getting-up time" looks. In fact, a number of children can tell time before they enter school; those who cannot usually show an interest in learning before the year is over.

Children are also interested in the calendar. Here the four- or five-year-old can measure time by intervals between holidays or by the relationship of some event to his birthday or to summer vacation. The teacher should take advantage of this interest in time relationships in her teaching.

Learning to tell time is a valuable foundation for more complicated arithmetic processes.

That children have some difficulty in understanding time relationships in spite of adult efforts to teach them is shown by the following incident:

> From Bedford Village, New York, Carol Chambers writes to tell about the five-year-old mind. "My daughter Martha . . . was acting impossibly the other day — after a long siege of angelic goodness. When I asked her why she was acting this way, especially on vacation at the shore, she said, 'Do you remember when I asked you why time seemed to go so quickly at the seashore? And you said because we were so happy?' I recalled this, and told her so. 'That's why I am bad now,' she said. 'I want it to last longer!' " [2]

Fractions. The meaning of "half," "third," and "fourth" is usually developed in the second grade, although some mature first graders are ready for it. The child can understand a fraction of a group of objects or a part of one object, such as a portion of a piece of pie, before he has an understanding of the concepts involved. But in general, in order to understand a fraction of a group of objects, he should have first been through the sequence described in the above paragraphs.

Learning the concepts and skills of arithmetic in a logical order is very important. The child must understand that "8" may represent eight children or eight apples or eight books, and that it can also represent six pennies and two pennies, or four pennies and four pennies, or five pennies and three pennies, or seven pennies and one penny. He must know how to recognize and combine groups and how to take them apart again. He must learn the purpose of zero as a place holder before he can handle 20 or 30 or any other multiple of ten. Before he can deal with these things in abstract form, he must be able to visualize them. Some children can visualize without the use of concrete objects and are consequently ready for the mechanical skills of reading-and-writing-numbers games. The teacher must keep in mind that there are differences in the way children learn and in the time that it takes them to learn.

Effective Teaching in Arithmetic

In a balanced program arithmetic is taught both as mathematics and as a social subject. In the former it is given meaning as a system of quantitative thinking. In the latter, it takes on significance through its social application. In the primary grades social arithmetic and mathematical skills are taught separately; this division of the two is for the purpose of clarification. In the nursery school and kindergarten social arithmetic and mathematical skills are so completely interrelated that there will be no attempt to distinguish between the two.

NUMBER EXPERIENCE IN THE NURSERY SCHOOL

Use of ordinal numbers. Janie, one of the three-year-olds, says, "I came down the slide first, and Martha came down last, and Robert came down

---

2 John G. Fuller, "From Bedford Village," *Saturday Review,* August 9, 1958, p. 6.

laster." The teacher says, "Janie came down first, and Martha came second, and Robert came third, and Robert was the last." As another child comes down the slide Janie says, "Now Ann is last. But what else is she?" Miss Andrews answers, "Ann is fourth." And she repeats the names, counting with each name — first, second, third, fourth, and last. The "game" is continued, Janie numerating each one until all eight children have come down, and each time she says, "Now Timmie is sixth and last," and so on. She has made the important discovery that there is a relation between a person's number and the fact that he is no longer last if other children keep coming; for when there are no more, she says, "Marie was the eighth and really the last one." The next day she remembers the game and plays it again and says correctly, "I am the third and the last until someone else comes, and then he is fourth and last."

Concept of time relationships. Several of the fours are playing train. Robert says, "When does the train go to Lincoln?" The teacher answers, "I don't know, but I could find out. Do you know how I could find out?" "From the man at the station." "How do you think the ticket agent knows?" Robert answers, "Oh, he just knows." "No, Robert," says the teacher, "he looks it up in a timetable that tells just when the train leaves Kansas City and when it arrives in Lincoln. I have some timetables. Let's look it up."

She finds the timetables, points to the towns and the time the train arrives in each town. For several days the children use the timetable to play train, "looking up" trains and stations and calling out the time. Some can read figures; they are the conductors.

Analysis. These two illustrations of number experiences at the nursery-school level show the natural way in which children arrive at the concept of ordinals and how they learn to see time relationships. The teacher helps to establish the concepts and to clarify ideas as needed. The number readiness of these children is well above the average for the age level. It will be extremely important for the teacher in the kindergarten to follow up and enlarge on their experiences with numbers when they enter kindergarten.

SOCIAL ARITHMETIC IN THE FIRST GRADE: A GROCERY STORE

Debbie's father owned a grocery store, where the first-grade children bought their orange juice and crackers. One day when Debbie's father forgot to send the crackers with the orange juice, the children decided it would be necessary to go to the store and get the crackers themselves.

When they were ready to leave the store, Mr. Hedges gave each child a lollipop to take with him. "Now," he said, "you can build a store at school. You know what one looks like." By the time the youngsters got back to school, Debbie said, "I'll be the clerk, I know how. Sometimes I wait on the customers at the store." "Who said we were going to build a store?" asked Tommy. Debbie said nothing more at that time.

Children learn the value of money by purchasing items and keeping accounts of their expenses.

The next morning during the planning period, the subject came up again. By this time Debbie succeeded in getting enough children interested in the project so that plans were made. They built the store, stocked it with empty orange-juice cans and cracker boxes, and put empty cartons on the shelves. The children marked the prices on the boxes and made signs for the articles. Two of the girls painted the awning during the work period. Michael, who knew how to write all the numbers, was in great demand. The interest in the grocery store afforded the children much opportunity for practicing social skills, for writing the prices on the packages, and for keeping accounts. The high spot of the interest in the grocery store was the day Mr. Hedges came to visit it himself to see how well business was doing at the first-grade store.

Analysis. The social situation of the grocery store stimulated the activities with numbers described and gave the children a chance to discuss, compare, and arrive at solutions to problems in measuring and constructing as well as in writing numbers. The use of the telephone, of the scales for weighing meat, and of the cash register gave additional opportunity to experiment with equipment useful in learning about numbers.

Subtraction in the First Grade

The children enjoy writing problems for their friends to work. Michael, who had shown little interest in this phase of mathematics, wrote a problem and placed it on Miss Steen's desk: "Gary had ten tickets for the merry-go-round. He gave five to Sandy. How many did he have left?"

Mary worked on the problem. She didn't need to use any objects to solve it. She just walked over to the blackboard and wrote:

$$\text{Five from ten leaves five:} \quad \begin{array}{r} 10 \\ -5 \\ \hline 5 \end{array}$$

Because some of the children did not understand the process, she illustrated it:

$$\begin{array}{cccccccccc} & X & X & X & X & X & X & X & X & X & X \\ X & X & X & X & X & & & X & X & X & X & X \end{array}$$

Gave away   Had left

Analysis. The take-away method makes it easy for children to understand subtraction. Without knowing the technical terms (that the minuend is the size of the original group, the subtrahend is the size of the group being taken away, and the difference is the size of the group that is left), the children had worked the problem. To prove that the answer was correct, the children added the difference and subtrahend to get the minuend.

Social Arithmetic in the Second Grade

One of the most popular units in February is always the valentine shop. A group of children decided they would make valentines, put them up for sale before school opened in the morning and at recess, and make enough money to buy a new chair for the library corner. They kept a record of the money they spent for materials. They worked during activity periods, and finally the shop was ready for business. Even the eighth-graders came and bought the valentines the children had made. During the week the shop was open, various children had the chance to sell, to work on the valentines, and to keep the shop in good order and the goods displayed attractively. They kept a record of the money, and found that they had made $6.94. They could buy the chair with the money that they made on the valentines plus what would be left from the party fund. They even decided to do with less food at the party, so that there would be enough money for the chair.

Analysis. The children learned to count the money as it came in each day, to write the prices on the backs of the valentines, and to determine how much money they would have to save from their party funds to add to the valentine money in order to buy the chair.

Mathematical Skills in the Third Grade

The eight-year-olds have a post office, and the principal allows them to sell stamps to customers in the school. The teachers try to remember to patronize home-town business. When the children run out of stamps during the noon rush, Mr. Redding, the principal, sells them some from his office. Kathy bought three stamps, but wasn't sure how much she should pay for them. The postmistress for the day asked the class to figure out the problem, and to show in three different ways that their answer was correct. These solutions were offered:

$$\text{Alice wrote:} \quad 4 + 4 = 8 \quad \text{and} \quad 8 + 4 = 12$$
$$4 + 4 + 4 = 12$$

John wrote: 4

4

4

———

12

Jeanne wrote:

$4 \times 3 = 12$

Cindy wrote:

0000

0000

0000

$= 12$

Jenifer wrote: 1111   1111   1111 $= 12$

James wrote: $4 + 4 + 4 = 12$
$4 + 8 = 12$

Analysis. The request to the pupils to solve the problem and work out proofs provided an opportunity for the individual pupil to work at his own level of ability and maturity. Multiplication is often considered a short process of adding, and some children are ready for it while they are in the first grade. It is the adding of like or equal groups. The multiplicand is the size of equal groups; the multiplier is the number of equal groups; the product is the total number of equal groups.

Instructional Aids

Visual and manipulative materials of good quality are available to schools today. They serve three purposes: to motivate the pupils by interesting them in a new step to be mastered, to help pupils discover meanings as a new concept is developed step by step, and to enrich the curriculum by providing applications in new situations.

Teachers will find evaluations of projection materials and an indication of where they may be obtained in the Fiftieth Yearbook of the National Society for the Study of Education.[3] Pictorial and manipulative materials are available commercially, although they can be made by teachers, and, indeed, some teachers prefer to make their own.[4] Such items as sticks, blocks, beads, clock faces, puzzles, play money, scales, balances, and one-inch cubes are necessary materials for the arithmetic center. There are many other materials

[3] Nelson B. Henry, Editor, *The Teaching of Arithmetic* (Chicago: The University of Chicago Press, 1951), pp. 177–185.

[4] See Grace Meek, "From Bottle Tops and Scraps," *Indiana Teacher*, 102:379–381, April 1958. The author includes pictures and direcions for making a number of arithmetical devices.

Number cutouts are perhaps the most popular instructional aids for teaching arithmetic to young children.

that are useful in teaching arithmetic and that may be used effectively in the primary grades. Some of them are:

Calendar	Sand	Toy telephones
Date stamp	Timetables	Telephone directory
Rulers	Berry baskets	Postage stamps
Yardsticks	License plates	Toy bank
Blocks	Stop watch	Toy cash register
Scales	Coins	Toy money
Measuring spoons	Price tags	Grocery pads
Fruit jars	Compass	Blank checks
Milk bottles	Adding machines	Egg cartons
Measuring cups	Metronome	Large clock dial
Dominoes	Thermometer	Tickets

Organizing the Class for Arithmetic

Children differ; so should experiences and assignments in arithmetic. Because children learn arithmetic as they do other subjects — at varying rates of speed — many teachers find that placing them in groups where they can succeed is desirable. In directing these groups, the teacher must avoid spending too much time with any one group. Children with above-average ability, for example, should not be left, as they frequently are, to shift for themselves. Then, too, the teacher who is alert to the capacities of the children will keep the groups flexible, so that children may move from one to another as their needs change. Such a system enables the teacher to give attention to individual needs, and it permits the children to progress at their own rate instead of being forced to learn arithmetic in lock-step fashion.

Generally speaking, groups are organized to meet the needs of the following types of children:

1. Children who understand concepts as they are explained and are immediately ready to go on to the next step. The bright pupil must be allowed to move on as quickly as he can. He does not need extra drill. He needs, instead, to get started with the new process and then go ahead on his own. After she has demonstrated the new process, the teacher is free to work with the next group.

2. The second group, although it needs no remedial work, includes children who must spend more time with concrete materials and who need specific drill after processes have been explained. In short, these children need to practice under teacher supervision. Practice does not make perfect, but it does make permanent. Too much unmotivated drill, however, often ends in inaccurate work.

3. The third group is the group that is not sufficiently sure of basic facts to give the correct response consistently. The teacher must be sure this group thoroughly understands each concept and the process involved before she assigns drill. Remedial work for the group that is not so able may start with attention to meanings. Once the pupils have shown an understanding of the number system, the teacher must plan a slow, step-by-step sequence of skills and provide carefully supervised practice. The use of incentives with this group is rewarding.

Evaluation

An adequate program of evaluation in arithmetic will measure growth in several phases:

1. Ability to make judgments in quantitative situations.
2. Ability to do mental arithmetic.
3. Attitudes toward arithmetic.
4. Appreciation of the uses of arithmetic.

It will make use of the techniques and devices of evaluation, such as teacher-made and standardized pencil-and-paper tests, interviews, problem situations, both real and contrived, dramatization, anecdotal records, growth charts, conferences, and others.

Some teachers feel more secure if they know what should be learned in the various grades. Schools normally provide a scope and sequence chart, a curriculum guide, or a statement of objectives to give the teacher a frame of reference for planning an adequate program. The teacher herself is, in the last analysis, the key to the better teaching of arithmetic. If she knows the subject matter of arithmetic, if she draws upon the interests of the children in planning the curriculum, if by her own enthusiasm she helps the child feel that arithmetic is fun, stimulating and rewarding, her pupils will be predisposed to succeed.

Summary

Improved instruction is essential if children are to learn arithmetic and be able to use it effectively. Since the teaching of arithmetic is a point of weakness in many classrooms, the staff in every school must engage in a cooperative effort that will have as its objectives:

1. To provide an in-service program in which teachers may reach a better understanding of the three essentials of arithmetic: the number system and its operations, the basic ideas of quantity and relationships, and the role of the social situation, in which quantity is predominant.

2. To provide opportunities for intensive study of the relationships of the mathematical and social aspects of the teaching of arithmetic and an understanding of arithmetic based on the theory of learning that emphasizes meaning, relationships, and understanding.

3. To encourage teachers to examine the various ways of teaching arithmetic and to work out a plan that is effective in their own situation.

4. To help teachers improve instruction in arithmetic through developing number readiness, basic number concepts, computational skills, concepts of measure, fractional concepts, through using drill effectively, through improving skills in solving problems, and through using adequate materials and effective evaluation techniques.

The scope and sequence of topics in arithmetic are influenced by many factors: scientific research, learning theories, the mental maturity of the child, the logical and sequential nature of arithmetic itself, the needs of the child in a particular environment, and the increased demand for mathematics skills.

The trend of the program for teaching arithmetic is toward providing a more challenging curriculum for children in the primary grades in order to prepare them adequately in the skills and understanding needed before they enter the intermediate grades, toward the elimination of material that is seldom used, and toward the introduction of more difficult topics as soon as children are mature enough to learn them. A desirable program in the primary grades must capitalize on and extend preschool learning as well as provide a program of learning activities that emphasizes both the mathematical and the social phases of instruction for children who can benefit from such a combination. It must, in short, provide learning experiences that include more than counting, addition, and subtraction. Furthermore, children should have practice in working with manipulative and pictorial materials in grouping and regrouping numbers, in reading and writing numbers, and in working with addition and subtraction, multiplication and division, the use of fractions, measurement, and money.

Assuming that the teacher recognizes the value of arithmetic in daily living and the importance of understanding relationships in arithmetic and knows how to teach them systematically, not only can children in the early years at school learn arithmetic, but with properly graded learning activities they will learn it happily and satisfyingly. Assuming these conditions, the individual classroom teacher becomes the key to an improvement in the arithmetic program.

QUESTIONS AND ACTIVITIES

1. Question a four- or five-year-old and see if you can determine his quantitative understanding.

   a. Have him estimate the distance from one object to another.
   b. Arrange simple objects in groups of four, five, six, and eight. See how many of the groups he can identify without counting their component parts.
   c. Ask the child which he would prefer, a quarter or a half-dollar, a nickel or a dime.
   d. Give the child objects that vary in size and weight. Ask him to tell you which is heavier, lighter, larger, smaller, narrower, wider, taller, or shorter?

2. How can a teacher utilize each of the following activities for teaching arithmetic in first grade? In third grade? In kindergarten?

   a. Collecting money for a Junior Red Cross Drive.
   b. Operating a school lunch program.
   c. Operating a school supply store.
   d. Weighing and measuring children.
   e. Participating in a paper drive.
   f. Collecting money for orange juice at mid-morning lunch.

3. Observe a classroom for two periods. List and examine the materials of instruction related to arithmetic. Was there an arithmetic center? How did the children use the center?

4. Observe the same classroom for several more periods. What is the range of achievement in arithmetic among the pupils? How does the teacher group the children to provide for these individual differences? How do the children in each group respond to the activities?

5. Examine two curriculum guides for arithmetic in the primary grades. Compare them as to grade placement of various phases of instruction.

6. Formulate the main principles that will guide you in teaching arithmetic. Give an example of each for the specific grade level you hope to teach.

7. Arrange role-playing situations for informing parents why one child is below the others in achievement in arithmetic; why visual and concrete materials are used in arithmetic class; why formal practice in the four fundamental processes is delayed until children understand the concepts.

8. Plan a panel discussion on the merits and weaknesses of developing an understanding of number concepts and processes before formal practice with the symbols alone.

9. Suggest ways in which the teacher can preserve the spontaneity, the creativity, the zest for arithmetic that young children have, and at the same time teach them to achieve speed and accuracy in the four fundamental processes.

SELECTED READINGS

Brownell, William A. "Meaning and Skill: Maintaining a Balance," *The Arithmetic Teacher*, 3:129–136, October 1956.

Buckingham, Burdette R. *Elementary Arithmetic*. Boston: Ginn and Company, 1947.

Clark, John R., and Laura K. Eads. *Guiding Arithmetic Learning*. Yonkers-on-Hudson, N. Y.: World Book Company, 1954.

Department of Elementary School Principals. *Arithmetic in the Modern Elementary School*. Washington, D.C.: National Education Association, 1950.

Finger Plays, Nursery Rhymes and Poems about Numbers: Grades 1–2. Waco, Texas: Superintendent of Schools, 1952.

Glennon, Vincent J., and C. W. Hunnicutt. *What Does Research Say about Arithmetic?* Washington, D.C.: National Education Association, 1952.

Grossnickle, Foster E., and Leo J. Brueckner. *Discovering Meanings in Arithmetic*. Philadelphia: The John C. Winston Company, 1959.

Grossnickle, Foster E., and William Metzner. *Use of Visual Aids in the Teaching of Arithmetic*. Brooklyn, N. Y.: Rambler Press, 1950.

Hickerson, James A. *Guiding Children's Arithmetic Experiences: The Experience-Language Approach to Numbers*. Englewood Cliffs, N. J.: Prentice-Hall, Inc., 1952.

Hollister, George E., and Agnes Gunderson. *Teaching Arithmetic in Grades I and II*. Boston: D. C. Heath & Company, 1954.

Johnson, Charles E. "Grouping Children for Arithmetic Instruction," *The Arithmetic Teacher*, 1:16–22, February 1954.

Martin, William E. "Quantitative Expression in Young Children," *Genetic Psychology Monographs*, 44. Provincetown, Mass.: Journal Press, 1951.

Morton, Robert. *Teaching Children Arithmetic: Primary, Intermediate and Upper Grades*. New York: Silver Burdett Company, 1953.

Morton, Robert. *What Research Says to the Teacher: Teaching Arithmetic*. Washington, D.C.: National Education Association, 1953.

Spencer, P. L., and Marguerite Brydegaard. *Building Mathematical Concepts in the Elementary School*. New York: Henry Holt & Company, Inc., 1952.

Spitzer, Herbert F. *The Teaching of Arithmetic*, Third Edition. Boston: Houghton Mifflin Company, 1960.

Stern, Catherine. *Children Discover Arithmetic*. New York: Harper & Brothers, 1949.

Stern, Catherine. *Structural Arithmetic*. Boston: Houghton Mifflin Company, 1951.

Swain, Robert. *Understanding Arithmetic*. New York: Rinehart & Company, Inc., 1957.

Upton, Clifford B., and Margaret Uhlinger. *I Can Count*. New York: American Book Company, 1950.

Wheat, Harry G. *How to Teach Arithmetic*. Evanston, Ill.: Row, Peterson & Company, 1951.

Wilson, Guy M., *et al. Teaching the New Arithmetic*. New York: McGraw-Hill Book Company, Inc., 1951.

14

Creative Activities

*. . . Suddenly a light, as it were, is kindled in one soul
by a flame that leaps to it from another, and thereafter
sustains itself.*

— PLATO

Children are creative. Each individual has within him potentials for creativity that have not been tapped. In the case of the prodigy, this is obvious.
Yet every average child has innate resources waiting to be developed. The
creative urge may take many different forms, though it all comes from the
same source. It can be expressed through the dance, rhythms, music, drama,
painting, or creative writing.

What shall teachers do to nurture creativity in the children they teach?
Not give out ideas ready-made, certainly, but help each child realize the tremendous possibilities that lie within him. Children cannot create in a vacuum. Creativity emerges from many rich experiences, from feelings, ideas,
reactions, and observations, from an atmosphere of freedom, encouragement,
and appreciation, from the experiments a child makes. The teacher who is

convinced that the aim of education is the fullest possible development of each individual's potential must attune her thinking to the child's areas of interest and ability, because in such interests lies the key to his capacities, talents, and achievement. Education cannot supply the child with capacities; they are innate. It can, however, stimulate and encourage his growth; it can guide him by understanding the media in which he chooses to express himself; and it can give him opportunity, materials, and time to develop his capacities.

Values of Creative Expression

Creative expression affords children a controlled emotional outlet. Children are creatures with strong feelings and an urge to express them. The arts offer a wide variety of media in which a child can express rather than suppress his emotions, and which will speed him on his way toward maturity. The child who discovers the art form through which he can best express himself is building inner resources that will bring him never-ending zest for living.

In addition, creative expression gives children a feeling of worth and achievement. Every child is anxious to succeed, to achieve, to do something of which he is proud and for which he receives recognition and approbation. The school, by providing an opportunity for boys and girls to express themselves creatively, takes seriously the responsibility for helping children achieve in at least one activity.

Creative expression helps children use leisure time constructively. It was Aristotle who said, "Education is the wise use of leisure time." Children in today's world are in danger of becoming spectators of life. "Their eyes, ears, and minds are so lotus-drugged from childhood by the constant impact of movies, radio and television that if we are not careful we will become a generation that prefers a succession of fleeting images that float before us on the screen to real drama, real music, [real art,] and real life." [1]

Creative expression helps children develop creative thinking. The spontaneity and imagination of the young child will die if it is not encouraged and nurtured. It is essential that we provide opportunities for the development of the unique personality and creative abilities of each child. Children must have time to work alone to develop these innate abilities. They must not be forced to adjust to the group at all times, to conform to the accepted pattern. The progress of civilization is dependent upon creative thinking. Steinbeck impresses upon us the importance of developing the creative power of the individual in one of his major novels:

> Our species is the only creative species, and it has only one creative instrument, the individual mind and spirit of man. Nothing was ever created by two men. There are no good collaborations, whether in music, in art, in poetry, in mathematics, in philosophy. Once the miracle of creation has taken place, the

[1] Walter Starkie, "U.S. Culture: No Apologies," *Saturday Review*, 41:14, July 26, 1958.

group can build and extend it, but the group never invents anything. The preciousness lies in the lonely mind of a man.[2]

Childhood, that period when the imagination is spontaneous and strong, is the time to cultivate the creative impulse, not the adult years when time has taken its toll.

Creative expression affords opportunities to grow in social understanding and cooperation. Not only must the child develop his creative powers and innate abilities; he must learn to live successfully with others. In order to do this he must understand them. One of the finest ways of learning to understand how others feel and think is through creative expression in dramatic play and creative dramatics.

Encouraging Creative Expression

Creative expression needs protection as well as encouragement and stimulation. Young children express themselves in rhythmic movement, in dramatic play, in song, line, color, design, and writing. The child, like the painter, reveals all of himself in every movement of the body, in every stroke of the brush, or in every movement of the pen. Often, of course, these expressions do not emerge in the form an adult may desire. But if creativity is suppressed because parents and teachers do not understand the meaning behind the expression, or if one child's efforts are compared with those of other children, the spark of genius may be forever lost. Children lose interest if pressed or constrained in their creative efforts. Thus the teacher has at once a challenge and a responsibility. It is a fine line she must tread, to give needed encouragement until a child builds confidence and his own style of expression and at the same time to be ready with help on techniques as help is requested. Benét says, "It is a very ticklish thing to endeavor in any way to direct so young a gift. It will find by instinct its own nourishment; that is my belief." [3]

How then are teachers to know when to offer a helping hand and when to keep hands off? Or does the teacher serve the child best by keeping hands entirely off? Fortunately, there are guideposts to help the teacher in making these decisions. As we discuss the role of the teacher in each of the creative experiences, we shall notice the way in which the three characteristics of creativity — a background of many experiences; the opportunity to observe, experience, feel, think, and react; an atmosphere of freedom, encouragement, and appreciation — act as clues to the teacher's role. We shall see when to guide, when to encourage, and when to forbear. In the moment of actual creativity the role of the teacher is that of the learner — that is her cue.

[2] John Steinbeck, *East of Eden* (New York: The Viking Press, Inc., 1952), pp. 113–114.
[3] William Rose Benét, introduction to Nathalia Crane, *The Janitor's Boy and Other Poems;* quoted by Hughes Mearns, *Creative Youth* (New York: Doubleday & Company, Inc., 1925), p. 16.

Only by fostering and developing creative activities of mind and body . . . can we hope to renew the much-needed spiritual aspects of our life today.

— GERTRUDE JOHNSON

CREATIVE ACTIVITIES

Rhythm and the Dance

Expression through spontaneous bodily activity is as natural to the child as is breathing. If this innate tendency is encouraged as the child develops, it will provide a reliable foundation for artistic expression in the dance. What is more important, it will provide an intensely satisfying way of expressing emotions in a creative art form. All children are, as we have said, creative, but they express this tendency in various ways. One child chooses to express himself in painting; another chooses the dance. Some few children are equally at home in all forms of the creative arts. The responsibility of the school, and particularly of the teacher, is to provide opportunities for experience, the time and space for experimentation, and a climate of interest and acceptance, all of which form the prelude to creativity in any art form. The actual creativity is the child's own province. If every child in every school were given the opportunity to experience dance as a creative art, then the child for whom rhythm is the particular form of self-expression would gain recognition and a sense of worth and achievement.

One has only to watch a child or a group of children to see that their natural response to music is bodily activity. Whether it be through dancing, or through experimenting with simple musical instruments, the young child must first feel the desire to respond rhythmically and then be able to translate his moods into rhythmical expressions.

The set-up for the rhythm period is fairly simple. There must be plenty of space and there must be a musical instrument or drum. The teacher who can follow the children's moods and patterns with her music is in an advantageous position for fostering a true appreciation of music.

If the teacher is a good pianist, she should by all means use the piano. If not, she should have a phonograph and build up a good collection of records.

In most kindergartens and primary grades there are some instruments on which the children can experiment. Often the children will get great satisfaction and a feeling for rhythm if they have a chance to play with rhythm sticks, bells, cymbals, clogs, tambourines, tuned bottles, and xylophones.

Principles Underlying Teaching of Rhythm

Creativity is a way of learning. The creative process, according to Andrews, "involves three phases, (1) the child and his creative power, feelings and imagination, (2) the action or interaction of his experiences, and (3) his outward form of expression."[4] Children need opportunities to see, touch, feel, taste, and smell. Young children are always exploring, investigating, and discovering things for themselves. Then, after they have had these experiences, they need the opportunity, inspiration, and encouragement to express what they have experienced. It is as simple as that. If the teacher recognizes and encourages this creative ability, the life of the child will be enriched and the life of the adult he is to become will be benefited beyond measure.

In creative expression the emphasis is on the process. The emphasis is on child, rather than on the product. The child expresses what he feels. No one looks to see if he is doing it "right." "It's right if it's right for you," the teacher says, and the child joyously moves around the room. Creative rhythmic movement is the child's interpretation of ideas and feelings, which

[4] Gladys Andrews, *Creative Rhythmic Movement for Children* (Englewood Cliffs, N.J.: Prentice-Hall, Inc., 1954), p. 21.

The child's natural response to music is bodily activity, which is easily transformed into dance patterns.

he expresses through the use of his body. Creativity, rhythm, and movement are the three constant elements, regardless of the term used.

Experiences in movement involve space and rhythm. Children discover that the body is an instrument and that movement is a medium of expression. They translate feelings, ideas, and thoughts into movement. A picture of trees hanging with Spanish moss turns children into slow-moving, droopy old trees in the swamps of Louisiana. Language arts, social studies, and other classroom activities can contribute ideas and impetus to rhythms. Children are fascinated with the discovery that the body is an instrument of expression.

Arranging the Environment

Creative rhythmic movement does not, any more than other art forms, take place in a vacuum. It requires the elements essential to any artistic expression: a permissive atmosphere, time to create, space, and guidance.

Permissive atmosphere. Children need an atmosphere in which they can be themselves and in which they are free to experiment, to let go and not be laughed at if they are clumsy. The teacher who is rigid, stilted, authoritarian, or repressive is not likely to be successful in this type of program. She would be happier teaching formal games or dances — and the children would be happier in such circumstances.

Time to create. It takes time to create, to plan, and to work, whether in groups or individually. It takes time to discuss and evaluate. If the creative rhythmic activity emerges as a part of the curriculum, that is probably better than having a specialist come in at designated periods. Flexible school programs enable rhythms to function as a part of the total school experience. If circumstances dictate that the period must be set at a specific time, the teacher should try to tie it to other school activities.

Space available for movement. A large gymnasium is neither necessary nor desirable for rhythm activity. In a large space the teacher may lose the intimate feeling that exists in the classroom. The ideal situation is, of course, a large classroom, kindergarten, music room, playroom, or outdoor space. Children in such a setting have space to gallop, jump, leap, and dance. They have space enough to move freely about, as well as to lie down and rest after such strenuous activity. Classrooms in which there are movable desks lend themselves well to rhythmic expression. Even in the old-fashioned rooms where desks are fastened to the floor, a resourceful teacher can work out an acceptable program. The music room, the corridors, the tennis court, the recreation hall, the council room, a stage, an auditorium, kindergarten rooms have all been used with greater or lesser success.

Teacher guidance. As in all phases of the educational program, the teacher plays the major role in selecting and motivating the opportunities for self-expression. Her attitude toward children and her ideas about the value of creativity in the life of an individual influence both the quantity and quality of creative experience in a given grade.

Although it is true that creative teachers encourage creativity in children, it is also true that more teachers possess creativity than give evidence of it. Teachers who are interested in child growth and development, who understand the need for creative expression, who think of creative experiences as alleviating some of the disciplinary problems, and who are not afraid to explore with children — such teachers can guide creativity successfully.

The extent to which teachers can be successful in helping children release the creative power within them depends not only upon their understanding of movement but upon their own ability to express themselves through this medium. Teachers should themselves enter into creative experience. They can, for instance, initiate the activity and then let the children take over. And of course they should allow the children to express themselves in their own way. The teacher's attitude, her interest in each child, her willingness to let children experiment, her ability to focus on the process, not the product, these are the keys to a successful environment for children. In addition, teachers need some specific suggestions as to what children can and will do in expressing themselves to music by means of movement. Examples of activities children enjoy will be presented with suggestions for teaching, getting the children started, developing a particular rhythmic response, and with examples of rhythmic activity.

Rhythmic Experiences

In the Nursery School

Young children who are happily engaged in satisfying activity will respond to music by dancing. They want plenty of opportunity to dance, to sing, to respond to music. The kinds of rhythmic activities the youngest children enjoy are swinging, bouncing, pounding, running, jumping, or pedaling a tricycle. Children like to swing in the inner tube from a large truck and sing "Bounce, bounce, bounce, while I swing, swing, swing!" They sing, too, as they go up and down on the see-saw. For young children music and dance have the greatest value if they are allowed to choose their own activity. When the teacher sets the pattern by saying, for instance, "Today I want all of you to be elephants; this is the way the elephant walks," and demonstrates, she blocks the child's use of music as a creative force. It takes only a little skill to fit the music to the child. Let the child express movement, and the teacher can take it from there.

Elaborate settings are not necessary in the nursery school. A little space, a friendly teacher, rhythm and music, opportunity to play the piano and to try out rhythmic instruments, all help in getting children to express themselves creatively. When teachers realize the value dancing offers to the child and the danger of patterning these expressions, the experiences they offer children will be limited only by their resourcefulness and by the physical environment.

IN THE KINDERGARTEN

In the rhythm program in the kindergarten the teacher attempts to give a child the opportunity to:

1. Experience the joy of expressing himself in another creative art form.
2. Develop motor coordination, posture, and poise.
3. Alleviate general strain and tension and provide emotional release.
4. Interpret his own impulses rather than imitate someone else's ideas and motions.
5. Develop an appreciation of listening and expressing.
6. Experiment with the piano, chimes, drums, and other instruments, such as sticks, clogs, bells, xylophones, tambourines, and cymbals.

How to start rhythmic expression.   The children are usually grouped on the floor near the piano. Sometime during the first few days of kindergarten, the teacher will notice during a free period that the children are engaging voluntarily in rhythmic activities. It may be that some children are swinging, running, skipping, or see-sawing. At the time the activity is observed, the teacher can sit down at the piano and accompany the rhythm of it. The children will probably leave what they are doing to come over and listen to the piano, and thus the first rhythm group will be formed.

The teacher may turn to the piano and play a lively, strongly accented bit of music. Not infrequently the children will begin to clap in time with the music. The teacher may ask if the children can make their feet tell a story while the piano plays. When the music stops, the children will stop. The children will enjoy listening to music and responding to it.

If the music used is changed frequently, the children will be led to listen not for certain tunes but for the mood of the music. The music used should become increasingly difficult to interpret, so that the child may develop.

An example of the use of rhythm.   The following account illustrates one way in which rhythms were developed with a kindergarten group. The use of questions and cues, the reactions of the children, and the progression of the lesson should be observed. Consider the following demonstration:

Teacher: "This is the time we listen to the music and make suggestions. Yesterday Miss Clark came and brought a drum and we did rhythms. Let's have a walk, and when the music tells us to walk on tiptoes or be giants, let's."

Children get up and walk around the room to the music. One child marches. Music changes to "giant" music. Children respond. Then the tempo quickens, and the children run on their toes.

Teacher: "Let's have a good skip; when I ring the triangle, you stand still and clap."

All except four children get up and skip to music. Those four remain seated. Two just clap. Some children skip on only one foot. Some gallop. One child joins group in skipping, then another, until at last all are skipping except one boy who stands and claps and one who remains seated.

Teacher: "Who knows another skip?"

Joan demonstrates a hop skip.

Teacher: "There's a side skip, too."

No one knows what a side skip is until Miss Campbell demonstrates. The children try, but it is too complicated. Most of them are still front-skipping. The teacher chooses girls alone. They gallop, or skip; only one or two do the side-skip. It is not easy. Boys are chosen.

Teacher: "Let's listen to what Miss Jones would like us to do. I have told most of the things."

Little response until the student teacher and Miss Campbell play with the children. The music is Brahms' *Lullaby*. The children sit down, and the teacher suggests they sway to it. She names the song.

It can be seen that the children in this demonstration were too much directed. They had little chance to respond to music or even to listen to it. They were told what to do and shown how to do it. If children are allowed to listen and express their feelings, something will happen.

IN THE FIRST GRADE

How a teacher approaches a group and how she starts depend upon her knowledge of children, their needs, their varying stages of development, their interests and previous experience. The teacher who is new to a first grade and to rhythms will feel more secure if she has a few questions thought out with which to begin the period. No one can prescribe what these questions should be. The spirit of the group, the group dynamics operating at the time, and the experiences the group has had in similar situations, all make it difficult to determine exactly what questions the teacher should ask. Among the questions that could be asked, however, are these:

1. Can we walk fast-fast-faster?
2. Are there any other ways we could walk?
3. What is another way we can move around the room without walking?
4. Can you skip and move your arms at the same time?
5. Can you skip around the room?
6. Can you take a jump and hop?
7. Can you move while sitting at your desk?
8. What is the difference between a skip, a hop, and a jump?
9. Did you skip in kindergarten?

10. How would you move if you were in a tiny box?
11. How would you move if you were the heaviest thing in the world?
12. Look at this picture. How is the horse going? Who can show us?
13. How did you walk to school this morning?

Define the problem for the entire group, limit the situation, and make it possible to move on from that point. When the children have exhausted one aspect, they should have an opportunity to try another.

Rhythm instruments (such as drumsticks), songs, or pictures of such things as a galloping horse, a zooming airplane, a rocket descending, a butterfly, a bee buzzing around a honeysuckle, animals at the zoo — any of these may be used to introduce children to movement.

IN THE SECOND GRADE

The teacher in one second grade began her approach to speech activities through movement and bodily action. She chose one-half of the group to go up on the auditorium stage and be "trees." The children moved about the stage freely in response to the music. Then the music changed:

Teacher: "Now let's be windmills."
>They respond. The second group is called to the stage and is given the opportunity to be trees swaying in the wind.
Teacher: "Let's try to be windmills. Straight arms, one up, one down. Everybody take a partner."
>The children face each other, and opposite hands move in rhythm to windmill music.
Teacher: "Now let's be birds."
>The children go through a variety of bird activities including walking, hopping, building nests, squeaking, and flying.
Teacher: "Sometimes birds just rest."
>Group rests, and then is encouraged once more to be birds.
Teacher: "Do something different now."
>A variety of bird responses follows, after which the children take their seats.

Notice that the teacher began this rhythms experience by asking the children specifically to be trees, instead of building up the idea of creating a dance pattern or moving to music in response to the rhythm. Though the children moved about freely, they were not encouraged to develop original ideas. Then the teacher changed the music, instructing the children to be windmills; here again was a lost opportunity. Too much direction, too much structuring of the rhythmic response defeats the expression, which should be creative and spontaneous. Next, the teacher's command to take a partner resulted in the usual confusion. On the other hand, when the group became birds, they showed the greatest creativity; here was an opportunity to do any of a number of things, and originality resulted momentarily — an indication of what freedom of expression could achieve.

In the Third Grade

The children are seated on the floor in the auditorium, and the pianist plays the music to the nursery rhyme, "Wee Willie Winkle."

"Remember Wee Willie Winkle? What was Wee Willie doing? I wonder how many of you would like to be Wee Willie Winkle? What could you be doing?"

One-half of the children are selected to go on the stage. The others repeat the rhyme in unison. The group on the stage repeats only, "Are the babes in their beds, for now it's eight o'clock?" The children respond creatively to the poem. They run up and down the steps, they rap on the window, they cry at the locks, they pantomime and put a great deal of original action into the play. Each group has a turn to play the scene three times, and the children use different actions as they repeat. It appears to be a favorite nursery rhyme.

For the remainder of the period the children separate into five groups. The teacher gives the following directions: "Today you could have a zoo. Would you like that? Stay in your places and decide which animals you want to be. Then come back to the zoo in your own groups and show the rest of us what animals you are. Who wants to be first?"

They have about three minutes to work out this action. Jimmie's group are elephants, Peter's group are kangaroos, Vicki's group are monkeys, Jane's group are birds, and Mamie's group are zebras.

Obviously the group had had experience in this type of creative rhythms before. They knew what to do, and there was no confusion, even though there were few specific directions. The teacher selected questions, cues, and experiences that appeared to stimulate the group to participate with enthusiasm. They seemed interested in trying to do it better each time, and evaluation was an integral part of the experience.

As early as 1922, Miss Eliot recognized the importance of free rhythmic movement.

Types of Rhythmic Activities

Rhythmic activities for children include free rhythms, nursery rhymes, singing games. They enable the child to develop rhythmic coordination and perfect certain skills, such as running, skipping, and the like. They also help the child to develop desirable social traits.

Listed below are various rhythmic activities and suggestions for teaching them:

I. *Natural Rhythms.*
   A. Walking (long, even beat).
      1. Clap out beats.
      2. Walk to music.
      3. Dramatize different types of walk.
   B. Running.
      1. Review walking.
      2. Play music faster until children are running.
      3. Combine running and walking.
   C. Hopping.
      1. Refer to some animal.
      2. Refer to skipping rope.
   D. Leaping.
      1. Develop from a long run.
      2. Compare with jumping over a puddle.
      3. Notice that in a leap one changes feet.
   E. Skipping.
      1. Sensitize to music (short, airy beat).
      2. Walk with a long and a short step, getting up on toes, and then off the floor.
   F. Gallop (long and short beat, heavy).
      1. Refer to horses.
      2. Always keep one foot ahead of the other.
   G. Suggested music.
      1. For walking: any march.
      2. For running: any march with time speeded up.
      3. For bouncing, hopping, and skipping: See Gladys Andrews, *Creative Rhythmic Movement for Children* (Englewood Cliffs, N. J.: Prentice‑Hall, Inc., 1954); and Dorothy LaSalle, *Rhythms and Dances for Elementary Schools* (New York: A. S. Barnes & Co., 1951).
      4. For galloping: "Police Horses" and "Fire Engines" from Dorothy LaSalle, *Rhythms and Dances for Elementary Schools.*
II. *Free Rhythms.*
   A. Ways of presenting a rhythm.
      1. Discussion.

    2. Pictures.

    3. Poems.

    4. An object.

    5. Correlation with other lessons.

B. How to teach a rhythm.

    1. Make the discussion natural.

    2. Have definite questions.

    3. Try to use the suggestions of the children.

    4. Try to guide the children, but let them make suggestions.

    5. Do not keep the children seated too long.

    6. Try to get originality.

    7. Avoid dragging out a rhythm.

C. Suggested music.

    1. Dorothy LaSalle, *Rhythms and Dances for Elementary Schools.*

    2. Gladys Andrews, *Creative Rhythmic Movement for Children.*

III. *Nursery Rhymes.*

A. Teaching suggestions.

    1. Teach words first.

    2. If a child knows the rhyme, let him recite it.

    3. Discuss the ways of dramatizing.

    4. Do just what the words say.

B. Suggested material.

    1. Gladys Andrews, *Creative Rhythmic Movement for Children.*

    2. Nursery rhymes.

        a. "Hickory, Dickory, Dock."

        b. "Ride a Cock Horse."

        c. "Little Boy Blue."

        d. "Pussy Cat."

        e. "Little Bo Peep."

        f. "Wee Willie Winkle."

        g. "See-Saw, Margery Daw."

IV. *Singing Games.*

A. Teaching Suggestions.

    1. Teach words first.

    2. Discuss the meaning of the verses.

    3. Teach only one verse at a time if the song is a long one.

B. Suggested material.

    1. Dorothy LaSalle, *Rhythms and Dances for Elementary Schools.*

    2. Gladys Andrews, *Creative Rhythmic Movement for Children.*

QUESTIONS AND ACTIVITIES

1. Observe in a nursery school or kindergarten and make a list of the rhythmic activities. Which were spontaneous and which were initiated by the teacher?

2. In some communities children are not permitted to dance because of parents' personal convictions. How would you handle a situation like this in nursery school? in third grade?

3. Some kindergarten teachers motivate the rhythms by dramatic play. The teacher says, "Today we are going to the zoo. I will play music that tells you to be an elephant; then I will play music that tells you to be birds; now you may be ponies." For each activity the teacher plays suitable music. The children know what the music tells them to do and they do it. Discuss this approach in terms of the idea of creativity you have gained from reading and observation.

4. Summarize the values of creative expression. How do you keep the values in mind and try to work toward higher goals of creative expression on the part of all the children?

5. How would you go about planning a lesson in rhythm or movement with a third-grade group? How would this differ from an experience in rhythms with a nursery-school group?

6. Are singing games suitable for use in kindergarten and primary grades? Select several that you believe would be enjoyed by children in the grade of your choice.

7. This is one teacher's formula for conducting a class in rhythms: "Feel the rhythm yourself. Increase your feeling by the way you play it. Show the children how to play it. Play the rhythm with them to make them feel it." How would you react to her formula? How might children react?

8. Evaluate this lesson plan: "Get the children to pretend that they are seeds in the garden (children may choose to be radish, lettuce, or onion seeds; they will run over to the garden to be planted); the wind, the sun, and the rains will come; one group of children may be gardeners, and they will prepare the ground; the seeds will grow in the prepared ground; after the seeds are grown, they will be harvested."

9. Observe a class in rhythms and try to find evidence of good feeling toward the group and toward the experience of working on problems together.

SELECTED READINGS

Andrews, Gladys. *Creative Rhythmic Movement for Children.* Englewood Cliffs, N.J.: Prentice-Hall, Inc., 1954.

Carabo-Cone, M. C., and B. Royt. *How to Help Children Learn Music.* New York: Harper & Brothers, 1955.

Kuhn, Jacqueline. *33 Rhythms for Children.* New York: Bregman Vocco and Conn, Inc., 1956.

LaSalle, Dorothy. *Rhythms and Dances for Elementary Schools.* New York: A. S. Barnes and Co., 1951.

Mason, B. *Drums, Tom-Toms and Rattles.* New York: A. S. Barnes and Co., 1938.

Morgan, Esther, and Hazel Grubbs. "An Approach to Rhythms for Children," *Childhood Education*, 29:383–387, April 1953.

Mukerji, Rose. "Creative Expression in Rhythms and Dance," *Childhood Education*, 34:15–17, September 1957.

Murray, Ruth Lovell. *Dance in the Elementary School.* New York: Harper & Brothers, 1953.

Music for Children with Special Needs. Sacramento, California: Music Professional Committee, California School Supervisors' Association, Southern Section, 1953–54.

Scheon, Elizabeth, and Emma O'Brien. *Rhythm in the Elementary School.* New York: A. S. Barnes and Co., 1951.

Sheehy, Emma Dickenson. *There's Music in Children,* Revised Edition. New York: Henry Holt & Company, Inc., 1952.

Staples, R. "Fun With Rhythm Instruments," "Fun with the Keyboard," "Fun with Melody Bells," "Fun with Classroom Harps," and "Fun with the Small Winds." *Musical Fun Books.* Chicago: Follett Publishing Company, 1955.

Waterman, Elizabeth. *Rhythm Book.* New York: A. S. Barnes & Co., 1936.

*Somewhere a child in the dawn is sing-
ing, free as a bird when it welcomes the
day .... We, too, need music to lift us and
cheer us. Come, then, and sing all our
cares away.*

— PETER DYKEMA

CREATIVE ACTIVITIES

Music

Singing is a completely natural and spontaneous activity for the child.
He hums as he hammers at the work bench; he sings as he paints on the
easel; he chants as he pulls a big load in the truck. For the child it is a
singing world.

Music can lift morale and spirit when a group of children and their teacher
enter into a partnership that makes music a creative art in the classroom.

Role of Music in Education

In education, particularly in preschool and the primary grades, music is
one of the vital human experiences in the lives of children. It is not the
skill based upon abstract patterns that perhaps it will become for them
later. Now music is just one more way for a child to express himself creatively. The fostering and nurturing of creativity in music requires conditions
and teaching techniques akin to those in the other creative arts.

Emphasis is on the growing, active, creative child, his enthusiasm for life,
and his natural inclination to respond to music. From the time he is an
infant he responds to his mother's voice, he reacts to music around him, he
responds with his body and with his voice. Listen to him as he sings about his
work and play. There is warmth, energy, and potential power for creative
growth as the child, without concern for technical perfection or mechanics of
performance, expresses his own feelings through song. He sings because it
makes him happy to sing. Sometimes he sings because he's happy; sometimes
he sings because he needs to, because the very singing makes him happy as he

expresses his own feelings and intuitive nature. He may not sing the song the way it is written, but he sings it. If he has the opportunity, he will develop creativity. But the teacher must provide day-by-day experiences in the classroom that have meaning for him. He needs to succeed in his experiences in music. If he can succeed in any of the phases of musical experiences, he and music will be inseparable for the rest of life. He will be forever singing or listening, dancing, or playing an instrument. He understands intuitively that spontaneous singing, sound and movement, song and dance are as much a part of life as are daily food, drink, and rest.

Role of the Teacher

Few children can have richer experiences and opportunities than their teachers can provide for them. If the teacher is to satisfy the need the child has for expressing himself in music, she must be prepared to make music an integral part of the classroom. She must take it upon herself to offer a balanced program in which the child sings, listens, plays instruments, and masters the technical skills that all arts require.

The teacher should try to help the child develop the craftsman's pleasure in the performance of beautiful music. The child needs to develop early the feeling of doing his best both when he sings and when he listens. There is an art in listening as there is in performance; he can be encouraged in the love of both. With a little encouragement he will listen to recordings during a free period.

The teacher should strive to set an example of the love of beautiful music, thus helping children find such joy in it that they will unconsciously turn to some phase of musical activity to satisfy the need for self-expression, communication, bodily action, or group association.

If the teacher takes some time each day to sing or play for the group, the children will know that she, too, needs music, that for her music is a vital means of expression.

Songs Children Like to Sing

Children should sing ten times as much as is now the custom in our schools, just as they should talk ten times as much as now is permitted in most schools. The old-time speechless school is thought to have thwarted the child's intellectual growth; the songless school probably stunts the child's emotional growth. Undoubtedly music should play a larger part in the life of the child in nursery school, kindergarten, and the primary grades than it now does. A variety of spontaneous musical activities in the classroom under the guidance of an understanding teacher will lay the foundation for a well-rounded experience in music.

The teacher must be familiar with a variety of songs and be able to share them with the children. The teacher can go back to the songs of her own childhood that have pleasant associations — folk songs, carols, songs in other languages, patriotic songs, community songs, children's songs, creative songs, experience songs, songs of the seasons, songs of holidays, lullabies, humorous songs, singing games, rounds, and counting songs. All these have a place in the musical program.

Children enjoy folk songs they know, such as *Skip to My Lou, Sweet Betsy from Pike, So Long, Home on the Range, Way Down Yonder in the Paw-Paw Patch,* and many beautiful Negro spirituals. These are songs that sing themselves.

Among the best-loved carols are *The First Noël, Adeste Fideles, Bring a Torch, Jeannette, Isabella, Good King Wenceslaus, We Wish You a Merry Christmas, God Rest Ye Merry Gentlemen,* and *Deck the Halls.*

Singing songs such as *Stille Nacht, Tannenbaum,* and others in their original language is always interesting to children. Even the youngest children like to sing in another language. This is another opportunity to help children understand people of other countries; through singing their songs children can develop better understanding.

Children at a very young age respond to the martial element in music. They feel the spirit of the songs and join lustily in such songs as *The Star-Spangled Banner.* There is a feeling of oneness with the group. Other songs they enjoy are *The Marines' Hymn, The Battle Hymn of the Republic, Yankee Doodle,* and *God Bless America.*

Children learn community songs by singing them with adults — for instance, *Loch Lomond, My Bonnie Lies over the Ocean, I Dream of Jeannie with the Light Brown Hair, Good Night, Ladies,* and a number of Negro spirituals that are easy to sing. Joining with parents at community sings or in school assemblies is a valuable experience for both children and teachers.

Books have been filled with songs written for and about children. Many of them are easy to sing, and children enjoy them. Songs of childhood, inspired by children, written about them and their world, as seen through the eyes of the composer; imaginative and realistic songs, both traditional and contemporary — all offer rich expression for the young child.

CREATIVE SONGS

The significance of creative songs is not in the product but in the process. It is what happens to the child as he sings or plays his own creation that is important. The teacher must be careful to leave the product as it is, not to polish it. She must be content with the product as it is expressed by the child. She must accept it for what it is — a work of art, the creation of a child's mind and heart. By providing a climate wherein expression finds fulfillment, she contributes in the most effective manner to creativity in the child's life.

Children learn to sing by imitating the teacher and by making up their own words and melodies when they cannot remember hers.

Children love to sing songs written about their own experiences and their own world — songs about swinging, dancing, running, jumping, walking, and skating, songs about dressing and undressing, about eating and sleeping, songs about boats and trains, airplanes and rockets, buses and automobiles, trucks and cars, songs about animals and birds, flowers and gardening, machines and construction. Children can learn dozens of these songs. They like to sing nursery rhymes and play them as they sing. Children like also to sing about summer, fall, spring, and winter. Some of the best-loved songs are *The North Wind Doth Blow, Jingle Bells, The Snowman, Good Morning Said the Crocus, Tirra Lirra Lirra,* and *Springtime.*

Three songs about a happy birthday are better than one. In addition to the traditional *Happy Birthday*, there are *He's Five Years Old Today*, and *[name] Has a Birthday, a Birthday, a Birthday.* The name can be filled in to fit the individual. If children are interested in the holidays, there are songs about Halloween, jack-o-lanterns, and pumpkins; there are Easter songs about bunnies, flowers, and Easter eggs. Christmas songs are, of course, numerous. The teacher can select the best and even compose some herself.

Boys as well as girls, in their early experiences with music, enjoy lullabies, which are a bridge to tie them to the home. Girls sing them in the doll house, and boys enjoy them during the rest period. A favorite is Brahms' *Cradle Song.* Others the children like are *Little Ole, Here Comes the Sandman, Rockabye Baby, Away in a Manger,* and *Sleep, Baby, Sleep.* Hearing the song in the language in which it was written is a rich experience for children, and perhaps especially so with lullabies.

In many schools children meet too little humor in the classroom. On difficult days — Mondays, pre- and post-holidays, Fridays, and in-between days — when children or teachers are not at their best, humorous songs can do much to make the classroom livable. Nonsense songs provide a welcome outlet for children. Among the perennial favorites are *This Old Man, Polly Wolly Doodle, The Bear Went Over the Mountain, I Know a Little Pussy, Aikem Drum, The Gingerbread Man, Will You Marry Me,* and *No, John, No.*

Singing Games

Children begin to enjoy singing games after they have been in school for a time. It makes them feel "grown up" to know such games because older children play them at recess and before and after school. Even some of the fours enjoy a singing game occasionally. Because children respond so spontaneously to rhythms, the singing games may be introduced whenever the children appear to be ready for such organized play. When that time comes, the teacher should be familiar with such games as *The Farmer in the Dell, Looby Loo, Here We Go Round the Mulberry Bush, Did You Ever See a Lassie, Round and Round the Village, Blue Bird, In and Out the Window, Little Sallie Waters,* and others. These games give the teacher an excellent opportunity to tell children about folk songs and how they were handed down to us and why there is more than one way of playing them.

ROUNDS

Children love to sing simple rounds. Among their favorites is *Frère Jacques.* Another one simple enough for small children is *Row, Row, Row Your Boat.* If there is an assistant in the group, or a student teacher, the children can be divided into two groups and follow the leader in a two-part round. The children will thoroughly enjoy trying to stay on their part. If one of the teachers has difficulty staying on her part, she might lead from the piano. Fives, sixes, sevens, and eights enjoy this type of musical activity increasingly as they become skillful in holding down the part and as they learn some of the more complex rounds.

COUNTING SONGS

Young children in kindergarten become very much interested in numbers before the year is over and they usually find a great deal of enjoyment and challenge in singing and dramatizing number songs, such as *Ten Little Indians, This Old Man, One Potato, Can You Count?, One, Two, Buckle My Shoe,* and *One, Two, Three, Four, Five,* and others found in music collections for young children.

How to Select a Good Song

An analysis of the songs mentioned above would give us a basis for selecting songs for children to sing. Songs should be chosen both to enrich the child's school life and to add to the pleasure of his home life. They should meet the following standards:

1. A song should be good musically. It should have melodic charm, be easy to sing, and have an enduring quality. In addition, it should have harmonic interest.

2. The song should have a rhythmic flow. There should be sufficient repetition of both rhythmic and melodic pattern, as well as of lyric content, to make it a song to remember.

3. The words should stem from and relate to a child's experience; they should express a genuine emotion in a childlike way. In some of the early song books, songs about the dainty rosebud babies or the personification of seasons were so removed from real life that they have long since been deleted from the collections of children's songs. What is required is a song to which a child can react emotionally.

4. The songs should be written in a range in which it is comfortable for a child to sing. The words and music should express the same idea. The song should be simple but not dull, short yet with a completeness and unity of harmony and melody.

In short, children's song material should come from three sources: the large collection of folk songs suitable for children, songs composed especially to be sung by children (written by people who have competency in the field in order to assure musical quality, literary value, and a strong appeal to the age group for which they are intended), and songs from the world's best music. It is from these three sources that the teacher will select the materials for children's musical experiences.

Understanding the Child's Voice

The high, sweet voice so often attributed to youngsters is not a true picture as far as many children are concerned. Often they sing with more gusto than quality. To be sure, some children have the ability to hear a tone and to reproduce it correctly; they have a keen sense of pitch and the natural ability to sing easily and accurately. There is, however, no such thing as a nonmusical child. Any child can respond to music in any of the forms we have mentioned throughout this chapter. Some children's voices lack flexibility and tend toward monotony. The teacher can help them improve both the speaking and singing voice and bring more color and variety into play. By encouraging the child to experiment with his voice, she can gradually help him become aware of the possibilities of using it more effectively. Any child should be encouraged to sing with the group if he enjoys it. Many a so-called monotone just has not yet found his voice placement.

The teacher will also need to come to terms with the fact that children at times sing with more vigor than she wishes. The test of the quality is the effect it has on the voice. Children can strain their voices more by singing with harsh, tense, small voices than they can by shouting. The teacher who is aware of the proper use of the voice can help children use it correctly. By knowing and providing a wide variety of music, the teacher can do much toward keeping a balance in the types of songs the children sing.

Developing Skills in Music

The teacher who is concerned with keeping music a creative, spontaneous experience might well ask about techniques. What about drill, the echo game, the singing games, the question-and-answer games? Is there a place for them? What about teaching children to read music?

A teacher who knows music and children will incorporate into her program the drills and the techniques as children are ready to profit from them. Indeed, children enjoy many of the so-called musical games if they are well directed in a spirit of fun. Of course, the child who is a poor singer should never be singled out; the game should be played for the fun and benefit of all. As long as the teacher keeps in mind the objectives of music in the life of young children, she will not go far afield from the course she should follow. Evaluation should be in terms of the child's previous progress, not in terms of progress made by other children.

TEACHING SONGS

The desire to sing is present in most children when they come to school. A child sings unconsciously as he works, as he plays, and sometimes as he rests. He learns his first songs by imitation. If the teacher has a large repertoire of songs and enjoys singing frequently with the children, they will share her enjoyment. She does not need to be a soloist or a highly trained singer, but she should have a voice that is accurate in pitch and sweet in tone. If she sings joyously, with correct phrasing and breathing, and enunciates the words clearly, she can expect the singing habits of the children to be good, for children reflect the singing habits the teacher exemplifies. If she really cannot sing, she can use recordings.

In teaching a song to a group, it is important for the teacher to *know* the song, to present it in a pleasant, engaging manner, in a direct and simple way with a good tone quality, and to interpret the mood. Discussions, explanations, and questions are likely to diminish the child's interest in learning the song. The teacher should sing the song in its entirety. She may then have the children join with her; and before she or the group realizes it, another song has been learned. Children learn singing as they learn anything else — by participating in the activity. They should be allowed to join in the singing as they feel ready and learn the song by singing it, not by reciting the words.

By the end of the kindergarten, a few children are able to reproduce a phrase after hearing it on only one occasion. By the end of the primary grades, all the children should be able to reproduce the phrase after hearing it only once. They may not be able to reproduce it accurately on pitch, but they all should make the effort.

In the second and third grades, children usually are ready to sing from books. They enjoy the thrill of the first experience in examining and following a musical score. This should be kept a happy occasion without concentrating on the structural analysis of the songs. As in previous grades, all singing should grow out of the children's needs and experiences.

Music in the Nursery School

Music should be an integral part of the nursery-school child's experience. Young children are not too much concerned with knowing the words; if they forget the words the teacher sang, they can sing new ones. The teacher who knows many songs, who can burst into song at the appropriate moment, encourages singing. Similarly, the teacher who can listen to children sing and record the music is well rewarded for her efforts. The sparkling eyes and other evidences of appreciation tell her what it means to Douglas when she announces, "Boys and girls, this is Douglas's song. I wrote it down while he was singing it. Would you like to hear it?" And the children hear:

> A little red bird flew up in the tree,
> He said tweet tweet to me.
> Will you come back another day?
> I asked him, as he flew away.

The teacher's main concern is that children enjoy music, that they shall have opportunity to sing, to listen to, and to appreciate beautiful songs.

The early experiences with music in nursery school are short, not more than five or ten minutes with the youngest children. As the year progresses, the time is extended. The four-year-olds listen for a longer period. They enjoy singing or even listening to recordings for some fifteen minutes. Children like to choose favorite songs to sing. These favorites are usually also the songs they sing best, and they sing them with gusto.

In one class the teacher played *Claire de Lune* for the children. Peter walked over to the easel and said, "That's blue music; I'll paint it." He painted a picture with circular movements that looked the way the music sounded. The quiet, peaceful rhythm of the composition was reflected in Peter's painting. Children may be permitted to leave the music group in this way to paint, when the teacher plays music that encourages the child to express his mood in art. As the individual child interprets the mood of the song, selecting his own type of response in singing, swaying, dancing, skipping, or drama, the rest of the group may continue singing. One group may express itself in various forms of music while another is singing, and vice versa.

A visit to a symphony orchestra makes the child realize that music is not isolated from living.

The teaching of songs in this way, as imitation and always as an outgrowth of intrinsic situations, should continue through the grades. The teacher's ability in this regard will be measured by her skill in making all singing an activity that has meaning and significance for the children. The child learns to express feelings and ideas in this form of creative art as he does in all other forms. The teacher's ability will be shown in the children's spontaneous desire to sing. To organize the classroom environment so that all children want to sing is one of the most challenging tasks of the teacher as she guides children from nursery school through the primary grades.

Music in the Kindergarten

Kindergarten children like to gather in an informal group around the piano. Sometimes the teacher holds a song book up for them to see, and they recognize the songs that they sing. When a new song is introduced, everybody listens to the teacher; even before she has finished, however, some of the children have started to sing. Then the teacher plays music to which all the children can respond.

Music in the First Grade

Activities begun in the preschool and kindergarten are continued in the first grade. There is much spontaneous rote singing of old and new songs without books until the second semester. Even when books are used there is no attempt to read music. For these children music is singing, dancing, creating, and playing in the rhythm band.

Music in the Second Grade

In the second grade, musical activities continue to emphasize creative experiences in a broadened rhythmic program, an expanded listening program, and in the wider use of rhythm and tonette bands as class activity. Water glasses, xylophones, and flower pots may be used to give additional experiences with music. Creative work in composing individual and group songs is extended and encouraged, and a definite program to develop readiness for the reading of music is launched. The latter consists of four phases: giving the child a broad background of melody, singing many kinds of songs, listening to music, and developing a feeling for the tonic chord. Books are put into the hands of children during the second semester to help build up readiness for reading music in the third grade, and songs are written on the blackboard.

Music in the Third Grade

The third grade presents a challenge to the teacher who teaches her own program. Sometime around this age, children become interested in reading music. They still have as the core of the music program the singing of songs — longer and more beautiful ones. They learn that certain types of songs have an accompaniment, which is an integral part of the song. They

Children should be encouraged to develop their own instrumentation for rhythm band selections.

continue to enjoy community and folk songs, and stress is placed on music of other countries as well as that of our own. If the teacher has the skill, this is the time to teach children to sing foreign songs in the language in which they were written. Such a practice serves a dual purpose: it has the educational value of broadening the child's cultural background by including a knowledge of other languages and cultures, and it adds the human-relations value of promoting better understanding among peoples. All countries have their favorite and significant songs. If by good fortune or foresight we bring to our children some of this musical literature, their lives as well as our own will be enriched. Once the group has given evidence of reading readiness, the teacher can begin to teach children to read music. She may use the approach of the number system or the scale and tonic chord sung by numbers and syllables. She must provide for drill in ear training. Listening activities continue; creative expression in composing songs is extended; rhythmic activities are broadened to include learning dances of our own and other countries; tonette and rhythm bands continue. In addition, children of this age like to organize choirs and give musical programs.

The Rhythm Band

Young children in kindergarten and primary grades enjoy experimenting with different effects on rhythm band instruments. The rhythm may be continued through the primary grades.

A suggested seating arrangement for a band of twenty might be:

Left	Center	Right
2 triangles	1 drum	1 cymbal
4 rhythm sticks	2 tambourines	6 sand blocks
	4 bells	piano

With practice and with emphasis on intelligent listening, children can learn to choose the instruments that convey the feeling of the different parts in the music. For example, light, airy music would be best accompanied by bells.

Music appreciation for young children is so closely connected with vocal, instrumental, and bodily response to music that it can scarcely be thought of apart from these activities. Though in all musical experience the children are encouraged to listen — to distinguish between music of different types and moods and to recognize melodies — yet often the child's first response upon hearing a bit of music is "Let's do it," "Let's sing it," "Let's play it."

A story or some suggestion as to what the child may hear will arouse a keen interest in new music. For example, to know that at some time while listening to the phonograph record of *In a Clock Store,* one may expect to hear tiny little clocks, great big clocks, and even an alarm clock, will be certain to make any child alert and attentive. Children enjoy using such records for the rhythm band.

Similarly, a single phonograph record or a few simple numbers played by skilled musicians on such instruments as the violin, the cello, the flute, or piano will mean more to the children than will an hour's concert, which may weary them.

QUESTIONS AND ACTIVITIES

1. Observe in a nursery school or kindergarten and in a primary grade to see how basic principles for music education are developed.

2. Can appreciation be taught? What is the role of the teacher in helping a child develop aesthetic appreciation? How does intellectual effort enter into the creative expression or enjoyment of music?

3. What is the best method of encouraging children who have no sense of pitch to participate in group singing?

4. Summarize the types of music children should be provided with in the pre-school and primary grades. How should the teacher go about selecting songs for the children to learn?

5. Observe in two kindergartens or primary grades to see if the same types of musical experiences are in evidence. If they are not, try to determine the reason.

6. Assume you are going to teach in a school in which the children seem to be repressed. What musical activities would you provide to help release these children? What would you have to consider in planning a program?

7. What is the educational value of playing records for young children and having them join in singing with the recorded music?

8. How would a nonmusical teacher provide adequate musical experiences for her pupils?

SELECTED READINGS

Barnett, David. *They Shall Have Music.* New York: George W. Stewart, Publisher, Inc., 1944.

Bresel, Ann Sterling. *Another Singing Time.* New York: Oxford University Press, n.d.

Brooks, Marian, and Henry Brown. *Music Education in the Elementary Schools.* New York: American Book Company, 1946.

Children and Music. Washington, D.C.: The Association for Childhood Education, 1948.

Children, The Music Makers. Albany, N.Y.: Bureau of Elementary Curriculum Development, 1953.

Coleman, Satais N. *Creative Music.* New York: The John Day Company, 1940.

Coleman, S. N., and A. G. Thorne. *Singing Time.* New York: The John Day Company, 1940.

Crowninshield, Ethel. *New Songs and Games.* Boston: Boston Music Company, 1951.

Crowninshield, Ethel. *The Song and Play Book.* Boston: Boston Music Company, 1944.

Fielder, Grace. *Rhythmic Program for Elementary Schools.* St. Louis: C. V. Mosby Company, 1952.

Foresman, R. *A Child's Book of Songs.* New York: American Book Company, 1948.

Fox, Lillian Mohr, and L. Thomas Hopkins. *Creative School Music.* New York: Silver Burdett Company, 1936.

Glenn, Mabel. *Listen and Sing.* Boston: Ginn and Company, 1943.

Grant, Parks. *Music for Elementary Teachers.* New York: Appleton-Century-Crofts, Inc., 1951.

Hamlin, Alice, and Margaret Gussford. *Singing Games for Children.* Cincinnati: Willis Music Co., n.d.

Hood, Marguerite V., and E. J. Schulz. *Learning Music Through Rhythm.* Boston: Ginn and Company, 1949.

Hunt, Beatrice A., and Harry R. Wilson. *Songs and Dance.* Chicago: Hall, McCreary Co., 1945.

Hunt, Evelyn. *Music Time.* New York: The Viking Press, Inc., 1947.

Landeck, Beatrice. *Children and Music.* New York: William Sloane Associates, Inc., 1952.

Landeck, Beatrice. *Songs to Grow On.* New York: Gerald Marks Music Co., 1950.

MacCarteneyer, Laura. *Songs for Nursery School.* Cincinnati: Willis Music Co., 1937.

McConathy, Osbourne. *New Music Horizons: Music in the Primary Grades.* New York: Silver Burdett Company, 1955.

Martin, F., and E. Burnett. *Rime, Rhythm and Song.* Chicago: Hall, McCreary Co., 1942.

Mursell, James L. *Music and the Classroom Teacher,* Revised Edition. New York: Silver Burdett Company, 1956.

Music Educators National Conference. *Music Education in a Changing World* (ed. Max Kaplan). Washington, D.C.: National Education Association, 1958.

Music Educators National Conference. *Music for Fours and Fives* (ed. Beatrice Landeck). Washington, D.C.: National Education Association, 1958.

Music for Children's Living. Washington, D.C.: The Association for Childhood Education, 1956.

Music Hour in Kindergarten and First Grade. New York: Silver Burdett Company, 1948.

Myers, Louise Kifer. *Teaching Children Music in the Elementary School.* Englewood Cliffs, N.J.: Prentice-Hall, Inc., 1954.

Nordholm, Harriet. *Singing and Playing.* New York: Mills Music, Inc., 1950.

Nye, R. E., and B. Bergethon. *Basic Music for Classroom Teachers.* Englewood Cliffs, N.J.: Prentice-Hall, Inc., 1954.

Pitts, Lula Belle. *Kindergarten Book.* Boston: Ginn and Company, 1951.

Pitts, Lula Belle, Mabelle Glenn, and Loraine E. Watters. *Singing All the Day.* Boston: Ginn and Company, 1957.

Play and Sing. Chicago: Meissner Institute of Music, n.d.

Seashore, C. E. *In Search of Beauty with Music.* New York: The Ronald Press Company, 1955.

Sehon, Elizabeth. *Rhythm in the Elementary School.* New York: A. S. Barnes & Co., 1951.

Sheehy, Emma Dickson. *There's Music in Children.* New York: Henry Holt & Company, Inc., 1952.

Siebold, Meta. *More Happy Songs for Happy Children.* New York: G. Schirmer Co., n.d.

Songs Children Like: Folk Songs from Many Lands. Washington, D.C.: The Association for Childhood Education, 1954.

Squire, R. N. *Introduction to Music Education.* New York: The Ronald Press Company, 1955.

Thompson, Carl, and Harriet Nordham. *Keys to Teaching Elementary School Music.* Minneapolis: Paul Schmitt Music Co., 1949.

Tooze, R., and B. F. Krone. *Literature and Music Resources for Social Studies.* Englewood Cliffs, N.J.: Prentice-Hall, Inc., 1955.

Wright, Frances. *Song Source Material for Social Studies Units.* New York: Columbia University Press, 1946.

SELECTED RECORDINGS

Anderson, LeRoy. *LeRoy Anderson Conducts His Own Compositions.* Decca.

Bartok, Bela. *Piano Music for Children.* Westminster.

Bartok, Bela. *The Voice of the Arts.* Vox.

Faith, Percy. *Festival.* Columbia.

Haydn, Franz Joseph. *Let's Listen to Haydn.* Haydn Society.

Luther, Frank. *Children's Corner.* Decca.

Marias, Joseph. *Songs of the African Veldt.* Decca.

Nelson, M. J., and Gladys Tipton. *Music for Early Childhood.* Silver Burdett.

Pitts, Lula Belle, Mabelle Glenn, and Loraine E. Watters. *Our Singing World.* Ginn.

Schubert, Franz. *March Militaire.* RCA Victor.

Seeger, Ruth. *American Folk Songs for Children.* Doubleday.

Tripp, Paul, and George Kleinsinger. *Tubby the Tuba.* Decca.

Waberg, B. J. *Dance Along.* Folkways.

Williams, Tex. *A & E Rag.* Capitol.

And children's faces looking up
Holding wonder like a cup.

— SARAH TEASDALE

CREATIVE ACTIVITIES

Dramatics

"The World and I" might well be the title of a child's creative activity, regardless of the medium through which he chooses to express himself — blocks, toys, movement, music, writing, paint, or words. Dramatic play looms large in the life of the young child. Long before he goes to nursery school, he has had many experiences in dramatic play. It is spontaneous; he needs no suggestions. He knows how to play, because play is the child's life, and dramatic play is "trying on" life. It is the way a child relives what he knows about his world. In terms of the child, this means that he is playing out the things he sees, hears, feels, and thinks about. He dramatizes his own emotions, his fears, doubts, anxieties, loves, and dislikes. By talking and dramatizing he rejects some of his erroneous ideas about the world and organizes events at his own level of understanding. Dramatic play has been called "the mirror of the child." Within the space of a morning a child may be a captain, a child, a mother; he may be a bird, a tree, a bear, a puppy, or a rocket. He can turn from being a mailman to being a conductor, the wind, or a plane. This delightful experience of make-believe that is real for the moment begins and ends spontaneously. Emphasis is on the play, not the performance; the process, not the product.

The younger the child, the less selective he is in choosing what he will be and the less time he will spend in being any one thing or person. When he is in nursery school or kindergarten his interpretation of the adult world around him and of his parents gives the teacher some idea of his attitude toward life as well as an understanding of his general behavior. Dramatic play thus affords opportunities to both child and teacher: to the child, to act out and "try on" life; and to the teacher, to gain an understanding of the concepts the child is forming about life.

Dramatic play is completely unrehearsed, spontaneous activity. It is not directed by the teacher. It may be as simple as a child's reliving a situation from past experience, from a recent television show, from a current happening, or from a movie.

Playmaking, the term used interchangeably with creative dramatics, is an inclusive term that takes in all forms of improvised drama. It includes dramatic play, pantomime, puppet plays, and story dramatization. It is extemporaneous, informal, created by the players. It may be original as to idea, plot, and character, or it may be based on a well-known story.

Creative Play in the Kindergarten

Creative dramatics in the kindergarten includes such spontaneous play as we have seen, where children act out their experiences without teacher guidance. It includes, too, another form of dramatics, in which the children act out nursery rhymes, poems, or stories they enjoy. In this form of drama the teacher is a guide, but *only* a guide. She does not put words into the mouths of the children. She stirs the imagination of the children, and they take it from there. Children will be encouraged to express themselves in spontaneous play more naturally if there is a physical as well as a social environment that affords opportunities for play — a playhouse corner, blocks, farm animals, toys, and centers of interest that suggest various activities.

Taking children on trips to see buildings going up, roads being made, machinery in action, or to the library to hear the librarian tell a story and to bring books back to school — all are instrumental in encouraging children to act out their experiences. When children have nothing to say, they are silent. Dramatic play that follows a trip should have some of the emotion of the original experience. Children should be encouraged to remember how they felt when they rode on the elephant, or slid down the pole at the firestation, or rode on the miniature train at the zoo. The questions the teacher asks are, "Can you show us how you felt when you were sitting on the turtle's back at the zoo?" "Did you feel like a fire chief when you sat beside the chief at the station?"

POEMS AND STORIES

Children like dramatizing or playing out favorite poems and rhymes. A poem that lends itself to action and feeling will be especially enjoyed. Such a poem is "Crescent Moon," by Elizabeth Maddox Roberts:

> And Dick said, "Look what I have found!"
> And when we saw we danced around,
> And made our feet just touch the ground.

We skipped our toes and sang, "Oh-lo.
Oh-who, oh-who, oh what do you know!
Oh-who, oh-hi, oh-loo, kee-lo!"

We clapped our hands and sang, "Oh-ee!"
It made us jump and laugh to see
The little new moon above the tree.[5]

They like, too, to dramatize the favorite Mother Goose rhymes, such as "Little Miss Muffit," "Jack and Jill," "Little Jack Horner," "Sing a Song of Sixpence," "Old King Cole," "Mary Had a Little Lamb," and others. The rhythm, the action, the feeling, and their familiarity make these favorites of children. In dramatizing nursery rhymes as well as in dramatizing poems and stories, the questions should be, "What does it make you feel like?" "What does it make you see?" "What does it make you hear?" "What do you see when you think about it?" "How do you feel inside?" First-hand experiences are excellent for sensitizing children to what they see, hear, smell, taste, and touch. The teacher should constantly be on the lookout for poems, rhymes, and songs that children can read with genuine feeling, that arouse in children a sense of appreciation as well as a sense of enjoyment.

[5] Elizabeth Maddox Roberts, "Crescent Moon," quoted in May Arbuthnot, *Children and Books* (Chicago: Scott, Foresman & Company, 1957), p. 142.

Familiar nursery rhymes, such as "Old King Cole," are excellent vehicles for original interpretation.

The Teacher's Role in Playmaking

Not only in the kindergarten, where it is used to a considerable extent, but also in the primary grades creative drama has real value for children. Unfortunately, some teachers feel that without specific training they are unable to do anything about drama in the classroom. As one teacher expressed it recently, "I never had a course in it; my critic teacher didn't know anything about it and wouldn't let me try it out. Now I'm afraid to try it."

This teacher would do well to attend a class or a summer workshop, and then experiment with dramatics when she returns. Even without such an opportunity, she can read books on creative dramatics, and if she understands the problems and responsibilities in creating an environment conducive to creativity, if she has a feeling for selecting the right stories to read to the children, she is on her way toward encouraging creativity in yet another form. Because the problems and responsibilities for creating the environment and providing the stories are similar in the kindergarten and primary grades, we will discuss the teacher's role without categorizing the various age levels. Children themselves differ in creative ability, and the teacher must adapt her teaching to the children. The creative teacher does this in every form of art and in every phase of teaching.

PROBLEMS OF SPACE, TIME, AND NUMBERS

The problems teachers face in these days of crowded classrooms and crowded schedules are very real. They are likely to center around too little space, too little time, and too many children.

As for the problem of space, it is very much the same as that in teaching rhythms. Here too, however, there are ways of coping with the situation. The teacher can have the children use pantomime standing beside their desks or tables and use the aisles as the need arises. The gym, auditorium, or outdoor play area may be available at times.

Dramatics can be planned for the last period of the day during a creative time when children are free to choose activities. Dramatics can also be a part of the program in literature or in the social studies on occasion. The children will finish their regular work promptly if they know there is to be time for playmaking.

As for the number of children in the group, creative dramatics has on occasion been used successfully even with as many as sixty kindergarten children. This is far too large a group, admittedly, but even with such a large group the children gained from the experience. In such an instance, half of the children can be the audience, while the other half play the story or experience, and vice versa. In pantomime, all the children may participate at the same time. Children learn early that some one needs to be an audience at least part of the time. Although twenty is an ideal number for creative dramatics, that number in a given grade or group is becoming more and more rare.

CREATING AN ENVIRONMENT FOR CREATIVE DRAMA

A creative teacher begets creativity — but more teachers are creative than are aware of it. The same permissive, yet organized, environment required in other creative arts is essential here. The group needs to know there is freedom to express, but freedom with control. There is sympathy and understanding on the part of teacher and children, but both also expect that each child will put his best effort into each experience. For young children all that is needed is a first-hand experience, a rereading of a favorite story, or a brief discussion of the story — and the play is on.

A Plan of Procedure

Although the children do the actual creating of characters, they must have the support and guidance of the teacher; and the teacher must have a plan of procedure with which she feels comfortable. Her responsibilities as a guide include motivating the children, presenting the material, planning the characters and action, and evaluating the whole activity.

MOTIVATING

No good teacher will wait for the inspiration of the moment. She goes out to meet it by motivating the group. The teacher must stir imagination, fire enthusiasm, and arouse curiosity. She may ask a question that sets the child thinking. Good motivation serves to kindle interest and engenders a feeling of excitement. For example, if the teacher were interested in introducing the nursery rhyme, "Sing a Song of Sixpence," she might ask, "What ever would you do if a bird flew by and snatched off your nose?" Or she might appeal to the child's senses. Listening with the children to the music of *Images on the Water*, by Ravel, might open the way for the story about Ping, the duck who lived on a boat in the yellow waters of the Yangtze River.

Another possibility is using activities within the community. These serve well as springboards for creative playmaking. Then, too, we are all familiar with seasonal motivation — the first snowfall, when the children run to the window and go dancing gaily back to their seats, making the way clear for the playing of "The Snow Had Begun in the Gloaming." Or at this point they might be ready for a story such as "The Big Snow," by Laura Ingalls Wilder.

The world of nature, with its frogs, spiders, bugs, and turtles, its flowers and sun, offers rich opportunities for creative play. A question such as, "Who likes the rain?" leads into dramatization of a number of activities.

A skillful leader will have something unusual to use to motivate children — a riddle, a joke, a secret, holiday material, or any delightful surprise. An ingenious teacher looks constantly for new ways to stir children's interest in creative play.

PRESENTING THE MATERIAL

It is in the realm of presentation that the teacher must draw upon her knowledge of literature and her skill in story-telling. She should choose her material from stories and poems to which she herself reacts with enthusiasm and to which she believes her group will react favorably. The story should be so familiar to the teacher that she can give her full attention to its interpretation and to the reaction of the children.

They must understand the story, the characters, and the plot from the way she tells it. The teacher brings the story to life, and brings life to it for the audience. Ruth Sawyer, a famous story-teller, once described the significance of this process: "One never knows the untold joy of the artist in taking substance, giving it form and color, blowing the breath of life into it, and then watching it take on life for others." In this case it is the teacher who knows the sequence of the story, keeps in mind the picture of the plot as it unfolds, and adapts it to the particular group to whom she is telling it.

One of the most important skills in working with young children is the ability to breathe life into a story, and this cannot be done with a colorless, monotonous voice. The teacher must be alive, both to the possibilities of the story and to the reaction of her audience. Nothing is more disappointing to children than to have a story read in a dull, unexciting fashion. The teacher who realizes the values of creative experiences will see to it that the children are inspired, not bored, by the way she reads the story or, preferably, tells it.

PLANNING ACTION AND CHARACTERS

The younger the child, the sooner the play should start. Young children are not interested in long discussion of what the characters are like. They want to hurry through the planning of the scenes, characters, and setting. The teacher may go into the play immediately with very young children.

Planning the scenes. The scenes should be decided on by the teacher and children together. If the class is playing *The Three Bears*, for instance, they might suggest four scenes: (1) the room where the bear family is getting breakfast, (2) Goldilocks's home, where Goldilocks is making her plans for the day, (3) the forest where the bears have gone for a walk, and (4) the home of the three bears upon their return. The children would not attempt the entire story at the first playing.

Planning the characters. Once a tentative plan of action has been set and there has been a brief discussion of each character, children "try on" characters by pantomiming. Teacher and children choose several characters. She may ask questions such as, "What kind of bear is the Father Bear? What kind of bear is the baby Bear? What about Goldilocks? Do you think she asked her

Giving life to the story effectively joins creative art and dramatics.

mother if she could go out for a walk? Are you ready? Let's pantomime the action together."

Planning a setting. In creative dramatics a setting is not essential. Children bring the setting to the experience with their imagination. Unless the setting is an integral part of the play, it is not needed. As for properties, only simple, suggestive ones should be used.

PLAYING

As far as the children are concerned, the play itself is the important event. The teacher helps the children understand that once the stage manager has announced the play, everyone is in character and remains so until the play is over and the audience applauds. The leader or stage manager says, "Cast on stage," or "Characters, take your places." A hush descends upon the room, and the play is on! Curtain may be called at the end of the scene or play, but the children will know when it is over.

EVALUATION

Praise is important in any creative activity. It is best to begin by telling the good things about the play. Such questions as, "What did you like about our play?" "What made it so good?" "How can we improve it if we play it again some day?" are helpful. Criticism should be kept on a positive plane. As children mature, they can evaluate the various phases of the play — the action, story characterization, dialogue, the manner in which the group worked together, and the audience reaction and behavior. Children in the audience should realize that they, too, have a responsibility — that of listening in order to bring enjoyment to the entire group. The longer the play, the more important it is that each scene be planned carefully. In the initial attempts at creative dramatics it is wise to choose children who can carry the play. Later the timid child will volunteer and enjoy it.

A Scheme for Evaluation

General
1. What did you think made our play interesting?
2. What did you think was particularly good about the way we played it?
3. How might we improve it?

Characterization
1. Were the characters in our play thinking and feeling like the characters in our story?
2. Were they convincing?
3. How did they make you feel they were real?
4. Did everyone stay in character throughout the entire scene?
5. Did the characters interact with each other?

Action
1. Was the play interesting to watch?
2. If you did not know the story, could you tell what was happening?
3. Did we keep the story going?
4. How do you think we might have helped it to move along a little faster?
5. Did we crowd the characters into too small a space or did we use the entire space?

Story
1. Was the story exciting and interesting, or did it seem ordinary?
2. Did our play tell the story?
3. Did we have a good climax?
4. Did you like the way it ended?

Dialogue
1. Did the dialogue help to move the story along, or did the characters talk about things not needed in the play?
2. How did the characters help each other to keep the dialogue going?
3. Did the dialogue seem to stop sometimes?
4. Did the dialogue seem real?

Cooperation
1. Did we all work together to create the scene?
2. How did the audience help?

3. How did the characters who were off stage part of the time cooperate for the good of the play?
4. Did any character call attention to himself rather than help to make the play important?
5. Was there a good spirit among the cast?
6. How did the players help each other?

Pacing
1. Did the play move along or did it drag?
2. If it dragged, what was the reason?
3. How might we improve it next time?

Voices of players
1. Did the players project their voices so that the audience could hear without straining?
2. How might the players improve their voices next time?

Audience participation
1. Did the audience take the responsibility of being good listeners?
2. Did they help us do our best work?
3. Did they laugh at the "right" places?

Time in preparation
1. Did we spend enough time in planning the play?

Suggested Material for Dramatization

Children react differently to different stories, but a few are perennial favorites with young children. Among those the author has used successfully with innumerable groups of kindergarten and primary children are:

Stories	*Nursery Rhymes*	*Poems*
Cinderella	Sing a Song of Sixpence	Hiding
The Three Bears	Old King Cole	Galoshes
The Three Pigs	The Queen of Hearts	Who Likes the Rain
The Three Billy Goats Gruff	Little Miss Muffit	The Snowman
The Runaway Bunny	Little Boy Blue	The Butterbean Tent
The Little Rabbit Who	Little Jack Horner	The Crimson Balloon
Wanted Red Wings	Ride a Cock Horse	Fancy Dress
Peter Rabbit	Three Little Mice	Choosing Shoes
The Little Wooden Farmer	Hickory Dickory Dock	Imaginings
The Bremen Musicians	Mary Had a Little Lamb	Firefly
The Elves and the	Daffy Down Dilly	What is Pink?
Shoemaker	Mistress Mary	Clouds
Three Little Kittens	Jack Be Nimble	The Swing
The Little Engine That		
Could		
Chicken Little Count to Ten		
Snipp, Snapp, Snurr and		
the Red Shoes		

Activity pantomime is another form of dramatization children like. This might include such activities as picking violets in the woods, eating an ice cream cone, hanging out the laundry, wrapping a gift, washing the dog, or sweeping the floor. Mood pantomime might include reading a letter containing exciting news, pretending someone is taking a splinter out of the child's finger, or watching television.

Creative Dramatization in a Third Grade

Presented here is an illustration of a typical third grade participating in a creative dramatization. This group has chosen language arts for the core of the curriculum. The teacher has read to the class many times the story of *Snipp, Snapp, Snurr and the Red Shoes.* "What is a good way to play a story as long as this is? . . . That's right, Marjorie. The best way to play it is in parts or scenes. Let's play just the first part today."

Without hesitation the children volunteer to be the characters; the mother, Snipp, Snapp, and Snurr are chosen. The children go up on the stage and prepare to act their parts.

"I don't know what the mother is doing," says the teacher, and she waits for the mother to decide. But the mother just stands there; she has no ideas. The teacher suggests several possibilities. Finally the mother decides to be reading a book. Because this particular group has had little experience with creative dramatics, they need many suggestions from the teacher.

"Boys, why don't you just be natural and do the things you normally do?"
The boys come in in a rather stilted manner. "Mother," they say, "we

In very young children dramatic play is a completely spontaneous and natural activity.

can't decide what to get you for your birthday. Tomorrow is the day. What would you want us to get for you?"

The scene ends, and Snipp, Snapp, and Snurr go out to play. This is better; they play basketball and get some action into it. But of course they are really on their way upstairs to get their banks, so they creep quietly up the stairs and try to get the money out. There is not enough, as we know, and the scene ends when each boy has found a job to earn enough money to buy the red shoes Mother wants.

Now another group comes up on the stage to play the same scene. They put more life into it. Mother says, "I wonder if anyone in my family will remember my birthday? I can't believe I'm thirty-two. I wonder if I'm getting gray. I should be, with those three boys to raise. Oh, well, they are pretty fine at that. When I think of poor Mrs. Svenson I count myself lucky. I'll have to stop thinking aloud; here they come now."

Snipp, Snapp, and Snurr hurry breathlessly into the room asking, "Mother, may we go out and play a while? It's such a beautiful day, and we promised Kim we'd come over for a while — that is, if it's all right with you. But first, Mother, tell us what you want for your birthday. We've been saving our allowance to buy you the best present there is, the best present for the best mother. Would you like a train, a wagon or . . ."

"I would like a pair of new red shoes," she answers. "Red is so popular this season. Mrs. Svenson has a pair, and you know I hate to have her get ahead of me. Your poor father hasn't been working much though; I'd almost given up hope. But I surely wish that you would get them for me."

The boys run out, but actually they go upstairs, and to their chagrin there is not enough money.

"I never realized shoes cost so much. What can we do?" asked Snipp.

"We could try getting jobs, although I know they are scarce."

"Let's try," chant the boys in unison.

And they are off. Before they end their scene, they have found jobs — one with a painter, one with a chimney sweep, and the third with a miller. The audience wishes the play could go on. This group is spontaneous and original in dialogue, full of action, and mindful of character; but the bell rings, and the class is over.

ANALYSIS

The first group apparently did not know the story well enough to put any originality into their performance. The teacher knew that they were really not ready for dramatization, because these children had had little experience in creative dramatics before they enrolled in their present school. However, they seemed to enjoy playmaking if they could be in a group where no one was particularly talented. They had come a long way but, of course, still had a long way to go. The second group had been playmaking since kindergarten. The place to start creative dramatics, as is evident from this experience, is in the nursery school and the kindergarten, not in the third grade. The first group might have reacted more favorably to playing a nursery rhyme or a poem in pantomime, but by this time they naturally wanted to do just what the other group was doing.

Evaluation

One of the most valuable elements of creative dramatics is the final evaluation, in which children discuss the play. The teacher can be sure that she is guiding dramatic play and playmaking creatively if she can answer some of the following questions affirmatively:

1. Do the children feel free to express themselves creatively?
2. Do they deal with the dialogue in a spontaneous manner?
3. Do they keep the attention of the audience?
4. Is the emphasis on the product or on the process?
5. Do I motivate them to the point where they want to do their best work?
6. Do I enter into the spirit of playmaking?
7. Do I stay out of it once the play has begun?
8. Do I try honestly to choose all the children?
9. Do I help children evaluate their performances in a constructive manner?
10. Do I help them ask the right kind of questions?
11. Do I take more interest in the participation and enjoyment of the children than in the setting and properties?
12. Do I help the children sense the responsibility of the audience?

QUESTIONS AND ACTIVITIES

1. Define and explain the following terms: dramatic play, creative dramatics, children's theatre, child drama, and playmaking.

2. Why are some children in nursery school unwilling to participate in creative dramatics? Why are some primary-grade children reluctant?

3. List some suggestions that would help a beginning teacher in her first experiences in creative dramatics in a primary grade.

4. The kindergarten teacher says, "I don't need to know anything about creative dramatics, because in kindergarten the children just engage in dramatic play. That leaves me out." Do you agree with her point of view? Why or why not?

5. Assume you are going to work with a first-grade group that has had experience in creative dramatics. The children are ready to plan a program in which they will "play" a story in the gym. Plan the characters, scenes, and so forth, with this imaginary group.

6. List a series of experiences children of a specific age level have that would dramatize well.

7. Indicate how dramatics could be utilized in units of work in areas such as music or social studies.

8. Indicate how a particular story children like might be adapted for creative dramatics.

9. Begin collecting poems that will be suitable for dramatization for the primary level. Examine story books that you feel will have possibilities for use in creative dramatics in the grade of your choice. Try to think through the type of motivation you would use in presenting one of these stories or poems to a group of children of the ages you hope to teach.

SELECTED READINGS

Batchelder, Marjorie. *The Puppet Theatre Handbook*. New York: Harper & Brothers, 1947.

Bowen, F. C. *Let's Play a Story*. Arts in Childhood Series 6, Bulletin 3. Nashville, Tenn.: Fisk University, 1951.

Brown, Corrine. *Creative Drama in the Lower School*. New York: Appleton-Century-Crofts, Inc., 1930.

Burger, Isabel. *Creative Play Acting*. New York: A. S. Barnes & Co., 1950.

Durland, Frances D. *Creative Dramatics for Children*. Yellow Springs, Ohio: Antioch Press, 1952.

Hagga, Agnes, and Patricia Randles. *Supplementary Materials for Use in Creative Dramatics*. Seattle: University of Washington Press, 1952.

Hartley, Ruth, *et al. Understanding Children's Play*. New York: Columbia University Press, 1952.

Huber, Miriam, and Blanton Huber. *Story and Verse for Children*. New York: The Macmillan Company, 1957.

Lease, R., and G. B. Siks. *Creative Dramatics in Home, School and Community*. New York: Harper & Brothers, 1952.

Mearns, Hughes. *Creative Youth*. New York: Doubleday-Doran and Co., Inc., 1925.

Mearns, Hughes. *The Creative Adult*. New York: Doubleday-Doran and Co., Inc., 1940.

Richmond, Arthur. *Remo Bufano's Book of Puppetry*. New York: The Macmillan Company, 1950.

Siks, Geraldine Brain. *Creative Dramatics: An Art for Children*. New York: Harper & Brothers, 1958.

Slade, Peter. *Child Drama*. London: University of London Press, 1954.

Slade, Peter. *With Younger Children*. Seattle: University of Washington Press, 1952.

Walker, Pamela Prince. *Seven Steps to Creative Dramatics*. New York: Hill and Wang, Inc., 1957.

Ward, Winifred. "Dramatics: A Creative Force," *School Executive*, 69:54–56, August 1950.

Ward, Winifred. *Playmaking with Children*, Second Edition. New York: Appleton-Century-Crofts, Inc., 1957.

Woods, Margaret S. *Creative Dramatics*. Washington, D.C.: National Education Association, 1959.

Not trees, but growth; not blossoms, but bloom.

— VINCENT VAN GOGH

CREATIVE ACTIVITIES

Art

No artistic expression is possible without experience. The way in which a child reacts to experience is primarily responsible for his expression, provided no factors prevent his free expression. The child is an artist. Like a true artist he expresses what he feels and believes. He expresses not only what is significant to him during the process of painting or modeling, but also the awareness present in his thinking, feeling, and perceiving. Through his art the child invites us into his inner world and shares with us his inner life. "Not trees, but growth; not blossoms but bloom" [6] — this is what his art is telling us if we but listen. It is through the art medium that the child attempts to give adults an intimate understanding of his relationship to the world and the things it represents. The greater his willingness to experiment, the greater his flexibility and breadth of concepts, the more harmoniously organized is his experience and the more meaningful his creation.

As the child grows and develops, his relationship to experience changes. Adults must become sensitized to this changing relationship in order to nurture and guide the artistic expression of children. Without such understanding, no effective motivation toward expression in the arts is possible.

Characteristics of Art Education

The most challenging concept in art education is the belief that all children are artists. Today's belief in the creativity of all — and the concomitant

[6] Vincent Van Gogh, quoted in Louis Untermeyer, *Makers of the Modern World* (New York: Simon and Schuster, Inc., 1955), p. 228.

recognition that some few have an even greater degree of creativity — has given new emphasis to creative expression in the classroom. The idea that every child can be helped to produce something that is new, superior, or unique when compared with previous performances, affords a greater challenge to the teacher than ever before.

Artistic expression does not emerge from a void. One cannot create in a vacuum. The painting of the artist reflects his thoughts and feelings, the result of his reaction to and interaction with his environment. In former years, children were told what to make and how to make it. Today the child is permitted and encouraged to experiment freely with tools and materials. No longer is the child given a step-by-step outline of what, how, and why. The teacher knows that she has a place in providing the materials, the tools, the time, the space, and the guidance in techniques, but the creative expression is the child's own.

The development of taste in art, as in music and in literature, is a specific objective of the program in the arts. There is too much evidence of bad taste in today's world.

Artistic skills should be used in meaningful situations as they are learned, for a skill is something to use. Related as it is to the needs and interests of the learner, it must develop as an integral part of the creative experience and not in isolation. Art, however, is more than the mechanical expression of skills.

All areas of the curriculum point to the development of good citizenship as a prime objective. In this respect art is no different from other areas. If the wise use of inner resources and of leisure time are desirable objectives, then it is obvious that art can help develop worthy citizens.

Responsibilities of the Teacher

The teacher's role in relation to creative expression in art is to provide the motivation that will serve to set off an artistic expression. This she does by providing the child with stimulating experiences and seeing to it that he has every opportunity to respond to them with the fullest possible sensory reactions. To see, to feel, to smell, to listen, and finally to react to an experience through one of the numerous art media provided by the teacher — this is the logical fruition of a stimulating, motivated experience. Once the child is ready to express himself in art, the teacher can help by showing a real interest in the product and by planning further experiences that will continue in the child the desire to create.

Young children are more creative when they are free to choose the media with which they are to work. But they want the teacher to help them in getting the materials ready, in writing the captions under the pictures, in asking about the pictures after they are finished. They do not want simply to work alone without any guidance from the teacher. What the teacher does for the children concerning motivation, the adult artist does for himself. The teacher helps kindle the child's talent from spark to flame and then helps it to be self-sustaining.

Most children are ready to begin work with an art medium in connection with some theme or experience almost as soon as the teacher has made the suggestion. Such questions as, "What does this make you think about?" or "What would you like to paint?" may help open the way for expression.

Teaching is the technique of helping children help themselves. It is concerned with the use of tools or materials and the composition or design. It is not concerned with the creation; that is the child's province. The two important problems facing the teacher are when to offer assistance and how much assistance to offer. The only way the teacher can honestly answer such questions is by asking herself if the child is ready for help. When the child is ready and asks for help, the teacher gives it. The learner who has not yet exhausted his own resources should not be pushed; he is not yet ready. The only way the teacher can be sure he is ready is to know the child well and to know the developmental stages of art well, so that she may match the two and recognize when help can be legitimately given. We will discuss briefly the stages of art development in young children in order to help the teacher decide at what point and to what degree help might profitably be given to a child. The problem might be phrased thus: In addition to motivating and setting goals, how much teaching should she do?

SELECTING THE MEDIA AND TOOLS OF EXPRESSION

The physical development of children has a bearing on the type of media that suit them best. At certain stages of development children have difficulty in using soft chalk and need a wax crayon. For little children who need to use large muscles paints are useful, and so are blocks. As the children grow older, they will choose media requiring smaller muscles, though some children, regardless of age, prefer the larger media. For this reason it is well to have many different types and to let the children choose the type with which they wish to work. The teacher must also offer a wide variety of tools in order to encourage the most effective creative expression.

Stages of Artistic Development in Children

THE AGE OF THE SCRIBBLER

Sometime between the age of two and four most children have their first adventure in creation in art. They scribble. They scribble with and on anything at hand. These first scribbles are as definitely related to painting and drawing as the first babbling sounds are to speech. A simple "Tell me about your picture" may handle the situation. If the child wants to tell a story while he is scribbling, the teacher listens and asks questions that lead to further activity. Easel paints are welcomed by children in the scribbling stage; so are blackboards and plasticene. Blocks are a welcome addition to art materials at this age and help the child to play out his experiences.

IN SEARCH OF A SYMBOL

The five-year-old, as he paints away at the easel, scarcely conscious of others around him so intent is he on the work of the moment, is searching for a symbol. He paints with deliberation, unhesitatingly, and without hurry. Throughout the process he steps back at intervals and surveys his product — at times with concern, but more often with satisfaction. Never should the teacher be too occupied to take time to look at the work.

Each child has his own style of painting and his way of working. A teacher makes an effort to help each child sign his product with his name or initial, but she learns to recognize the style and can help a child identify his product even if there is no name.

Children from four to six are searching for a symbol. They may draw self, mother, father, brother, sister, or teacher. The head is usually the size of the rest of the figure. No background or setting is used.

THE SYMBOL IS FOUND

Beginning somewhere between the ages of five and six, and continuing until the ages of eight or nine, is the "schematic" or "symbolic" stage. Two chief characteristics of this level of development are the use of a standardized formula for representing the human figure and the use of a base line to indicate space relationships between the objects in a picture.

Having found his own formula, the child repeats it many, many times with evident satisfaction and delight. This formula expresses his concept of a human being in a way that temporarily satisfies him.

It is important for the teacher to realize that the child will continue to

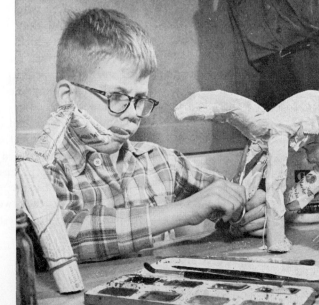

Every venture in creative art can be exciting not only for the child but also for the teacher.

paint his symbol until he has had an experience that jolts him out of it. At this point he should be encouraged to express his new experiences. Merely telling the child to draw something else for a change will not accomplish the desired result. It may, on the contrary, hinder the child and block his expression entirely for a time, or induce him to revert to conventional patterns of figure drawing. It would be more effective to take him on a trip to the zoo or to the airport.

In regard to the base line across the bottom of the page to indicate space relationship, the teacher should remember that the time to give the child help is when he asks for it — not before. Undue emphasis on technique at this early stage is not warranted. Similarly, restrictive activities such as coloring an outlined picture, using the crayons in a very precise manner, or using only bright colors, make children feel insecure and they often tend to withdraw. Sometimes teachers are disappointed when a child who has talent just stops creating for a while, but they should not put pressure on the child.

The greatest contribution the teacher can make to the child is to put up his pictures for everyone to see. Let him realize that he is an artist, that he has ideas worth expressing. The six-year-old needs to be assured and reassured.

Pitfalls in the Teaching of Art

Many teachers do not recognize the fact that children react unfavorably to dictatorial teaching practices. An experiment was conducted in which an attempt was made to ascertain some of the results of inappropriate teaching methods on 120 children five and six years of age. For a month before the experiment all the children enjoyed a creative art program. Some were in the schematic stage of development, but most were searching for a symbol. All were creative in their expression. The children were grouped according to mental maturity, sex, and emotional maturity into two groups.

Group A consisted of 60 children who had their creative program brought to a halt; for a two-month period they were told what media to select in art and what type of activity in which to engage. There was no attempt made to dictate the topic or subject for the art period, but there was a definite assignment of media and activity. For the month previous to the experiment a child could choose any media and any activity. During the experiment he was not allowed to choose.

At the end of two months Group A had ceased doing anything in the way of creative art. They worked on a project only about seven minutes as compared with fifteen to seventeen minutes during the creative period. They gave only brief descriptions of their pictures, such as, "A design," "I don't know," "I wanted to paint," "I don't care."

During the ensuing two months they were permitted to go back to the creative program, while Group B was restricted to the dictatorial method

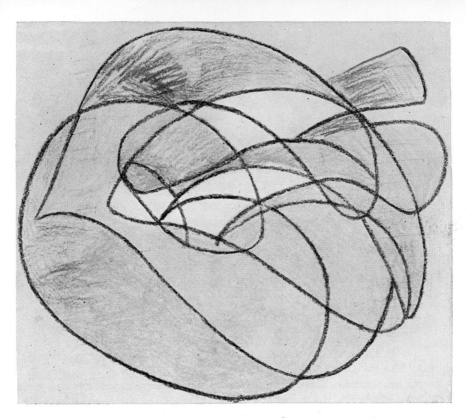

A "good" piece of creative art is not only a matter of technique but also one of expression.

after three months of creative activity. Later the two groups reverted to their original programs. A record was kept of the pictures that were made in easel paint, crayon, and water color. All of the children in Group B showed growth both in art and in language development as it related to the stories they told about their drawings and paintings. Not only had they had a two-month longer period in the creative program at the beginning of the year, but they had ended the year with the creative program. Group A, on the other hand, had been cut off in their creative program at the first of the year, and, as it turned out, they were cut off again at the end of the year. In all, although the difference in the creative program amounted to less than two months, Group A never recovered from the first shock of change. Group B was able to snap back each time, even though their over-all progress was perhaps not quite so outstanding as it might have been under the creative program for the entire year. If depriving children temporarily of choice of media and choice of activity makes such a difference, one may well ask what it does to a child who never is permitted a choice.

The following is a list of media with which children should be encouraged to experiment:

I. Crayons.
   A. Appropriate ages: kindergarten and first grade.
   B. Characteristics.
      1. Large wax crayons that produce brilliant color.
      2. A box with six or eight colors for each child.
   C. Techniques.
      1. Crayons should be pressed hard upon the paper to produce a dark, rich color.
      2. Children should draw with the crayon flat to the paper, producing the result of coloring and drawing.

II. Scratch Board.
   A. Apply a bright or light wax crayon over glossy paper, tag, or lithoboard, repeating the colors.
   B. Next apply dark colors over the crayoned area in very thick proportions. Upper-grade students may use India ink.
   C. Reverse the point of a pen in the holder and scratch a design on the board.

III. Chalk.
   A. Apply colored chalk with a flat surface, blending with finger tips.
   B. Dampen paper before using colored chalk to make the colors richer.

IV. Poster Paint (Calcimine).
   A. Caution children against using a light overcolor before a darker undercolor is completely dry.
   B. Sponge painting with tempera.
      Use small square of rubber sponge and dip into dishes of poster paint. Cover large areas by this method.

V. Stencils.
   A. Pouncing.
   B. Brushing (positive and negative stencil).
   C. Crayon stenciling.
   D. Spatter print with stencil.

VI. Block Printing.
   A. Potato blocks.
   B. Felt blocks.
   C. Linoleum blocks.
   D. Backings for block printing.
   E. Wood, pencil, cork, spool, potato, stamp pad, or sticks.

VII. Water Color.
   A. Colors as intense as possible should be used, since one-third or more of the color is lost when the paper dries.
   B. Apply as in tempera painting, background areas first. Sketch the picture lightly on the paper, and paint from the background to the immediate foreground.

VIII. Oil Painting (not recommended for the elementary grades).

IX. Cut Paper.
   A. Enjoyed by children of all ages.
   B. Techniques: scissored shapes may be curled, snipped and tucked, folded, pleated, or crushed to make many fascinating objects such

as fish, fowl, flowers, or animals. The paper may also be pulled between thumb and scissors or curled around a pencil.

X. Others.
  A. Collage (an adaption of sculptured paper work).
  B. Montage (the selection and mounting of pictures).
  C. Fountain brush pen (for quick lettering).
  D. Finger painting (enjoyed in all grades).
  E. Starch paper (used with finger painting).
  F. Clay
  G. Plaster of Paris.
  H. Papier-mâché.[7]

Criteria for the Teaching of Art

Since research and investigation have tentatively indicated that the following are the essential qualities of a good experience in the arts, they may serve as criteria to guide the evaluation of a classroom program.

1. Through the media of art the teacher is trying to help each child express honestly his own ideas, feelings, and experiences in his own way. In arithmetic there is only one answer to a problem, but in art a child's originality is prized. Here the child is approved for making a picture different from the others. The day is past when every child makes a picture of a daffodil, and every daffodil is identical. The "right answer" to an art problem comes when the individual child achieves what is for him the right answer; and surprisingly enough, he knows when it is right. If you have ever watched a group of kindergarten or primary-grade children at dismissal, you will often have seen some child surreptitiously crumple his painting or coloring and put it in the wastebasket or throw it on the floor for the janitor to pick up. He knows when it is good work, and in his judgment he is comparing it with his own work of yesterday, not with that of someone else.

2. Through art the child will perceive with all his senses the world in which he lives. He will become interested in and aware of the art that exists in his surroundings — the things of nature and the things of man. Through an awareness of the relationship of the seemingly unorganized, unrelated elements in his environment, the child develops a concept of design. By means of such a concept he then begins to see possibilities for beauty in the structure of a flower, the branches growing from the trunk of the tree, the bird spreading its wings in flight, and the flame of a sunset. As he travels through the countryside, he will see design in the furrows of the fields and, from the air, in the pattern of the landscape and terrain. New vistas will open up to him, and he will express not only what he experiences and feels, but what he sees.

[7] From Irma Paine, *Art Aids for Elementary Teaching*, Revised Edition (Minneapolis: Burgess Publishing Co., 1953), pp. 37–47.

The wise use of inner resources helps the child develop a self-satisfying personality.

3. Through art the teacher can provide a base from which the child may solve his problems in and out of the classroom. When art is related to something the child knows, feels, and understands, he is more inclined to react favorably to it.

There should be no pressure to reproduce the details of a textbook illustration the teacher sketches on the board for the children to copy and color. An extreme example, although not altogether rare, is for a teacher to assign a coloring lesson to a small child in which he must color a hectographed turkey because it is near Thanksgiving. Rather, the art the child produces should give the teacher an objective measure of what a learning experience has meant to a child. Art should be related to the school program, but in a meaningful fashion. The culmination of a unit very frequently is some type of art project: painting a mural, designing a book, constructing a diorama, making a movie of a favorite story, or setting up an exhibit.

4. Through activities in the realm of art the total growth of the child is promoted. Much research has been done on the child's art experience as an index of his social, emotional, intellectual, and total personality characteristics and of his general needs as a person.

An Indian Unit

The following Indian unit is an example of how two teachers used art as a center for organizing a unit:

I. *Introduction.*

The people of America should appreciate the Indian, what he has contributed and is continuing to contribute to American life. In our changing world the Indians live and work today quite differently from the way they did when Europeans first settled the continent.

By studying how Indians solved their problems of food, clothing, and shelter, the child will be led to appreciate the fact that people in early days were dependent on the resources around them.

Some of the tribes of Indians were merely roving, hunting bands, who lived a hand-to-mouth existence. Other tribes lived in more-or-less permanent settlements, adapting their lives to what their environment had to offer them for food, clothing, and shelter.

II. *General objectives.*
  A. In the primary grades an Indian unit may be used to acquaint the children with primitive cultures.
  B. Such a unit may show how the Indian adapted to his environment in satisfying his needs for food, clothing, and shelter.

III. *Specific objectives.*
  A. To learn about the food, clothing, and shelter of the Indians in different parts of the country.
  B. To learn about the manners and customs of the Indians.
  C. To develop an understanding of the contributions of the Indians to early American culture.
  D. To stimulate creative efforts by a study of Indian arts and crafts.
  E. To learn about and appreciate Indian traditions and legends.
  F. To contrast present living conditions of the Indians with those of their ancestors.
  G. To clarify any confusion that exists in the children's minds concerning the Indians of pioneer days and the Indians of today.
  H. To help children understand the reasons for friction between the Indians and pioneers, thus giving them a glimpse of pioneer life and leading to a possible unit on pioneers.
  I. To provide opportunity for cooperation in a group project.
  J. To provide opportunities for a variety of resource experiences.
  K. To provide an opportunity to participate in the purposeful use of the language arts as related to the unit.

IV. *Initiation of the unit.*
  A. Setting the stage through use of the bulletin board.
  B. Visiting the museum.
  C. Arranging an exhibit in the classroom of curios and relics brought by the children.
  D. Singing Indian songs.
  E. Reading Indian stories and poems.
  F. Showing movies, filmstrips, slides, and so forth.
  G. Going on an excursion to the library to find books.
  H. Making charts.
  I. Inviting a Boy Scout, or some person who has spent some time studying the Indians, to the classroom.

V. *Development of the unit.*

    A. What were the five main living areas of the Indians in what is now the United States?

        1. Northwest Coast Tribes

        2. California Tribes

        3. Southwest Tribes

        4. Eastern Woodlands Tribes

        5. Plains Tribes

    B. How did the American Indians live?

        1. Dwellings

        2. Food

        3. Dress

        4. Tools, weapons, and utensils

        5. Religion, beliefs, superstitions

        6. Signs and picture writing

        7. Arts and crafts

        8. Music

        9. Wampum

    C. What were the means of communication and transportation used by the Indians?

    D. How does the way the Indian lives today contrast with the way his ancestors lived?

    E. What influence did the white man have on the Indians?

        1. Missions

        2. Reservations

        3. Wars

    F. What contributions did the Indians make to the life of the white man?

VI. *Art.*

    A. Make a mural of Indian life.

    B. Make Indian dolls using pipe cleaners dyed with coffee or iodine, brown-paper toweling for clothing, yarn for hair. For moccasins use bits of foam rubber, into which the pipe-cleaner legs are stuck.

    C. Make tom-toms from boxes or tin cans covered with paper, and use crayons to decorate them with Indian designs. Stretch inner tubes, or repair patches for inner tubes, over the top.

    D. Make rattles by placing gravel in capsule boxes or two small foil pie-plates. Run a knitting needle or meat skewer through each box as a handle. On one end fasten a cork and feathers.

    E. Make ceremonial dresses and suits from small cleaner bags; fringe and decorate.

    F. Make head bands from brown paper with feathers stapled on.

    G. Make a top by using a cork or spool decorated with bright colors and spin on a lollipop stick or pencil.

    H. Color stick macaroni by means of water colors, break it into pieces and string it for jewelry, using dried seeds and pods for ornaments.

    I. Make an accordion booklet of Indian picture language. Make booklets of stories that the children have written together.

J. Make tepees from drinking cups or wrapping paper.

K. Make pottery from clay.

L. Make totem poles from paper cylinders, various sized boxes, clothes-pins; or carve them from soap, candles, or spools.

M. Make bows and arrows.

N. Make paper canoes.

O. Make maps showing where various Indian tribes lived.

P. Make an Indian village.

Q. Make Indian war masks from paper bags.

R. Make a papoose in a cradle. Use a large match box for the cradle, a clothespin for the papoose, and lace in with heavy twine.

S. Make an Indian diorama.

VII. *Arts as related to the unit.*

A. Language arts.

1. Make a booklet of Indian stories written by members of class.

2. Prepare oral and written reports on Indian life in different sections of the country.

3. Prepare an Indian poem suitable for choral reading.

4. Write letters to various Indian localities asking for portfolios and free booklets on Indian tribes: Chamber of Commerce, Flagstaff, Arizona; Chamber of Commerce, Sante Fe, New Mexico; Chamber of Commerce, Albuquerque, New Mexico.

5. Make a dictionary of the new and important words.

6. Prepare a quiz program.

7. Choose an Indian name, then write a story telling why you chose that name.

8. Write an original play about Indians.

9. Dramatize Indian stories.

10. Prepare a pantomime of Indian activities.

11. Select an Indian story to read to the class.

12. Prepare reports on various Indians, such as Pocahontas, Rain-in-the-Face, Squanto, Geronimo.

13. Memorize a poem or a favorite stanza from some Indian poem.

14. List new words for speaking, writing, and spelling vocabulary. Suggested word list:

cliff	warrior	pemmican
bow	war dance	plateau
arrow	trading post	mountains
tribe	weapon	travois
chief	quiver	mesa
brave	papoose	decorate
canoe	tepee	shield
forest	wigwam	prairie
desert	swamps	tom-tom
valley	totem pole	canyon
pottery	Pueblo	skins
plains	moccasin	war paint
flint	wampum	potlatch

dugout	ceremonials	medicine
loom	hogan	pottery
arrowheads	weave	reservation
maize	treaty	tomahawk
cliff dwellers	signal	legends
adobe	buffalo	blanket
squaw	birch bark	weapon
Seminole	Cherokee	Navajo
Hopi	Zuni	Apache
Iroquois	Tecumseh	Hiawatha

B. Music

   1. Songs

      a. Theresa Armitage, *et al. Merry Music*, Book III. Boston: C.C. Birchard and Company, 1950.

      b. John Beattie, *et al. American Singer*, Book II. New York: American Book Company, 1954.

      c. Marguerite Hood. *Singing Days*. Boston: Ginn and Company, 1950.

      d. Osborne McConathy. *New Music Horizons*. New York: Silver Burdett Company, 1950.

      e. Osborne McConathy, *et al. The Music Hour*. New York: Silver Burdett Company, 1949.

      f. Marie Westevelt. *Indian Songs and Rhythms*. Cincinnati: Willis Music Company, 1952.

   2. Recordings

      a. *Indian Lullaby*. RCA Victor.

      b. *Music of the Sioux and Navajo*. Folkways.

      c. *Cowboys and Indians*. Allegro.

      d. *There Were Three Indians*. MGM.

VIII. *Games.*

   A. "Big Chief Black Hawk" — Grades 1–6: One child is chosen to be Black Hawk, the Chief, and two others are his guards. They stand in any place within the designated area, with one guard on either side of Black Hawk. The rest of the children represent a hostile Indian tribe and are spread out over the entire playing area. Black Hawk and his guards start walking around within the playing area, while the Indians try to dodge the guards and touch the chief. If an Indian is successful in touching Black Hawk, that Indian changes places with him and becomes the new chief. However, if any of the hostile Indians should be touched by a guard before they touch the chief, they become prisoners and must sit down in a "stockade" at one end of the playing area. After about five minutes, they are released and two of them chosen to replace the old guards, who in turn become Indians. Play may continue indefinitely.

   B. "Ride, Indian, Ride." — Grades 1–6: Children are divided into two equal teams with the members of each team standing one behind the other, back of a starting line. The leader of each team has a broom placed between his legs as if he were riding a pony. At a signal, each leader starts "riding" the broom toward the turning line about 30 feet in front of him. As soon as he crosses this line, he may take the broom in any manner and run back to the starting line with it, handing it to the next player in his line, who "rides" to the turning point. The team that first has all of its players back in the original starting position and sitting down is the winner — provided it has not committed any errors along the way. These are errors: (a) a player leaves the starting line before the one ahead of him gets back across it; (b) a player does not cross the turning line; (c) a player does not "ride" the broom correctly.

C. "Keep It Up" — Grades 1–6: Children are divided into two equal teams, but remain in their seats until it is their turn. One child from each team is chosen to go to the front of the room to represent his team. Each of them is given a feather, and at a signal must hold it over his head, let go of it, and then try to keep it in the air longer than his opponent by blowing it. The player who is able to keep his feather in the air the longer of the two wins one point for his team. When these players return to their seats, two new players are chosen, one from each team. Play continues until all of the children have had a turn. The team having the greatest number of points is the winner.

IX. *General evaluation.*

  A. Determine whether certain desirable abilities and skills have been acquired.

    1. Have children learned how to use books in locating information?

    2. Can children give satisfactory reports?

    3. Can they read maps, graphs, and pictures?

    4. Have they learned how to participate in committee work?

  B. In the final analysis the teacher will evaluate the learning experiences in terms of their contribution to the child's personality and character development.

    1. Has the unit broadened the child's interest in the world and its people?

    2. Does the child realize that differences in physical environment have caused man to make different types of responses to environment in fulfilling the essential needs for food, shelter, and clothing?

    3. Is the child a more cooperative member of a group because of experiences during the unit?

    4. Has he learned to abide by the will of the majority, and to be loyal and cooperative once a group decision has been made?

    5. Has he gained in creativity and appreciation of art?

X. *Evaluation of this unit.*

  A. Have the children learned:

    1. About the different phases of Indian life?

    2. Some of the contributions the Indians have made to us?

    3. How they looked, dressed, and so forth?

  B. Have the children learned to appreciate:

    1. The long period of development of Indian civilization?

        2. The excellence of their art?

        3. The beauty of their dances and music?

        4. How the Indians overcame the difficulties of environment?

    C. Have the children seen that environment affects the lives of people:

        1. In the food they eat?

        2. In the clothing they wear?

        3. In the homes they build?

    D. Have the children made progress:

        1. In oral and written expression?

        2. In the ability to seek facts through reading?

        3. In the ability to spell correctly the words they used in connection with the written work of this unit?

        4. In their speaking vocabulary?

XI. *Culminating activities.*

    A. Program for parents.

    B. Exhibit for another class.

    C. Summary given by committees.

    D. Class scrapbook of original pictures.

    E. Creative writing relating to the unit.

    F. Assembly program for the school.

    G. Dramatization of an Indian legend.

    H. Play or story illustrating various beliefs and ceremonies.

    I. Party with children wearing headdresses or costumes they made.

XII. *Children's bibliography.*

Abeita, Louise. *I Am a Pueblo Indian Girl.* Eau Claire, Wis.: E. M. Hale and Company, n.d.

Beals, Frank R. *Chief Black Hawk.* London: Oliphants, Ltd., 1943.

Bleeker, Sonia. *Apache Indians.* New York: William Morrow & Co., Inc., 1951.

Britannica Junior Encyclopaedia. Chicago: Encyclopaedia Britannica, 1949.

Brewster, Benjamin. *The First Book of Indians.* London: C. A. Watts & Co., 1950.

Buff, Mary. *Dancing Cloud: The Navajo Boy.* New York: The Viking Press, Inc., 1937.

Clark, Ann Nolan. *In My Mother's House.* Eau Claire, Wis.: E. M. Hale and Company, n.d.

Clark, Ann Nolan. *Little Navajo Bluebird.* Eau Claire, Wis.: E. M. Hale and Company, n.d.

D'Aulaire, Ingri, and Edgar d'Aulaire. *Buffalo Bill.* New York: Doubleday & Company, Inc., 1946.

D'Aulaire, Ingri and Edgar d'Aulaire. *Pocahontas.* New York: Doubleday & Company, Inc., 1946.

Dearborn, Frances. *How the Indians Lived.* Boston: Ginn and Company, 1927.

Deming, Therese. *Indians of the Wigwams.* Chicago: Albert Whitman & Co., 1938.

Deming, Therese. *Indians in Winter Camp.* River Forest, Ill.: Laidlaw Brothers, 1931.

Deming, Therese. *Little Eagle.* River Forest, Ill.: Laidlaw Brothers, 1931.

Elting, Muriel H. *The Land of Little Rain.* Philadelphia: The John C. Winston Co., 1950.

Fletcher, Sydney. *Big Book of Indians.* New York: Grossett & Dunlap, 1950.

Insley, B. *Indian Folklore Tales.* New York: Exposition Press, 1952.

Jenkins, M. *Before the White Man Came.* Portland, Ore.: Binfords & Mort, 1951.

Lindermann, F. B. *Indian Why Stories.* New York: Charles Scribner's Sons, 1926.

Moon, G. P. *Book of Nah-Wee.* New York: Doubleday & Company, Inc., 1932.

Moon, G. P. *Chi-Wee.* New York: Doubleday & Company, Inc., 1937.

Moon, G. P. *One Little Indian.* Chicago: Albert Whitman & Co., 1950.

Running, C. *When Coyote Walked the Earth.* New York: Henry Holt & Co., Inc., 1949.

Seton, J. M. *Indian Creation Stories.* Hollywood, Calif.: House-Warven, 1952.

XIII. *Teacher's bibliography.*

Appleton, LeRoy. *Indian Art of the Americas.* New York: Charles Scribner's Sons, 1950.

Benedict, Ruth. *Patterns of Culture.* Boston: Houghton Mifflin Company, 1934.

Childcraft. Chicago: Quarrie Corp., 1945.

Compton's Encyclopedia. Chicago: Compton, 1950.

Edwards, R. M. *American Indians of Yesterday.* San Antonio, Texas: Naylor Co., 1948.

Embree, E. R. *Indians of the Americas.* Boston: Houghton Mifflin Company, 1939.

Encyclopaedia Britannica. Chicago: Encyclopaedia Britannica, 1952.

Hamilton, C. (ed.). *Cry of the Thunderbird.* New York: The Macmillan Company, 1950.

Mason, B. S. *Dances and Stories of the American Indian.* New York: A. S. Barnes & Company, 1950.

National Geographic Magazine. September 1925; September 1927; November 1937; November 1940; December 1940; January 1945; September 1947; February 1948; September 1948.

Salomon, J. H. *Book of Indian Crafts and Indian Lore.* New York: Harper & Brothers, 1928.

Schwalbach, James. *Fun Times Crafts.* Chicago: Children's Press, Inc., 1949.

Thompson, Laura, and Alice Joseph. *Culture in Crisis.* New York: Harper & Brothers, 1950.

Wissler, Clark. *North American Indians of the Plains.* New York: American Museum of Natural History, 1948.[8]

---

[8] Elzada Hall and Henrietta Seibert, *An Indian Unit,* Mount Vernon Elementary School, Mount Vernon, Indiana. Adaptable to grades 2–6.

Summary

Throughout this chapter on the creative arts we have pointed out ways in which the teacher can work with children to develop their creative powers. The teacher is the most important factor in fostering and nurturing creativity. She sets the stage so children will feel free to express themselves.

There are other things she can do. The teacher who herself is creative will find it easier to understand the thrill that comes to the child when he creates. Teachers themselves have untapped reservoirs of creativity waiting for expression. They are, therefore, in a position to understand why the child "dawdles before he writes." They are in a position where they are able to help release creativity.

The teacher has a responsibility, too, for helping children have rich experiences in all the arts. How can she do this unless she herself has a knowledge and appreciation of the arts? The teacher who participates in the enjoyment of art, music, and literature can bring much more to the children than the teacher who does not recognize the difference between a Watteau and a Van Gogh, a Beethoven sonata and a Brahms symphony, a sonnet and a ballad. The broader the teacher's horizons, the broader will be her pupils'.

The teacher should also be an encouraging person. It is not enough to teach; she must inspire.

QUESTIONS AND ACTIVITIES

1. What are your reactions to current theories of art instruction? Visit a classroom and look for evidences of them in operation.

2. Describe any situation you have observed in which children disliked art. Explain how the attitude might have come about, and indicate ways in which it could have been corrected.

3. Observe the art supervisor in your city. Note especially:
   a. The motivation she uses.
   b. The manner in which she helps children establish goals.
   c. The way in which she teaches or gives help as children need it.

4. Describe the steps you might take if confronted by the following:
   a. A group of third-grade boys who think art is "sissy."
   b. A second-grade group who are untidy and waste their materials.

5. Take the following test and score it. Compare your results with those of the other members of the class:
   a. Do you respect the child's own personal and sensitive expressions or do you regard them as careless and immature?
   b. Do you call upon the child's own imagination, or do you put up examples of work for him to copy.
   c. Do you encourage the child to explore and invent his own pattern or do you have him follow a precise pattern? Do you give the child prepared materials, such as printed shapes, for him to color neatly?

d. Do you allow only crayon and pencil because they are neat, or do you provide a variety of materials even though they are messy and require particular effort to keep in order?

e. Do you stimulate the child to improvise his own forms and materials freely and expressively?

f. Do you measure achievement on the basis of child values or do you expect adult or professional standards? [9]

SELECTED READINGS

Art for Children's Growing. Washington, D.C.: The Association for Childhood Education, 1955.

Boylston, Elsie Reid. *Creative Expression with Crayons.* Worcester, Mass.: The Doirs Press, 1953.

Cole, Natalie Robinson. *The Arts in the Classroom.* New York: The John Day Company, 1942.

Creating Materials for Work and Play. Bulletin No. 5. Washington, D.C.: The Association for Childhood Education, 1957.

Dewey, John. *Art as Experience.* New York: Milton, Balch and Company, 1934.

Easel Age Scale. Madison, Wis.: California Test Bureau, 1955.

Erdt, Margaret H. *Teaching Art in the Elementary School.* New York: Rinehart & Company, Inc., 1954.

Gaitskell, Charles D., and Margaret Gaitskell. *Children and their Art.* New York: Harcourt, Brace & Company, 1958.

Goodenough, F. L., and D. B. Harris. "Studies in the Psychology of Children's Drawings, II," *Psychological Bulletin,* 47:369–433, 1950.

Heffernan, Helen. "Art Experiences in Kindergarten," *Grade Teacher,* 75:16, April 1958.

Johnson, June. *Home Play for the Preschool Child.* New York: Harper & Brothers, 1957.

Larkin, L. Marie. "Creative Expression in Art," *Childhood Education,* 34:11–13, September 1957.

Lowenfeld, Viktor. *Creative and Mental Growth,* Revised Edition. New York: The Macmillan Company, 1957.

Mendelowitz, Daniel. *Children Are Artists.* Stanford: Stanford University Press, 1954.

O'Brien, Mary, *et al. Developing Creativity in Children's Use of Imagination: Theoretical Statement,* Union College Studies in Character Research, I:17–26, 1953.

Schultz, Harold A., and Harlan J. Shores. *Art in the Elementary School.* University of Illinois Bulletin. Urbana, Ill.: College of Education, 1948.

Shaw, Ruth F. *Finger Painting: A Perfect Medium for Self-Expression.* Boston: Little, Brown & Company, 1934.

Tomlinson, R. R. *Children as Artists.* Baltimore: Penquin Books, Inc., 1944.

[9] Victor D'Amico, "Understanding Children's Creativeness," *The Instructor,* 67:5, April 1958.

THE PROBLEMS

WE FACE

V

Young children have a right to educational experiences that will develop maximum capacities. They have a right to certain group experiences in nursery schools, kindergartens, and the primary grades. They have a right to a foundation that will eventually enable them to become contributing members of society.

In Part IV we shall consider how the school can most effectively discharge its responsibilities to all children — the gifted, the mentally retarded, the children with problems of adjustment, and the physically handicapped. We shall discuss the problems of organizing the curriculum to meet the needs of these children. We shall stress the importance of creating a classroom environment in which every child will be accepted by the teacher and the group. Finally, we shall look at the problems that face us in the wake of large enrollments, crowded classrooms, and shortages of teachers.

The problems are not new. Neither are they insurmountable. Indeed, as teachers, administrators, and parents recognize the urgent need to face these problems and to work together to provide the best possible solutions, they will discover means whereby their educational objectives can be realized for all children. Above all, they will recognize the importance of providing well-qualified teachers who can inspire children through creating a learning environment in which the pursuit of knowledge is equated with the search for truth, creativity in the arts, understanding of the natural and social forces that shape our world, and devotion to the ideas of free men. This they will accomplish for the gifted and the slow learner, for the self-starter and the dullard, for the inquisitive and the disinterested, and for the artist and the artisan.

15

The Exceptional Child

What is good for the handicapped is good for the "normal."

— WENDELL JOHNSON

Education in America is dedicated to the proposition that each child is entitled to an education that will develop his highest potential. This concept implies teaching the exceptional as well as the average child. The exceptional child has needs that are similar to those of the average child, and the average child has needs similar to those of the exceptional child. What is good for the exceptional child is good for the normal child. Each has, in addition, needs that are different and that must be met in different ways. To preserve what is normal as well as to make the most of what is exceptional is the aim of education. It is to this end that teachers should direct their efforts.

About fifteen per cent of the present elementary school enrollment consists of children who are handicapped in some respect: those with physical disabilities, the mentally retarded, the speech handicapped, the emotionally unstable, and those with behavior problems.[1] Yet, according to the National Society for the Study of Education, in cities that have developed programs for educating exceptional children, only six per cent of the child population is enrolled in special schools or classes.

The following chart gives some idea of the number of exceptional children, including the physically handicapped.

Numbers and Types of Exceptional Children [2]

Types of Exceptional Children	Number of Children	
	Exceptional	*Normal*
Mentally gifted	2	100
Mentally retarded and slow learning	5	100
Crippled (including cardiacs)	1	500
Blind	1	2,000
Partially seeing	1	500
Deaf or deafened	1	1,000
Hard of hearing	1	25
Maladjusted (behavior problems)	2	100
Epileptic (convulsive disorders)	2	100
Glandular deficient	14	100
Defective in speech	12	100
Showing lowered vitality	15	100

The figures in the table include only those children who are markedly exceptional. In fact, these ratios probably represent more nearly the one-third or one-fourth of our children whose deviations are most marked and who later, when they enter school, cannot be educated safely or profitably in a regular school. The White House Conference Report indicates that approximately 22 per cent of all children need some kind of individualized opportunity or special service at some time during their school attendance.[3]

The school is committed to the task of providing programs that will meet the needs of all children. It should make specific provisions for the early identification of diseases and for the prevention of accidents and any other experiences that may cause disability or affect negatively the strong emotions; early diagnosis to determine each child's capacities, needs, and limitations; and education that will challenge the capacities of each child and simultaneously be adapted to his level of maturation and his ability to profit from the experiences. Finally, programs for exceptional children must provide for all areas of the child's mental growth, social experience, and physical health.

[1] "The Primary School: Stop! Look! Evaluate!" Bulletin No. 61 (Washington, D.C.: Association for Childhood Education International, 1952). Quoted in Hazel M. Lambert, *Teaching the Kindergarten Child* (New York: Harcourt, Brace & Company, 1958), p. 267.
[2] National Society for the Study of Education, *Early Childhood Education,* Forty-sixth Yearbook, (Chicago: The University of Chicago Press, 1947), p. 317.
[3] *Ibid.*

To kindle those, the gifted ones
With lambent flame that soars and sings
Or fit one with Pegasus' wings
Till world on worlds before him rise.

— JOSEPHINE LESTER

THE EXCEPTIONAL CHILD

The Gifted Child

In spite of the implications inherent in the statements of responsibility of the school toward exceptional children, the gifted child has received little attention. In most schools, not enough is being done to enable the bright child to realize his potential. Too often standards are geared to the average pupil, with the inevitable consequence that the more brilliant child finds the assignment too easy and loses his drive. Education must allow for differences. The curriculum should be modified to meet the needs of the talented youngsters as well as of the retarded; of the able as well as of the physically handicapped. We should concern ourselves with the uncommon, by identifying the best qualified — the gifted — and educating them to the highest level of which they are capable, then using their genius in profitable ways. The need in our country today is for creative thinkers, trained minds, and skilled workers. It is in the classroom that we discover these individuals, in whose hands our destiny lies.

Identifying the Gifted Child

Many gifted children can be identified before they enroll in school. Parents frequently ask for a yardstick by which to measure their children. Some criteria that may help them arrive at an accurate estimate are the following:

1. Did the child walk and talk early? Many gifted children speak by the time they are eight months old and can say whole sentences at two.

2. Did the child begin to read early? Many gifted children read before they are four. They teach themselves, and parents are not always aware of

the fact that they can read. They enjoy picture books by the time they are two. They are also very much interested in atlases, dictionaries, and encyclopaedias.

3. Does the child have a retentive memory? There are children who understand and remember the meaning of a word at a very early age.

4. Does the child know the relationship between cause and effect? Though the average four-year-old is constantly asking questions, he does not always care about or remember the answers. The gifted child not only wants to know the cause of everything and its effect, but he remembers the explanation and is guided by it in future action.

5. Can the child follow directions? A gifted six-year-old can carry out in order three simple directions given him at one time. Normally this is an accomplishment of the eight- or nine-year-old. The gifted five-year-old also has developed this ability.

6. When did the child learn to tell time? The gifted child can tell time before he enters kindergarten. He is interested in calendars and measurement of all types.

7. Does the child have a good attention span? The normal child of five can give attention for 15 to 30 minutes. The gifted five-year-old can remain absorbed in something for nearly an hour.

8. Can the child handle abstractions? Often a gifted six-year-old can explain a word like *charity* or *phenomenon* — an achievement on the twelve-year-old level.

9. Does the child have broad interests? At all ages, gifted children show an interest in practically everything in the universe.

10. Does the child show the capacity to get along alone? Gifted children are able to occupy and amuse themselves well at all ages. They have so many hobbies and interests that they do not need other people. This does not mean that they are withdrawn; it means that they have developed inner resources.

11. Is the child proficient in drawing, music, or other art forms?

CREATIVITY AND THE GIFTED CHILD

Much emphasis is being placed on the element of creativity in the identification of the gifted. Giftedness, we are discovering, consists in more than a high I.Q. For years the concept of a gifted child has been that of a physical weakling, a book worm, a social misfit who isolates himself from all contacts, and one who possesses an I.Q. ranging from 130 to 175 or above. Contrary to this popular belief, research has discovered that the gifted child is generally a physically superior, attractive, and rather well-rounded individual with a zest for living. He is modest and well-adjusted socially, enjoys association with children who are several years older and two, three, or four years above him in school.

Intelligence tests, which in the past have been used to identify the gifted,

Creativity in many different forms is usually a characteristic of the gifted child.

measure intelligence in academic and scholastic achievement but do not discover the child who is creative or talented in the arts. The child who has a high I.Q. does not necessarily possess the characteristics of creativity, which is coming to be considered a significant factor in achieving success in life.

Gifted children should, if possible, be identified before they enter school. The intelligence test has been widely used for such purposes. Children of I.Q. 130 are generally referred to as gifted; in some instances 125 is used as a criterion for giftedness. The I.Q., however, takes into consideration only one dimension of giftedness, for it identifies those who possess in high degree verbal or abstract intelligence. Experimentation in the field of new techniques for measuring intellectual ability should yield more inclusive data for measuring giftedness.

IDENTIFYING CREATIVITY

Here are some characteristics of exceptional creativity that an intelligence test may never reveal:

1. The highly creative child is more sensitive to problems than his less creative peer. Not only is he more aware of their existence, but he wants to solve them.

2. The highly creative child comes up with unusual but effective ideas.

He does not conform to a pattern; he is not interested in reproducing another's ideas. He is flexible in his thinking as he looks at a problem; he sees its relationships in a new way, avoids commonly held or widely accepted points of view, and goes about finding his own solutions.

3. The highly creative child is interested in a large number of projects, activities, and ideas at any given time. He is brimming over with ideas and enthusiasm.

4. The highly creative child persists in the face of frustration, distraction, or temporary defeat. He is able to concentrate on what he is doing without giving in to the annoyance of physical stimuli or distractions in the environment. He is so able to lose himself in an activity that he is oblivious to what is going on around him. A child who had been studying the piano and who was allowed to take organ lessons became so engrossed in practicing that on one occasion she stayed for three hours in an organ loft where the temperature was over ninety degrees without realizing the discomfort of the heat. As she said to her mother, "It was so heavenly I didn't notice it was warm up there."

5. The highly creative child often prefers individual activities to group activities. He is not concerned with conformity to the mores of the group.

6. The highly creative child is *not necessarily* at the top in academic achievement. There seems to be little correlation between academic success and creative productivity.[4] It is highly possible that the creative child has not been rewarded for his efforts in the traditional school environment. It is possible that if his gifts were more adequately rewarded and appreciated, he might perform better in the academic tasks assigned to him.

IDENTIFYING ARTISTIC TALENT

The Committee on Human Development of The University of Chicago conducted a research project in Quincy, Illinois, part of which centered on the identification of gifted children in various fields. The committee proposed the following criteria for discovering children talented in art:

Which of your pupils stands out in these characteristics when compared with the rest of the class?
1. Draws a variety of things (not just people, jets, horses, or houses).
2. Puts depth into pictures. Plans pictures and uses good proportion.
3. Takes art work seriously. Seems to find much satisfaction in it.
4. Shows originality. Draws things in ways no other children do.
5. Is willing to try out new materials and experiences.
6. Fills extra time with drawing and painting activities.
7. Uses art to express his own feelings, his own experiences.
8. Is interested in other people's art work. Can appreciate and learn from others' work.

[4] Studies show there are relatively low or negligible relationships between test-intelligence and measures of ability in music, art, and other areas. See, for example, Paul Witty, "How to Identify the Gifted Child," *Childhood Education*, 29:315, March 1953.

9. Likes to model clay, carve soap, or work with other forms of three-dimensional art.[5]

IDENTIFYING MUSICAL TALENT

Some children may show more talent in music than in art. Unless the teacher is alert to the possibilities of the child's musical interest, this talent may be wasted. A nursery-school or kindergarten teacher is in a strategic position to identify the musical child. The following criteria can help:

Which of your pupils stands out in these characteristics when compared with the rest of the class?
1. Responds more than others to rhythm and melody.
2. Sings well (on pitch and with good quality).
3. Puts verve and vigor into his music.
4. Is interested in music. Listens to records. Puts himself out to hear music.
5. Enjoys harmonizing with others or singing in groups.
6. Uses music to express his feelings and experiences.
7. Makes up original tunes.
8. Plays one or more instruments well.[6]

IDENTIFYING A TALENT FOR WRITING

We have already discussed creative writing in Chapter 10. Here is specific behavior for which to look:

Which of your pupils stands out in these characteristics when compared with the rest of the class?
1. Can develop a story from its beginning, through the build-up and climax, to an interesting conclusion.
2. Gives a refreshing twist, even to old ideas.
3. Uses only necessary details in telling a story.
4. Keeps the ideas organized within his story.
5. Chooses words that show perception.
6. Includes important details that other children miss and still gets across the central idea.
7. Enjoys writing stories and poems.
8. Makes his characters seem life-like. Captures the feelings of his characters in writing.[7]

In creative writing the experiences and the variety of ideas that a child has are the significant factors to look for in identifying giftedness. Correct spelling, grammar, and punctuation are not a part of the creative experience but must be taught as skills in a separate period. They are needed by the child as techniques for putting his ideas into communicable form, but the possession of these techniques does not ensure creativity.

[5] Jack Kough and Robert DeHaan, "Identifying the Children Who Need Help," *Teacher's Guidance Handbook*, Part I (Chicago: Science Research Associates, Inc., 1955), p. 66.
[6] *Ibid.*, p. 82.
[7] *Ibid.*, p. 72.

IDENTIFYING SCIENTIFIC TALENT

Scientific ability, like every talent, needs early discovery. Pupils who place in the ninetieth percentile and higher in the SRA *Test of Primary Mental Abilities,* especially on the subtests for Verbal Meaning, Reasoning, and Numbers, have the essential characteristics required for high-level work in science. Ability in science may also be indicated by the extracurriculum activities pupils choose, such as maintaining an aquarium, making insect or rock collections, experimenting with chemistry sets, studying the stars, or raising hamsters, mice, or snakes. Early interest in science, however, does not always persist. In Chapter 12 we pointed to the ways in which an original interest in science might be continued. A child who is good in mathematics, who can read at an advanced level, who works on special projects, and who spends considerable time on assignments of interest to him may well be on the road to a career in science.

Parents, too, should be aware of their responsibilities in this regard. Instead of discouraging the early scientific projects of children as " smelly," "messy," or too time-consuming, they should encourage the child who has talent and aptitude. The important thing to remember is that to be successful in any of the creative pursuits the child must begin early to apply himself to the discipline.

Providing for the Gifted Child in the School

Having identified the gifted child, what can be done to take care of his needs? Perhaps it might be well to cite some of the methods that are being used and briefly describe each.

ACCELERATION

Acceleration consists of skipping a grade or in some other way moving along at a pace appropriate to the individual's ability and maturity. For example, instead of having the bright child skip one or more grades, he may be placed in a rapid advancement class, in which he completes three years' work in two, or four years' work in three. One plan in use allows children of similar chronological age and social and emotional maturity to move along at the rate of speed that ability, maturation, and social conditions indicate is for the best interest of the child. The bright child is accelerated; the average child completes his primary education six semesters after kinder-garten; the slow child is permitted to remain in the primary school seven or eight semesters before he enters the traditional fourth grade. Regrouping, which takes place at the end of the semester, helps both the accelerated and the retarded child. Acceleration has the advantage of enabling the able learner to start early in his profession. Such acceleration made on an individual basis need not cause either social or emotional maladjustment.

An Enriched Environment

Some children will gain from an environment in which they are allowed to use their ability in stimulating projects and challenging experiences. There are those in every classroom who will read widely, engage in research projects, carry on scientific experiments, and participate in creative activities. A stimulating environment will provide these opportunities, but is this enough for the gifted child?

The advantage of enrichment is that it keeps the talented child with his own age group and with children of varying abilities. Yet he has additional work and more extensive opportunities to study subjects in which he is particularly interested.

The disadvantage of such a scheme is that in the regular classroom an intolerable burden is placed on the already overloaded classroom teacher. Enrichment is not easy for a teacher to manage, particularly when she has pupils of such a wide range of abilities as is found in the average classroom. Because such a program is cheap, easy for principals to administer, and does not single out the talented child unduly, it is a popular program, although admittedly not an effective one in the majority of cases. In short, enrichment can be only as effective as time, teacher, instructional materials, and physical facilities allow.

Additional Subjects

Within the framework of the curriculum of the average public school it is possible to include one or more additional classes in the gifted child's schedule. Since he can carry the regular program with ease, an extra class in a foreign language, in music, art, advanced mathematics, or science, or in creative writing or dramatics may be added. Obviously, this step alone is inadequate to meet the needs of the gifted; but it is preferable to letting him waste his time and talent.

Subgrouping Within the Regular Classroom

Many teachers make an effort to provide for individual differences in the classroom by offering opportunity for the gifted child to do advanced study, to work on special projects, or to explore a common or individual interest. This program requires, however, that the teacher be skillful in determining the abilities of individual children and that she have time to study their interests and provide materials. She must have adequate physical facilities, small classes, a wide variety of instructional and reading materials, adequate scientific equipment, a wide knowledge of group processes, and a broad knowledge of various subject matters. Given an ideal situation, all this might help the gifted child. The fact is, however, that there are few situations in the average classroom where the needs of the gifted are adequately met in this manner.

The gifted child has greater powers of concentration and retentiveness.

SPECIAL GROUPING

Sometimes the pupils are grouped homogeneously for all or part of the day. Such a scheme may be handled in one of several ways. The gifted pupils from several schools may be brought together in a single special group, as in the Major Work Groups in Cleveland. Children may be arranged by intellectual ability into two, three, or four groups for a given grade. Or talented children may be put into special groups for a part of the school week. These classes usually consist of about ten children, who carry on special projects that are often shared with the entire school or with a given grade.

SPECIAL CLASSES

Children may be placed in ordinary classes with a heterogeneous group for most of the time and then selected for special classes in their particular interests; or they may be placed in such classes for the entire program. For example, they may be placed in science, foreign language, mathematics, art, music, creative writing, and social studies classes.

There are many advantages of special classes: (1) They simplify the problem of enrichment, even including subjects, such as foreign languages, that are not usually included in the regular curriculum. (2) They make possible a certain amount of acceleration. (3) Competition with those of similar intellectual capacity provides a challenge to excellence that is a valuable experience for the child; it makes for habits of industry and efficiency rather than for those of sloppiness, laziness, and dawdling. (4) Children of similar interests, abilities, and tastes are likely to find congenial friends in such classes, and thus to have a happy social experience.

The hazards in planning for special classes are far from insurmountable but should be known and kept in mind. There may be some jealous reaction to such a program if it is not planned carefully. The attitude of gifted children occasionally needs training. They should be made to study the lives of men and women who have made great contributions to humanity, to ward off any feeling of superiority. In most cases the gifted child is not egotistical; usually he is a humble individual who does not regard himself as anything special. A final danger is a too narrow acquaintance with the activities and interests of others. This, too, is uncommon. On the whole, children in special classes share a healthy interest in other people and other activities and are concerned with wide interests of their own and others.

SPECIAL SCHOOLS

In large cities certain schools are specifically geared for pupils with special talents or gifts. Admission is based on a designated I.Q. score, on a satisfactory command of the skills of communication and computation, and on the recommendation of teachers and principal. One of the best known is the school connected with Hunter College, in New York City. This school enrolls children of extremely high I.Q.'s, and there is a waiting list for each grade, from the preschool on through the high school. Such schools provide grouping of gifted pupils for the purpose of giving children an environment in which they may be stimulated by especially qualified teachers and conditions conducive to maximum learning. Children can go as far and as fast as they are able and they can follow some of their individual interests.

So far, much more has been done in providing special training for children of limited capacities than in caring for the needs of those children upon whom rests the future leadership of the nation. It is by no means democratic to provide for the mentally retarded, the physically handicapped, and the speech defectives, while ignoring the gifted. Some methods by which the gifted may be helped to reach their potential have been cited. Four of these methods involve administration: (1) acceleration, (2) special groups, (3) special classes, and (4) special schools. Enrichment, on the other hand, is primarily a teaching procedure. It is largely in this area that the classroom teacher is able to make a contribution.

The Gifted Child in the Classroom

Too often in the past the problem of providing for the gifted has been shrugged off by administrators with the explanation that the public gets what it wants. Something should be done, they agree, but there is no money, no time, and no interest on the part of the teachers. Yet teachers are now asking for help in teaching the gifted.

AN ENRICHMENT PROGRAM

The following list of enrichment activities illustrates the kinds of things the teacher can encourage the gifted children to do in the areas of language arts and creative arts. Of course, for any particular group not all of these are workable or stimulating to the children.

Listening

1. Listen critically to debates, discussions, newscasts, and talks to form opinions, to hold discussions, and to draw conclusions.
2. Listen to radio and television performers to discover errors or difficulties in speech, new words, beautiful and appropriate words.
3. Make recordings to discover errors or difficulties in speech.
4. Listen for and make a list of sound effects used on a particular radio or television program and find out, through research, how these sounds are produced.

Speaking

1. Interview resource people in preparation for an oral report.
2. Develop and use techniques for debates, panel discussions, and parliamentary procedures.
3. Tell the class original stories.
4. Select poems suitable for choral work and arrange them for a choral-speaking group.

Reading

1. Use library resources such as the card catalog, atlases, yearbooks, and the *Readers' Guide* to locate and gather information on a topic.
2. Read materials to broaden interests.
3. Read materials to understand human relationships.
4. Select poems and stories that illustrate specific styles of writing.
5. Use dictionary, glossary, and thesaurus to improve the range of effective vocabulary.
6. Design and follow a balanced, leisure-time reading program.

Writing

1. Learn the techniques of speedy and accurate note-taking.
2. Learn the skills of outlining.
3. Learn to use abbreviations.
4. Compile a list of new words learned.
5. Edit a room newspaper.

Arts and Crafts

1. Plan stage settings, design costumes.
2. Design and construct puppets.
3. Plan and arrange bulletin boards in hall or classroom.
4. Arrange exhibits.
5. Construct scale models.
6. Make scale drawings.

7. Draw cartoons of current events — local, state, national.

8. Plan and carry out a decorating theme for a special occasion.

9. Express ideas and feelings through painting, clay modeling, sculpture, and dioramas.

10. Create stories or pictures to interpret musical selections or poems.

Music

1. Study the origin and historical significance of folk songs, folk dances, and patriotic songs.

2. Make a study of the development of certain musical instruments, such as the piano, violin, or harp.

3. Write original songs.

QUESTIONS AND ACTIVITIES

1. How do you account for the lag in providing for the needs of the gifted in this country? What evidence do you see of a trend in a new direction?

2. What methods are open to a school system in caring for the needs of the gifted?

3. Visit a primary-grade classroom and see in what ways the teacher provides for the gifted child.

4. Visit the office of the administrator of schools in your city. Try to find out what method is being used to deal with the gifted.

5. What qualifications would a teacher of the gifted need? In what way are these similar to those of the teacher of the average group? Of the slow learners?

6. As you read the enrichment program on pages 381–382, try to evaluate the effectiveness of the suggestions in terms of gifted children in the kindergarten through the third grade. Which activities apply to only one age level? Which could be used with all?

SELECTED READINGS

"A Way to Go to College While You're Still in High School." Editorial, *Good Housekeeping,* August 1958, p. 146.

Abraham, Willard. *Guide for the Study of Exceptional Children.* Boston: Porter Sargent, Publisher, 1956.

Baker, Harry J. *Introduction to Exceptional Children.* New York: The Macmillan Company, 1947.

Barclay, Dorothy. "The Private Life of the Gifted Child," *New York Times Magazine,* May 12, 1957, p. 46.

Birch, J. W., and E. M. McWilliams. *Challenging Gifted Children.* Bloomington, Ill.: Public School Publishing Co., 1955.

Brumbaugh, Florence N. "The Intellectually Gifted," *Special Education for Exceptional Children,* Vol. III. Boston: Porter Sargent, Publisher, 1956.

Cutts, Norma Estelle, and Nicholas Moseley. *Teaching the Bright and Gifted.* Englewood Cliffs, N.J.: Prentice-Hall, Inc., 1957.

DeHaan, Robert Frank, and Robert J. Havighurst. *Educating Gifted Children.* Chicago: The University of Chicago Press, 1957.

Hall, Theodore. *Gifted Children.* Cleveland: The World Publishing Company, 1956.

Havighurst, Robert, *et al. A Survey of the Education of Gifted Children.* Chicago: The University of Chicago Press, 1955.

Hildreth, Gertrude Howell, *et al. Educating Gifted Children at Hunter College Elementary School.* New York: Harper & Brothers, 1952.

Langdon, Grace, and Irving W. Stout. *Helping Parents Understand Their Child's School.* Englewood Cliffs, N.J.: Prentice-Hall, Inc., 1957.

Russel, Donald W. "A Functional Approach to the Study of the Gifted," *Elementary School Journal,* 57:45, October 1956.

Scheifele, Marian. *The Gifted Child in the Regular Classroom.* New York: Columbia University Press, 1953.

Small, J. J. "Developing Superior Talent," *School and Society,* 86:219–227, May 10, 1958.

Stoddard, Alexander J. *Schools for Tomorrow: An Educator's Blueprint.* New York: The Fund for the Advancement of Education, 1957.

Strang, Ruth. "The Mental Diet of our Gifted Children," *NEA Journal,* 44:265, May 1955.

Terman, Lewis M. *The Discovery and Encouragement of Exceptional Talent.* Test Service Notebook No. 14. Yonkers-on-Hudson, N.Y.: World Book Company, 1954.

Terman, Lewis M., and Melita Terman. *The Gifted Child Grows Up.* Stanford: Stanford University Press, 1947.

Wiener, Norbert. "Analysis of the Child Prodigy," *New York Times Magazine,* June 2, 1957, p. 15.

Witty, Paul (ed.). *The Gifted Child.* Boston: D. C. Heath & Company, 1951.

Worcester, D. A. *The Education of Children of Above-Average Mentality.* Lincoln, Neb.: University of Nebraska Press, 1956.

Yuhas, T. Frank. "The Gifted Child in the Classroom," *Educational Administration and Supervision,* 43:429–438, November 1957.

And when into the commonplace
Some bit of leaven is instilled
To mingle with the mediocre
And lift it quite beyond itself,
— This is reward.

— JOSEPHINE LESTER

THE EXCEPTIONAL CHILD

The Slow Learner

Nowhere is the close relationship between satisfaction and quality of work more evident than in teaching slow-learning children. When teachers find ways of understanding the slow learner, of diagnosing his problems, of adjusting the curriculum to meet his special needs, frustrations are at a minimum.

Today's teacher has a professional understanding of the slow learner. She accepts him mentally; but does she accept him emotionally? Learning to accept him with his limitations, to discover his assets as well as his liabilities, to appreciate him as a unique personality, is the first step on the road to success in working with him.

Identification of the Slow Learner

Very early in his school experience, the child suspected of being exceptional should be given a thorough examination to obtain a complete picture of his medical, psychological, and educational needs. Once these needs have been established and a diagnosis made, recommendations for the educational program of the child should be made and a sequence of learning activities planned. He should be placed in a special class or a special school, where his educational growth can be guided effectively, where he can learn at his own rate, taught by a teacher who has been trained in the education of such children.

Specialists tell us that the great majority of persons with I.Q.'s below 70 have the potential to be satisfactorily employed if they are properly trained.[8] But to be most effective, help should be offered as early as possible; the value of early investment is inestimable. Those who have worked with the handicapped testify that "one dollar invested in special education is worth at least a hundred dollars invested in institutionalization."[9]

STUDY AND DIAGNOSIS

In general, a program providing for the needs of the slow learners follows a pattern similar to the one presented here:

(1) A survey is made of age-grade records for grades 1–5 to discover the children who are two years or more below average.

(2) Teachers are asked to give recommendations concerning children who are having undue difficulty in keeping up with their grade level.

(3) A careful check is made of the cumulative health record and the social history of the child to ascertain obvious causes that have contributed to retardation. Scores on intelligence tests are checked.

(4) Group intelligence tests are administered.

(5) If the mental retardation appears to be due to emotional factors, a thorough study is made by a qualified psychologist. Included in this study are an individual intelligence test, a performance test, a personality and social maturity test, and achievement tests.

SUMMARY AND RECOMMENDATIONS

The summary and recommendations are made by a team consisting of the teacher, principal, school psychologist, and counselor. The final recommendation must take into account such considerations as social and emotional development, physical growth, mental and educational factors, and the child in relation to the rest of the special class.

ASSIGNMENT TO A SPECIAL CLASS

In the special class the child has opportunity to work in an environment in which he is allowed to progress at his own rate, in which the group is limited in number, and in which the teacher is trained. The scope of her work requires that the teacher have personal characteristics suited to working with children who are slow in learning. She must have endless patience, kindness, insight, and a genuine love for children, as well as a spirit of missionary endeavor. She must have specialized teaching competencies as well as a working knowledge of closely related fields. The latter includes a knowledge of medical conditions, the ability to help a child with his personal adjustment, acquaintance with tests and methods used in evaluating the child, a knowledge

[8] Salvatore G. DiMichael, *Counseling and Psychotherapy with the Mentally Retarded* (Glencoe, Ill.: The Free Press, 1957). Quoted by John Kidd, "Special Fulfillment of a Promise," *The Elementary School Journal*, 58:457, May 1958.

[9] John Kidd, *op. cit.*, 456.

of the curriculum, a knowledge of teaching techniques and materials, knowledge of professional literature, and good interpersonal relationships, manifested in an ability to work with parents, staff, children, and welfare agencies.

The Slow Learner in the Regular Classroom

Although it is ideal for the retarded child to be in a special class, it is not always possible. Sometimes the mentally retarded or the slow learner is placed in the regular classroom, under the direction of a teacher who may be untrained in the methods and materials of special education. When this is done, for whatever reason, the teacher should talk with the school psychologist or special educational consultant about each retarded child in order to understand him better. In an average class of thirty to forty youngsters, one to four are likely to be retarded. The classroom teacher needs some guiding principles for working with them. Among the principles that make the wheels turn more smoothly are these:

(1) The teacher must respect the individuality of the child. If she is unable to do that, she should not teach, for, in spite of the shortage of teachers, schools can get along better without her.

(2) The teacher must take the learner where he is and help him at his own rate of learning. The readiness materials may continue for weeks and months beyond the time usually allotted. Frequently the slow learner takes one-and-a-half school years to accomplish what the average child does in a school year.

(3) The slow learner needs motivated drill, but it need not be all of the same type. The teacher must be ingenious in devising new approaches to the material.

(4) The teacher must make use of concrete materials and concrete learning situations.

(5) The slow learner needs generous praise for effort and needs to be constantly reassured. Extrinsic rewards — a star on his paper, a bright-colored toy, his name in colored chalk — stimulate his interest.

(6) The teacher should help the child to look as attractive as possible in order to make the most of his assets. Good grooming will go a long way toward getting the group to accept the child.

(7) Children who learn slowly need to keep short-range plans and short-range goals before them.

(8) Formal school subjects should be delayed until the child is ready. Since the slow child is usually two years behind the other children (his mental age is usually two years below his chronological age), he should be expected to achieve on the level of a younger child.

(9) Success for child and teacher is the result of patient planning and thoughtful guidance during an extended readiness period before going into the regular school program.

(10) Repeating kindergarten is frequently desirable for the slow learner, since most children enjoy kindergarten so very much. It is usually the parents who must be convinced that it is a good thing for a child to have another year in which to develop some qualities of leadership. In the end they will usually be willing, although not happy, to cooperate. If a child cannot profit from a regular classroom after two years in a grade, he should be referred to a special class.

EDUCATIONAL ADJUSTMENTS

In the primary grades educational adjustments should be made for retarded children enrolled in the regular classroom. The teacher may recommend the following, singly or in combination: delay in school admission, extended kindergarten instruction, part-time attendance at school, repetition of a grade, or frequent conferences with parents.

Classroom teachers who work with slow learners or retarded children for the first time are frequently unprepared for the experience. Some orientation to such children is important in order to ascertain whether an individual teacher is equipped to work with these youngsters. Let us look in on a class in which all the children have an I.Q. rating of 75 or less, and see how happy, how relaxed, and how purposeful they are.

These children are in a special room at the end of the long corridor in the kindergarten-primary unit of an elementary school. You observe that they have their own entrance, their own playground. They have the usual equipment on the playground, but the playground is empty. When you step inside the room, no one rushes over to greet you to tell you about the interesting things that are happening today; but as you go over and sit beside the reading table, Lulu looks up shyly and smiles through a mop of black hair. This is progress for Lulu. The first time you came and sat beside her at the reading table she got up and left. John comes over and takes you by the hand. He doesn't say anything, but you know from the smile that something special has happened, and you walk with him over to the other side of the room. There he shows you the baby chicks that have hatched since you were there last. The children set a hen and cared for it each day, and now he says, "See the baby chicks."

The room is large and cheerful, and the pace is slow and relaxed. Only thirteen children, you think; this would be wonderful — to live with children and get to know them. With only thirteen, one could teach them. But when you look around the room, you wonder. Over in a corner two eight-year-old boys are playing with the blocks. They are painstakingly constructing a high building similar to the one five-year-old Billy constructed the other morning in kindergarten, but Billy did it in a few minutes and rushed over and said, "Look, Miss Piner, see, I built a large department store. I'm the manager, and Buddy is one of the clerks. What do you want to buy? Or are you just looking?"

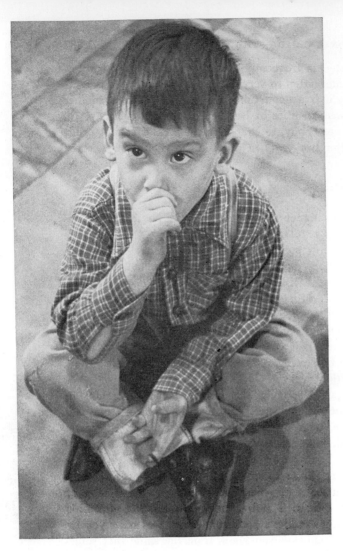

The slow learner needs as much additional time in which to make social and emotional adjustments as he needs to learn academic skills and communication techniques.

Here no one is talking — just going carefully and painstakingly about the job of building. Communication? Yes, but of a different kind. Over at the doll house three little girls are playing. They are getting ready for lunch. They have set the table with the blue and white checked cloth, and have put on the blue goblets. This is apparently a special day. "Somebody's birthday?" you ask. Again, no answer. They seem to have a way of communicating without words.

Way over in the other part of the room in front of the fireplace are the twins. You know them, and they know you, for they live down the street from your home. As you walk over, Mike, the smaller one, says, "Hi." His brother, Matt, bigger but shyer, says nothing but shows you the book he's "reading." These two are inseparable. You wonder what would happen if they were separated next year in first grade — and then you remember they won't be in first grade next year. They will still be in kindergarten.

You look over to see where the teacher is. She is helping Janie read. The children do not come up to the front of the room and read in a circle. Here the children read individually as they are ready for it. The teacher provides books and gets them interested in stories, but there is a great difference in their readiness for reading. Mostly they are still absorbed in their building, cutting, pasting, playing in the doll house. Janie is the only one who is interested in reading. Perhaps tomorrow there will be another.

As you wonder about the schedule, you see that it is almost time for outdoor play. How do they respond to directions? Here is an opportunity to see. The teacher in a calm, quiet voice calls, "Let's put the blocks and work away. When we finish, we will come over to my chair and talk about what will happen next." Although there is no rush, things get done. There is no confusion; how does the teacher get them to understand? Remember, this is March. These children have been living together since September. They know what is expected of them. They know they can trust the teacher to plan for them. They know they can achieve. Each child has learned that much.

He has learned that at school he can do many things he never knew he could do. He knows he has friends — friends who are like him — and a teacher who cares what he had for breakfast and when he gets a new pair of shoes. His teacher is happy when he tries to do his best and when his behavior is good; he tries to let her know he appreciates her interest. He does not of course realize that she is a superior teacher, that she is, in fact, a gifted teacher. He knows only that when she is in the room, he feels good inside. And so he smiles his slow, shy smile and walks over to put his hand in hers, because today it is his turn to be the leader when they go to the playground.

Teaching the Slow Learner

Some teachers think that the slow learner covers the same ground as the fast learner; they suppose he just needs more time. Actually, he requires different teaching procedures. Teaching the slow learner is like teaching children who are immature in experience or intellectual development. The slow learner learns best if the teacher provides:

1. Shorter units of instruction.
2. More concrete associations — things to see, hear, feel, smell.
3. More motivated drill, or review.
4. More specific directions, and feedback to make certain the directions are understood.
5. More time to complete work.
6. More illustrative and audio-visual material.
7. More supervision and guidance.
8. Personalization of experience.

9. More motivation, often extrinsic.
10. Immediate application of the learning, relating it to something important to the child.
11. Greater variety of stimulation and materials.
12. Stress on developing attitudes in such subjects as social studies and citizenship, as opposed to factual learning.
13. Greater variety of pupil response in a given area of learning.
14. Emotional involvement in the activity, as in dramatics, dancing, and art.
15. Praise for work that shows any indication of worth.

Approximately twenty per cent of all school children are classified as slow learners. Often the slow learner needs an entirely different curriculum from that of the normal or gifted child. Such children need more real-life situations. They should be helped to do the things in which they can succeed: to make change, to use the city transportation system, to tell time, to know the value of money, to play games, to care for personal needs. As soon as possible they should be taught the basic rudiments of reading, writing, and numbers. Slow learners need more time, more encouragement, and more motivation. The best teacher is one who respects their worth, encourages their strengths, and helps them live with their weaknesses.

ADAPTING READING INSTRUCTION

Since reading is so vital in the life of every individual, some suggestions to help the teacher adapt the reading program to the abilities of the slow learners in the classroom are in order:

1. Delay actual instruction with formal reading material until the child evidences readiness.
2. Introduce all phases of reading more gradually than for the average child.
3. Select reading materials carefully on the basis of interest as well as level of ability of the child.
4. Plan frequent short periods of instruction.
5. Emphasize the readiness activities in the reading lesson.
6. Fill the reading period with vital, concrete, and diversified activities.
7. Plan an appropriate program of word recognition. Use ear-training activities, word games. Build a sight vocabulary.
8. Help the child evaluate his own progress.
9. Read below as well as at the child's reading level.
10. Review reading materials frequently, but provide incentives for the re-reading. For instance, read to dramatize a story.
11. Begin reading only after the child has had experience with stories he helps compose — stories about his home, family, pets, and so forth.
12. Make reading significant to the child by using functional reading for motivation — reading the notices on the bulletin board, daily plans, directions for a game.

The slow learner needs more motivated drill in order to complete his work successfully.

13. Enrich the child's experience. Often the slow learner has had few experiences to bring meaning to the printed material.

14. Expect less of him than of the average child. Remember his I.Q. ranges from 75 or 80 to 90 at the highest.

In working with slow learners try to keep in mind the fact they are not responsible for their lack of ability to learn; try to motivate them and praise them for each effort.

QUESTIONS AND ACTIVITIES

1. Observe a class of exceptional children. Note particularly the following:
   a. Curriculum adjustments.
   b. Special equipment.
   c. Physical surroundings.
   d. Teaching techniques.
   e. Curriculum resources.
   f. Apparent nature of the handicaps.
   g. Relationships between teacher and pupils.
   h. Relationships between teacher of special class and regular classroom teachers.
   i. Teaching aids.
   j. Provisions for individual differences.
   k. Atmosphere in the classroom.
   l. Special qualities of the teacher.

2. Describe the apparent homogeneity or heterogeneity in terms of age, grade placement, specific handicaps.

3. Observe in a regular classroom. Indicate the number of children who might be classed as exceptional. How are the mentally retarded and slow learners provided

for? How does the classroom teacher handle unusual problems, such as wide range of achievement, scheduling, resources?

4. How can the classroom teacher make provision for individual differences?

5. What are some specific methods of teaching the slow learner in addition to individualizing the instruction?

SELECTED READINGS

Featherstone, W. B. *Teaching the Slow Learner.* New York: Bureau of Publications, Teachers College, Columbia University, 1951.

Goodenough, Florence L. *Exceptional Children.* New York: Appleton-Century-Crofts, Inc., 1956.

Hagerman, Helen. "The Slow Learner," *Grade Teacher,* 71:24, May 1954.

Heck, Arch O. *Education of Exceptional Children.* New York: McGraw-Hill Book Company, Inc., 1953.

Hilleboe, Guy L. *Finding and Teaching A-typical Children.* New York: Bureau of Publications, Teachers College, Columbia University, 1930.

Ingram, Christine P. *Education of the Slow-Learning Child.* New York: The Ronald Press Company, 1953.

Jenkins, Gladys Gardner. *These Are Your Children,* Expanded Edition. Chicago: Scott, Foresman & Company, 1953.

Johnson, Orval. "The Teacher and the Withdrawn Child," *The Education Digest,* 22:14–22, April 1957.

Kirk, S. A. *Teaching Reading to Slow-Learning Children.* Boston: Houghton Mifflin Company, 1940.

Kirk, S. A., and G. O. Johnson. *Educating the Retarded Child.* Boston: Houghton Mifflin Company, 1951.

Lightfoot, Georgia. *Characteristics of Bright and Dull Children.* New York: Bureau of Publications, Teachers College, Columbia University, 1953.

Lloyd, Frances. *Educating the Sub-Normal Child.* New York: Philosophical Library, Inc., 1953.

Noel, Elizabeth. "A New Look at Slow Learners," *The Instructor,* 67:6, 80, December 1957.

Redl, Fritz, and William W. Wattenberg. *Mental Hygiene in Teaching,* Second Edition. New York: Harcourt, Brace and Company, 1959.

Scheidemann, Norma. *The Psychology of Exceptional Children.* Boston: Houghton Mifflin Company, 1931.

The Slow Learner in the Average Classroom. New York: Metropolitan School Study Council, Subcommitte on the Slow Learner, 1954.

Taba, Hilda. "Acceptance and Rejection in Primary Grades," *Childhood Education,* 30:23–26, May 1954.

Yackel, Martha L. "Purposeful Reading for Slow Learners," *The Instructor,* 66:7, June 1957.

We all have a different timbre,
  some reeds are double,
  some single,
Some of us speak to the bow . . .
      we sound in
  different ways.

— NATHANIEL BURT

THE EXCEPTIONAL CHILD

Speech Defectives

The language and speech patterns that the child learns will influence him for his entire lifetime. Although he may consciously make changes when he is an adult, the early patterns have a tendency to come through in times of stress. For this reason it is important that parents and teachers set the best possible examples themselves and that they insist on the child's speaking his best for his level of maturity and development.

On the other hand, many speech problems are the result of parents or teachers setting standards that are too high for the child's development. Each child has his own design for development; few children are average. For this reason it is important to know the progression of development in speech skills, recognizing that a child in kindergarten may be normal in speech development even though many sounds are not yet included in his vocabulary. Scolding a child because his skill in the use of language does not equal another child's can result only in frustration for all concerned.

Because in these early years there is such a wide range in the acquisition of the various motor skills at each chronological age, it is important that the teacher should know what is normal for the child's age. But deviation from this norm should not cause undue concern unless it is well over a year off.

General Development of Speech

Speech is an acquired skill in the use of muscles and organs that have biological functions far removed from speech. We breathe to sustain life, but incidentally we control the expulsion of the breath to make sounds. The larynx contracts and the glottis is closed when the body strains. Here the biological function takes over. Yet we can close the glottis voluntarily and emit air under pressure through it to make sounds.

Fortunately, the child performs these various functions involuntarily. He cries in protest against being left alone, against being hungry, or just "because." Soon he learns the pleasure of making sounds other than those of crying. Near the sixth month the child enters the stage of random vocalization, or babbling. Here he first uses the variety of vowels and consonants that will lead to the development of language. As crying is a form of protest, babbling is an expression of the child's pleasure. Other factors being equal, the happy child has a better opportunity of developing speech skills than the protesting, crying one.

During this babbling stage the child utters a wide variety of sounds. Many of them seem very strange to us. Only a phonetician or linguist can recognize them. Those that the child finds bring the most pleasant response, he keeps. The others eventually will be lost. The baby should be encouraged in this prelingual phase of his speech development. He is forming patterns now for true speech.

About six months later the child enters the next phase of his speech development. He has apparently become entranced with the sound of his own voice. He repeats sounds that are pleasurable to him. The child, listening to himself, is gaining the skill of making sounds at will. This leads him into the next stage of development, where he imitates sounds he really hears.

In this echolalia stage the child consciously tries to repeat the sounds made by his mother or other adults. Here is the true beginning of the child's native speech. Sounds that he has been making but that are now not given to him by the adult tend to disappear. He retains only those sounds that bring response from the people on whom he depends.

By the time the child is two years of age, he should be talking. He will have learned the names of those who are near him and of the objects and actions that most concern him. The jargon that he has used in imitation of the adult's speech in his effort to capture their fluency is rapidly vanishing. Instead, he has become concerned with communication with the adult world. This means that he must use the oral symbols that are meaningful to them. At first he uses mostly nouns, because these are usually the names of things he can see, feel, and hear. Sixty-five per cent of the words used between thirteen and twenty-seven months are nouns. By the time the child is three to four years of age, only twenty per cent of his words are nouns.

The visibly made sounds are the first to appear in the child's meaningful speech. The labials (lip sounds), *p, b, m,* and *w,* are used in connection with the vowels that have appeared and have been practiced during the jargon and echolalia stages. The next to appear are the front tongue consonants, *t, d,* and *n.* The back-of-the-tongue consonants are usually next, *k, g, ng.*

The *l* and *r* sounds, which are more difficult, are comparatively late in appearing. *S*, *z*, and *sh* are the last.

Helping Children Develop Normal Speech

Teachers of young children have a great responsibility in the area of language development. First of all, they must set an example in their own speech that will give the children correct models to follow. Their voices should be free of harshness and strain. Their articulation should be free of deviations. Needless to say, they should use correct grammar and diction.

In the nursery school and kindergarten emphasis should be placed on word games that the children can play together. Children who have developed the skills of speech will enjoy the games, while those who are having difficulty can participate in speech drills without having any feeling of pressure or any awareness of differentness. Children at these ages are thinking more rapidly than they can speak. They must search for words. In this silence they may lose their chance to speak. Hence they sometimes resort to meaningless sounds, or they may prolong the initial sound until they are sure of the word. The teacher who does not realize that all children have normal nonfluencies in their speech tends to label them as stutterers. This appellation often starts a distressing and unnecessary cycle. The child, made to feel that he is different, becomes fearful. Either he withdraws from speaking situations entirely, or in the ensuing struggle to speak he actually develops stuttering.

Many of the speech problems of children in these early years will be taken care of by the simple process of maturation. An awareness of this on the part of the teacher will make life more pleasant for both teacher and child. This does not mean, however, that the teacher is to do nothing.

An examination of the child by his family doctor should reveal any actual physical abnormalities that handicap him in his speech. These, of course, should be corrected if possible. The removal of adenoids, for example, though making it possible for the child to speak more clearly, will not guarantee that he will. If speech habits have been set, he will need a period of retraining under the guidance of a speech correctionist. More often, the child can make the correct sounds but has not learned the habit of making them. The teacher should not make an issue of changing the speech pattern. Very few classroom teachers have the necessary training to be speech correctionists. But all classroom teachers, and especially those teaching young children, should understand the development of speech and what can — and even more important, what cannot — be done in regular classroom routines. The permissive atmosphere created by a wise and understanding teacher will do much to help children over these early difficult years of mastering oral communication.

In the school systems where there are teachers of speech correction assigned to one or several buildings, the classroom teacher has her greatest ally in working with children with speech problems. No one person can do the job alone. Though the correctionist with her specialized training can give the child the individual, skilled help that he needs, all her work can be undone by an unsympathetic or a jealous teacher. Both the correctionist and the teacher are needed for the best development of the child. The minutes each week taken from the classroom routines for the child with a speech problem can mean the difference between success and failure in life for him. The art lesson missed, the reading lesson slighted, the explanation of the arithmetic lesson that was conducted during his work with the correctionist should be considered by the teacher as slight payment for the help the child is receiving in fitting him to take his place more securely with his fellow pupils through his improved speech skills.

Because of the close relationship between the skills of reading and speaking, all teachers of young children should have some work in speech correction. The child who has articulatory problems will usually have reading problems as well. Often it is better to work with the speech problems first.

One of the best ways of helping all children develop better speech habits is through the use of speech games. Before any effective work can be done with speech exercises, however, the children must be relaxed.

RELAXATION EXERCISES

1. Have the children be "rag dolls." The teacher recites:

> Let's play rag doll
> Don't make a sound
> Fling your arms and bodies
> Loosely around.

The children will bend from the waist and let their trunks and arms swing until they are completely relaxed. Have them drop their jaws and roll their heads. The teacher may walk among them and swing an arm to see if it is properly relaxed.

2. Another game the children enjoy is "Scarecrow." In this the children stand. They become scarecrows gradually, beginning with the feet. Have the children make their feet as tense and stiff as they can — then their legs — their hips — their trunks — their chests — their arms out straight — their necks. When they are as stiff and tense as they can be, in short, "scarecrows," have them immediately become "rag dolls." This exercise is especially good for the children who have difficulty in relaxing. Nearly all can tense themselves. The natural reaction from great tension is relaxation.

3. Preschool children like to "float" when they take their rest. They can float on a cloud, drifting slowly through the sky. They must be relaxed, or they will fall off. Lift an arm to see if there is any tension. Let them float, too, on the water; any stiffness, and they will sink.

4. Have the children be "trees" with the wind blowing their branches. They sway in the breeze, gently at first. Then the wind gets stronger. They toss their trunks as the wind sweeps over them. The wind dies down and they again stand silently.

ARTICULATION GAMES

When the children are relaxed is the time to do articulation games. The primary children should understand how the various sounds are made as they practice the sound games and poems. During the practice periods let them exaggerate the movements of the lips, tongue, and jaw to get the feel of the movements. Care should be taken, though, that the children do not think that this exaggerated movement is to be used outside of the practice period. Some suggested games follow:

1. When the children come in from recess have them pant like dogs. This gives them good exercise for breath control. Have the dogs lap up water. This is excellent for developing control of the tongue. Now let the dog run his tongue around to get every drop of water on his lips. The dog is tired. He puts his head on the desk and relaxes all over.

2. Let the children pretend they are tires on a car. The car has a flat tire. Hear the air going out — s-s-s-s-s-s-s-s. A child pumps the tire. Have all the children fill their cheeks with air. The tire goes flat again, s-s-s-s-s-s-s-s.

3. Take listening walks. Let the children make the sounds they heard, and the others guess what made them.

4. Give the children a sound. The children say words beginning with the

Articulation games, such as using the telephone, are most effective when the child is relaxed, yet alert.

sound, with the sound in the middle of the word, with the sound at the end of the word. Have the children give the sounds and judge if they are made correctly.

5. Let the children exercise their jaws. Snap jaws like a snapping turtle; round the lips and say *oo*. Now say *ee*. Exaggerate these. Have the children say *ah* so the dentist can work on the back teeth. While the children are working on these for flexibility of the lips be sure that the quality of the voice is good.

6. Have children talk in high voices, in low voices. If any children are having trouble with certain sounds, have all the children work on them as games.

Exercises for the Jaw

John Cook's Grey Mare

John Cook had a little grey mare,
  Hee, haw, hum;
Her legs were long and her back was
    bare,
  Hee, haw, hum.
John Cook was riding up Shooter's
    Bank,
  Hee, haw, hum;
The mare she began to kick and to
    prank,
  Hee, haw, hum.

John Cook was riding up Shooter's
    Hill,
  Hee, haw, hum.
His mare fell down and made her will,
  Hee, haw, hum.
The bridle and saddle were laid on the
    shelf,
  Hee, haw, hum;
If you want any more, you may sing
    it yourself,
    Hee, haw, hum.

Bow! Wow! Wow!

Bow, wow, wow, whose dog art thou?
Little Tom Tinker's dog, bow, bow,
    wow.

The Old Billy Goat

In a lot near our school
  Is an old Billy Goat.
  Baa, baa, baa!
He has a long beard
  And a warm wooly coat.
  Baa, baa, baa!
The children at noon
  Throw him bits of their lunch.
  Baa, baa, baa!
And laugh as they watch
  Old Billy Goat munch!
  Baa, baa, baa!

Frog's Chorus

"Yaup, Yaup, Yaup!"
Said the croaking voice of a frog:
  "A rainy day
  In the month of May
And plenty of room in the bog."

"Yaup, yaup, yaup!"
Said the frog as it splashed about:
  "Good neighbors all,
  When you hear me call,
It is odd that you do not come out."

"Yaup, yaup, yaup!"
Said the frog: "It is charming weather.
  We'll come up and sup
  When the moon is up,
And we'll all of us croak together."

The Old Black Crow

An old black crow flew into a tree.
  Caw, caw, caw!
And what do you think he could see?
  Caw, caw, caw!
He saw the sun shine on the lake.
  Caw, caw, caw!
And tiny splashes fishes make.
  Caw, caw, caw!

The Jolly Little Clown

I'm a jolly little clown,
  Yak, yaw, yah!
I can smile and I can frown,
  Yak, yaw, yah!
I can drop my jaw far down!
  Yak, yaw, yah!

EXERCISES FOR THE LIPS

Tu-whit! Tu-whoo!

The owl by day can't see, 'tis said!
  OOoo, OOoo, OOoo!
He sits and blinks, turns his head,
  OOoo, OOoo, OOoo!

But when the stars come out at night,
  Tu-whit, tu-whoo, tu-whoo!
He calls his mate with all his might.
  Tu-whit, tu-whoo, tu-whoo!

The Chee-Choo Bird

A little green bird sat on a fence rail,
  Chee-choo, chee-choo, chee!
Its song was the sweetest I ever have
    heard,
  Chee-choo, chee-choo, chee!
I ran for some salt to put on its tail,
  Chee-choo, chee-choo, chee!
But while I was gone, away flew the
    bird,
  Chee-choo, chee-choo, chee!

Pitty Patty Polt

Pitty Patty Polt
Shoe the wild colt;
  here a nail
  and there a nail,
Pitty Patty Polt.

Pussy Cat Mew

The Pussy-Cat Mew jumped over a
    coal,
And in her best petticoat burnt a great
    hole.

Poor Pussy's weeping, she'll have no
    more milk,
Until her best petticoat's mended with
    silk!

Playing Clown

I'm a funny little clown,
I say. "Ah-oo-ee-oo."
My mouth is open wide
When I say, "Ah, ah, ah."

My lips are very round
When I say, "Oo, oo, oo,"
I draw my lips far back
When I say, "Ee, ee, ee."

Ah — oo — ee — oo,
Ah — oo — ee — oo
I'm a funny little clown.

EXERCISES FOR THE TONGUE

Hickery, Dickery, Dock

Hickory, dickory, dock,
The mouse ran up the clock;
The clock struck one and down he
    ran;
Hickory, dickory, dock!

Thomas A. Tattamus

Thomas A. Tattamus took two T's
To tie two tups to two tall trees,
To frighten the terrible Thomas A.
    Tattamus.
Tell me how many T's there are in
    that.

Dotting the Roof

My tongue can dot
The roof of my mouth;
  Dot — dot — dot.

It touches the front,
And middle and back;
  Dot — dot — dot.

Can your tongue dot
The roof of your mouth?
  Dot — dot — dot.

Can it touch front,
And middle and back?
  Dot — dot — dot.

The Two Crows

There were two crows sat on a stone,
  Fal, la, la, la, lal, de.
One flew away and then there was one,
  Fal, la, la, la, lal, de.
The other crow found himself alone,
  Fal, la, la, la, lal, de.

Lapping Milk

Little kitty laps her milk,
  Lap, lap, lap!
Her tongue goes out,
Her tongue goes in,
  Lap, lap, lap!

Little kitty likes her milk,
  Lap, lap, lap!
Oh, see her tongue
Go out and in,
  Lap, lap, lap!

Exercises for Plosives

Baa, Baa, Black Sheep

Baa, baa, black sheep,
  Have you any wool?
Yes, sir, yes, sir, three bags full;
  One bag for Bobby,
And one bag for Bill,
  And one bag for Betty,
Who lives on the hill.

A Farmer Went Trotting

A farmer went trotting,
Upon his grey mare,
  Bumpety, bumpety, bump!

With his daughter behind him,
So rosy and fair,
  Bumpety, bumpety, bump!

A raven cried "Croak!"
And they all tumbled down,
  Bumpety, bumpety, bump!

The mare broke her knees,
And the farmer his crown,
  Lumpety, lumpety, lump.

The mischievous raven
Flew laughing away,
  Bumpety, bumpety, bump.

And vowed he would serve them
The same day,
  Lumpety, lumpety, lump.

Jack-in-the-Box

Jack jump out,
And Jack jump in!
Jack jump up,
And Jack jump down!

Shake your head!
Look out and in!
Go in and shut
The cover down!

Peter, Peter

Peter, Peter, pumpkin eater,
Had a wife and couldn't keep her,
He put her in a pumpkin shell,
And there he kept her very well.

Pump, Pump, Pump
Pump, pump, pump, pump,
Water from the spout;
Plish, plosh, plish, plosh,
Water gushes out.

Pour, pour, pour, pour,
Fill the doggie's pan;
Pump, pump, pump, pump,
Quickly as you can.

Brown Birdie
Little brown birdie is bobbing his head,
  Bobbety, bobbety, bob.
Looking for something behind the shed,
  Bobbety, bobbety, bob.
If his dinner will be a fat bug or worm,
  Bobbety, bobbety, bob.
Whichever it is, I think it will squirm,
  Bobbety, bobbety, bob.

The Little Bird
Once I saw a little bird
Go hop, hop, hop,
I said, "Little birdie, Will you stop, stop, stop?"

He looked me up and down
With a peep, peep, peep,
And across the grass he went
With a leap, leap, leap.

Bubble Bath
Bubble bath, bubble bath
  In a white tub.
Hear the little bubbles go
  Bub, bub, bub.

The Birches
The little birches, white and slim,
  Gleaming in the forest dim,
Must think the day is almost gone,
  For each one has her nighty on.

In the third grade the children can begin a scientific study of the voice organs. In health class they can study charts of the throat, mouth, and nose to see how sounds are produced and resonated. They can begin to understand the reasons why their voices become tired and hoarse when they strain them. If there is a packing house near, the teacher or a group of the pupils may be able to secure the larynx of a pig or sheep. If the lungs are attached, all the better, as then they can see how the air goes from the lungs up through the larynx. They can see, too, the vocal folds and get an idea of their smallness. If the child's attention is drawn to the fact of how tired his large muscles get when he uses them a great deal, he can better understand the need of careful use of the very small muscles that govern his speech organs.

QUESTIONS AND ACTIVITIES

1. Visit a kindergarten and observe the children you think have speech defects. Make a list of the sounds that are missing and the ones that are substituted. Do these fit into patterns of normal speech development?

2. Observe a third grade. Compare the number of children with defective speech with those in the kindergarten. What sounds are involved here? Explain your findings.

3. From the books listed in the bibliography and other sources, make a scrapbook of speech games and drills for the primary grades.

4. Make a scrapbook of pictures that could be used to test articulation in the preschool. Check a list of suggested words in a speech correction book. Be sure to include words that will use the sounds in the initial, medial, and final positions.

5. Observe a speech correctionist as she works with small children. Ask her about her concept of her relationship with the classroom teacher.

SELECTED READINGS

Akin, Johnnye. *And So We Speak.* Englewood Cliffs, N.J.: Prentice-Hall, Inc., 1958.

Anderson, Virgil. *Improving the Child's Speech.* New York: Oxford University Press, 1953.

Arnold, Genevieve. *A Practice Manual for the Correction of Speech Sounds.* Houston: Speech Clinic, University of Houston. 1950.

Beasley, Jane. *Slow to Talk.* New York: Bureau of Publications, Teachers College, Columbia University, 1956.

Berry, Mildred, and Jon Eisenson. *Speech Disorders.* New York: Appleton-Century-Crofts, Inc., 1956.

Carter, Eunice, and McKenzie Buck. "Prognostic Testing for Functional Articulation Disorders among Children in the First Grade," *The Journal of Speech and Hearing Disorders,* 23:124–133, May 1958.

Chipman, Sylvia. *The Child's Book of Speech Sounds.* Magnolia, Mass.: Expression Co., 1954.

Eisenson, Jon. *The Improvement of Voice and Diction.* New York: The Macmillan Company, 1958.

Eisenson, Jon, and Mardel Ogilvie. *Speech Correction in the Schools.* New York: The Macmillan Company, 1957.

Hahn, Elise. "An Analysis of the Delivery of the Speech of First Grade Children," *Quarterly Journal of Speech,* 35:338–343, October 1949.

Johnson, Wendell. *Your Most Enchanted Listener.* New York: Harper & Brothers, 1956.

Johnson, Wendell, Spencer Brown, James Curtis, Clarence Edney, and Jacqueline Keaster. *Speech-Handicapped School Children.* New York: Harper & Brothers, 1956.

Nemoy, Elizabeth. *Speech Correction Through Story-Telling Units.* Magnolia, Mass.: Expression Co., 1954.

Nemoy, Elizabeth, and Serena Davis. *The Correction of Defective Consonant Sounds.* Magnolia, Mass.: Expression Co., 1954.

Newby, Hayes. *Audiology.* New York: Appleton-Century-Crofts, Inc., 1958.

Ogilvie, Mardel, John Pruis, and Elise Hahn. "Bibliography of Speech in the Elementary School," *The Speech Teacher,* 2:262–265, November 1953.

Pruis, John. "General Speech Training in the Elementary School. *Quarterly Journal of Speech,* 36:524–527, December 1950.

Templin, Mildred. *Certain Language Skills in Children.* Minneapolis: University of Minnesota Press, 1957.

Tjomsland, Lily. "Santa's Toys." *The Speech Teacher,* 5:309–312, November 1956.

Van Riper, Charles. *Speech Correction.* Englewood Cliffs, N.J.: Prentice-Hall, Inc., 1954.

Van Riper, Charles. *Teaching Your Child to Talk.* New York: Harper & Brothers, 1950.

Van Riper, Charles, and Katherine Butler. *Speech in the Elementary Classroom.* New York: Harper & Brothers, 1955.

Walsh, Gertrude. *Sing Your Way to Better Speech.* New York: E. P. Dutton & Co., Inc., 1947.

Wise, Claude M. *Introduction to Phonetics.* Englewood Cliffs, N.J.: Prentice-Hall, Inc., 1958.

Wood, Alice. *Sound Games.* New York: E. P. Dutton & Co., Inc., 1948.

Yoakam, Doris A. "Speech Games for Children," *Quarterly Journal of Speech,* 30:85–87, February 1944.

Zedler, Empress Young. *Listening for Speech Sounds.* New York: Harper & Brothers, 1955.

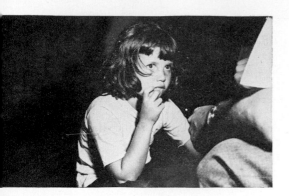

Life is a problem for everybody.

— SIGMUND FREUD

THE EXCEPTIONAL CHILD

Problems of Social and Emotional Adjustment

Normal children have their areas of stress and conflict, but one characteristic of normality is the ability to resolve conflicts through socially approved activities. The normal child uses legitimate avenues of release from emotional tensions; for example, he may release tensions through play, construction, art, music, writing, the dance, drama, or similar creative activities.

Some children, however, are not able to release their tensions and emotional conflicts without help from adults. Their problems, indeed, may be of such a serious nature as to require the help of trained personnel from the guidance clinic, a psychologist, or a psychiatrist. In these cases, the responsibility of the teacher is merely to identify the child who needs more help than she can give. She should refer him to the proper agencies and then cooperate with these agencies in working out a solution to the problem.

In order to determine which children the teacher can handle in the classroom and which children have emotional disturbances with which the teacher should not try to cope, it is necessary to know the particular situation, the child, the relationships between teacher and child, parent and child, and the teacher, child, parent, and school. Teachers react differently to behavior problems; children react differently to teachers. We shall discuss some of the types of emotional and social problems that many teachers in nursery school, kindergarten, and primary grades must meet and cope with.

Types of Problems

THE SPOILED CHILD

One of the types of children most in need of special help from the teacher is the child who is labeled, for want of a better term, "spoiled." The term in itself indicates that something should have happened long ago, but didn't, to prevent what is happening now. Such a child is not accepted by others because of his behavior; and since he is not accepted by others, he does not accept himself.

The teacher must find the cause, not treat the symptom. Treating the acts of the spoiled child ignores the underlying roots of the problem and fails to take into account the fact that this behavior is a surface substitute for the kind of behavior and growth the child really wants. But he needs help. Since the "spoiledness" is frequently his reaction to real or imagined rejection, he may need more than firm limits to help him change.

The teacher or parent who must face living with such a child at school or in the home must stand up to him and see him as he is. It is frequently not a pretty picture. The teacher must be able

> . . . to face the child with all his destructiveness, hyperactivity, and impulsiveness, to stand fast before his accumulated fury and at the same time to live through his experiences with him, comforting and supporting him even when he resists . . . and becomes utterly unable to face himself.[10]

A spoiled child knows well when his parent or teacher is afraid of him, of what he may do or say, and of the intensity of his own fears. Parents and teachers have put off reckoning with him; they have failed to brace themselves to meet him because it is easier to go on as they have been doing.

The problem is that the emphasis has shifted from his own growth, his own development, to the effect he has on other people. Adults have been concerned with his destructiveness rather than with his growth. His teachers and parents have tried to find ways of making him responsible instead of recognizing that he acts irresponsibly because he has been deprived of a requirement for effective living — he needs to be loved. This is apparent in those rare moments when he is a genuinely lovable child who is giving you a glimpse of what he would like to be — of what he could be — if someone would only help him. Such occasions should be used to form a new relationship and to strengthen and solidify it once it has been initiated. Parents and teacher too, sometimes, during these brief interludes of desirable behavior in which the defenses of the child momentarily break down, overlook completely the need the child has of taking a new look at himself. They are so grateful for the temporary relief of changed behavior that, though they give the child approval and reward him, they do nothing to help him

---

[10] Clark E. Moustakas, "Spoiled Behavior in the School-age Child," *Child Study*, 35:17, Winter 1957–1958.

maintain this new, desirable behavior; thus, he lapses into his old pattern.

Sometimes there is little the teacher can do. It may be that the child needs to be referred to the child guidance clinic after consultation with the parents and principal. The therapist can take a more objective look. There is nothing personal involved for him, no long-standing sensitive feelings. Sometimes in the quiet of the playroom, in the relief of hearing a restrained adult voice, the child calms down and feels there is someone who wants to know him and who is not impressed by his destructive behavior. By treating the child as a person he would like to know, by failing to be impressed with his tantrums, by showing that he disapproves of the actions but not the child, the therapist may be able to help.

If, long before, the parents or the first teachers had made it clear to the child that they, too, liked him, that they were not afraid of him, and that there could be a close relationship between them, the child might have become a person he himself could admire. This would have been the beginning of a chance for him to express a positive feeling toward someone who believed in him. Accepting him and treating him like a person who wants to change his behavior is the first step now toward helping him be a normal instead of a spoiled child.

Here, as in every other phase of teaching, the personality and understanding of the teacher loom large in establishing the kind of relationship the child needs. The best sight is still insight. Insight comes largely from accepting and studying children, from trying to find the cause of their problems, and then changing the environment, removing the cause, or changing the child. The child who feels he has a friend in the teacher is already helped toward a happier adjustment.

Children must be helped to gain confidence in themselves.

THE TIMID CHILD

The timid, withdrawn child in school gives very little trouble, rarely speaks out of turn or fights with anyone. Though one cannot blame parents for being worried about the timid child and urging him to "show some spunk," they will need to do more than urge him.

Why is he so lacking in self-assertion? It may be that he still has not had enough experience in social activity. In order to help children develop confidence in themselves, parents and teachers must be willing to step back and let a child try his mettle; but they must only step back, not go out of sight. They must be available if the child needs them. If the child is confident that the adults in his life will be there when he needs them, progress toward mature behavior will be facilitated. For him independence means neither rebellion nor rejection. The challenges that adults later present to guide him toward greater independence are accepted for what they are — challenges to be met with confidence, not with fear.

THE AGGRESSIVE CHILD

The overly aggressive child poses a problem for the teacher in the classroom and on the playground. He must be restrained from harming other children, guided to a more realistic understanding of his own role and importance in the scheme of things, and helped to accept limitations imposed by the group. Even threes and fours can learn to abide by such rules as "No hitting with things, no biting, scratching, kicking, or poking. No hitting in the face. No kicking the other fellow when he's down." It is not enough, at times, to say, "We play nicely together in this school," or "We don't fight." Children have to know specifically what they can do and what they cannot do.

Children can be helped to understand that mature behavior for a given age level demands consideration for the other person. Most of them want to be mature. As the child learns to trust the adult — both teacher and parent — and knows that they have his interest at heart, he may feel, if he is the timid one, that he has a backer beside or behind him; if he is the aggressive one, that he can get along increasingly well without his fists. He knows that the teacher will help see that he is treated fairly and squarely. As his confidence in adults grows, his confidence in himself will grow, and much of the undesirable behavior will disappear. The teacher should emphasize the positive. She should set limits, have a warm personal relationship with the child, help him realize his strengths and limitations, and give him experiences that will increase his social skills.

THE HYPERACTIVE CHILD

The child who cannot sit still is a very real problem to the teacher in the primary grades. This is particularly true in a school in which the program is formal and little legitimate provision is made for moving about. Making a child "toe the mark" does not solve his problem. The teacher should provide legitimate ways in which he can release excess tension without building up feelings of guilt.

THE HOSTILE CHILD

Resentment interferes with the child's healthy development. The teacher needs to understand that the hostility the child is expressing as he strikes out at the world has a basis in a situation. Among the most common sources of hostility and resentment are a new baby in the home, having to keep clean, having to share the teacher with so many children that the child fails to get the instantaneous response he gets at home, harsh methods of control at home or in school, wanting to be big and self-reliant, and rebelling because he is dependent upon adults. The teacher must discover the reason — whether one of the above or some other — responsible for the child's hostility and then cope with it. He may need a vigorous type of release. She may help interest him in working on something that is very difficult. He may become interested in vigorous outdoor play. He may be permitted to come to nursery school or kindergarten only a couple of days a week until the group stimulation has a less negative effect on him. During this time the teacher will work with him, trying to help him reduce the feelings of frustration, building up his feelings of security and adequacy, accepting him as he is, but helping him to find better ways of solving his problems.

THE BULLY

Many teachers are confronted with a child whom, for want of a better term, they call a "bully." This child looks upon the room and the playground as his domain. He feels it is his business to dominate, to beat up and boss. Nearly always the answer to his problem lies in the home or neighborhood. It is a recognized fact that when children are dominated by parents, older brothers or sisters, or neighborhood children, they retaliate at the level at which there is no retribution. The child picks on some one smaller, weaker, or just more courteous than he. Some parents contribute to this behavior by an exhortation to "Fight your own battles; that's the only way you'll get anywhere in this world."

If the teacher looks into such a situation, tries to find its causes, and delays interpretation of the bullying behavior until she has sufficient evidence and has worked out a tentative plan of action or treatment, it is likely that she can help the child find a better way of satisfying his needs.

THE OVEREMOTIONAL CHILD

The child who is overemotional, who has an unreasonable fear of dogs, other children, fire drills, or anything else, can be a problem. Children of

Confused ideas of the teacher's expectations subject even normal children to occasional stress.

nursery-school and kindergarten ages are quick to react to the child who is afraid. If a dog comes to the playground and frightens one child it may cause a chain reaction. The first thing the teacher knows, the number crying has more than tripled. The teacher needs to be on hand to assure the child if the feared object is around; but just saying, "There, there, the dog won't hurt you," does not restore the child's equilibrium automatically. Fear is a learned response. It takes a new learned response to erase the old.

THE CHILD WITH TEMPER TANTRUMS

Unless a beginning teacher has been prepared for such eventualities, temper tantrums can be very upsetting. The child momentarily loses all control. He has received attention for this behavior in the home, and so, according to his way of thinking, why should it be any different at school? The teacher must show by her attitude that such actions do not win approval here, either from the other children or from her. She can wait for a lull in the storm and ask the child if he would like to rest a few minutes until he feels better. In cases of persistent behavior of this type, the author has found that helping a child up on an elevation — a table, the teacher's desk, or a cupboard seems to have a calming effect. Merely holding him on one's lap, talking to him, or isolating him from the group does not necessarily calm him. In time, when the child is anxious for the teacher's approval and that of the group, when his fear and anger have subsided, he will wonder why he ever acted that way. The teacher must always remember that the child who is overemotional is as much in need of help as any other disturbed child. He needs the calm, reassuring hand of the teacher patting his head.

The Child Who Swears or Uses Vulgar Language

The child who has added to his vocabulary some words that are forbidden in the classroom must be helped to understand that certain language is acceptable and other language is not. With some children, ignoring undesirable language may be effective; this is not, however, always the case. Some children use the language to show off to the other children, to shock the teacher, and to draw attention to themselves. To allow a child to continue to use such language in the belief that he will outgrow it is to ignore the responsibility a teacher has to the rest of the group. Helping him learn new, interesting, and colorful words and phrases to substitute for the undesirable language is the teacher's responsibility.

Helping Children Who Have Problems

The teacher has a threefold-responsibility for helping children with emotional and social maladjustments; to study each child and know as much as possible about him, to supply as much help to each child as she is able, and to identify those problems that are beyond her skill or time to solve and to refer these to the proper personnel. As the teacher interprets the child's problems, she should try to find out their cause. There are various concepts that contribute to the interpretation of problems — needs, barriers, conflicts, defensive mechanisms, or descriptive traits.

QUESTIONS AND ACTIVITIES

1. Observe in a nursery school or kindergarten, and try to determine which children have problems of personal and social adjustment. In what categories would you place these problems? How did the teacher handle these situations?

2. What was the attitude of the teacher toward the withdrawn or shy child? With what type of behavior did she seem to be most concerned?

3. Observe and report a situation in which a problem arose because the teacher in charge failed to define limits for the children. How might she have avoided this particular problem?

4. Which of the behavior problems of children discussed in this section would you find the most difficult to meet? Why? What might help you cope with the particular type of problem?

SUGGESTED READINGS

Almy, Millie. *Child Development.* New York: Henry Holt & Company, Inc., 1955.

Axline, Virginia. *Play Therapy.* Boston: Houghton Mifflin Company, 1947.

Develyn, Katherine E. *Meeting Children's Emotional Needs.* Englewood Cliffs, N.J.: Prentice-Hall, Inc., 1957.

Moustakas, C. E. *Children in Play Therapy*. New York: McGraw-Hill Book Company, Inc., 1953.

Moustakas, C. E. *The Teacher and the Child*. New York: McGraw-Hill Book Company, Inc., 1956.

Prescott, Daniel A. *The Child in the Educative Process*. New York: McGraw-Hill Book Company, Inc., 1957.

Prescott, Daniel A. *Emotion and the Educative Process*, A Report of the Committee on the Relation of Emotion to the Educative Process. Washington, D.C.: American Council on Education, 1938.

Redl, Fritz. *Understanding Children's Behavior*. New York: Bureau of Publications, Teachers College, Columbia University, 1949.

Redl, Fritz, and David Wineman. *The Aggressive Child*. Glencoe, Ill.: The Free Press, 1957.

Soper, Daniel W. "Importance of Children's Feelings." *How Do Your Children Grow?* Washington, D.C.: Association for Childhood Education International, 1959.

Stouffer, G. A., Jr. "Behavior Problems of Children." *Mental Hygiene*, 36:271–285, April 1952.

Ziman, Edmund. *Jealousy in Children*. New York: A. A. Wyn, Inc., 1949.

There were doors all round the hall, but they were all locked. She walked sadly down the middle, wondering how she was ever to get out again.

— LEWIS CARROLL

THE EXCEPTIONAL CHILD

The Physically Handicapped Child

The Crippled Child

About 3 cases per 1000 children is the figure usually given for the number of orthopedic handicapped children. The crippled child may suffer from a minor handicap, which restricts him very little in his activity, or he may suffer to the extent that he is bedridden. The broad definition of a crippled child is an individual under 21 years of age who is handicapped in the use of his body due to defect at birth or through accident or disease.

The handicap may be so slight that it does not interfere with the child's normal activity. Gail visited kindergarten one day to see whether this would be a good place for him. He was a highly intelligent little boy of five, with a limp caused by infantile paralysis. He was a sensitive youngster, with a fine sense of humor, but was fragile in appearance, and the children began to protect him to the point where experience in school was not helping him develop any resourcefulness. His problem was not his physical condition; no one paid any attention to that. It was his appearance. He had blond curls and his mother dressed him in Little Lord Fauntleroy suits. The kindergarteners, convinced he was a girl, treated him with the courtesy they accorded the gentler sex. Gail in turn was very unhappy because the boys would not play with him.

Finally the teacher persuaded his mother to cut his hair, dress him in boy's clothes, and let him act like a regular boy. In no time at all he was accepted and treated like a boy. In addition to the pleasure the association with other children gave Gail, he was benefited intellectually, emotionally, and physically. He was a fine singer, and that gave him status in the group. The teacher, who had been worried by the thought of having a crippled child in the classroom, found that he provided stimulation to the group. He had the same needs the other children had, he required very little extra care, and he was completely cooperative.

Indeed, the biggest problem with the crippled child in the regular classroom lies not so much with the child as with the protective attitude of the parent. It is sometimes difficult for parents to let go. Often they let go with the mind but not the hand. The child needs to become independent.

Blind Children

As a group, blind children are perhaps the most seriously handicapped of the exceptional children. Normal children use their eyes for a great deal of their learning about the world in which they live. The blind child tends to develop fears because he is unable to see where he is and what is around him. Of course, today's child is fortunate to be able to use radio as a medium for learning.

Every effort should be made to educate the blind child in order that he may live as normal a life as possible. Lee and Vincent, standing by the Pestalozzian principle in dealing with the blind, point out that we should never do anything for a child that he can safely or succesfully do for himself. They also emphasize the fact that society is interested in what the handicapped children can do, not in what they cannot do, and in having them make a real contribution to the social welfare.[11]

Children with Partial Sight

Children with partial vision are less handicapped than the blind, but they are very seriously handicapped in that their visual imagery is distorted. Frequently, also, they wear thick glasses, which do not add to their attractiveness. In addition, being clumsy and awkward in play, they are not often selected for games even when they do play. Indeed, the danger of being injured in play is so great that some authorities recommend the abstention of partially seeing children from active games, particularly those in which the risk of accident is high.

Such children should of course be given medical attention and fitted with proper glasses, and they should have specially prepared materials for reading and other academic work, with type large enough for them to see. They need, in addition, frequent rest for eyes and body. Games that require auditory acuity are fun for them because this skill, which they have highly developed, gives them an opportunity to excel.

[11] John J. Lee and Lee M. Vincent, *Exceptional Children* (Chicago: The University of Chicago Press, 1947), p. 328.

Children with Defective Hearing

Children with defective hearing fall into three categories: the deaf, the deafened, and the hard of hearing. Both the deaf and the deafened are extremely handicapped. The deaf suffer the greatest loss. They are those who have lost all perceptual hearing before they had an opportunity to acquire normal speech. The deafened have lost their hearing after they have acquired speech. The hard of hearing have partial hearing.

The deaf, because they have no concept of sound, must have very special training. The deafened must also have special training, or they will lose the concept of sound. The hard of hearing probably should be fitted with hearing aids to conserve what residual hearing they have. Ideally, every child should have a hearing test each year. As it works out, most children get a hearing test about three times during the elementary school years — usually in the first, fourth, and seventh grades. Kindergarten children should be tested at any time the teacher deems it necessary. This is true, in fact, for all grades in which tests are not regularly scheduled.

For all of these children it is important to be seated where they can see the teacher, so that they may read her lips. With or without training, such children learned to read lips, faces, and bodily action long before they read books.

The handicapped child can be a stimulating factor in the group if children are taught to accept him for his abilities.

It is extremely important that loss of hearing be discovered very early in childhood and that treatment be secured to remove or at least minimize functional hearing losses. In addition, one must have an accurate diagnosis to determine the extent of the child's hearing loss. Once this is accomplished, the program of education, protection, and care of these children can begin. They need a balance of parental love and affection and an opportunity for independence.

The deaf and deafened must be placed in special schools in order to have their needs met. Usually state schools for the deaf, and some city schools, have programs not only to educate the children but also to educate the parents. Nursery-school education is especially helpful to children with defective hearing, because it helps them adjust to other children. In addition, it tends to raise the I.Q. level.

Teachers who are interested in working with children suffering from these handicaps should visit schools that have lip-reading classes. Children who are merely hard of hearing can get along in regular classes if they are seated in the front of the room, if they receive regular lip-reading instruction, and if the person who is speaking faces them. The other two types of children — the deaf and deafened — must be cared for in special classes or schools.

Summary

A consideration of children with problems that require special education or training shows that these children not only profit from early identification and specific training or treatment but that they are entitled to receive it. The exceptional child is one who because of deviation from the average requires special education or training to reach his potential.

The concept of social responsibility for the education of all children is broadening currently to include not only education and training in the traditional sense, but also diagnostic and remedial services, social and personal adjustment, and prevention of handicaps where possible.

Children at the nursery-school and kindergarten level, too, are entitled to the educational privileges accorded exceptional children — the gifted, the mentally retarded, the speech defectives, the children who suffer severe emotional tensions or who appear to be moving toward social maladjustment, and the children with physical handicaps.

QUESTIONS AND ACTIVITIES

1. Observe in an elementary classroom and determine what special attention the teacher gives any handicapped child. What is the nature of the handicap? Would you deal with it in a way differing from that the teacher uses? Why?

2. Visit a school for the blind or the deaf and report on the special teaching techniques used.

3. What kinds of medical and health programs do you think the school should supply for the physically handicapped? How should they differ from those provided for normal children?

SELECTED READINGS

Baker, Harry J. *Introduction to Exceptional Children.* New York: The Macmillan Company, 1945.

Burt, Sir Cyril. *The Causes and Treatment of Backwardness.* New York: Philosophical Library, Inc., 1953.

Crowder, Thora H., and James J. Gallagher. "Adjustment of Gifted Children in the Regular Classroom." *Exceptional Child,* 23:353–63, May 1957.

Cruickshank, William, and Norris G. Haring. *A Demonstration: Assistants for Teachers of Exceptional Children.* Syracuse, N.Y.: Syracuse University Press, 1957.

Cutts, Norma E., and Nicholas Mosely. *Teaching the Disorderly Pupil.* New York: Longmans, Green & Co., Inc., 1957.

DeHaan, Robert F., and Robert J. Havighurst. *Educating Gifted Children.* Chicago: The University of Chicago Press, 1957.

Forney, Katherine. *Up and Away: The Education of Handicapped But Exceptional Children.* New York: Exposition Press, 1957.

Frampton, M. E. *Special Education for the Exceptional Child.* Boston: Porter Sargent, Publisher, 1955.

Gardner, D. E. M. *The Education of Young Children.* New York: Philosophical Library, Inc., 1957.

Graham, J. P. "When You Build, Don't Forget the Handicapped," *Illinois School Board Journal,* 24:7–10, Sept.–Oct. 1957.

Hall, Theodore. *Gifted Children, The Cleveland Story.* New York: World Book Company, 1956.

Harris, Grace. *Language for the Preschool Deaf Child.* New York: Grune & Stratton, Inc., 1950.

Heck, Arch O. *The Education of Exceptional Children.* New York: McGraw-Hill Book Company, Inc., 1953.

Illinois Annual School for Mothers of Deaf Children. *If You Have a Deaf Child.* Urbana, Ill.: University of Illinois Press, 1953.

International Council for Exceptional Children. *Books, Art, Music for the Exceptional Child.* Lexington, Ky.: Blue Grass Chapter, International Council for Exceptional Children, 1956.

Kvaraceus, William C., and Jane E. Dolphin. "Selected References from the Literature on Exceptional Children," *Elementary School Journal,* 58:407–18, April 1958.

Louttit, C. *Clinical Psychology of Exceptional Children,* Third Edition. New York: Harper & Brothers, 1957.

Patterson, C. H. *Counseling the Emotionally Disturbed.* New York: Harper & Brothers, 1958.

Rogers, Dorothy. *Mental Hygiene in Elementary Education.* Boston: Houghton Mifflin Company, 1957.

16

The Classroom Environment

"How do you do it?" we asked at last.
"But I don't do it," he protested ...
"I take off the lid, and other art masters
Clap the lid on — that is the difference."

— Cizek

The child receives his first impression of school when he walks through the open door, and here before him is — his room. This is the room that will determine his attitude toward school, the room in which he will spend so many hours. The effect of the physical environment upon the budding personality is of singular importance.

The Physical Environment

Every structure should be a three-dimensional translation of the kind of life that is to be lived in it. For young children this life includes functional purpose, physical activities, and sensory reactions.

CHILDREN NEED SPACE

The physical set-up of a school — the building and equipment — influences the human relationships in the school. The problems of planning and equipping each room should be solved in terms of the needs of the people who will use it. A well-planned classroom enables the teacher to get around and give help to more children. It lessens her fatigue, leaving her with more energy to teach. Naturally, she will do a better job when there are fewer limitations due to physical arrangements. The teacher who is worn out dragging equipment long distances and taking a group of children up and down flights of stairs to get to the play area is limited by the nature of the situation in her ability to be a creative teacher.

Housing facilities for young children should be close to the ground, with direct access to the outdoor play area and the playroom. Young children need to be able to get to the toilet easily. Architects sometimes forget this. For the youngest, indeed, satisfactory toilet facilities are first on the list of desirable building features. A nursery school needs, in addition, an isolation room, a kitchen (if it is to be an all-day arrangement, this is a must), an office for the director, and a storage room for supplies and the janitor's equipment.

There must be space, space in which to work together or singly. Children need enough space in which to work and play cooperatively, happily, and successfully together. Of course, the teacher must be able to get to all parts of the playground, the playroom, and the workroom with reasonable facility, but too much space is rarely the problem. Ample space is an invitation to creativity and play.

CHILDREN NEED BEAUTY

Most teachers have little to say about the structure of the building or even the size or type of room in which they teach. Sometimes they are consulted, but only rarely are they consulted early enough to influence decisions. Let us assume that the room is there, the paint is on the walls, and that is about all that is there. All the equipment is stored in the cupboards, the curtains are not up, if there are curtains, and the room is devoid of pictures, flowers, plants, toys — everything that gives it life and invites the child to learn.

In spite of this, this is still the most important room for the child who is to enter the door and find the joys of shared experiences. The teacher must take heart, ignore the sallow tan paint, and recite, "May the brightness of my enthusiasm envelop its poor entrance, its bare room. May my heart be more a column for it and my goodwill more golden than the columns and gold of wealthy schools. . . ." [1]

One advantage of a subdued color is its lack of stimulation. If the group

[1] Gabriela Mistral, Chilean poetess and winner of Nobel Prize for Poetry, 1945.

is large, the children themselves will furnish stimulation enough; the clothing of the children, added to the toys and plants they bring in, will give variation in color. The total effect the teacher wants is not one of a dizzying busyness in the room, but rather a general feeling of friendliness and warmth, not too exciting. Children react to color, and too much color can play havoc.

If the teacher is lucky, there will be light chalkboards in place of the old blackboard, ceilings with a high reflection factor, and light-colored furniture for beauty and hygiene. Since windows occupy a considerable area, the whole color scheme will be comparatively light in order to achieve brightness and balance. Though children like primary colors, it is not good to use them in large areas. As accents of color, they give a friendly and even gay atmosphere. There is no need to exclude cool colors or to exaggerate the use of warm ones; colors ranging from yellowish tones to greenish blues are all attractive, and the choice depends largely on the teacher's personal taste. If the room is to be painted during the year, the children might well have a voice in the selection of the color.

In the modern scheme of things, the teacher usually has an opportunity not only to visit the classroom before school opens in the fall but to get the room ready for the children during the orientation period.

How much the teacher should do is debatable. Surely the children will want to feel it is their room and that they have a part in making it livable. Yet their reaction to school is colored by the impression they have when they see their room for the first time. The teacher who remembers what it is to be a child will not go wrong in planning the physical environment for children. She should provide enough color and life to make the room inviting, but not enough to shut the child out should he wish to bring plants, pictures, and objects of art to make the room lovely.

When the teacher can step back and survey the room with the feeling that it is an easy, relaxed room in which to live, she has probably done all that she should do. Her next stop is to arrange centers of interest that will invite exploration, manipulation, socialization, dramatization, and individual activity.

CHILDREN NEED CHALLENGE

Among the interest centers that children enjoy and find stimulating are a doll corner or doll house, a science center, a library corner, a music center, an arithmetic center, a workbench, a sand table, a number of easels, a sink and work space, a reading corner, a block center, and an art center. There should also be space for supplies, preferably along the windows, bulletin boards, chalkboards, cloak racks, storage shelves, the teacher's desk, and a filing cabinet.

There is no longer such a difference between the nursery school, the kindergarten, and the primary rooms as there once was. Recognition of the needs of children has resulted in bright, cheerful rooms for primary children. Because of crowded conditions, however, many undesirable rooms are being used and the teacher must make a real effort to make them not only livable but also attractive.

It is desirable for the furniture to be movable in order to make way for dramatic activities and rhythms in the classroom, for construction in connection with units of work, and simply for rearrangements in the furniture. Preferably it should be light in weight and color. There should be plenty of storage place easily accessible to the children. Supplies and materials should be located where children can get at them easily and have no difficulty in putting them away. For each activity children should be able to go to and from their interest centers easily. The middle of the room should be free of furniture. Informal and flexible grouping of furniture and interest centers makes for a happy, contented group.

Children Need Equipment

Equipment sets the stage for learning. The amount of equipment and its usefulness depend partly upon the resourcefulness and imagination of the staff and partly upon the size of the budget. Minimum essentials in equipment are suggested by the needs of children. Some of the equipment serves the fives as well as the twos; for example, a sand box is used by both groups, but it is used differently. Other essentials are blocks of varying sizes and shapes, packing boxes, walking boards, barrels, a small ladder or two, a large telephone pole, a jungle gym or other climbing apparatus, wheeled toys, see-saws, swings, and a merry-go-round for the older children. Paints and

The teacher should provide a wide variety of activities to keep the young child interested.

easels, clay, and homemaking equipment are also necessary. Included with this type of equipment should be cooking utensils to use in the sand pile.

As children mature, space for running and for playing games becomes increasingly important. This is particularly true if there is little equipment for outdoor play. In this case the teacher is responsible for helping the youngsters organize group games, dramatic play, and rhythms. If the play area adjoins the room, it is sometimes possible to carry on indoor and outdoor activities simultaneously. Such an arrangement makes it possible to share facilities and to avoid overstimulation by dividing the group on the basis of the children's selection of equipment. If there is an assistant or student teacher, the supervision of both areas at one time will be facilitated. Weather permitting, work periods or periods of self-chosen activity may be outdoor periods much of the time.

Further items of useful equipment include a record player and instruments for the rhythm band; materials for manipulation, for dramatic play, and for exploration; puzzles and nested wooden blocks; clay, art materials such as easels, easel paints, chalk, water colors, finger paints; educational toys, large peg boards, beads; wood, tools, and a workbench; housekeeping materials such as dolls, doll clothing, a doll bed, bed linens, a doll dresser, a doll buggy, and unbreakable dishes; kitchen utensils such as a stove, sink, cupboard, broom, dustpan, tea table and chairs, rocker, refrigerator, and telephone; and "dress-up" materials.

Toys used in dramatic play might include trains, dump trucks, derricks, cranes, boats, airplanes, cars, buses, sand toys, wooden spoons, shovels, pans, sifters, pails, wooden animals, farm animals, circus or zoo animals.

Much of the material that appeals to young children is obtainable at little or no cost.[2] A telephone pole lying flat on the ground lends itself to dramatic play, offering children numerous opportunities for imaginary trips. Old tires, especially large truck tires, wheels of various sizes, hoops, and boards are other free items enjoyed by the children.

It is not enough to have the equipment needed. It is essential that the teacher know the significance of arrangement as it affects the group. Arranging the equipment in a desirable way permits social experiences. The use the children make of wheeled toys, musical instruments, or blocks will in each case be influenced by their arrangement in the room. The teacher must continually study the effect of the physical environment on children's intellectual, physical, and social growth. Placing the equipment so that activity is suggested, keeping in mind both the attractiveness and the utility of the arrangement and the needs of children for solitary as well as group play, and introducing new materials gradually, all these are factors that influence the growth and behavior of the child.

[2] See "Creating With Materials For Work And Play," *ACEI Bulletin*, No. 5, Washington, D.C., n.d.; Association for Childhood Education International, Study Conference, *The Best Toys In Life Are Free*, a functional display catalogue published annually.

Today's teacher recognizes the importance of the physical environment as it influences children's behavior. Today's teacher knows, too, that, essential as the physical environment is to the design for development, the social environment that she creates with it is immeasurably more significant.

Social Environment

How does a teacher help a child become a contributing member of a large, heterogeneous group and at the same time preserve his indentity as an individual? Too often the teacher thinks only of the group. "Today," she is likely to say, "the group will take a trip to the feed store. They're interested in the chicks over there."

Are they? Well, the group may be, but what about Mary, who is afraid of dogs and cats and people? Is this trip good for her? Isn't the group made up of many Marys? What about individual needs? In the effort to plan group activities the teacher must not ignore the individual children.

TEACHER-PUPIL RELATIONSHIPS

Every day when the first child enters the room the teaching day begins. The teacher must take time to talk with him, to find out his concerns, his interests, his problems. How else can she guide him? How else will she know which doors to open for him?

Behavior ranges from eager participation to rejection, and the teacher must be ready to cope with both. Here is the point at which her human sympathy and interest in people stand her in good stead. She anticipates and accepts the behavior stemming from a child's sense of insecurity when he finds himself alone in new surroundings with adults he doesn't know and children he hasn't met. She plans various ways to meet the need of the child for love and acceptance as she tries to ease the transition from home to school.

If a child is one who has attended the orientation conference the previous spring and has had an opportunity to see his room and meet his teacher, it may be easier. He already knows his room. What is more, he knows his teacher. He likes her, and he is pretty sure she likes him. He had a chance to look around the room when he was here before. He is on his way to making a good adjustment to school. Sometimes, to ease the tensions of the first days, the mother is invited to stay until the child feels secure enough to accept the teacher as a mother-substitute. If he appears to be making it on his own, however, the mother will leave sometime during the morning.

If, on the contrary, he shows little evidence of being ready for a group experience in nursery school, the teacher and his mother may decide to wait to enroll him until he is more mature. The teacher learns to observe reactions of children and to determine whether a particular child has been weaned from his mother. School is not the place for the weaning process. That must precede enrollment.

A good teacher is aware of the needs of the individual as well as those of the group.

Many children are, however, ready for school when they arrive and are ready not only to allow their mothers to leave but to accept other children. The teacher helps the child solve the problem of his initial adjustment to school by taking an interest in him as a person and by adapting the environmental factors to his basic need for security. If the teacher is free to be with the children, if she is relieved of clerical duties, such as enrolling children, collecting rental fees, and other activities, especially on the first day, the initial adjustment is simplified for the child. There should be another individual — a parent, an assistant, the principal, or a student teacher — to look after other details. The teacher should be free for her most important job — that of getting to know the boys and girls as they come in, getting to know how they react to new experiences, what interests them, and what their needs are.

The teacher's attitude toward each child in the class is the basis for group morale and does much to set the tone of group behavior and discipline in the classroom. We do not imply that there will be no disciplinary problems if the teacher arranges the physical environment and the social climate in a desirable manner, but the problems will be reduced to a minimum. Frustrations will decrease, and satisfactions will mount.

THE TEACHER AND THE GROUP

The teacher is concerned, and justifiably so, with the question, "What will they be like as a group?" She knows that the group is not merely additive; it is also dimensional. Factors of dynamics that are not in evidence when each child is alone operate in a group. What is so disturbing to the inexperienced, and at times to the experienced, teacher is the fact that as individuals the teacher can cope with them, as a group she cannot.

During the first few days at school the children are individuals; group dynamics are operating at a subnormal tempo. Children are likely to be somewhat retiring, they are not yet quite at home with the surroundings, the teacher, and the other children. During this period, in which everyone is getting acquainted, the teacher and children can sit down together and plan the kind of school they want. They can talk about the kind of relationships they want for their school and the standards of behavior they will set and uphold. Children want limits; they need them. They are happier and more secure if they know that certain standards of behavior are required. Although they need to know that the teacher will love them even if they do not always meet the standard, they also need to know that she is expecting them to grow in their behavior so that they will soon experience the satisfaction that desirable behavior brings. Such comments as, "We surely like the way William is growing; today he helped Karen find her mittens," (a few weeks ago he had hidden them) give children recognition for desirable behavior and growth.

The teacher and the group work together, plan together, and solve problems together. The teacher realizes that human beings are capable of several levels of problem solving. At the lowest level, for example, the children decide whether to have milk or ice cream for the Valentine party. This being a simple problem, the solution may be almost instantaneous. In more complex problems that have to do with day-by-day living in the classroom, the teacher must remember that problem-solving skills are developed; children are not born with them. They are not ready for making weighty decisions on such things as discipline in the group and the control of behavior. They need to feel that adults are in charge, for they realize that they themselves have not the maturity to regulate their lives. They realize, too, that they feel more secure when there is consistent guidance and discipline, and they want to know what limits are placed on their behavior. If they are permitted to do what they please, they wonder if their parents or their teachers care what happens to them. They need to know they are wanted and that they are loved, but that they are expected to help the group by their behavior.

Discipline

Group Control: The Province of the Teacher

As we have said, children do not have the foresight or wisdom to take responsibility for classroom control. Many teachers have interpreted the child's need for experience in problem-solving and in the planning of a democratic classroom environment to mean that the group should have power to reward or punish individual children. This assumption is dangerous.

The teacher has and must assume the responsibility for meting out reward and punishment. Children can be very cruel to a child they do not accept. The classroom climate should foster kindness, sympathy, understanding — not retribution, judgment, and hostility. The young child has difficulty making decisions. If he is given power to make decisions for another, it is evident that the teacher is attributing to the child powers that he is too immature to assume. Self-discipline — yes; that is the child's province. But discipline for the group — no. That is the teacher's function.

Another hazard of allowing the group to discipline is that it makes the group too powerful as a socializing agency. The pressure of a group used unwisely can be very undesirable control. Children become afraid of the group, feeling its pressure and knowing themselves judged by individuals who have neither the maturity, the insight, nor the authority to stand in judgment. Conformity to the group, indeed, has been a factor that has negated some of the values teachers try to build in children. As they arrive at the age when group approval becomes increasingly important, there needs to be careful scrutiny of group authority, action, responsibility, and discipline.

Used with discretion, of course, group action has a definite place. Participation in planning and evaluating does not mean, however, that the group

Discussion is an important factor in establishing rapport between teacher and pupils.

takes over the responsibilities of the teacher. She is there to guide, to set limits, to direct. What is teaching if it is not directing children, guiding them from immaturity to maturity, from dependence on others to increasing dependence upon oneself for wise choices and decisions?

An atmosphere of laissez faire permits almost total freedom in the group. The teacher, though present, offers little or no guidance, direction, or control. Each child does what he wants if he wants; within wide limits he follows his own desires. "The gym is yours, boys; do what you want. If you need me, I'll be at my desk." This means that the teacher might help settle a dispute or offer advice if asked or if she deemed it necessary. This type of action used with immature pupils leaves the individuals with limited goals, little growth, and much frustration. It cheats them out of their rightful heritage of learning and results in conflict among individuals and confusion and disintegration on the part of the group. Such a teacher has failed to realize that children cannot be turned loose suddenly to assume responsibility for their behavior. Adequate limits must be set.

The autocratic discipline, on the other hand, such as we remember reading about or hearing about from our fathers or grandfathers, is a thing of the past. We have come a long way from the day when children's knuckles were cracked by the schoolmaster, and the stereotype of discipline was the teacher walking up and down the aisle ready to use his cane at the slightest provocation. We have come a long way, too, since books published for teachers contained exhortations to be more sympathetic in the matter of punishment. The following is an excerpt from a text written for teachers to show the "new trend" in discipline in 1893 in this country:

> Human sympathy is always a motive sufficiently powerful to lead a whole class to watch with deep interest, if not strong feeling, the administering of punishment on a fellow pupil. The punishment may usually be given with advantage in the presence of the class, but not while the class should be working. Between lessons or at the close of the forenoon or afternoon is a suitable time.[3]

In pulling away from such rigid authoritarian discipline, the pendulum swung for a time to a permissiveness that literally let children do anything they pleased. This permissiveness was illustrated by the cartoon of a child saying, "Do I have to do what I want to do again today?" It had no greater impact on any level than on the nursery schools. This being the period of rapid growth for schools for young children, it was natural that they felt the full effect of the swing away from the old-fashioned type of discipline.

In misinterpreting and misapplying the new idea that children should be free to follow their natural inclinations and interests, many schools, eager to let the children express themselves, carried unlimited freedom to absurd extremes. The story is told that Dewey once visited a nursery school and discovered his own son helpless on the floor where a bigger boy was pounding

---

[3] J. L. Hughes, *Securing and Retaining Attention*, (Chicago: A. Flanagan Co., 1893), p. 69.

him. The teacher explained smugly, "This is a part of our progressive education. There is so much cruelty in the world that he might as well begin to learn it now."

Another story is told of a time when Dewey entered a classroom to observe children in a primary school. In the midst of the general confusion he found a boy sitting quietly reading a book. The teacher apologized for this strange behavior, explaining, "He's been with us only a week. You must excuse him."

The pendulum is now swinging in the other direction. Children are being directed again. They are being challenged to achieve and given recognition for achievement. A quest for knowledge, a pursuit of truth, and a premium on excellence are once more attaining importance in the educational pattern. The design for development embraces the concept of the teacher guiding the children in self-government so that they want to do what they need to do in harmony with social, physical, and natural laws. Children are not satisfied until they know that they have done their best, and the best they can do is the measure by which they determine achievement and performance.

Kindergarten teachers, too, went through the period in which children were allowed to express themselves — to the extent of using the teacher's glasses to throw pennies at or throwing blocks at visitors without being reprimanded. "Just ignore it" was an overworked phrase. "Don't even mention discipline. If your environment is structured well, there will be no disciplinary problems." The modern teacher, on the other hand, looks discipline squarely in the eye, admits that there is a problem, and does something about it. She is wise. She uses the problem-solving techniques that have been discussed repeatedly. She takes the first step — she recognizes that there is a problem — and then she looks for possible solutions.

Principles of Discipline

Discipline is self-government. It is the affinity for wanting to do what you have to do in harmony with social, natural and physical laws. In dealing with young children, discipline involves six basic steps to help build better human relationships and healthier individuals:

1. Accept the child, even when you cannot approve of his behavior.
2. Set up necessary limits.
3. Provide creative activities for the release of tension.
4. Encourage and support the child when he needs help.
5. Praise him for his efforts to express himself in desirable behavior.
6. Allow time for the child to learn and to conform to the standards.

These principles should be kept in mind and the children should be made aware that although the teacher is their friend, she will tolerate no nonsense. If the teacher is creative and teaches because she enjoys it and is herself a growing individual, there is every reason to believe that problems of discipline will be at a minimum. The high quality of academic achievement and of creative activity, and the good feeling stemming from interpersonal relationships in the classroom, in the home, and with the staff will make the classroom a desirable place. Children will want to come to school. Even when conditions are not ideal and when classes are too large, the teacher and pupils will find ways of solving the almost insurmountable problems that come in the wake of large enrollments, lack of space, and double or triple sessions.

Large Enrollments

While many teachers are struggling with large classes and trying to keep the quality of instruction high, experts are saying that a classroom of 25 children is an ideal situation. It is obvious that for the time at least we shall have to find stop-gap measures to take care of the numbers of children knocking at our doors. Long-range plans for new buildings are admirable, but, as one teacher pointed out to her principal, "That won't help my situation; I'll be retired then. In the meantime I have 38 children and only 33 desks."

The younger the child, the more guidance he needs. Consequently, if early attitudes towards school are to be positive, the young child should be in a group small enough to guarantee maximum attention.

Let us look at a kindergarten group in which 65 children are enrolled in one session and see how this group worked out its problems.

In a kindergarten. We arrive at the kindergarten at 8:30 and observe that the teacher and the assistant are making plans for the day. The program has to be well structured to permit as much individual attention as possible for the large number of children. When the children arrive, Miss Stem, the teacher, greets the children who come in at one door, and Mrs. Goldman greets those who enter the other door. There is general conversation, and the children look around the room. They go to see the goldfish, look at the avocado to see how it is growing, go over to have a look at the turtle, and put the flowers they brought to school in vases. The room, although old and not particularly well suited to the needs of small children, is pleasant and airy, and the children's works of art are in evidence.

To avoid undue stimulation, the children sit in separate groups of about 30 at either end of the room. They know which group is their own group, and when the teacher calls the roll, they answer. Such formality is necessary in this school, as the attendance must be recorded at the office a few minutes after school begins. To be sure the number is correct, children in each group are chosen to count the boys and girls. A child writes the total for his group on the board, and the assistant checks it.

A music period follows, in which all the children sing with a great deal of enjoyment. They dramatize a number of nursery rhymes, including *Sing a Song of Sixpence, Mary Had a Little Lamb, Old King Cole, Little Boy Blue* and *Jack and Jill.* Children from both groups are chosen, so that neither group gets more attention than the other. The teacher plays the piano while they sing.

After music, one group goes to the bathroom with the assistant, and one group remains in the room to talk over interesting news. The children enjoy sharing-time. They express themselves freely and have much to talk about. Cindy has a new baby brother. Russell went to visit his grandmother last evening. Donna has a new television, and Rhonda had a letter from Merton, who recently moved to Detroit. This conversation time continues until Group One returns from the bathroom. This is the cue for Group Two to go with the assistant to get ready for outdoor play. They take their graham crackers with them, because they will have mid-morning lunch and rest after play. They leave with no show of reluctance, because they know they will be back in an hour ready for *their* work period.

Group One comes over and sits down to make plans for the work period. Since this day is near the end of the year, the children are interested in planning a trip to the park. In this kindergarten, a mother comes in every Friday to help the group, so that they can take excursions or carry on activities that require one other adult. They talk about the park and the store they will pass on the way. They decide to build a store in their room.

During the period that follows, the children choose various activities — building with blocks, playing with transportation toys, looking at books, playing games at the interest centers, playing in the doll house, painting at the easel, finger painting and clay modeling, water coloring, chalking at the easel, and coloring at the coloring table. Some of the girls play with the little doll house and miniature furniture, and two girls cut out paper dolls. The teacher makes the rounds to see what everyone is doing, offers a word of encouragement here, a pat on the shoulder there, and a word of caution to Douglas as he dashes over to the doll house to invite the children to come to the store.

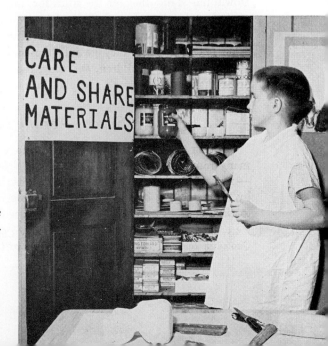

Children must learn to accept the rules and responsibilities necessary in group living.

The work period progresses with a minimum of confusion. The children are relaxed, and the teacher appears to be. She helps them with their names if they wish to identify their work and helps find the supplies they need. Douglas asks her to come to the store so he can read new books to her from the store's library. She listens to him, and as he reads to her, others gather. Before long, about seven children are hearing him read "Chicken Little Count to Ten." Although no effort is made to teach children to read in kindergarten, if a child does read, he is allowed to choose that activity as he would any other of his own interest.

"About ten o'clock," Miss Stem says. "The other group will soon be here. I wonder if we could have the room in as good shape for them as it was when you started to work." After clean-up, there is time to sit down and tell about the work and make a few plans for tomorrow. Then Tom says, "The other group is here. I saw them come up the stairs when I hung my paint apron up in the hall." "Goody," says Marjorie. "Now it's our turn for out-door play and crackers."

The children in Group One go over to the door, where Mrs. Goldman is waiting to take them to the bathroom, then to the room for crackers and rest, and then outdoors until it is time to get ready to go home.

Group Two, which has just come in, has had outdoor play, rest, and a story before they came up to the room for the work period. Because they are more tired than Group One was when they started, the teacher has them relax a bit. "I'm a little rag doll, my head is limp, my arms are limp, my legs are limp, I'm a little rag doll."

The children then have their work period and sit down to talk about it before they go home. When it is time for them to go, they get their wraps and line up ready to sing their goodbye song, "Our happy school is over, and we are going home. Good-bye, good-bye, be always kind and true." Down the stairs they go to wait for mothers or the drivers of their car pools to take them home. The other group is also waiting for their parents with Mrs. Goldman. The teacher and Mrs. Goldman wait until the last child is on his way before they go into the building for lunch. After lunch there will be sixty more children, and they, too, will be divided into two groups in order that they may work and play in a reasonably sized group.

Space — or the Lack of It

"During the past year nearly every school building has been overcrowded — many rooms with seats for 60 have had from 70 to 120 pupils in attendance — many sitting upon the floors and platforms — others standing and sitting by turns, making it impossible for teachers in such rooms to do justice, either to the pupils or to themselves." [4] These words were written not in 1958 but

[4] From the Eleventh Annual Report of the Chicago Board of Education, 1864–1865. Quoted in *Journal of the American Association of University Women*, 51:158, March 1958.

Lack of adequate facilities means that some children learn in sub-standard conditions, as does this class, which is housed in a fire station.

in 1865. Obviously, the problem of large enrollments and lack of space is a persistent one, one that has not been solved in the last hundred years or more.

Teachers are concerned as they watch space disappear and children crowd into classrooms, as they read that some 800,000 children are on half-day sessions.[5] They know, on the one hand, that these are stark realities; and they know, on the other hand, they can teach more than forty-five children with only a modicum of effectiveness. As they try to find possible ways of handling the situation, they carry on a two-pronged program: to inform the public of conditions, and to do the best job of teaching possible, despite limitations.

They can work on the long-range program by asking friends, neighbors, and civic groups to study the situation and suggest remedies. But the problem at hand must be faced. Each teacher tries to answer the question, "How can I make better use of the space I do have?" There is no panacea, but some suggestions may be gleaned from the following descriptions of programs in which good teaching occurs in spite of, not because of, limitations.

On the stage. A group of 40 first graders crowded onto the stage and began their day's activities. One child said, "This used to be the place where we came to listen to a program. Now there are no programs. We use it all the time for school. I don't like school this year. It's so dark, I can't read."

[5] "Changing Times," *Schools and Colleges*, 12:29, August 1958.

In the corridors. Children used to enjoy walking up and down the corridors at Christmas, singing Christmas carols for the different grades. That was fun. Having classes in the hall is not. It is even worse when other classes are passing. The teacher tries to get attention, but distractions are great. Conditions for effective learning are conspicuous by their absence, and everyone is tense, including the teacher. "How can you teach them anything in this place?" she asks. "There's no incentive for art work. We have no place to hang things. We sing a lot, though, and that helps. And we have the playground. No gym, though, because they're using that, too."

In basement rooms. Substandard basement rooms are used in increasing numbers. "At first it was fun to talk about being downstairs if we had an air raid, but we are so close to the outdoor play area that reading is next to impossible. We are so far away from the bathroom that it takes what seems like hours for 50 of us to go."

In the auditorium. Classes are now being held in auditoriums. In one such arrangement the room is divided into eight sections by curtains. In the first grade there are 80 children with one teacher. Although there is some talk of getting a teacher's aide, so far nothing has been done. The children strain to hear, and the teacher is worn out. "When the third grade practices tonettes, we might as well give up," the teacher said.

In Sunday School rooms. If the class meets in Sunday School rooms, on Friday afternoon the teachers must lock away all the materials, clear bulletin boards, move the blocks, dismantle construction projects, and take down the art work. The conscientious teacher spends at least an hour on Fridays and Mondays getting the room in shape. In short, good time and energy are being taken from the teacher's real job — teaching.

In rooms planned for 30 but holding 50. "Chaos, clamor, and confusion best describe the situation I had last year," one teacher said. "Desks were so closely arranged there was no room for me to walk down the aisle. The children were seated by reading groups in alternate desks so there would be an empty desk as they came up for reading. Before that, there was so much fighting it wore me out. I changed jobs and I have only thirty-two this year. We have room to breathe and time to have some art again. It was either change jobs or go to an institution. I changed jobs. I wonder whom they got. No one I know."

In double sessions. Double and even triple sessions are not uncommon, but the problems involved are legion. Among the most obvious is the fact that children have no personal belongings, since they must share the desks and the books. Bulletin boards must be shared. Children who come in the afternoon are fatigued, and so is the teacher. The lack of space leaves little room for individual work. There is little time for the teacher to plan or to make the room attractive. It is like a factory shift instead of an educational program. Because the room is in such constant use, it is difficult to have it cleaned thoroughly.

Effects of Crowding

Danny, after his first morning in kindergarten, expressed what many children feel when he told his teacher, "I'm going home now. I'll be back when there aren't so many kids."

Children who are crowded into a small space, who have to share desks, lockers, and materials with others, who have to share a teacher with many other children, are anxious and worried. There are just too many children. They cannot keep track of their wraps; they cannot find a coat or a hat when it is time to go home. There never is time. It takes forever just to go to the bathroom, to put on boots, or to put on wraps. There is pushing, fighting, pinching, and hitting; there are too many tears.

That is what crowding does to the children. What of the teacher? Working with young children is in itself strenuous. If the teacher does a good job, she must know the children, provide the equipment, plan the activities, help each child reach his potential, help him find areas in which he can achieve, and help him develop social skills as well as gain academically. She must become acquainted with his parents, be active on committees, continue her professional study, participate in community activities and still have time for a life of her own. In all this, what is most difficult to accept is the thought that children are not getting what they need, that they are being neglected. The teacher must be in the room with the children at all times; she has no time for a break or rest period if her groups are unduly large. One teacher felt badly because she no longer could call to mind a particular child if she met his parent and was asked "How is Johnny getting along?" She could not reply except in broad generalities, because she just could not remember Johnny. Another teacher was unable to tell the succeeding teacher about the children she had had the previous year; she could not remember a third of them. The records, the reports, the other mechanics take time that the teacher needs in teaching.

What Can Be Done

The picture presented here is not entirely dark. Teachers and children, for the most part, accept the impaired working and living conditions that large enrollments and overcrowding produce. They make an effort to achieve maximum educational experiences even as they are looking for and experimenting with more effective ways of teaching and learning.

Teachers' aides can relieve the teacher of many of her clerical and routine chores, such as mixing paints, watering plants, arranging materials for work, cleaning blackboards, mixing orange juice, bandaging skinned knees, monitoring lunch rooms, policing the playground, putting on snow suits, collecting funds for dozens of causes, and filling out elaborate monthly and annual attendance reports and cumulative records. Aides can do many of these routine chores, leaving the teacher free for teaching. The problem here is to determine what is routine in teaching; but that is less of a problem than for the teacher to carry the entire load.

Groups can be rotated, so one group can use the classroom for a work period while the other group has an outdoor, rest, lunch, or story period. The two groups can begin the day together. This type of solution was described earlier in this chapter.

Careful staff planning can make the most effective use of the time, space, and personnel and instructional resources of the school. A program of team teaching can be worked out whereby one teacher will take two groups for music, story hour, choral speaking, or gym, while another teacher has a free period. At another time the other teacher reciprocates.

Parents are often willing to help with the lunch duty, the playground, or hall supervision, in order to free the teacher to have a period away from children in the morning and afternoon, to help ensure her good mental and physical health.

Double sessions can be used as a stop-gap measure until a sufficient number of classrooms are built.

We have talked a great deal about using problem-solving techniques in helping the child. These techniques are also significant in helping a teacher and staff improve their teaching.

ACTION RESEARCH

Action research is the art of being as objective and scientific as possible while trying to improve a situation. It represents a technique between that of pure research and simple problem solving. Compared to pure research it has the following characteristics:

(1) In action research the design may change as research moves along.

(2) Action research is successful if it results in improvement in practice. Traditional research is successful if the same results are found when the experiment is repeated, and if the conclusions are of wide applicability.

(3) Action research is cooperative; the researcher must take into consideration the ideas, experiences, and opinions of pupils, teachers, administrators, and parents.

(4) In action research the teacher works with children in a specific classroom. In traditional research random sampling is used.

(5) In action research statistical techniques are deliberately reduced to a minimum.

The motivation for action research comes from within the teacher, who feels a desire to improve her own classroom situation or practices. When she participates in such research, she will learn more than if she merely reads an account of what some other school or some other teacher has done to solve the problems.

A creative approach to problems and a positive attitude toward them will minimize frustrations caused by conditions beyond the teacher's control. The teacher might well remember that the limitations are influenced by what she herself will do.

The Shortage of Teachers

Among ways in which the teacher shortage may be alleviated are these:

1. Utilize the reserve teaching corps made up of mature women who have taught and would like to return to the classroom.[6]

2. Investigate the possibilities of educational television. Although it may not always be feasible to use television as a substitute for teachers of young children because of the need for a close rapport between teacher and child, it is possible that the teacher shortage might be relieved at the upper elementary level, thus releasing teachers for younger children.

3. Encourage more highly qualified young people to select teaching as a profession by a strong program of recruitment, in which the classroom teacher takes a position of leadership. The best advertisement for teaching is a successful and happy teacher.

Summary

The key to meeting the needs of children effectively is the teacher. It is she who has the responsibility for creating an environment in which learning is made more desirable, more effective, and more creative through the use of sociology, psychology, education, and good human relationships.

The teacher must create a climate in which each child feels he is part of the group. The atmosphere must be happy and permissive, but the limits must be defined if the child is to be secure and the teacher successful.

QUESTIONS AND ACTIVITIES

1. Visit two classrooms, one in which there is a normal-sized group and one in which the enrollment is extremely large. What real differences do you observe in:

   a. Behavior of the children?

   b. Achievement in academic subjects?

[6] John H. Niemeyer, "Career After Forty," *Journal of the American Association of University Women*, 51:153–158, March 1958.

c. Teacher domination?

d. Type of control used?

e. Opportunity for creative expression?

2. Under what class sizes are various teaching techniques successful?

3. How can research help the teacher solve her problem? What is action research?

4. What is the most important factor in the development of discipline?

5. What is meant by a two-pronged approach to the problems of crowding in the classroom?

SELECTED READINGS

Benne, J. Kenneth. "Studying the Classroom as a Group," *Phi Delta Kappan*, 39: 224–228, March 1958.

Bush, Robert Nelson. "Principles of Successful Teacher-Pupil Relationship," *Phi Delta Kappan*, 39:271–274, March 1958.

Corey, Stephen. *Action Research to Improve School Practices*. New York: Bureau of Publications, Teachers College, Columbia University, 1953.

Cunningham, Ruth. *Understanding Group Behavior of Boys and Girls*. New York: Bureau of Publications, Teachers College, Columbia University, 1951.

Foster, C. R. *Guidance for Today's Schools*. Boston: Ginn and Company, 1957.

Jenkins, Gladys Gardner, Helen Schacter, and William W. Bauer. *These Are Your Children*. Chicago: Scott, Foresman & Company, 1953.

Larson, Roy E. "Schools Are Strengthened by Radio, Press, Movies," *Childhood Education*, 28:61, October 1951.

Leonard, E. D. Van Denan, and L. Miles. *Counseling with Parents in Early Childhood*. New York: The Macmillan Company, 1954.

Leton, Donald A. "Group Processes: Some Implications in the Field of Education," *Education*, 73:136–144, October 1952.

Lofgren, Ruth. "What Makes a Good School," *Educational Horizons*, 36:148–215, Spring 1953.

Martin, William, and Celia Burns Stendler. *Child Development: The Process of Growing Up in Society*. New York: Harcourt, Brace & Company, 1953.

Millard, Cecil V., and John Rothney. *The Elementary School Child: A Book of Cases*. New York: The Dryden Press, Inc., 1957.

Mills, Clarence A. "Weather and Your Moods," *Life and Health*, 72:16–21, March 1957.

National Society for the Study of Education. *Mental Health in Modern Education*. Chicago: The University of Chicago Press, 1955.

Nixon, Norman. "A Child Guidance Clinic Explores Ways to Prevention," *Children*, 4:9–14, February 1957.

Prescott, Daniel. *The Child in the Educative Process*. New York: McGraw-Hill Book Company, Inc., 1957.

Read, Katherine H. "Discipline in the Nursery School," *The Association of Childhood Education Journal*, 32:322–326, March 1956.

Redl, Fritz. *Understanding Children's Behavior.* New York: Bureau of Publications, Teachers College, Columbia University, 1949.

Redl, Fritz, and W. Wattenburg. *Mental Hygiene in Teaching*, Second Edition. New York: Harcourt, Brace & Company, 1959.

Report of the Sixth World Conference. Athens, Greece: Organización Mundial Educación Pre-escolar, 1956.

Seagers, Paul W. *Providing an Environment for Effective Learning.* Washington, D.C.: National Education Association, 1952.

Shane, Harold, and Wilbur A. Yauch. *Creative School Administration.* New York: Henry Holt & Company, Inc., 1954.

Taylor, Donald W., and William L. Faust. "Twenty Questions: Efficiency in Problem Solving as a Function of Size of Group," *Journal of Experimental Psychology*, 44:360–368, November 1952.

Waechter, Heinrich, and Elizabeth Waechter. *Schools for the Very Young: An Architectural Record Book.* New York: F. W. Dodge Corporation, 1951.

Wiles, Kimball. *Supervision for Better Schools*, Second Edition. Englewood Cliffs, N.J.: Prentice-Hall, Inc., 1955.

Photograph Acknowledgments

Index